Computer
Networking and
Scholarly
Communication
in the
Twenty-First-Century
University

SUNY Series in Computer-Mediated Communication
Teresa M. Harrison and Timothy Stephen, Editors

Computer Networking and Scholarly Communication in the Twenty-First-Century University

Edited by
Teresa M. Harrison
and Timothy Stephen

State University of
New York Press

ABE 9153

Published by
State University of New York Press

© 1996 State University of New York

Printed in the United States of America

For information, address the State University of New York Press,
State University Plaza, Albany, NY 12246

Production by Bernadine Dawes • Marketing by Nancy Farrell

Library of Congress Cataloging-in-Publication Data

Computer networking and scholarly communication in the twenty-first-century
university / edited by Teresa M. Harrison and Timothy Stephen.
        p. cm. -- (SUNY series in computer-mediated communication)
    Includes index.
    ISBN 0-7914-2853-2 (hardcover : acid free paper).
    -- ISBN 0-7914-2854-0 (pbk.: acid free paper)
    1. Information technology. 2. Scholarly publishing--Data processing.
3. Learning and scholarship--Data processing. 4. Computer networks. I. Harrison,
Teresa M., 1952–   . II. Stephen, Timothy, 1952–   . III. Series.
T58.5.C655   1996
001.2'0285'46--dc20   95–47786
                                                                         CIP

1   2   3   4   5   6   7   8   9   10

CONTENTS

—————————————— *PART III* ——————————————
COMPUTER NETWORKING, RESEARCH, AND
ACADEMIC DISCIPLINES

——————————————— *PART V* ———————————————
USING COMPUTER NETWORKS TO DISSEMINATE KNOWLEDGE

——————————————— *PART VI* ———————————————
NAVIGATING THE NETWORK: AN INTRODUCTION

Preface

During the past decade, we have witnessed the beginning of a revolution in scholarly communication, which, it is now widely acknowledged, will be comparable only to the invention of the printing press in its impact upon research and education. The availability of international computer networks and the widespread proliferation of computer-mediated communication within the academy signifies a radical break with forms of scholarly communication of the past and promises that a diverse set of electronic research, educational, and publication practices will comprise scholarship in the twenty-first-century university.

This collection of essays explores how computer networking and computer-mediated communication is changing research, teaching, publication, and other professional activities in the university of tomorrow. In addition to examining changes that computer-mediated communication is already stimulating in research and education, the essays in this volume speculate liberally about the processes, the forms, and the products of scholarly communication in the decades to come.

Computer networking and computer-mediated communication are trans-disciplinary phenomena. We have assumed that a volume about the implications of this new set of communication practices is likely to be of interest to a broad range of academic audiences: higher education administrators and policymakers, information technology support staff in computer centers and libraries, and researchers, educators, and students across the curriculum interested in using computer-mediated communication in their own scholarly projects. The collection thus addresses a wide range of computer networking applications in research, teaching, and publication undertaken within a diverse array of disciplinary and professional contexts.

In 1990, when we first conceived of this project, we worried that there might not be quite enough to write about to justify a volume. Three years later, when we were at last able to begin work on this collection, we found it frustrating to have to choose among all the networking applications that could have been featured. But we feel fortunate indeed to have attracted to the volume such a distinguished group of authors, most of whom have been directly responsible for having initiated or championed one or more computer networking projects in the service of their disciplinary or professional constituencies. We acknowledge and applaud their efforts and those of our colleagues in colleges and universities around the world whom we have not been able to mention in these pages; this small army of innovators is reconstituting the academic world.

*Part I*_____

AN INTRODUCTION TO COMPUTER NETWORKING AND SCHOLARLY COMMUNICATION

Computer Networking, Communication, and Scholarship

Teresa M. Harrison and
Timothy Stephen

It has taken an unexpectedly long time for the academic world to be transformed by the computer, although there have always been great expectations about the dramatic changes that the computer would introduce in education and research. It was anticipated, for example, that the computer would revolutionize teaching, enabling students to learn at their own pace and freeing teachers for more personalized activities with students; some even feared that computers would make teachers obsolete (Roszak 1994). Higher education has not given up on the promise of computing technology to change the process and outcomes of teaching, but, in the face of decades of failure to realize this vision, there has been a significant effort to reevaluate precisely what its impact might be (Jacobson 1993).

No one has ever questioned the usefulness of the computer for scholarly research. The computer's ability to quickly process large amounts of information, easily perform complex and extensive calculations, and effortlessly manipulate text and graphics enables scholars in many disciplines to pursue research programs that would not have been feasible without the power and flexibility afforded by the computer. But neither have these capabilities had the effect of transforming on a wholesale level the process or products of scholarship. Computers have surely changed much about the way that research is done, but the social organization of academic disciplines, the forms taken by knowledge products, and the processes of knowledge dissemination and archiving have all so far remained relatively untouched.

Given this history, it may seem foolhardy to advance yet another prediction about computing and the academy. Nevertheless, we contend that our age will witness the reconfiguration of the academic world and, again, we see the computer as a central player in this

3

revolution. But it is not the computer alone to which we now attribute these dramatic effects upon the character and substance of the academic world. Instead, the technology that will be responsible for this largely unforeseen revolution in the practices, the structure, and the products of scholarship is the computer network.

The fact that computers can be connected physically to each other—through telephone, cable, satellite links, or radio links—means that they can be used to exchange information and ideas in a variety of ways. Individuals linked through computers can share data files, use computer systems and data resources that are geographically distant, send mail to others, converse in real time, and participate in conferences on topics of mutual interest. This set of interactional capabilities is made possible by what is no less than an entirely new medium for communication. The introduction of computer networking is changing the way that scholars communicate, creating novel practices as well as novel genres of discourse. The net impact of this will be to stimulate a vast array of changes in the conduct of scholarship.

As yet, there is no definitive history of computer networking; but Rheingold (1993) describes some of the impetus, motives, and visions of the individuals and institutions involved in the creation of the computer network now known as the Internet. The precursor to the Internet, a project of the Department of Defense's Advanced Research Projects Agency known as ARPAnet, was a network of military computers, originally interconnected in order to establish a communications system that could survive a disastrous nuclear attack. ARPAnet developers soon recognized that their network could also be used for resource sharing and other exchanges of information, and they realized further that enabling systems operators to communicate with each other facilitated these applications. Thus, ARPAnet was programmed with electronic mail facilities and, over time, communication applications began quickly to rival other uses of the mainframe machines involved.

But, as Rheingold (1993) points out, even before ARPAnet went online, a few of those responsible for developing this system had already grasped the implications of the new technology and were writing about them. These individuals were no doubt among the first to see that computer networking constituted a new medium for communication—one that could "change the nature and value of communication even more profoundly than did the printing press and the picture tube. . . . " (Licklider, Taylor, and Herbert, 1968, 22). This would happen, they claimed, through the creation of online communities of individuals with common interests, whose interaction was made possible through computer networks. And they foresaw that when people do their informational work "at the console" and "through the network," telecommunication will be as natural an extension of individual work as face-to-face communication is now. The impact of that fact, and of the marked facilitation of the communication process, will be very great—both on the individual and on society. (31)

Although computers have always provided their users with *access* to information, the major innovation in the development of computer networking is the ability to *share* on a widespread and nearly instantaneous basis both information and ideas in a variety of symbolic forms (text, numbers, images, sound, color, etc.). The sharing or communication of information and ideas is the foundational activity of scholars working within a discipline. Whether conversing, collaborating, presenting papers, teaching, or writing scholarly articles, scholars are exchanging information and ideas of some kind with each other. Scholarship is at root a social activity; research products become knowledge only when ratified by the disciplinary community. Scholars obviously engage in many activities in addition to communication (like analyzing, observing, conducting experiments, and synthesizing), but the products of those activities are not regarded as knowledge until they enter into the stream of disciplinary discourse through which knowledge is created, justified, disseminated, and archived.

Various forms of technology for computer-mediated communication have been available for several decades. Some of the first experiments using such technologies for scholarship were conducted in the 1970s, on systems in which geographically separated users accessed a common host mainframe through commercial data carriers (see, for example, Hiltz 1984; Hiltz and Turoff 1993). However, two more recent technological developments have fueled the explosive growth in scholarly applications of networking that has taken place in the late 1980s and early 1990s. The first was the development of increasingly inexpensive personal computers, which made computing both affordable and convenient for many students and faculty. The second was the development of free-access, global area networks of computing facilities in academic institutions (e.g., Bitnet, JANET, and the Internet), which provided students and faculty at connected institutions with a virtually no-cost medium for interaction. Personal computers equipped with modems could function as terminals interacting with mainframe machines, placing the resources of wide area academic computer networks at the fingertips of a large audience within North American higher education systems.

The ability to share data files or use the capacities of very large and powerful ("super") computers from remote sites has been a major impetus for investment in the development of computer networks in the last decade, as government and educational institutions sought to create an infrastructure that would provide the United States with a scientific, technical and, ultimately, commercial edge over other countries (Bloch 1988; Poore 1988). However, personal computing power combined with access to networks has also made it possible to integrate networking into the more mundane daily research activities of practicing scholars across many disciplines.

Through the use of relatively simple technology such as electronic mail, scholars can replicate, on a dyadic basis, many of the informal communication activities that sustain "invisible colleges" (Crane 1972) of research interests, such as exchanging manuscripts, seeking advice or support, and even conducting group discussions on topics of mutual interest. Beyond electronic mail, numerous other applications for group or public information sharing and interaction have since been developed with more sophisticated and powerful communication capabilities that can be used to further the development and dissemination of knowledge within a discipline.

In this book, we present a broad overview of the ways that faculty, students, researchers, librarians, and professional organizations across the academic spectrum are using computer networking. We do not intend to be exhaustive, for this would hardly be possible. New applications of networking within academic disciplines germinate on a daily basis; it is impossible for anyone to keep up with them. We have chosen not to treat any particular discipline in great depth, although some have clearly become more heavily involved in computer networking than others. And we will not focus on any particular aspect of scholarship, preferring to range over the substantial terrain demarcated by Boyer (1990), which included discovery, integration, application, and teaching, and even beyond to encompass issues related to the storing and dissemination of scholarly products.

Instead, we are concerned with how networking is being used in the service of any activity in which knowledge is created, made meaningful to others through teaching and application, and rendered available to others through formal scholarly channels of communication or knowledge repositories. We sample a diverse number of disciplines with the goal of identifying trends, tendencies, minor perturbations, and even only marginal possibilities introduced by networking that may grow to fruition to constitute the academic world in the twenty-first century.

It is too soon to make any definitive statements about how computer networking will ultimately recast the shape and structure of academic life. As many of the essays in this volume make clear, computer networking threatens to disrupt existing disciplinary social structures based on print technology, restructure traditional student-teacher relationships, and destabilize longstanding economic, legal, and professional interdependencies in the dissemination of academic research. If we are in fact poised on the threshold of a dramatic and far-reaching transformation of the world of scholarship, then the time it will take for such changes and their outcomes to be fully manifested will surely eclipse our lives. But it is not too soon to attempt to catch a glimpse of the futures made possible through networking, and to cultivate some preferences among those possibilities. Indeed, it is only in undertaking such explorations that we can begin actively to build the twenty-first century university.

In the remainder of this essay, we address two tasks central to such explorations. First, we sketch a general framework for understanding the relationship between technological change and social change. More specifically, we argue against a simple technological determinism in which computer networking is viewed as the unproblematic cause of a set of changes in the organization of the academic world that can be expected to unfold naturally in the coming years. We suggest instead that the effects of innovative material capabilities afforded by the network will be negotiated within the social, professional, political, and economic contexts of the academic fields in which they are introduced. Second, we introduce readers to five major applications of academic computer networking, as well as some of the issues that such applications engender. Within the context of this discussion, we also introduce readers to the individual essays in this collection.

The Adoption of Computer Networking by Academic Disciplines

As the essays in this book make clear, there are marked differences in the extent to which computer networking has been adopted and used for scholarly purposes, as well as differences in the sophistication of the network tools that are employed within academic disciplines. Some fields, such as ornithology, which is described by *Jack Hailman* in this volume, rely principally upon electronic mail applications of networking (such as "Listserv"-based communication forums), with apparently little investment in more sophisticated tools. In other fields, such as medieval studies, described in the chapter by *Deborah Everhart*, scholars have moved relatively quickly to adapt the technology of the World Wide Web, through which users are offered a wide range of scholarly resources. In still other fields, such as high energy physics, individuals *have invented* new network tools such as the World Wide Web (Hughes 1994), presumably in an effort to respond to their own particular research exigencies. Thus, the pattern of adoption and use of computer networking has not been uniform across the disciplines and may appear at first glance to be nothing less than a crazy-quilt, with no apparent rationality or consistency informing or explaining deviations between the disciplines.

Is there a way to explain differences in the rate of adoption and kinds of applications that various disciplines are pursuing? Before attempting to answer this question, it is important to stress that it would be a mistake to think of networking projects in terms of a single institution, such as *a* discipline or *a* research field, moving as a unit to adopt the new technology. Although this is a convenient way to write about what is happening within academic fields, it is misleading. In most cases, specific individuals have acted initially to make computer networking technology available to others within their fields—by informing them about the existence of the technology, by adapting the technology to uses perhaps somewhat idiosyncratic to their fields, or by writing entirely new software to create technologies that are relevant to their fields. These individuals work within the contexts of their disciplinary communities; they have been trained within the discipline, understand the needs and exigencies of disciplinary inquiry, and have the technical background to be able to imagine how networking technologies might be used in the service of the field. Such innovators have designed resources and undertaken projects related to the interests of those within their disciplines, and, frequently without financial support, taken the initiative to make these services available to their audiences.

It is also a mistake to think of computer networking as one technology. It is instead a cluster of technologies involving a variety of hardware configurations (e.g., personal computers, workstations, mainframes, network connection technology) and software tools. Each hardware and software configuration can provide a wide but delimited array of functionalities, with somewhat different advantages and disadvantages. Readers unacquainted with network infrastructures and their software resources will benefit from reading the essay by *John December* in this volume, which provides an introduction to the vocabulary and resources of network navigation.

And it is a mistake to think in terms of coherent and unitary disciplines responding in some uniform way to the potentials of computer networking. Instead, different fields of inquiry within a discipline or across disciplines may react quite differently to various network capabilities, depending upon the tempo, the levels of interdependence and ongoing communication, and the rate of change within these research areas.

To advance any broad generalizations regarding the brief history of network use by academic disciplines at this point would imply the existence of a relatively well elaborated theoretical framework that could lend itself to the formulation of *a priori* predictions about the diffusion of new communication technologies across social contexts. While some things are known about the diffusion of innovations (see, for example, Rogers 1984), such a framework simply does not exist. Instead, we can make some sense out of this ongoing evolution by examining briefly how communication theorists and historians have explained the deployment of new technologies of the past and the changes these technologies are credited with stimulating. The outcome of this examination will be to suggest that changes within academic disciplines associated with computer networking will have as much to do with prevailing patterns of media use, more or less idiosyncratic demands for communication, and existing social organization within a research field as they do with new capabilities afforded by the technology.

The introduction of any new technology in a social context takes place within an ongoing set of social tensions among competing, cooperating, and coexisting social groups. Initially, technologies must perform some service regarded as valuable, frequently just enabling individuals to do something they have always done, but more quickly, more efficiently, or obtaining some other advantage hitherto not achievable. As with any new communication technology, the introduction of computer networking within a social context threatens to disrupt prevailing patterns of media use and, in turn, to destablize the social interdependencies within communities that are predicated upon them. Marvin (1988), who has studied the history of the electric light and telephony, observes that "[e]arly uses of technological innovations are essentially conservative because their capacity to create social disequilibrium is intuitively recognized amidst declarations of progress and enthusiasm for the new" (235).

Thus, networking technology alone will not *determine* particular changes in the academic world. The transformations that we casually attribute to new technologies are more accurately viewed as the emergent products of negotiations among social actors and groups over time, through which questions such as *how* the technology will be used, *who* will use it, and *what groups* will benefit eventually get answered. These negotiations involve strategic maneuvering to realize opportunities and achieve objectives through the rearrangement of previous social interdependencies, the creation of new groups and organizations, as well as social conflict and its resolution. But they also encompass consequences of individual actions, which, despite their best efforts, individuals are unable to control or influence completely. Although we assume that people use technology intentionally to achieve their goals, unintended consequences arise simply through the effects that the technology may have upon the attitudes, beliefs, and values of users.

This brings us to the question of what role technology *does* play in social transformations, and, more specifically, the role that we expect it to play in transforming the academic world. While, as we have argued, technology does not determine social change, technology does offer material capabilities for new kinds of action. In Cherry's (1985) words, new technology presents certain "liberties of action" (74), making it physically possible for individuals to organize and behave in new ways. The presence of such capabilities does not guarantee that they will be used or that these uses will ever gain widespread significance, but they do provide for certain kinds of potentials that can be manipulated and exploited.

Innovative material capabilities of new technologies also threaten existing social orders, as they present advantages or disadvantages that are biased in ways that benefit some individuals or groups at the expense of others. As Winner (1986) has pointed out, whether or not a technology is developed at all and what specific features are included in the design of a technology are decisions whose answers favor the political, economic, or social positions of some individuals or groups and distress others. Further, choices to use or develop a technology "tend to become strongly fixed in material equipment, economic investment, and social habit" and "[i]n that sense technological innovations are similar to legislative acts or political foundings that establish a framework for public order that will endure over many generations" (Winner 1986, 29).

Thus, the introduction of any new communication technology always takes place, as Marvin (1988) notes, within a tension created "by the coexistence of the old and the new . . . " (8). Existing social orders and new communication capabilities are mutually accommodated and, in the process, social change takes place, for "[n]o matter how firmly custom or instrumentality may appear to organize and contain it," new communication technology carries the seeds that subvert existing social orders (Marvin 1988, 8). It is important to recognize that the processes of change just described are essentially indeterminate, and that it will be

> difficult, if not well-nigh impossible, to guess what will be the future uses, significance, and values of radically new inventions of our own day—especially those pertaining to human communication. The reasons are . . . namely, that we do not know what will be the social conditions of the future, what will be the new customs and habits, the new institutions, the political and economic changes. (Cherry 1985, 59)

But this is not to suggest that we should allow change to unfold unmonitored and without critique. Simply because these processes are indeterminate does not mean that we should abandon attempts to influence and control them. In fact, quite the opposite. It is because the process of change is a negotiated one, and because actors can exercise influence over these negotiations, that these processes are indeterminate. The history of new technology is one in which social actors—scientists, researchers, engineers, industrialists, policymakers, humanists, and educators—have made active choices among technological alternatives, albeit sometimes in favor of development consistent with preexisting distributions of power (Marvin 1988; Noble 1984; Winner 1986), but not exclusively so. As others have pointed out, individuals and groups frequently "appropriate" technical expertise and new communication technologies for their own uses, much to the dismay of some engineers and designers (Giddens 1990; Poole and DeSanctis 1990).

Following Giddens' (1984) more fundamental position regarding human agency and its constraints, we regard human beings as social actors, enmeshed in the business of making choices about future actions, relatively knowledgeable about what they are attempting to accomplish, monitoring in an ongoing and reflexive way the outcomes of their actions and those of others in the environment, and adjusting action in ways consistent with their intentions. Actors are constrained in numerous ways by existing social practices, social norms, and power relations, but their behavior is not predetermined in any necessary way. Further, social actions can produce outcomes that are not predicted or fully understood by the actors who undertake them. Even in the face of new technologies, social action may reproduce existing social conditions, but change is an ever-present potential outcome of any human action. We are convinced that substantial and wide-ranging changes in the social organization of disciplines, in the process and products of higher education, and in the form, distribution, and storage of scholarly products are now beginning to emerge. But we also acknowledge that, to the extent that these very general predictions are realized, such changes will be the products of incremental social action, practiced by individuals and accumulating over time, and will take particular forms not entirely consistent with our current best guesses.

Thus, the history of the introduction of computer networking technology in the academic world is just beginning to be written. In the maelstrom of innovation stimulated by the development of computer networking, existing requirements for information sharing and communication within fields of inquiry, prevailing patterns of media use, relations of power among ongoing social groups, levels of technical expertise among members of a field, access to hardware and the networks, new methods for engaging in traditional disciplinary activities, and entirely new technological capabilities for exchange and discourse—all these factors and the interdependencies among them will be implicated in the process of change, which, as we have argued, is still essentially open-ended. Since some of the consequences of using new technologies will be unintended and unforeseen by users and designers, it would be reckless indeed to assume that any particular path of evolution has been set irrevocably in motion. But, as we observed earlier, the choices we make today regarding how and whether new technology is used are more likely to become fixed in the world that is constituted tomorrow. Thus, as we explore further in a later chapter (see *Stephen and Harrison* in this volume), it is of immense importance that we think carefully about how computer networking may be used in the service of academic objectives, and that we engage in an ongoing process of critique as these applications emerge.

Major Applications of Academic Computer Networking

In the remainder of this chapter, we shall explore our claim that computer networking is stimulating the development of new research practices, new ways of teaching and learning, and new ways of distributing and archiving scholarship. Some of the changes that we describe as "new" are perhaps more accurately regarded as traditional disciplinary practices that technology now enables us to perform in different, perhaps better, ways. In other cases of change, we can detect the glimmers of more radical innovation, consisting of potentially new forms of discourse, new forms of knowledge products, new forms of social organization, and perhaps even the emergence of new conceptions of what knowledge is. In partial support for our claim, we turn to particular chapters of this book, which describe applications of computer networking designed to accomplish particular communication objectives within fields of research or teaching, or assess their potential for doing so. Before reading about these applications in greater detail, it may be useful to situate them within a more general and broader view of the uses to which computer networking is being applied within academic fields.

Gaining Access to Computer Networking

Inititially, whether or not computer networking is used by members of a field or discipline appears to depend upon a variety of factors that enable an individual to gain access to the technology, such as obtaining the necessary hardware and software, and gaining affordable access to the network. It is also necessary to master the technical skills required for using network tools and resources. None of these are trivial obstacles, and they have not been completely overcome; but their ability to inhibit the diffusion of networking in institutions of higher education has declined significantly over the last decade.

As we noted earlier, decreases in the cost of computers and related peripherals have enabled many faculty members and students to acquire the equipment necessary to use computer networks at their convenience. Owning or having direct and perhaps exclusive access to equipment is important because, as Schaefermeyer and Sewell (1988) point out, those who possess personal computers and modems in their homes and offices are more likely to be heavy users of computer-mediated communication. It is certainly not the case that the average faculty member or student can afford to purchase workstations with sophisticated graphics and multimedia capabilities. But, even in the humanities and social sciences, many faculty members, if not most, can either afford or have obtained institutional access to basic computing equipment that makes network connections possible.

Markus (1987) has argued that universal access is required for the diffusion of an interactive medium with a community. Without such access, the medium threatens to split a research community into "haves" and "have-nots," precluding many of the potential advantages associated with using computer networking to support research or teaching. However, institutional subscriptions to academic computer networks such as the Internet and Bitnet have burgeoned over the last decade, supplying members of thousands of educational organizations with virtually no-cost (at least at this point in time) access to computer networking. This has enabled an immensely fertile period of experimentation, giving members of academic institutions the time to learn about networking and to launch projects that encompass increasingly larger audiences within their disciplines and fields.

As these technical and financial hurdles were beginning to be overcome for significant numbers of faculty and students, it became increasingly possible, in principle, for a critical mass of users to physically access the network; it therefore became increasingly conceivable to use the network as a tool for scholarship. We first began using electronic mail to exchange drafts of collaborative research papers between Rensselaer Polytechnic Institute and West Virginia University in 1984, but it soon became apparent that the network could be used in the service of broader scholarly objectives. Initially, we surmised that this could be accomplished through the development of software ("file-servers") that would enable individuals to contribute to and draw from an automated repository of files encompassing information of one kind or another that might be useful to those within a disciplinary community. We envisioned that such a resource might deliver bibliographies, syllabi, drafts of research papers, conference announcements, and other useful documents. It also occurred to us that the network might be used to establish online groups of faculty and/or students with similar interests who would be able to exchange documents, as well as conduct ongoing online conversations, in support of their research or teaching interests. We were not the only ones to arrive at these insights.

But a further impediment to diffusion of networking has been the difficulty scholars have experienced in learning how to to use the network. Academic computer networks were not designed originally to be used by those without computer science backgrounds; network vocabulary was and continues to be arcane, and procedures generally non-intuitive; computer center staff were frequently not skilled at communicating with networking novices. Furthermore, documentation for network protocols and procedures was in short supply and, when available, difficult to understand.

In designing our own disciplinary service for communication scholars, we were sensitive to the need to make using the network a relatively painless as well as rewarding experience. Thus we created our own software system called "Comserve" (see *Stephen and Harrison* in this volume and Harrison and Stephen 1992), which required only that users learn how to send and receive electronic mail. Once that skill was mastered, users could begin immediately to avail themselves of the professional resources offered by Comserve, which, in 1986 when the service was inaugurated, consisted of an online resource library, a self-service professional directory to enable scholars to locate the network addresses of others, and periodic newsletters. Computer conferencing was added one year later, following the development of the "Listserv" software.

Up until the mid-1980s, existing computer conferencing facilities (e.g., Usenet) were relatively inaccessible to unsophisticated users, or required financial resources to install or to become connected. In 1986, the appearance of the Bitnet-based "Listserv" software (available at that time to the higher educational community for free and supported voluntarily by systems operators at colleges and universities across the U.S.) enabled the first wave of network innovators within a wide variety of disciplines to initiate their own online "lists" or electronic conferences organized around particular themes or topics. Listserv (and later Eric Thomas's "revised Listserv") was immensely popular because it was free and, while requiring some network expertise, it was not necessary for an individual to know how to program in order to initiate a conference. The availability of this software meant that, with a little knowledge about how the network operated, virtually anyone could create and operate an electronic conference. Further, Listserv conferences were relatively easy for novice networkers to join and the procedures standard across conferences or "lists." Once a user learned how to join and participate in one conference, that user could join nearly any conference.

Thus, simply by learning how to use the electronic mail facility at their home institutions, most interested individuals could join the vast majority of academic electronic conferences and participate "asynchronously" in professional dialogue using the network. In such conferences, electronic mail to participants can simply be sent to the conference's computer address, where the software then accomplishes distribution to list members; electronic mail from the conference address is sent directly to each participant's computer address where it accumulates in participants' electronic mailboxes to be read at their convenience. All that was then required was the creation of conferences that served one's own interests. Network innovators have moved quickly to meet this need; the number of academically oriented electronic discussion lists now reaches nearly 1800, a dramatic increase from its initial count of 517 in 1991 and a second count of nearly 800 in 1992 (Okerson 1994; Kovacs 1992; Kovacs 1994). It seems unlikely that any field of significant academic inquiry is unrepresented by an electronic conference.

Interacting in a Networked Environment

Although more sophisticated networking technologies may produce more dazzling effects, there seems little doubt that fundamental changes in scholarly practices at a grass roots level received their primary and initial impetus from scholars' participation in electronic conferences. The ability to send electronic mail enables scholars to keep in touch with each other on a dyadic basis; the ability to reach extended groups of recipients in electronic conferences through electronic mail has meant that scholars could participate in dialogue with colleagues who share their research and teaching interests. As Harasim (1993) argues, network conferencing creates a kind of "social space." For academics, this space resembles a perpetual academic conference where scholars gather in virtual hallways, bars, and public presentations to share information about each other's research, offer consultation regarding research problems, debate issues relevant to their fields—in short, to practice the kind of discourse that is the essence of informal communication in scholarly communities (Crane 1972).

As the chapter by *Jack Hailman* illustrates, electronic conferences have permitted members of particular research specialties (in his case a small speciality within the field of ornithology), who are internationally dispersed and who might otherwise meet face-to-face at infrequent conferences, to share an ongoing forum for information exchange. But electronic conferences also enable individuals in interdisciplinary research fields, such as medieval studies, described in the chapter by *Deborah Everhart*, to establish channels for interaction that are easily accessible to all. Such electronic conferences frequently offer services similar to those provided by professional organizations, such as directories of information about members, notices of international meetings, grants, legislation and other news related to the field, and forums for posting article and paper abstracts and reference materials.

Academic electronic conferences vary widely in content, structure, and the extent to which substantial academic work is accomplished. Some conferences are free flowing and general forums, in which any topic may be introduced and pursued if there is sufficient interest. They may exist purely to broadcast or exchange information or for engaging in spontaneous interaction. Some conferences are moderated by individuals, who monitor content more or less loosely for appropriateness and relevance to the audience and objectives of the conference, and who may, at times, stimulate discussion on useful topics (see, for example, Conner 1992; McCarty 1992).

In still other conferences, great pains are taken to insure that the audience can participate or "lurk" in a forum engaged in focused and directed scholarly discourse. For example, the University of Chicago Philosophy Project offers an array of conferences that are guided by moderators and consist of particular types of discussion relevant to philosophy, such as "(1) comments on and exegesis of sections of a philosophy text, (2) attempts to elucidate difficult arguments in the text, (3) interpretative argument between participants over parts of the text, (4) papers by the participants that are related to the text in some way, and (5) general discussion of the text by participants" (Welcome to The University of Chicago Philosophy Project 1994). *Deborah Everhart's* essay describes the structure of "Interscripta," a medieval studies conference in which discussions are carried out in a "round table" format, addressing particular topics for six weeks at a time, and moderated by an individual who subsequently shapes the content of the discussion into a summarizing article that is distributed to participants for revision before publication in the companion electronic journal.

Although electronic conferences are not likely to supplant the need for face-to-face interaction, their ability to link geographically dispersed scholars in a research field, transcend disciplinary boundaries, and be used in the service of significant scholarly discourse makes them powerful interactional tools. It should not be overlooked that this form of contact has the additional advantage of being more widely inclusive of scholarly populations. While the problem of access to the technology has not disappeared, and is particularly acute in non-Western countries, more and more scholars and students are gaining access. Further, as numerous researchers and commentators have noted, computer-mediated communication minimizes social presence cues (such as physical features, status identifiers, speech disfluencies), thus making it easier for some individuals to interact, disagree with others, or support unpopular positions under these conditions (see Spears and Lea 1992 for a review).

In the best of circumstances, online conferences produce a new and intriguing textual product. In traditional scholarship, a formal, artificial type of dialogue is carried out through a series of extended monological texts, from article or book to article or book, across long expanses of time. In contrast, texts produced through online conferences reflect a more authentic scholarly dialogue: distinctions between authors and readers become blurred as participants function in both roles, their voices represented as distinct even as their particular contributions get woven into synthetic and emergent products (see *Jean-Claude Guédon's* essay in this volume and Harrison and Stephen 1992). In such texts, it may be possible to see the dialogical process of scholarship at work. The fact that substantial scholarly work is accomplished through network interaction (and that network discussions are the site for other types of significant social action as well) makes them a source of information that scholars increasingly wish to cite within their research. *Laura Gurak's* essay describes the problems she has confronted in using such texts as research information, and explains how she has reasoned through issues of authorship, copyright, and citation conventions to conduct her study of the network-based protest against the development of a marketing software product.

However, beyond their ability to broadcast information, electronic conferences may be more or less useful for various disciplines as forums for scholarly discourse. *David Rodgers*, *Kevin Curnow*, *Drury Burton*, *Greg Ullmann*, and *William Woolf*, who describe experiences of the American Mathematical Society in a chapter in this volume, note that interest in Listserv conferences devoted to mathematics has been limited, while public access to online services that automate the delivery of professional and scholarly information has been quite robust. It is possible that disciplines may differentially value information versus interaction, or certain types of interaction, in the service of their research programs. For example, researchers in some humanities and social science disciplines may rely more heavily upon discourse and interaction for idea generation, while those in scientific fields may value quickly disseminated information about recent research (cf. Cronin 1982). These kinds of distinctions, which would surely affect the way in which different kinds of electronic services are received within scholarly communities, must await empirical verification.

Sharing Resources in a Network Environment

In the meantime, it is clear that computer networking has been used by individuals, universities, professional associations, and educational and research organizations in a wide number of disciplines to offer services that facilitate access to professional and scholarly resources. Space permits only a few illustrations of the burgeoning library of scholarly resources that exist on the network. Chemistry students and researchers, for example, can use the network to explore the Cambridge Structural Database, which contains bibliographic information for organocarbon compounds produced by X-ray or neutron diffraction and is maintained by the Cambridge Crystallographic Data Centre (Cambridge Structural Database 1994). Humanities scholars can conduct online searches of the Catalogue of Projects in Electronic Text maintained by the Center for Text and Technology at Georgetown University. This database documents information about electronic text projects that provide machine-readable files of primary materials from humanities disciplines (Catalogue of Projects in Electronic Text 1994). Michael Hart's impressive"Project Gutenberg" is one example of an electronic text project that seeks to convert texts of 10,000 enduring works to electronic form to create an electronic library by the year 2001 (Hart 1994). Increasingly, network services offer access to full text materials in the scholarly literature as, for example, the Distance Education Database, maintained by the International Centre for Distance Learning, which supplies online search and retrieval for the full text of over one hundred papers and reports in distance education (Melton 1994).

The latter raises the larger issue of how texts, regardless of disciplinary content or form (article, book, report, etc.) can be distributed in a way that facilitates scholars' ability to analyze them. As *Brian Gaines* points out, electronic publications that do not allow scholars to analyze and restructure text sacrifice part of our ability to organize, index, search, and use knowledge contained within them. However, the development of incompatible text analysis systems is both frustrating and wasteful. This problem is addressed by *Susan Hockey* and her collaborators in the Text Encoding Initiative, an encoding scheme for humanities texts based on the Standard Generalized Markup Language (SGML). The SGML-based system increases the usability of electronic texts by providing descriptive labels for their various parts and by documenting the particular text transcription, both with a common set of conventions that allow electronic texts created anywhere on the network to be used by scholars anywhere on the network.

Unfortunately, such efforts to organize resources for networking are the exception rather than the rule. Until recently, even simple access to most network resources has been technically difficult and haphazard for users, which is the negative side of the unmanaged, sprawling evolution of the network and the voluntaristic ethic that has spawned the creation of network services. The result has been that an enormous number of scholarly and other resources, characterized by one science writer as the "Storehouse of Human Knowledge, Department of Grass Roots" (Gleick 1994), are dispersed across thousands of host computers with varying protocols, producing a situation that has resisted the creation of a systematic method for cataloging or developing collections of services. Only the most intrepid and persistent of users have penetrated cyberspace on behalf of their disciplines to find out what resources exist and what one needs to know to gain access to them. Even now, volunteers circulate a monthly "Internet Hunt" that challenges users' network navigational and detective skills.

However, a set of sophisticated technological tools for using the network (we refer here to Gopher systems, Mosaic, the World Wide Web and other network tools, which are described in the chapter by *John December*) that enable individuals to overcome technical obstacles to locating resources has quite recently come of age. Further, such tools make it possible for scholars or organizations within research fields to construct automated links ("hypertext" links) between network resources, thus facilitating users' ability to identify and gain direct access to those resources related to a field of inquiry, but located at diverse computer sites.

But even with these technological tools, it has become increasingly apparent that efficient and productive use of the network requires the development of forms of social organization that complement and enhance the ability of the medium to serve as a mechanical conduit for information. As guardians of print resources, librarians, who might have headed down a slow but steady path to obsolescence, have instead become champions in the campaign to make their academic constitutencies aware of the revolutionary potential of the Internet, to provide technological and social support in finding valuable network resources, and to call attention to the complex issues that face us in re-structuring the academic world for electronic communication. Librarians have taken on the task of organizing "field guides" to resources that exist on the network, some of which appear in print publications for the purpose of alerting uninitiated users to the value of network (see, for example, Dowling 1994; Fehrmann 1993; Glazier 1994). In this volume, the chapter by *Lyman Ross, Paul Philbin, Merri Beth Lavagnino*, and *Albert Joy* describes one university library's efforts to incorporate network resources into the collections it makes available to patrons.

But certainly one of the most common forms of social support for the network has consisted of lone individuals or ad hoc groups who have taken the initiative to identify resources related to a field of study and been generous in making their information available to others. For example, Arthur McGee has for several years compiled lists of electronic conferences, online bulletin boards, news services, and other online resources related to African and African-American affairs, international development issues, and indigenous, native, or aboriginal affairs, which are broadcast through relevant electronic conferences. His labor, and that of countless other network volunteers, receives no financial support. The group of scholars collaborating in the design of Labyrinth project discussed by *Deborah Everhart*, present a particularly compelling example of volunteers forming a social structure that complements sophisticated network technology in organizing access to network resources for their field. This project, like so many others, was undertaken initially without financial support.

It is now becoming more common to see the development of network projects supported by the government, by research centers and universities, and by scholarly societies whose mission is to organize network resources in the service of disciplinary inquiry. For example, the Department of Energy has funded the High Energy Physics Network Resource Center housed at FermiLab, providing physics researchers with a central location for identifying online resources (Welcome to HEPNRC, 1994). Increasingly, research centers and professional societies have become active in facilitating their disciplines' use of the network. For example, the Center for Computing in the Humanities maintains an online archive for syllabi and other course materials in humanities computing (McCarty 1994). As of July 1994, sixty-five professional academic organizations now maintain their own "Gopher" systems, which are used to provide access to professional information and to identify and link relevant resources wherever they may exist on the network (University of Waterloo Library, 1994).

As we have seen, the network is an excellent mechanism for the distribution of information. But this distribution capability is only as good as the information that is transmitted. Thus, a critical issue in using the network for academic research is determining what kind of content is most appropriate to deliver, how to guarantee its quality, and how to ensure that it will be maintained over time. Such decisions can probably best be made by disciplinary insiders who understand what their colleagues will see as valuable and credible. As the social organization supporting the network becomes increasingly elaborated, issues of content, quality, and currency will begin to be confronted directly. For the forseeable future, however, academic networkers need to be somewhat cautious about the resources they obtain from the network, as too many resource sites fail to maintain their materials.

Despite this rationale for a conservative approach to networking, scholars have initiated increasingly bold attempts to exploit the potential of the medium to support research. One of the most dramatic applications of networking is the development and use of systems that automate the distribution and archiving of preprints. In certain rapidly evolving scientific fields, like high energy physics, new information circulates quickly among selected individuals through the exchange of preprints. Traditionally, researchers have maintained their own preprint lists, inevitably leaving some researchers out of the loop. In 1991, Paul Ginsparg of the Los Alamos Research Laboratory developed software that allowed anyone in the high energy physics field (and beyond) to identify, obtain, and archive papers prior to their publication in print journals, which typically can take months (Broad 1993; Publication by Electronic Mail Takes Physics by Storm 1993). Electronic preprint distribution has been so successful in taking the place of paper preprints, as Okerson (1994) reports, that the Stanford Linear Accelerator Center has recently decided to cease their paper preprint distribution because more than half of them had already circulated widely on the Internet. Such a distribution channel appears to be making print media functionally irrelevant to the process of doing research in high energy physics.

Following this example, individuals in other disciplines are organizing to provide similar electronic preprint distribution services. Individuals in research fields related to physics have tended to use Ginsparg's software to administer their services. Other organizations, both formal and ad hoc, have designed and developed their own software. *Rodgers, Curnow, Burton, Ullmann*, and *Woolf* discuss some of the issues considered by American Mathematical Society in undertaking their preprint distribution service. It will be interesting indeed to see if such services are received as enthusiastically in the humanities and social sciences, as disciplines such as philosophy and economics begin experiments with preprint distribution (International Philosophical Preprint Exchange 1994; Economics WPA World Wide Webb Service 1994).

Collaborating in a Network Environment

These combined interactional and informational resources suggest that the network is a potentially useful site for new types of collaborative research. And it has been the case that scholars, especially in multi-, trans-, or interdisciplinary research projects, have marshalled network capabilities to support their work. This is not to say, however, that the network will prove uniformly useful as an interactional tool across all such projects. *Duncan Sanderson's* carefully drawn distinction between cooperative and collaborative work reminds us that offering opinions, providing information, sharing data, and other activities characteristic of cooperative work is quite different from the commitments of time and energy, the complex coordinated actions, and the development of common understandings that are more characteristic of collaborative work. While networks may be seen as easily supportive of cooperative work, more than just technology is required for genuinely collaborative work. As *Sanderson* further observes, some researchers, such as the atmospheric sciences team he studied, may prefer to use face-to-face meetings instead of the network for their interaction. Whether or not the network can be used successfully to support collaborative work may depend on the personalities of individual researchers as well as the conventions for discourse and interaction within particular disciplines.

Nevertheless, computer networking has been used for some projects that appear to be genuinely collaborative. One of the longest and most visible examples is Principia Cybernetica, "a collaborative, computer-supported attempt to develop a complete cybernetic and evolutionary philosophy" (Heylighen, Joslyn, Turchin 1994). This network of engineers, philosophers, physicists, and other forms of systems theorists, which leaders began to organize in 1989, has supported its work with both computer networking (beginning with one Listserv-type conference) and face-to-face research forums; the group has received several research grants to support its work and now maintains its own hypertext server with a searchable index.

In this volume, *Fay Sudweeks* and *Sheizaf Rafaeli* relate their experiences using the network to organize a large, multidisciplinary, and international research team in the creation of a database for research studies addressing the character and content of computer-mediated communication. In addition to discussing the ethical, mechanical, and conceptual issues involved in assembling such a database, their chapter provides a glimpse into the complexity of using network technologies in support of task communication among a large group of researchers.

A provocative set of technologies causing significant speculation about their potential for collaborative scholarship are networked text-based virtual reality programs, which provide real time conferencing environments for members who collaboratively program the construction of their world and the objects that furnish it. The class of interactive technologies known as MOOs and MUDs are controversial; many see them as frivolous wastes of time and some colleges have even outlawed them (Bennehum 1994). In contrast, *John Unsworth* argues that MOOs are contexts in which play can serve as a possible foundation for productive scholarship. PMC-MOO, developed by *Unsworth* as a real-time interactional supplement to the relatively well established electronic journal *Postmodern Culture*, embodies an evolving community whose participants experiment with postmodern concepts through discussion and programming. *Michael Day*, *Eric Crump*, and *Rebecca Rickly* describe their experiences in MediaMOO, a well-known environment because of its democratic aspirations (Bennehum 1994), which provided a context for informal collaboration among a group of composition faculty. The playful nature of MOOs, the very quality that has called into question their academic integrity, is precisely what advocates claim is intrinsic to their potential as contexts for academic collaborations. *Peter Lyman* reminds us that we know very little about how play can be used in learning and teaching. MOOs may well supply contexts that help us to observe something about that relationship.

Pedagogy in a Networked Environment

An important implication of computer networking technology is that, in principle, nearly all the resources and services available to scholars through the network can be used by students as well, stimulating a wide range of potential educational benefits that educators have been enthusiastic to realize. We cannot hope to survey all of the innovative educational applications of the network with which faculty are now experimenting. Instead, we will highlight here some of the most interesting of these applications and benefits and refer interested readers to other sources for a more detailed picture (see Burge 1992 and two forthcoming volumes by Berge and Collins).

As we noted earlier in our discussion of scholarly electronic conferences, computer-mediated communication creates an interactional environment that encourages more active participation. Diminished social presence cues reduce interpersonal and status differentials among participants, even between teachers and students, and creates a sense of anonymity, even when real names are used. Further, in online conversations, there is no need to compete for speaking time; everyone can be "read" in an online discussion. These characteristics encourage students who might otherwise be reticent in face-to-face discussion, such as women, to participate more actively. Moreover, discussions are more likely to be directed by students' interests and choices, instead of following the teacher's plan (Faigley 1992; Tuman, 1992). And, as both *Linda Harasim* and *William Graziadei* argue in their chapters, computer networks make it possible to distribute learning experiences over greater distances and more time zones, thus minimizing or eliminating such barriers for students whose lives cannot accomodate the traditional classroom experience.

Complementing the participative character of this new form of communication, the network enables students to engage directly resources that enrich their education. *J. R. Lemke's* vision of an educational environment comprised of interconnected, digitized, and networked multimedia documents is one that puts a premium on the capacity for decentralized, independent learning. The primary mission of teachers in Lemke's model of online education is to enable students to pursue their own questions by helping them to acquire the "literacy" skills—information retrieval, navigation, and authoring skills—required to negotiate a global hypermedia network. The chapter by *William Graziadei* describes his attempts to encourage this kind of skill development and inquiry by incorporating network tools and other technological enhancements in his biology courses.

One of the most valuable resources the network can offer students is, of course, access to other inquirers, including both students and established scholars participating in their academic communities. Using a Bitnet conference to enable an online semester-long conference between her undergraduate history students and a network of "consultants" that spanned several institutions and a range of related disciplines, *Carolyn Schriber* illustrates how such interaction can contribute to the development of community in the class, extend the time available for discussion beyond the physical duration of the class, and model the process of idea exchange and critical thinking that is the heart of many humanities and social science disciplines.

Such online "discussions" are, ironically, conducted through acts of writing, which suggests that the medium of computer-mediated communication traverses the oral/written continuum and encompasses qualities associated traditionally with both forms of communication (Wilkins 1991). Educators suspect that numerous advantages can be derived from this aspect of the new medium. The asynchronous writing environment constituted by most online conferences (in which electronic postings await replies in an electronic mailbox or conference space) enables individuals to compose at their own pace and receive lots of peer feedback, a process that produces more thoughtful and rigorous exchanges and may actually improve students' writing. Some of these themes are reflected in the essays by *Schriber* and *Graziadei*.

A somewhat different perspective is offered in the essay by *Michael Day, Eric Crump*, and *Rebecca Rickly* who use *real time* or *synchronous* network conferencing through a tool called Internet Relay Chat (described more fully by *John December*) to teach composition. The oral character of this online medium and its ability to involve individuals in rapidly evolving interaction creates a synergistic brainstorming session in which the tendency to self-evaluate can be short-circuited temporarily. This environment frees students to experiment with ideas, grammar, and forms of expression and allows them to observe and play off the reactions of others. The medium thus constitutes a tool for invention, audience analysis, and for providing feedback that teachers may find particularly valuable.

One further theme in the literature of online education, strongly articulated in the chapter by *Linda Harasim*, is the potential for collaborative education. The ability to transcend institutions, geography, and time means that individuals from anywhere on the globe can be brought together within the same social space to pursue educational objectives.

This has encouraged many colleges and universities to experiment with distance education programs that offer students the ability to receive college credit and degrees through courses that increasingly rely upon computer-mediated communication.

However, the implications of these programs extend beyond the ability of a single insitution to increase its student base. In his chapter, *Jeff Taylor* shows that computer-mediated communication can be used successfully to forge an alliance between a distance education program in labor studies and the Canadian Union of Public Employees. Such an arrangement provides labor educators in both organizations with a medium for cooperation, offers workers across the country an opportunity to continue their education, and, as, *Taylor* argues, supports the kind of interaction that is essential to workers' education. Further, as the BESTNET (Binational English-Spanish Telecommunications Network) (Bellman, Tindimubona, and Arias 1993; Watkins 1994) project has demonstrated, networking can bring students and faculty from various countries into courses, research projects, and other forms of intercultural contact with each other. The BESTNET project, which currently encompasses seven institutions in the U.S. and four in Mexico, is being extended to Africa, where it offers scientists an array of electronic conferences focusing on development, management, biomedical research, and social sciences and the humanities (Bellman, Tindimubona, and Arias 1993).

At the heart of all the research and educational innovations discussed so far is the theme of inclusion. More than any other medium, computer networking has the potential to encompass greater numbers of faculty and students in ever-expanding opportunities for information, interaction, and collaboration. Among these are audiences that have been historically excluded due to physical or learning disabilities. The ability to participate in computer-mediated communication is made possible through adaptive technologies that can compensate for disabilities. As *Sheryl Burgstahler* and *Tom McNulty* argue in their essays, with access to adaptive technologies, scholars and students with disabilities can participate independently in distance education programs, forums for disciplinary interaction, and collaborations in teaching and research. Educational institutions are legally required to provide computer and network access to those with disabilities when such access is necessary for academic studies. *Burgstahler* argues that, rather than retrofitting at a later point, a more effective and less expensive way for educational institutions to provide such access is to integrate technologies for the disabled in the planning phases for developing computing and networking facilities.

*Distributing and Archiving Knowledge in a Network
Environment*

One final arena in which computer networking is stimulating innovation is scholarly publishing; the changes underway and those envisioned encompass both a reevaluation of the form of scholarly products and the potential reorganization of the economic and social relationships that have constituted our systems of knowledge dissemination. As we noted earlier, the ability of the network to automate preprint distribution has called into question the continued viability of traditional journals in certain disciplines as primary media for scholarly communication. The crisis in serials pricing has been an important source of pressure for electronic journal publication, as librarians and scholars search for strategies that can decrease the costs of journal publication. And scholars have realized that certain network capabilities can be used to support other desirable scholarly practices too cumbersome, inconvenient, or impossible to realize through the medium of print on paper.

The first forays into electronic scholarly journal publication took place more than a decade ago; these experimental publications appeared on single host machines that were accessed by geographically distant users (Pullinger 1986; Turoff and Hiltz 1982). The development of wide area computer networks has partially alleviated the problem of critical mass and attendant worries about citation potential that plagued such systems, and has buttressed other arguments in favor of electronic publication, such as the speed and relatively low costs of production and dissemination as well as the ability to publish more and longer articles.

Arguing that under the current system of publication, commercial publishers receive the economic benefits of scholarship produced at public expense, librarians have been among the first to advocate the publishing alternative afforded by the networks (see *Kenneth Arnold's* essay in this volume, as well as Okerson 1990; Rogers and Hurt 1989; Yavarkovsky 1990), and to support the fledgling efforts begun by a handful of scholars sprinkled across the curriculum. In October 1990, the Association of Research Libraries, led by Ann Okerson, and the Library at North Carolina State University sponsored the first conference on refereed academic electronic publishing projects, enabling the new generation of network journal editors to meet face-to-face and exchange information about the projects and problems they faced. Twelve projects were reflected in the mailing list generated by that conference, a number that has grown more recently to seventy-four

(Okerson 1994), indicating that, even with a potentially greater risk of journal mortality, avid interest exists among scholars in exploring the potential for electronic journals.

Although the economic advantages of electronic journal publication are compelling, scholars who have initiated electronic journals have been motivated by the possibility of incorporating research innovations not easily realized through traditional print publication. The creation of some journals, such as the well known *Online Journal of Current Clinical Trials*, was undertaken with the eventual goal of using hypertext links to connect relevant articles as well as any commentary that might be attached to them (such as letters, rebuttals, and retractions) within a larger electronic archive of disciplinary work (see, e.g., Kellar 1991). Such archives can enhance access and information retrieval within a body of literature to a degree not previously available. As a further example, the *Electronic Journal of Communication/Revue électronique de communication*, offered under the auspices of the Comserve project, will soon be accompanied by a software system that facilitates the ability of subscribers to read articles on their computer screens, rather than downloading them to print. The display program attempts to overcome some of the traditional limitations of reading text on a computer screen, for example, enabling readers to move directly from text citations and footnotes to references via hypertext-style links, and allowing them to annotate text in a pop-up notation space that can be saved for future inspection (Harrison and Stephen 1993).

Scholars are also using electronic journals to reconceive traditional peer review processes as well as to recover the ancient dialogic character of scholarly communication, which has always been poorly reflected in print publication. Stevan Harnad (1991) has argued that when journals are distributed through the network, scholarship can progress at a speed and tempo more similar to that of natural thought and speech. *Psycoloquy*, the electronic journal founded by Harnad, has thus been designed to automate the delivery of current research reports and peer responses, reducing time lags from months to hours and preserving the interactive quality that ideally should characterize such processes. *Postmodern Culture* solicits self-nominated peer reviewers by issuing a call to all subscribers with descriptions of essays recently submitted to the journal; this speeds up the process of peer review and allows the editors to gauge the level of interest in particular submissions.

Another way that editors have used networking to enhance the dialogic quality of scholarship is by associating Listserv conferences or MOOs (see, e.g., *John Unsworth's* essay) with their electronic publications. In his essay on the history of print publication and the future of electronic publication, *Jean-Claude Guédon* suggests that the ability to incorporate comments and arguments from readers in online discussion about articles may itself yield a new form of scholarly product—one in which the integrity of a monological text produced by a single author is eroded, gradually giving way to the creation of a text in which distinctions between authors and readers are blurred in the "flow-like" production of an online text.

Other journal projects have been conceived with the goal of allowing readers to access various types of information relevant to the articles published, such as images, and graphical and quantitative data. For example, the online *Journal of Statistics Education* plans to store articles within a database that will allow readers to retrieve associated data sets and graphics as well as the text of the article (Solomon, Arnold, and Dietz 1992). Similarly, the *Journal of Fluids Engineering* will enable subscribers to read the results of research in an article as well as to examine the raw data associated with that particular research study (Ekman and Quandt 1994).

It should be apparent that the variation in form and function possible through electronic journal publication is considerable indeed. In his essay in this volume, *Brian Gaines* discusses the kinds of technological options available in electronic journal publication and calls attention to the problems and potentials such options present for refashioning the traditional print-based model of the scholarly journal. He presents an agenda of objectives that might be realized through electronic publication that can also be used to guide the development of current and planned electronic journals.

Most of the new electronic journals appearing on the network have been initiated by scholars themselves, effectively bypassing traditional academic publishers, although some editors have sought and received the support of their professional organizations. The majority of these journals have been offered to subscribers over the network for free. It is too soon to say what the eventual outcome of such innovations will be and how long such journals can continue to be offered without an attempt to recover costs; clearly there are many factors affecting the degree to which network-based publications will be received positively by their academic constituencies. However, the ability of the network to support these grass-roots publications, scholars' apparent willingness to perform editorial roles without immediate financial support, and positive reception by the library community has given rise to speculations about how scholars, publishers, and the library community will be positioned in a publication system that relies upon network distribution.

While lagging behind scholars and librarians in recognizing the potential of electronic publication, non-profit and commercial scholarly publishers are becoming increasingly involved in their own attempts to explore how the network can be used for electronic publishing. Several university-based and professional society publishers, such as the Johns Hopkins Press' Project MUSE (DeLoughrey 1994) and the University of California Press (Ekman and Quandt 1994) are making available over the Internet the contents of several established humanities journals. A similar project to make archives of the *Physical Review* available is being undertaken by the American Physical Society (Thomas 1994). In one of only a few examples of a new publisher-supported academic journal, MIT Press in conjunction with the MIT Libraries is planning to offer the *Chicago Journal of Theoretical Computer Science* through the Internet, using a site licensing fee arrangement (described in more detail in the essay by *Brian Kahin*). Finally, in their essay in this volume *Cliff McKnight, Andrew Dillon*, and *Brian Shackel* describe several collaborations comprised of various combinations of commercial academic publishers, software companies, research organizations, professional organizations, universities, and academic libraries, who have joined together to create electronic versions of print publications that attempt to recreate the "look and feel" of the printed page (see also DeLoughrey 1993) and to determine how they can become economically viable.

As *McKnight, Dillon*, and *Shackel* point out, the use of computer networks to deliver academic publications has called into question the structure of the entire system of scholarly publishing, as well as some of the conceptual foundations upon which that system is based, such as, for example, the meaning of copyright. As commercial publishers, university presses, university librarians, and the legions of technology companies now finding themselves in the business of publishing information jockey for position, it will be important for scholars to think clearly about whose interests are served by the flood of new models that are starting to appear. Some of the issues involved in the coming transition are taken up in more detail in the essays by *Brian Kahin* and *Kenneth Arnold*.

Kahin's essay calls our attention, on one hand, to the problems that nonentrepreneurial university presses and libraries experience in recovering costs for risky electronic publication projects and, on the other hand, to the ability of commercial organizations to impose serious restrictions on the flow of scholarly information through information licenses and software patents. He argues for the development of university-based alternatives to conventional publishing, in which copyright is held jointly between academic authors and the universities for whom they work, rather than assigned to commercial organizations. *Kenneth Arnold*, representing the publishing community, raises concerns about what such a vision of publication might entail, arguing that universities are not equipped to undertake management of a system for scholarly communication, that there are roles within such a system that only academic publishers—commercial and non-profit— are able to play. The authors differ in their assessments of the requirements for a new system of scholarly communication; both *Arnold* and *Kahin*, however, agree that a new system is needed and needed quickly, before universities are forced to operate within an environment for scholarship that has been designed by those with purely commercial interests.

The Future of Academic Networking

The introduction of hypertext, networking, and multimedia computing has made it apparent that much of the way we think about research and education, even the way that we define knowledge, is predicated upon the medium of print. Until quite recently, it has been possible to take print-based conceptions of knowledge for granted as natural, necessary, and objective; what other form could knowledge take in most disciplines but as journal articles or books? But as electronic alternatives stimulate our imaginations and offer ways to supplement print and avoid or transcend its constraints, we are now beginning to recognize how arbitrary indeed are the print-based conventions that have structured our view of the academic world (Tuman 1992). And we can begin to imagine how such conventions will be changed as the world of print is supplemented by or gives way to a world of electronic discourse.

One vision of the electronic text is Richard Lanham's (1993) multimedia discourse, in which words, images, sounds, and color are inextricably intertwined to produce a literature in which the expressive arts are interchangeable. This is a discourse, as Lanham points out, that re-enfranchises those lacking a natural proclivity for print, and one that allows each of us to use the full range of our sensory capabilities in the service of inquiry. One catches a glimmer of what such a discourse can bring to scholarship in recent efforts to make available to medieval scholars around the world images of the Beowulf manuscripts (Kiernan 1993) and David Zeitlyn's (1994) World Wide Web distribution of digitized sound recordings of Mambila language transcribed in print, in his article on kin talk appearing in *Man*, for linguists and anthropologists. There are many technical, organizational, and economic problems to be overcome before any such visions can be put in place. *David Austin's* chapter on providing networked access to visual information impresses us with how much work needs to be done before we can realize the promise of a multimedia text. And *Tom McNulty* reminds us that an electronic multimedia discourse that enfranchises many may also exclude disabled scholars unless designers keep in the mind the needs of these scholars and students as they create electronic texts and the technologies used to display them.

Although we cannot now be sure of all that an electronic discourse will entail, it seems certain that the evolution from print to the networked electronic text will culminate in new conceptions of knowledge that are, as *Peter Lyman* argues, different from, but not opposite to, those embedded in the media of print. *Lyman* hypothesizes that such new forms of knowledge will restructure many of the social relationships that constitute the academic world: relationships between words, human emotions, and human actions; relationships between authors, texts, and readers; relationships that impart value to texts; and the reformation of social institutions such as libraries, campuses, and disciplinary communities.

Computer networking has captured the collective imagination of the academic world because it has presented us with the ability to realize more fully certain scholarly ideals that traditionally we have been forced to compromise—unending and inclusive scholarly conversation; collaborative inquiry limited only by mutual interests; unrestrained access to scholarly resources; independent, decentralized learning; and a timely and universally accessible system for representing, distributing, and archiving knowledge. Our review of networking applications has been brief, but even so it is apparent that computer networking has reawakened consideration of these ideals and reinvigorated our efforts to achieve them within the contexts of our ongoing research and teaching. It is also apparent that our very attempts to realize these ideals harbor the seeds of disciplinary, pedagogical, and organizational innovation that will create a new academic world for the twenty-first century, with ideals that we must now begin to invent.

References

Bellman, B., Tindimubona, A., and Arias, A., Jr. (1993). Technology transfer in global networking: Capacity building in Africa and Latin America. In L. Harasim (Ed.) *Global networks* (237–254). Cambridge, Mass.: MIT Press.
Bennehum, D. (1994). Fly me to the MOO: Adventures in textual reality. *Lingua Franca* 4(4):22–36.

Berge, Z. and Collins, M. (forthcoming). *Computer mediated communications and the online classroom: An overview and perspectives*. Cresskill, N.J.: Hampton Press.

Berge, Z. and Collins, M. (forthcoming). *Computer mediated communications and the online classroom in distance education*. Cresskills, N.J.: Hampton Press.

Bloch, E. (1988). A national network: Today's reality, tomorrow's vision, Part 1. *Educom Bulletin* (Summer/Fall):11–13.

Boyer, E. (1990). *Scholarship reconsidered: Priorities for the professoriate*. Princeton, N.J.: Carnegie Foundation for the Advancement of Teaching.

Broad, W. J. (1993). Doing science on the network. *The New York Times* (May 18):C1, C10.

Burge, E. (1992). *Computer mediated communication and education: A selected bibliography*. Toronto: Ontario Institute for Studies in Education.

Cambridge Structural Database. (1994). URL:http://csdvx2.ccdc.cam.ac.uk/csd.html#CSD.

Catalogue of Projects in Electronic Text. (1994). URL:gopher://Gopher.Georgetown.edu/).

Cherry, C. (1985). *The age of access: Information technology and social revolution*. W. Edmondson (Ed.). London: Croom Helm.

Connor, P. (1992). Networking in the humanities: Lessons from ANSAXNET. *Computers in the Humanities* 26:195–204.

Crane, D. (1972). *Invisible colleges: Diffusion of knowledge in scientific communities*. Chicago: University of Chicago Press.

Cronin, B. (1982). Invisible colleges and information transfer: A review and commentary with particular reference to the social sciences. *Journal of Documentation* 38:212–236.

DeLoughrey, T. J. (1994). Journals via computers. *Chronicle of Higher Education* (March 9):A25–A26.

Dowling, T. P. (1994). Internet resources for engineering. *College and Research Libraries News* 55(6):352–353, 357.

Economics WPA World Wide Webb Service. (1994). URL:http://econwpa.wustl.edu:80.

Ekman, R. H. and Quandt, R. E. (1994). Scholarly communication, academic libraries, and technology. URL: gopher://arl.cni.org/00/scomm/scalt.

Faigley, L. (1992). The achieved utopia of the networked classroom. In L. Faigley (Ed.) *Fragments of rationality: Postmodernity and the subject of composition* (163–199). Pittsburgh: University of Pittsburgh Press.

Fehrmann, P. (1993). Internet resources for psychology. *College and Research Libraries News* 54(9):510–511.

Giddens, A. (1990). *The consequences of modernity*. Stanford: Stanford University Press.

Giddens, A. (1984). *The constitution of society*. Berkeley: University of California Press.

Glazier, M. (1994). Internet resources for women's studies. *College and Research Libraries News* 55(3):139–141, 143.

Gleick, James. (1994). The information future: Out of control. *The New York Times Magazine* (May 1):54–57.

Harasim, L. (1993). Networlds: Networks as social space. In L. Harasim (Ed.) *Global networks* (15–34). Cambridge: MIT Press.

Harnad, S. (1991). Post-Gutenberg galaxy: The fourth revolution in the means of production of knowledge. *Public-Access Computer Systems Review 2*: 29–41.

Harrison, T., Stephen, T. and Winter, J. (1991). Online journals: Disciplinary designs for electronic scholarship. *Public-Access Computer Systems Review* 2:18–28.

Harrison, T. and Stephen, T. (1992). Online disciplines: Computer-mediated scholarship in the humanities and social sciences. *Computers and the Humanities 26*:181–193.

Harrison, T., and Stephen, T. (1993). *The case of EJC/REC: A model for producing, consuming and delivering electronic journals electronically.* Paper presented at the University of Manitoba International Conference on Refereed Electronic Journals, October.

Hart, M. (1994). NEWUSER.GUT. URL:ftp://mrcnext.cso.uiuc.edu/etext/ NEWUSER.GUT.

Heylighn, F. Joslyn, C., and Turchin, V. (1994, March 10). An overview of the Principia Cybernetica Project. URL: http://pespmc1.vub.ac.be/ NUTSHELL.html.

Hiltz, S. R. (1984). *Online communities.* Norwood, N.J.: Ablex.

Hiltz, S. R. and Turoff, M. (1993). *The network nation: Human communication via computer.* Cambridge, Mass.: MIT Press.

Hughes, K. (1994). Entering the World Wide Web: A guide to cyperspace. May. URL: ftp://ftp.eit.com/pub/web.guide.

International Philosophical Preprint Exchange. (1994). URL:gopher://Phil-Preprints.L.Chiba-U.ac.jp.

Jacobson, R. L. (1993). As instructional technology proliferates, skeptics seek hard evidence of its value. *Chronicle of Higher Education* (May 5): A27–A29.

Kiernan, K. S. (1993). Digital preservation, restoration, and dissemination of medieval manuscripts. In *Scholarly Publishing on the Electronic Networks, 1993: Gateways, Gatekeepers, and Roles in the Information Omniverse.* URL:HTTP://www.uky.edu/ dhart/dhart.html.

Kovacs, D. (1994). Directory of scholarly electronic conferences, 8th revision. URL: FTP://ksuvxa.kent.edu/library.

Kovacs, D. (1992). Academic discussion lists and interest groups. In A. Okerson (Ed.), *Directory of electronic journals, newsletters, and discussion lists.* 2nd ed. (83–241). Washington, D.C.: Association of Research Libraries.

Licklider, J.C.R., Taylor, R., and Herbert, E. (1968). The computer as a communication device. *Science and Technology* (April):21–31.

Marvin, C. (1988). *When old technologies were new.* Oxford: Oxford University Press.

Markus, M. L. (1987). Toward a "critical mass" theory of interactive media. *Communication Research 14*:491–511.

McCarty, W. (1992). HUMANIST: Lessons from a global electronic seminar. *Computers and the Humanities 26*:205–222.

McCarty, W., (1994, April 9, 15:12:02 EDT). Archive of syllabi. Electronic message to Internet discussion group Humanist@BrownVM.BITNET.

McGee, A. (1994, Feb. 22, 17:37:31 CST). Black/African/Development Info. Electronic message to Internet discussion group PACS-L@UHUPVM1. UHU.EDU.

McGee, A. (1994, Feb. 22, 17:37:45 CST). Indigenous/Native/Aboriginal Info. Electronic message to Internet discussion group PACS-L@UHUPVM1. UHU.EDU. See also URL:ftp:// ftp.netcom.com/pub/amcgee.

Melton, L. (1994, Feb. 21, 13:23:14 CST). International Centre for Distance Learning–Database. Electronic message to Internet discussion group Pacs-L@Uhupvm1.Uhu.Edu.

Noble, D. (1984). *Forces of production.* Oxford: Oxford University Press.

Okerson, A. (1994). Introduction. In A. Okerson (Ed.) *Directory of electronic journals, newsletters, and academic discussion lists.* 4th ed. Washington, D.C.: Association of Research Libraries. URL: Gopher://arl.cni.org/00/ scomm/edir/eintro.

Okerson, A. (1990). Incentives and disincentives in research and educational communication. *Educom Review* 25:15.

Poole M. S. and DeSanctis, G. (1990). Understanding the use of group decision support systems: The theory of adaptive structuration. In J. Fulk and C. Steinfield (Eds.) *Organizations and communication technology* (173–193). Newbury Park: Sage.

Poore, J. H. (1988). Funding the national network. *Educom Bulletin* (Summer/ Fall):49–51, 58.

Publication by Electronic Mail takes Physics by Storm. (1993). *Science* (February 26):1246–1248.

Pullinger, D. J. (1986). Chit-chat to electronic journals: Computer conferencing supports scientific communication. *IEEE Transactions on Professional Communications PC* 29:23–29.

Rheingold, H. (1993). *The virtual community.* Reading, Mass.: Addison-Wesley.

Rogers, E. (1984). *Diffusion of innovations.* 3rd ed. New York: Free Press.

Rogers, S. J. and Hurt, C. S. (1989). How scholarly communication should work in the 21st century. *Chronicle of Higher Education* (October 18): A56.

Rosczak, T. (1994). *The cult of information.* 2nd ed. Berkeley: University of California Press.

Rowland, J.F. (1994, March 31, 9:19:29 EST). Report on ELVYN Project. Electronic message to Internet discussion group Vpiej-L@Vtvm1.Bitnet.

Schaefermeyer, M. J. and Sewell, E. H., Jr. (1988). Communicating by electronic mail. *American Behavioral Scientist, 32,* 112–123.

Solomon, D. L., Arnold, J. T., and Dietz, E. J. (1992). Starting a new journal in statistics education. In A. Okerson (Ed.). *Visions and opportunities in electronic publishing: Proceedings of the second symposium* (19–28). Washington: Association of Research Libraries.

Spears, R. and Lea, M. (1992). Social influence and the influence of the 'social' in computer-mediated communication. In M. Lea (Ed.) *Contexts of computer-mediated communication* (30–65). New York: Harvester Wheatsheaf.

Thomas, T. R. (1994). Welcome to the Prototype Physical Review Online Archives. URL: http://www.c3.lanl.gov:8080/apswelcome.

Turoff, M. and Hiltz, S. R. (1982). The electronic journal: A progress report. *Journal of the American Society for Information Science 33*:195–202.

Tuman, M. (1992). *Word perfect: Literacy in the computer age*. Pittsburgh: University of Pittsburgh Press.

University of Waterloo Library. (1994). Gophers and Other Servers of Scholarly Societies. URL: gopher://watserv2.uwaterloo.ca/00/servers/campus/scholars/about).

Welcome to HEPNRC. (1994). URL:http://www.hep.net/hepnrc.html.

Welcome to The University of Chicago Philosophy Project. (1994). URL: http://csmaclab-www.uchicago.edu/philosphyProject/philos.html.

Wilkins, H. (1991). Computer talk: Long-distance conversations by computer. *Written Communication 8*:56–83.

Winner, L. (1986). *The whale and the reactor*. Chicago: University of Chicago Press.

Wouters, A. (1994). Internet services for philosophers. URL: Gopher://gate.oxy.edu/00/Internet.

Yavarokovsky, J. (1990). A university-based electronic publishing network. *Educom Review 25*:14–20.

Zeitlyn, D. (1994, April 4, 05:37:34 +0000). World Wide Web speaks Mambila. E-mail note sent to Humanist electronic discussion group.

*Part II*_____

ISSUES IN COMPUTER NETWORKING AND SCHOLARSHIP

How Is the Medium the Message?

*Notes on the Design of
Networked Communication*

Peter Lyman

Although the Internet is often defined as "the network of networks," the sociology of the network is more than the sum of its technical parts. An analysis of the importance of cyberspace for teaching and learning must begin by investigating the character of digital technologies and networks as they are used, not as they are constructed—as essentially social, not technical, phenomena. Although the personal computer has been used to produce printed texts, it is essentially a medium for information design—the creation, management and use of information—not an automated typewriter. Similarly, the network is not essentially a technology for linking computers, it is a new medium for communication, the characteristics of which are still largely undiscovered.

Technical language mirrors the embryonic history of this innovation. Vestigial words reflect the origin and development of this technology, yet obscure its nature as a medium for communication. The word "computer" is itself anachronistic, since today the network is used for information management more than computation. The names and uses of the parts of the keyboard—keys named "control," "break," "escape," and "command"—derive from a cybernetic "command and control" philosophy, reflecting the military development of computation to sustain hierarchy. Technology design itself reflects for control: the technical infrastructure was based upon centralized "mainframes" controlling "dumb terminals," essentially the technological equivalent of a master/slave command relationship. Today, network social relations tend to be egalitarian or communal, and mainframes have been replaced by "client/server" architectures originally developed to support collaborative scientific research. In each case, the design of technology reflects social organization more than it causes it. If we do not yet have an appropriate language to describe the social relationships that are occurring on the network, this is a sign that we may be living in an age of genuine social innovation.

Networked information is in an experimental phase that might yet be shaped by a vision of the uses of digital communications for education. Technology is a design for human activity shaped by social vision, not an independent historical force with its own inexorable logic. An evolutionary strategy from print to digital communication would imprison teaching and learning within the designs of a cybernetic command and control culture that is inappropriate for educational social relationships. Thus, the following notes toward the design of an appropriate sociology for networked teaching and research are only hypothetical, questions and inferences based upon experiments such as those described elsewhere in this anthology.

Knowledge as a Material Culture

Is there a difference between the way print technology and computer representations of knowledge shape communication and therefore mediate human relationships? Early experience suggests that printed and networked texts are not opposites—all texts are instantiated in technical artifacts—yet they are not the same. In focusing upon knowledge as "content alone," we often lose track of the way that texts are created by a material culture of technical objects and craft activities, governed by disciplines that still function like guilds in some respects. But networked information inevitably draws our attention back to the crafts and tools with which we create and consume digital documents, if for no other reason than that they are new, and still being created.

It is often said that we are in the midst of a historic change, perhaps a renaissance in which new forms of knowledge and new arts have been made possible by technology. Yet even if this is true this is not a change from a world in which ideas and communication were not mediated by technology. For half a millennium, ideas have been expressed and exchanged through a mechanical process of printing; we are beginning an age in which ideas will also be mediated by digital communication technologies. This change in the media within which ideas are represented and exchanged will, sooner or later, be fundamental. History suggests that in the first stages of innovation, the new technology typically is adapted to reproduce the old (e.g., Eisenstein 1979), but gradually experimentation produces parallel but separate knowledge cultures. It is very likely that print and digital media will continue to coexist, the way print and oral cultures have coexisted.

We must begin by recognizing that our assumptions about the creation, content, and use of knowledge are deeply embedded within the tacit crafts of knowledge built upon the use of printed texts. This recognition will enable us to understand the ways that electronic knowledge is different from, but not the opposite of print mediated knowledge. A corollary is that digital works are unlikely to substitute for the cultures of knowledge built upon print. The specific characteristics of printed commodities—for example, the facticity of the form of the book, newspaper, and journal—has defined the rhetorical rules that organize knowledge, and the social institutions that have developed from them. Networked information, in contrast, lacks fixed material form; form may be dictated by the user, and may be copied and changed at will. In sum, as will be explored later in this essay, there is a phenomenological link between the technical format of a text, the rhetorical rules within which it is constructed, and its content.

The definition of intellectual property as copyright, for example, emerged when the expression of an idea took material form as a printed commodity regulated by a market. An idea cannot be owned or easily regulated, but a printed object that contains the expression of an idea may be part of a "marketplace of ideas." Indeed, the process of production itself can be regulated by law, as in the literal meaning of the word "copy-right." In a networked environment in which information has no particular material form that can effectively be regulated, what kind of a concept of intellectual property is appropriate and enforceable? The answer to this question is not simply legal, but social and economic: what form must intellectual property take in order to create economic incentives for the production of high quality information in a networked environment? In this emerging pluralistic world, research and education will have many expressions, each in a technological format appropriate to its content, to the social relations and cultural values that it serves, and each, if it is to be viable, commanding a price in a marketplace.

History also suggests that it is not the technology itself that causes innovation, it is cultural and social needs, which are latent but unmet by the old technologies. Consider this description of the impact of the printed book upon the sociology of knowledge in Europe.

> the printed book was something more than a triumph of technical ingenuity, but was also one of the most potent agents at the disposal of western civilization in bringing together the scattered ideas of representative thinkers. It rendered vital service to research by immediately transmitting results from one researcher to another; and speedily and conveniently, without laborious effort or unsupportable cost, it assembled permanently the works of the most sublime creative spirits in all fields. . . . Fresh concepts crossed whole regions of the globe in the very shortest time. . . . The book

> created new habits of thought not only within the small circle of
> the learned, but far beyond, in the intellectual life of all who used
> their minds. In short . . . the printed book was one of the most
> effective means of mastery over the whole world. (Febvre and
> Martin 1976, 10)

Technologies have withered when they come into direct conflict with
power structures, but flourish when they renew core cultural values
and reinforce social change. Fundamentally, technical innovation always occurs within the context of social relationships and cultural
ideals; thus, an analysis of the possible impact of the network upon
higher education should begin by discovering how innovations using
networked information resolve problems or meet a latent educational
need.

The Relation between Texts and Actions

How do different kinds of textual media shape the relationship between words, human emotions, and actions? Some early experiments
suggest that digital words are more intimately linked to emotion and
action than printed words: it is not yet clear whether this link is dependent upon the social context with which we use texts, or whether
print literacy skills become tacit in early education, while digital literacy skills still require conscious attention and engagement only because most of us are learning them long after we have learned to read
print.

The most fundamental starting point in defining the similarities
and differences between digital and printed text is obvious, yet little
noted. While written texts are the interface both between humans and
books and between humans and computers, there may be important
phenomenological differences between texts represented by printed
words and as words on a computer screen. Digital words may have a
relationship to actions that printed words do not have; they are a
doing, a performance, that has the capacity to evoke something like
the feelings we normally associate with relationships between human
beings.

Computers sometimes evoke an emotional engagement, making
them a genuine field of play. In play, thought and action are unified
in a sense of "flow," in which the sense of time disappears (cf.,
Csikszentmihalyi 1990). This sort of human-tool relationship is not
unprecedented, for musical instruments are also tools that become a
medium for expression, which seem to become one with the body in

a skilled performance which is disciplined yet often experienced as play (Sudnow 1979). Sherry Turkle's ethnographic studies (1980; 1984) suggest that the computer's responsiveness unites the emotional power of play with learning, by enabling the user to "work through" life contradictions and issues.

The power of this feeling of play has often been observed in computer based entertainment, and yet we do not yet know much about its use in teaching and learning. Studying the human/tool relationship reminds us to pay more attention to the experience of learning and to the crafts of knowing, and less to the automation of teaching and the content of knowledge.

In each case, the human/tool relationship must be understood in the context of the experience of using the tool in use in a skilled performance, and not merely as an object of inspection. Books too are very different when inspected as objects, in contrast to their presence in the activity of reading: "The availability of a book to the hand, its presence on a shelf, its listing in a library catalog—all of these encourage us to think of it as a stationary object. Somehow when we put a book down, we forget that while we were reading, it was moving (pages turning, lines receding into the past) and forget too that we were moving with it" (Fish 1972, 401). The capacity for a sense of play makes both books and computers very successful media for entertainment, yet however engaging reading books may become, the sense of emotional engagement in digital work seems to be more likely to be experienced as a social relation with an "other," if not a person.

Tools, books or computers, contain instantiated technical cultures, which demand literacy skills, whether defined by the technical design decisions within the computer system or the lexical and rhetorical structure of a book. The very power of the experience of play in music or games is dependent upon these tacit rules that require skill and concentration; thus, it is not necessarily technical order or the need to master the skills that are part of virtuosity that constitutes the problem of technical literacy. The emotional issue is whether technological order is experienced as domination or empowerment by the user. Turkle, for example, studied educational environments, not the social contexts of computers at work, in which the computer dominates the worker, imposing technical authority that anonymously plays the same role as personal supervision in the factory.

Networked information, such as electronic mail, is an even more complex human/tool relation than reading a book or a computer screen, for social relationships themselves are directly mediated by the network. A clue to the dynamics of networked communication is suggested by an analysis of "flaming," the tendency of electronic mail "conversations" to become emotional and extreme. Sproull and Kiesler (1986) suggest that it is the absence of social context cues that allows e-mail exchanges to become hostile, but flaming itself might also be due to the absence of a common culture (or the presence of a common culture that tolerates and values aggressiveness), or the still primitive development of rhetorical cultures that might govern networked communication.

Each of these studies suggests the important point that "information" is never socially or emotionally neutral; it always occurs within social contexts, whether those implicit in the human/tool relationship or those in machine-mediated communication. The very word "information" has a scholastic origin, and deliberately contains a connotation of training, the instilling of certain attitudes or values, in contrast to the modern technological sense that "information" is by definition "objective." If we can understand the emotional and social contexts of networked information, these very characteristics make the network of much greater value for teaching and learning.

What is the Relationship between Author and Reader?

How, in a specific phenomenological sense, do different media shape the social organization of knowledge? As Fish (1972) described reading above, the printed page is a tool which mediates a serial, yet distinctly human relationship between writer and reader. For example, ideally the activity of reading reconstructs in the mind's eye a kind of dialogue, in which the writer speaks and the reader listens. Structurally, there is an economic and legal relation as well, in which the writer is an author, owning rights that define the proper use of the text. These relationships are tacit for us, ingrained in the habits that we call literacy and property. And yet, the same text in a digital environment may generate very different social and economic relationships; this is the reason a digital text is unlikely to "replace" a printed text. Even more importantly, there are some texts that may only exist in digital and networked environments, which will generate unprecedented relationships between reader and writer. Networked information is raising profound questions about the relationships between ideas, media, and the law: intellectual property is an important form of capital for which there is a market that must be regulated, but which also raises important epistemological questions about legal responsibility for the validity of published information.

These issues are reflected in Michel Foucault's argument that the concept of an "author" arose simultaneously with the printed book. With development of a commercial market for books, the expression of an idea in print placed it in the public domain, and thereby generated issues concerning liability and legal responsibility.

> Texts, books, and discourses really begin to have authors to the extent that authors became subject to punishment, that is, to the extent that discourses could be transgressive. . . . Once a system of ownership for texts came into being, once strict rules concerning author's rights, author-publisher relations, rights of reproduction, and related matters were enacted—at the end of the eighteenth and the beginning of the nineteenth century—the possibility of transgression attached to the act of writing took on, more and more, the form of an imperative peculiar to literature. (Foucault 1984, 108)

The idea of "author" thus links writing both to legal responsibility, and to property right; the idea of a literature thus inevitably has a political and economic context. How will "authorship," understood to contain these linked notions of responsibility and ownership, change in a networked medium? If the idea of authorship changes, how does the activity of reading change, and the tacit relationship of writer to reader? How does the "unit of knowledge" change from print to network, and thereby our concept of a scholarly "literature" or discipline? Of a library or classroom?

The writer's status as author is reinforced by the inflexibility of the printed page; but the digital page can be redefined by the reader. These new relationships between reader and writer have led to the creation of new textual artifacts, in which the boundary between reader and writer is unclear, and the authority of the writer and the reader's "rights" are transformed.

Hypertext is a textual artifact that reflects the reading style of technical readers, in which the reader becomes author, interrogating the text with questions. This style of reading is familiar to us most when we read reference materials. Some texts, like dictionaries, contain entirely non-sequential writing, but any narrative text might be read as hypertext if it is treated as information. This principle is illustrated by a study that compares reader comprehension of a statistics textbook which was presented in different formats—print, online, and as hypertext (Egan, Remde, Landauer, Lochbaum, and Gomez 1989). Readers understood printed texts better than the same text as it "scrolled" by on a computer; yet when placed within the hypertext program, comprehension was higher than in the print version. Of course, different kinds of knowledge have different rhetorical structures; an encyclopedia is a kind of reference material that lends itself to hypertext in a way that a narrative text such as a novel would not. While the format or medium must be appropriate to the content and structure of the knowledge in which it is presented, it is equally true that reading is an activity that may have many purposes, and readers are always free to impose their own structure on a text.

What Makes Texts Valuable?

How does the network give information a distinctive value, different from the value of printed information: its provenance? structure? its use by new kinds of communities? its timeliness? What is the epistemological status of digital simulation? How will education develop the kind of critical methodologies for evaluating digital information that now exist to evaluate printed information?

Writing is always a design for reading. In a networked environment, this design must include a design for navigating a global information infrastructure that has been designed without a consistent structure; the Internet is organized around technical standards for moving information, with almost no attention to organizing the content of information. Writing has always tacitly been designed as the expression of the recorded knowledge of a community of readers; who is that community when knowledge is global? What is the editorial process by which "truth" or inclusion in a "literature" is constituted in a networked environment?

Each of these questions is posed by online text. McGraw-Hill's Primus project placed textbooks and magazines in a database, to be edited and printed on demand. Two things were surprising about the use of the database: (1) readers combined materials from different disciplines; and, (2) readers treated the paragraph as the fundamental unit of knowledge, removing information from its narrative context. As a consequence, some authors refused to place their work in the database. Because digital texts are malleable, the association between author and writer weakens, and the opposition between writer and reader will evolve into a continuum. For example, the notion of the writer's property right becomes ambiguous when groups of people create texts as a collaborative act; every reader becomes a writer when text can be copied from the network, perhaps changed, and republished in new form. Similarly, the idea of a scholarly literature changes when the documentary record is malleable. Because printing has required substantial capital investment, the act of "publication" has implied both quality and editorial control as well as distribution. However, networked information may be distributed globally by any writer. And even where editorial control over networked information exists (and the electronic journal movement is a substantial series of experiments in this area), the traditional forms of scholarship may change. Will the traditional representation of data through text or graphics in the printed journal article continue to command authority when a networked journal article can directly contain a data field, when peer review may be appended as a continuing discussion, when a group of scholars may create a real-time database?

While printed publication is a useful distortion of the process of discovery, a picture of what is known at a given point in time, it is a substantial distortion of the continuous process of discovery and criticism.

All knowledge is open-ended on the network; in principle, there need be no microcosm of knowledge like the encyclopedia or textbook, in that links can be provided to the data, to other texts, to the tools for analysis, ultimately which might enable the reader to rewrite the text. A text might include performances in a real-time live video window, or link changing real time information with recorded knowledge in text, graphics, and sound. The notion of knowledge as a "literature," a systematic body of texts within which judgments about the validity of information are made by reference to the system itself, has led to the understanding that knowledge is theoretical. This in turn subjects the learning process to the authority of the teacher, which is in turn derived from the literature. In a networked environment, however, knowledge requires a skilled performance, learning and research are a doing, not a literature. Technical culture, in this sense, is a tacit agent of change, embedded in technical objects, introducing the pedagogy of learning by doing, by iteration, by reducing error. It also introduces the value of collaborative, rather than competitive, social relations in learning. The discipline becomes a strategy for learning, which requires navigating the network to find access to the right information, making judgments about its quality, and knowing how to integrate it into one's own work.

Finally, what is the epistemological status of digital simulations, like the dinosaurs in *Jurassic Park* that appear to be real, but exist only as a simulation of the real? From an aesthetic point of view, digital simulations appear to hold the full status of an analog based text, but they have a uniquely different provenance, originating within a mathematical model, not a correspondence to the real; "what is simulated is no longer the territory, an original substance or being, but a model of the real . . . from now on it is the map that precedes, and thus generates, the territory " (Popper 1993, 58). Digital criticism must distinguish between the truth value of analog and digital, between representation and simulation, between an image that makes reference to the real and one that makes reference to a model of the real.

The Electronic Library as a Social Institution

The idea of an electronic library thus far has focused upon the automation of the printed library, rather than upon the social functions and culture of the library as an institution. What kind of social institution is an electronic library? What kinds of subsidies can it command in the marketplace? What kinds of literacies will it require? If the library has been the center of the campus, for what kind of campus will the electronic library be a center?

The printed codex made possible the idea of a library, with all that word now implies: a coherent and cumulative scientific literature; publication and intellectual property rights; preservation and access to ideas; and a global intellectual culture (Febvre and Martin 1976). As a technology for the organization and transmission of knowledge, print was the foundation upon which new kinds of institutions evolved, such as science and invention, democracy and the marketplace.

Today, the most distinctive definition of the network as an institution is the idea of the electronic library, a global reference room in which every citizen can publish information and find access to the information published by others. There was substantial reason to envision the network as a library when the idea emerged in 1992. MERIT statistics indicate that by 1992, nearly two-thirds of the use of NSFNet by scientists was for the organization and access to information, not computation. In 1992, OCLC research (Dillon, Jul, Burge, and Hickey 1992, 12–14) estimated that the Internet, Bitnet and Usenet together contain 3.1 million FTP files, 337 library catalogs, 111 listserv sites each containing many more uncounted computer lists, 3,275 electronic conferences, 26 electronic journals, 72 newsletters, 16 digests, and 3,794 newsgroups. The 1992 Directory of Electronic Journals, Newsletters and Academic Discussion Lists (Strangelove and Kovacs 1992) published by the Association of Research Libraries includes 36 electronic journals, 697 scholarly lists and 80 newsletters.

The ideal of an electronic library is important as a first approximation of the use of the network to build institutions for the organization and management of information on a global scale. Ideally, an electronic library would remove inequalities in access to information created by distance, particularly in an era in which intellectual capital is the foundation of economic wealth.

And yet, the idea of the electronic library is as interesting for what it does not include as for what it does. As yet there is no concept of how to establish or regulate a market in intellectual property on the network, no quality standards of publication or pricing and marketing, no strategy for creating network literatures, or for the preservation of networked information. The radical democratic vision of the electronic library contains the best elements of the traditions of the public library in American society. While the fiscal basis of free (subsidized) access to information in the public library was taxation, the fiscal basis of access to networked information thus far has largely been the subsidy provided by federal defense and scientific research, research universities, and the donated labor of innovators (such as the publishers of electronic journals). The future of the electronic library will be defined somewhere between the metaphor of the public library and the metaphor of pay television; federal policy debates suggest the latter, while technical visionaries prefer the former.

In either future, there will be a new kind of literacy, the skills needed to "navigate" the global reference room. Finding the right information is no longer a problem of scarcity, it is a problem of quality control and selection from an information explosion. This is as fundamental for the future of teaching and learning as it is for the design of new technical systems. The problem of teaching will be focused increasingly upon creating lifelong skills of learning, not upon communicating a particular set of information. The problem of learning will be focused increasingly upon developing the crafts of creating knowledge from the tools and information sources available ready at hand on the network. In this sense, networked teaching and learning will resemble library research more than classroom lectures.

By extension, then, if the library has been the center of the campus, what becomes of the campus in a world of networked information? The origin of the campus was in the concentration of scarce intellectual resources, teachers and books. But is it possible that the fundamental components of education could be decentralized in a society that is saturated with information resources? Looking at the question from a different perspective, might what we call education potentially be vastly expanded, to include entirely new kinds of students and new kinds of skills, based upon new modes of teaching and learning?

A City in Cyberspace?

If the network will change the social relationships implicit within the artifacts with which we represent knowledge, might it also create entirely new kinds of social relations, social forms, organizations, and institutions? Scholarly publications are artifacts produced to enable communication among scholars who belong to scholarly communities: what kinds of scholarly communities can be nurtured by the network? Early experiments suggest that genuine communities can develop and be nurtured on the network among participants who have never met face to face, even on a global scale. What is the nature of electronic communities, their use for education, and what are their limits?

In networked environments, this same dimension of performance has the power to give rise to a sense of membership in a community; it is, in fact, a new kind of community, that can grow without face to face experience. Consider a most radical case, the consequences of a rape in cyberspace (Dibble 1993). The case study concerns Lambda MOO, a MUD (multi-user dimensions), a house built entirely of words, which was the home to a community of fictional personae created by people geographically distant from each other who, in fact, had never met face to face. Lambda MOO might adequately have been described as a computer game, but for a series of rapes enacted by one character on an other. The virtual rapes had the same kind of consequence for this community that a real rape might: those raped felt emotionally violated, and demanded punishment. One evening there was a meeting and discussion, and as a consequence the rapist was banished from the community, executed or ostracized, by having his access canceled. Dibble concludes, "I have come to conclude that [virtual realities] announce the final stages of our decades long passage into the Information Age, a paradigm shift that the classic liberal firewall between word and deed is not likely to survive intact" (42). This "conflation between speech and act" makes computer-mediated communications a genuine kind of human relationship with great promise for education, yet one thus far used more for entertainment than for learning.

Networked information implies far more than global distribution of printed information, although that alone would be an achievement of great importance in a world in which information economies are dependent upon access to intellectual capital. Scholarly journals reflect the work of disciplines, few of which have world-wide scale outside of science, technology, and medicine. The global reach of the network will vastly expand membership in the scholarly communities which disciplinary societies represent, and subject national literatures to international use and criticism.

By extension, might other social structures change? In the 1970's, Daniel Bell created the idea of an information society and commented, "The revolutions in transportation and communication, as a consequence of technology, have created new economic interdependencies and new social interactions. New networks of social relationships have been formed (preeminently the shift from kinship to occupational and professional ties); new densities, physical and social, become the matrix of human action" (Bell 1973, 189).

What is the fate of indigenous knowledge and culture in a global networked environment? Just as corporations have used electronic communications and digital networks to grow from national to transnational status, might the network become a medium for cross-cultural exchange and learning, or perhaps for the formation of new kinds of ethnicity? In the 1990s, it may be that the idea of the nation itself changes; in that ethnicity is now transnational, ethnic groups having been subjected to global diasporas, nations without nation state status might form around the network, establishing "literatures" without a foundation in a nation state. "All in all, then, life and thought in the third phase of Modernity will be shaped as much by activities and institutions on non-national levels—whether subnational or transnational, international or multinational—as by our inheritance from the centralized nation state" (Toulmin 1990, 207).

The five-hundred-year consequence of print is measured by the social formations it enabled, not by the technology of movable type. The very history of the network—a global communications medium created in less than ten years without a central planning authority—suggests it is best constructed as the expression of a shared culture. A vision of higher education on the network must begin with the cultures of scholarship, teaching, and learning, and adapt technology to those values and social relationships. Cyberspace, not computers, is the innovation of use to higher education.

References

Bell, D. (1973). *The coming of post industrial society*. New York: Basic Books.

Csikszentmihalyi, M. (1990). *Flow: The psychology of optimal experience*. New York: Harper and Row.

Dibble, J. (1993). A rape in cyberspace. *The Village Voice* (December 21):36–43.

Dillon, M., Jul, E., Burge, M., and Hickey. (1992). Assessing information on the Internet: Toward providing library services for computer-mediated communication. *Annual Review of OCLC Research 1991–1992*. Dublin, OH: OCLC Online Computer Library Center.

Egan, D., Remde, J., Landauer, T., Lochbaum, C., and Gomez, L. (1989). Behavioral evaluation and analysis of a hypertext Browser. *ACM CHI '89 Proceedings* (May):205–210.

Eisenstein, E. (1979). *The printing press as an agent of change.* Cambridge: Cambridge University Press.

Febvre, L. and Martin, H-J. (1976). *The coming of the book: The impact of printing 1450–1800.* Translated by David Gerard. London: Verso Editions.

Fish, S. (1972). *Self-consuming artifacts.* Berkeley: University of California Press.

Foucault, M. (1984). What is an author? In P. Rabinow (Ed.). *The Foucault reader.* Translated by Josue V. Harari. New York: Pantheon Books.

Lyman, P. (1984). Reading, writing, and word processing. *Qualitative Sociology* 7(1/2):75–89.

Popper, F. (1993). *Art of the electronic age.* New York: Harry Abrams Publishing.

Sproull, L. and Kiesler, S. (1986). Reducing social context cues: The case of electronic mail. *Management Science* 32:1492–1512.

Strangelove, M. and Kovacs, D. (1992). *Directory of electronic journals, newsletters and academic discussion lists.* Washington D.C.: Association of Research Libraries.

Sudnow, D., (1979). *Ways of the hand.* New York: Bantam Books.

Toulmin, S., (1990). *Cosmopolis.* Chicago: University of Chicago Press.

Turkle, S. (1980). The computer as Rorschach. *Society* (January/February): 15–24.

Turkle, S. (1984). *The second self.* New York: Simon and Schuster.

Institutional and Policy Issues in the Development of the Digital Library

Brian Kahin

The information revolution is electronic, digital, and networked. It brings the efficiency and economy of magnetic and optical media and character encoding. It brings "smart text"—machine-readable, linked, manipulable. And it brings ubiquity, the emancipation of text and image from points of origin and processing. These changes will radically transform many institutions, none more so than publishers and libraries.

In the networked environment, the pipeline model of publishing collapses. Authors can speak directly to readers. Publishers and libraries find themselves in the same business: providing access to information. Under the old model, publishers saw that books and journals were manufactured and physically delivered; libraries cataloged and archived books and journals from many publishers and made them available to one user at a time. In the new model, these classical functions, and the neat division of labor that characterized the pipeline model, disappear.

Publishers traditionally evaluate, assemble, and integrate products. Libraries evaluate products, and assemble and integrate multipublisher environments. But is CompuServe a publisher or a library? It publishes its own material, mounts material provided by others, provides gateways for other publishers, and offers forums for user interaction. Is cable television a publishing operation or a library service? Are these simply contemporary equivalents of commercial lending libraries, offering access not by rentals but by the drink, by the hour, or by flat monthly fees?

*This paper was presented at the International Conference on Scholarship and Technology in the Humanities, Elvetham Hall, England, April 1994 and also appears in *Networking in the Humanities: Proceedings of the Second Conference on Scholarship and Technology in the Humanities held at Elvetham Hall, Hampshire, UK, 13–16 April 1994*, edited by Stephanie Kenna and Seamus Ross, British Library Research, London: Bowker Saur, 1995 (ISBN 1 85739 064 4).

Libraries traditionally represent the interests of end users, whether members of an academic community, employees of a company, or the general public. Commercial publishers, of course, represent the interests of their shareholders, but they must also meet the needs and desires of their customers, i.e., both authors and users. Nonprofit publishers, such as university and society presses, may claim to represent the entire community of users and producers, as well as the public interest in maximizing the dissemination of knowledge. The key difference is that libraries lack the strategic position in the distribution chain that publishers, commercial or noncommercial, have. Libraries are not inherently entrepreneurial, because their users are captive. And although they are often an important part of the chain, their role is not exclusive, because many consumers of information buy directly from publishers or bookstores.

Like other institutions, both nonprofit publishers and libraries are captive to long-established policies and practices. In addition, their nonprofit structure makes it difficult for them to capitalize new modes of doing business. As an alternative, libraries characteristically look to cooperative cost- or resource-sharing enterprises to spread costs and risks of new activities. OCLC's (Online Computer Library Center) Online Union Catalog and the Research Libraries Group's Research Libraries Information Network are classic examples of cooperative resource-sharing that date from the mainframe era. Other resource-sharing enterprises have arisen independent of libraries within specific academic communities: the Inter-University Consortium for Political Science Research (ICPSR), ARTFL (the Project for American and French Research on the Treasury of the French Language), and Comserve (for communication studies). All of these have been around for some time. Why, given the continually dropping costs of mounting electronic information, the growth of the Internet, and the increasing capabilities of academic users, are there not many more?

The Cost-Shared Journal

The *Chicago Journal of Theoretical Computer Science*, a peer-reviewed electronic journal under development by the MIT Press, provides a promising new model for applying cost-sharing and risk reduction to academic publishing. In return for annual subscription fees of $125, libraries are licensed for unlimited use of the journal at their institution. The journal can be mounted locally or accessed over the Internet. It will be archived at MIT by the MIT Libraries, so that subscribing libraries will not have the burden of archiving as they do with paper journals. The *Journal* will take advantage of its electronic form by including executable computer code.

The market for the *Chicago Journal of Theoretical Computer Science* is fairly clearly defined: perhaps four hundred research libraries worldwide. Since there will be virtually no market for separate individual subscriptions, the economics are nearly transparent. There is no press run, no shipping costs, no inventory to maintain. As for marketing and promotion, the Internet puts scholarly communities (and their libraries) in such virtual proximity that marketing costs are trivial. The opportunities to streamline the processes of solicitation, review, and editing promise to further reduce the costs of operating a scholarly journal.

The core managerial and editorial functions will remain. These include the often intangible front-end costs of attracting a prestigious advisory board, reviewers, and contributors. These initial costs will be greater than normal because electronic journals lack the acceptance and broad reach of print journals.

Ironically, the startup costs are increased by the very fact that early electronic publications have been distributed free of charge, often with limited or no peer review. While free distribution has much to commend it, it does not instill confidence that the journal, or the authors represented, will endure. The result is that the electronic journal has been stigmatized as an underfunded, technologically-driven novelty—a periodic bulletin board.

The *Chicago Journal of Theoretical Computer Science* takes aim at the gulf between the free information and unmetered environment that characterizes the current Internet and the tightly metered world of online publishing. MIT Press must put effort and resources into selling the model, but that burden will diminish for those that follow. Basically, electronic scholarly publishing must be capitalized as an institution, although much of the required capital may take the form of prestige and other intangibles. The commitment must span the entire academic enterprise—faculty, libraries, computing services, and administration—encompassing tenure and promotion decisions, acquisition and licensing policies, and infrastructure development. And it must be a mutual commitment entered into by a critical mass of the most respected universities.

As the problem of global capitalization is solved, commitment to support individual electronic journals can and should be analogized to the periodical subscriptions that libraries have entered into for the past two centuries. The library pays a fixed amount of money for a reasonably fixed flow of information of known quality. This predictability helps simplify and rationalize the process of scholarly communications.

But while it is helpful and probably necessary to focus on the journal as an enterprise, the individual article is really the fundamental unit, and it is the citations and links between articles that define scholarly communications. Whereas print journals constrain the flow and format of information, digital technology and networks make it possible to quicken, enhance, and intelligently order information in new ways. The difference is as dramatic as the difference between the one-way analog channels of cable television and the packet-oriented environment of the Internet. For the near term, however, it is challenging enough to wrestle with accountability at a journal level of granularity.

Site Licensing for Cost Recovery

While digital technology provides opportunities for many different kinds of added value supported by greater accountability, other characterics push the other direction. With marginal costs approaching zero, networked digital information behaves increasingly like a pure public good, suggesting that there may be consumer welfare loss associated with strict controls. Thus, the local site license (allowing unrestricted local use) looks highly desirable, if the licensor can be reasonably confident of controlling leakage from institution to institution.

This usually means circumscribing the community of authorized users more rigorously than simply those individuals with accounts on the institution's computers. Licensing practices for electronic journals could well follow definitions and security procedures that have been developed for commercial databases under institutional site license. Some may feel uncomfortable with this unless the license preserves universal access within the walls of the institution's library—so that the library does not have to erect internal barriers to access and use.

More generally, the challenge is how to balance the need for accountability at an institutional level with options for occasional access by others. In some fields (including, quite possibly, theoretical computer science), there may be a relatively neat fit. Virtually all users would be expected to subscribe, especially if the scope of the enterprise is small (like a specialized journal) and the cost of unlimited local access is affordable. However, if the field is interdisciplinary or otherwise ill-defined, and as the enterprise grows to a library-like scale with commensurate costs, then the need to accommodate occasional users grows. Furthermore, the larger the enterprise the greater the costs of capitalization—and so the necessity of discriminating between the initial funders and those that buy in later when the enterprise has proved viable.

In some disciplines, the potential users will be very mixed. Whereas users of humanities journals and databases may be almost exclusively academics, users of medical resources will be an extremely heterogeneous lot: academic researchers, industry researchers, practicing professionals. Among the professionals, some may be in lucrative private practice; others may work in adverse conditions in developing countries.

Under the traditional library model, such issues of market segmentation and/or equity are obscured. The library is a local service that is taken for granted, not a global service accountable to the many institutions that support it. Library use is without direct cost, because copyright law does not require accounting to rights holders for simple use, and because both efficiency and equity militate against cost allocation based on use. In the United States, there is no public lending right, so that even loans for use outside the library require no accounting. There continues to be great ambivalence about accounting for interlibrary loan, even though the recent Association of Research Libraries study shows per-transaction costs of greater than $30. Electronic publishing, by contrast, proceeds from a model in which access to information (whether direct or through an online vendor) is contracted for on a usage-sensitive basis.

Both the free loan/free use model and the metered use model have been modified to fit particular circumstances. Some libraries charge user fees for some services (such as access to online databases) where the library incurs direct costs. However, a number of online databases are made available to educational institutions on a library-like fixed-fee basis, in large measure for the purpose of building a future customer base.

Public libraries, in contrast, are seldom offered promotional pricing and must face the fundamental problem directly: How does the library as an institution maintain the principle of universal access in a networked environment where all transactions are increasingly contractual and accountable? What replaces the lending library, where those who cannot afford to buy a book can borrow it? Do we perpetuate the tradeoff between cost and convenience by creating electronic queues, where anybody can wait to get free information they could get instantly if they were able and willing to pay for it?

Defining the Digital Library

The term "digital library" has become widely used within past five years, but there is considerable uncertainty about what it means. Nonetheless, it can be contrasted with conventional libraries in important respects:

— The conventional library is local and generalized (even if it is focused on a specific field or discipline); the digital library is a unique, specialized, global resource.
— The conventional library is supported as a line-item in an agency, institutional, or corporate budget; the digital library is supported by memberships, subscriptions, and service fees.
— The print library is a cataloged repository of mass-produced physical objects; the digital library is software-enabled environment of nearly uniquely located virtual objects.
— The conventional print library differs fundamentally from the mass-produced objects it contains, which are global and specialized; the digital library is functionally similar to the electronic journal, although there may be significant differences of scale and editorial control. Both are specialized and globally centralized, like books and unlike conventional libraries.

Other characteristics of the digital library are less clear. Will it be an extension of publishing? Or is it a product of user needs to access information in a diverse multipublisher environment? To what extent will it be an extension of academic networking and computing infrastructure?

Quite possibly, the answer varies from discipline to discipline. Perhaps the humanities are at one end of the spectrum, and technical information, where most of the market is outside academia, is at the other end. University presses are heavy at the humanities end and weak in applied sciences and technical information. Will this be the natural state of affairs for digital libraries as well?

One hopes not. The university press model is fundamentally a sub-market model, in which the university subsidizes publishing that in general cannot be supported in the commercial marketplace. It contrasts with the role the universities have played in the development of the Internet, where, with help from the public sector, they have been in the vanguard. Indeed, the computer networks that give coherence and scope to the emerging information infrastructure of higher education and research have been driven in large part by uses in the sciences, including science applied to problems such as global climate change.

Two factors have been critical to this growth and leadership in infrastructure. One is the compelling economic and political case for resource-sharing which led to National Science Foundation funding of access to computer science centers (CS-NET in 1979) and to supercomputers (NSFNet in 1986). The synergy between networking and resource-sharing has led to a proliferation of volunteered resources on the Internet, most of which are available at no charge, including the preprint bulletin boards which have become so important to communicating new knowledge in high-energy physics and other sciences.

The other factor has been the remarkably close relationship between academic research in computer science and the development and implementation of TCP/IP-based computer networking, with the Internet serving as a common testbed. Substantial federal funding for computer science provided a base of resident expertise and leverage for the development of an in-house infrastructure. As network users, computer scientists have had a strong professional interest in advancing networking technology and infrastructure.

More generally, the growth of distributed computing, personal computers, and the availability of inexpensive leased lines created important opportunities to develop academic infrastructure. Use of these technologies is characterized by fixed costs, which have made it easy to bring in other academic uses at the margin—i.e., virtually for free, provided that occasional congestion can be tolerated. This has been particularly evident at large research universities where network capacity has been driven by remote visualization and other high-bandwidth uses and it has been possible to achieve large economies of scale.

Control of Information

The remarkable strength of academic information infrastructure at the network level contrasts with remarkable weakness at the information level. Here universities find themselves having to buy back research information that their faculty and staff have generated, especially in the sciences. It is in this context, with journal costs rising rapidly, that interest in the electronic journal as university-based alternative has been most intense. Preprint bulletin boards have sprung up to provide fast and, in some respects, nearly costless means of disseminating new research.

The basic problem is this: Once established as a critical channel of communications within a new field, a specialized journal can grow with the field, occupying it very effectively to the exclusion of the others. For potential entrants, the risks of starting a new journal are compounded by the risks of taking on a known journal of record. Secure from competition and owning the primary means of communication within the field, the journal which successfully occupies its niche has considerable latitude to raise prices, which it may rationalize by increasing its frequency or the number of pages per issue, further entrenching itself in the process.

From the academy's perspective, this problem is aggravated by the routine assignment of copyright by academic authors of journal articles. The loss of copyright to commercial publishers means that any alternatives to journal subscriptions (beyond interlibrary loans under "the rule of five") will be subject to copyright fees entirely within the discretion of the publisher. As institutions cancel subscriptions, publishers will rely on copyright fees to recover lost revenue. The fees are likely to become an increasingly visible element of interlibrary loan, document delivery service, and classroom copying ("course packs").

As we have seen, much of the value added by publishers in the case of the print journal is unnecessary to the electronic journal. Beyond the individual articles, the enduring value is added by the editor, who is likely to be an academic, and the reviewers, who are typically uncompensated academics and professionals. As publishing becomes network-enabled and less encumbered with costly physical processes, the opportunity for universities to repatriate and internalize the publishing process grows. (See the report of the Association of American Universities Task Force on a National Strategy for Managing Scientific and Technical Information, May 1994.)

However, there is presently no institutional framework to enable this transformation. In some respects, academic societies are positioned to do so, in that they provide global services on a cooperative basis. But their resources are minuscule, and those that publish journals are often reluctant to disturb an established member benefit and source of income. For the most part, only the largest scientific societies have been able and willing to experiment with electronic publishing.

Recasting the Legal Issues

There has been much concern within the library community that publishers will seek to sidestep copyright provisions on fair use, including interlibrary loan practices, by licensing information under restrictive contracts. Networks facilitate contracting and avoid the problems of shrink-wrap licenses (i.e., the difficulty of establishing contracts concerning products that appear to have been sold outright). Copyright remains as a powerful means of dealing with uses that are not explicitly permitted under the contract. In fact, direct network delivery makes copyright more powerful than ever because the copyright holder's distribution and public display rights are not vitiated by the first sale doctrine. The first sale doctrine applies when copies are sold into commerce, but if instead access is licensed by the copyright holder, then those rights are enforceable. If public display is forbidden under the license, it is not only a violation of the license, it is a violation of copyright. Arguably, use of information in violation of a contract could even work to limit a fair use, because it would color the "character of the use," which is one of the four statutory factors that determine fair use.

The ability to license access to information effectively makes it easier to exercise market power. The legislative history of the U.S. Copyright Act makes it clear that Congress did not intend copyright to preempt freedom of contract under state law. Even if that were the case for libraries, as some have argued it should be, content owners would be inclined to cut off access to libraries altogether and deal only with users who can enter into enforceable contracts. At least this would be the case for much scientific and technical information where there is substantial demand outside academia. In the U.S., publishers might well try to treat their information as a trade secret. Given the strong American regard for freedom of speech, it is improbable that content owners could be compelled to "publish" information rather than circulate it in private.

The answer, in my opinion, is not to look nostalgically back at the conventions of the print environment but to develop the information infrastructure of the academy aggressively to provide effective cost-based alternatives to conventional publishing. This includes implementing institutional policies that discourage wholesale assignment of copyright to commercial interests. In the case of scholarly publication where academic authors do not expect compensation (i.e., articles, but not textbooks), copyright should be held jointly by authors and their institutions with the understanding that publishers will normally be granted a right of first publication. Allowing a reasonable degree of exclusivity (depending on the subject matter and publisher's ability to reach the whole of the potential audience) to the first publisher will not disrupt or jeopardize the operation of the present system.

A New Model: Functional Integration of Distributed Resources

Steps to rationalize and reform the conventional system must be combined with the continued development of generic infrastructure and the validation and enhancement of new means of organizing, presenting, and accessing information. This leads to the view of the digital library not as an institution, but as functional infrastructure—the distributed, unbounded global information infrastructure enabled by Gopher, the World Wide Web, and other high-level protocols. It is embodied in the Mosaic software created by the National Center for Supercomputing Applications that integrates much of this functionality under an elegant user interface.

Just as the Internet is not a network but a metanetwork of many autonomous networks, Mosaic and the underlying protocols define a metalibrary of autonomous interlinked "libraries." These libraries may be all original material, or they may be collections from multiple sources. They may be electronic journals, bulletin boards, or archives. They point as they wish to other libraries and objects within those libraries.

They arise and evolve independently, leveraged by their own ad hoc networking and standardized means of access. As in the Internet, the centralized functions associated with the metalibrary are the development, maintenance, and enhancement of the software, standards, and conventions that enable the linked libraries to appear and interoperate as part of a common environment.

The Patent Threat

The functionality of the networked digital environment, at both library and metalibrary levels, is subject to preemption by patents in the United States. In Europe, the presence of certain statutory exceptions to patentable subject matter, such as "presentations of information," together with a more conservative attitude in the European Patent Office and national patent offices, has discouraged the patenting of software processes. However, in the U.S., erosion of judicially developed limits on patentable subject matter, promotion of patents by the patent bar, lack of patent examiner expertise, and the absence of pregrant publication of patent applications have led to a flood of patents on software processes. In general, this has pleased the hardware industry and the patent bar, while it has forced software companies to engage in "defensive patenting" and engendered considerable anxiety among content-driven multimedia developers and publishers.

The academic community has not reacted coherently to the explosion of software patents. While computer scientists seethe with contempt for the patent office (which did not hire computer scientists as examiners until early 1994), they assume that software patents, as ludicrous as many are, will not directly affect academic interests. The voice of academia on patent policy is the Association of University Technology Managers, which takes the perspective of the university as a small non-manufacturing licensing entity—not as a builder of a highly complex and interdependent information infrastructure.

The one incident that came closest to affecting academic interests involved the X Windows system developed by MIT and licensed free to the computer industry as a public platform, just as the Internet protocols are available for public use and implementation. After Windows had been widely implemented by the industry, AT&T sent letters to commercial licensees claiming that X Windows infringed on a patent it held. Although X Windows was developed at MIT independently of the AT&T work, independent creation is not a defense to patent infringement.

Ironically, it is the very breadth and integrative power of Mosaic—as well as its growing ubiquity—that makes it commensurately vulnerable to U.S. patents. Furthermore, because of the complete secrecy of the patent application process in the U.S., we will not know until 1996 or 1997 or even later what patents may be infringed by the current version of Mosaic. It is important to note that while AT&T may have compunctions about going after educational and research institutions for patent infringement, small licensing companies who hold strategic patents are much less concerned with public perception or relations with a large customer base. Their dominant ethical concern is: "Is it fair to our shareholders?" States, including state universities, are now fair game with deep pockets, because Congress saw fit to abrogate state sovereign immunity for patent infringement in 1992.

If there are any doubts about the relevance of patents to the conduct of research and education, consider the following recent spectacles:

1. At a major computer trade show, the executive vice-president of Compton's New Media announces that Compton's has been awarded a patent on accessing text and images through multiple entry paths, and that Compton's is inaugurating a licensing program that would have virtually the entire multimedia industry pay tribute on every sale. The patent creates such an uproar that the Commissioner

of Patents and Trademarks takes the extraordinary step of ordering a rexamination.

2. The president of Optical Data Corporation, a publisher of multimedia instructional materials, writes a friendly letter informing the state educational technology directors in Florida, Texas, and California that the company had been granted two patents which most videodisc-based curriculum products were probably infringing. He thereby implicitly informs the states that they will be liable for triple damages, since henceforth their infringement would be willful.

These are not examples of technology companies fighting it out with other technology companies but publishers using the patent system to hamstring competing publishers. This is not the genteel world of copyright, where there must be an actual taking somewhere along the line to find infringement. This is a world where first in time is first in right, regardless of how many others independently arrive at the same result. It is a world in which state-sanctioned monopolies cover not only copying and public use, but all use, private as well as public—and not only use of processes but the use of products of patented processes, so that merely reading a document created with a patented process infringes the exclusive rights of the patentee. This is a world that exalts technology over content by allowing patent holders to control the flow of information and knowledge.

In the United States, despite our love of free expression and the free flow of information, the order and syntax of interactive speech is up for grabs. So, too, is the design and operation of the digital library—especially the new fabric of the global metalibrary that is taking shape on the Internet. The promise of a technology-enabled knowledge infrastructure built on the accumulated wealth of human enterprise and expression has been stood on its head. Such aspirations are hostage to secret proceedings in a federal bureaucracy, where speculators in abstract processes tough it out with the electrical engineers who examine the patents.

Conclusion

The full realization of the digital library challenges the higher education and research community in several distinct ways. It requires universities to cooperate in new and unfamiliar ways. Instead of bricks and mortar or faculty positions, it asks for a commitment to an intangible inter-institutional infrastructure. It asks for a considerable short-term investment in the expectation of long-term returns. At the same time, it means reorienting internal communities that have developed their own intramural practices and cultures—and reconstructing many well-worn practices.

Along with this entrepreneurial and managerial challenge comes a challenge to develop public policies that support the creation, management, and dissemination of knowledge within the emerging information infrastructure. The higher education community, with its enormous stake in these processes, its experience and leadership in information infrastructure development, and its ability to draw on a wide range of faculty experts, is uniquely positioned to provide such stewardship. However, such policies must not be merely reactive and protective of established practices and short-term interests. Nor can they be abstract or speculative. They must be informed and tested by hands-on experience in developing and maintaining alternative forms of publication, and by the actual design and implementation of digital libraries as functionally sophisticated global enterprises.

Assessing the Costs of Technopoly

Constructing Scholarly Services in Today's Network Environment

Timothy Stephen
Teresa M. Harrison

Neil Postman (1993) has argued that the United States has become a "technopoly"—a society dominated by a scientific ethos in which technology is pursued almost exclusively for its own sake. The counterpoint to a technopoly is a "tool using" society, in which technologies are subordinated to shared cultural values. In technopolies, technologies and the processes of science responsible for them run away with culture, fundamentally realigning a culture's value system by placing it in the service of technological evolution. The preeminent goal of such a culture becomes the maintenance and further development of its technologies. This same criterion serves as a predominant moral standard for judging the merit of competing courses of action or social policies. In a tool using society, by contrast, technologies are embraced only when they advance preexisting cultural values. They may be ignored or suppressed when they conflict with them.

Postman's argument was published just ahead of the recent explosion of dialogue about the Internet and the information superhighway. Had his book come out just one year later he surely would not have been able to resist a chapter on computer networking, because there is no more interesting case of the attempted abduction of culture by technology. This has been so vivid in American institutions of higher education that it may now be prudent to take a step back from this process and reflect upon whose interests are principally served in the Internet's current organizational configuration (those of the information technology industry, whose economic future is advanced by widespread investment in internetworking, or those of the academic community). Another way of approaching this issue is to ask who is willing to take responsibility for nurturing and sustaining existing efforts at melding research and educational activities to the Internet.

This volume contains many examples of pioneering applications that enhance or extend scholarship and education, of innovative projects that have seized upon one or another potential of wide area networking to assist traditional objectives. However, most current network projects are the offspring of innovative individuals meeting up with fortuitous circumstance—the right person with the right idea at the right time—rather than the planned productions of carefully administered programs of technological implementation designed to enable, nurture, and sustain specific valued capabilities within the education and research community. For better or worse, the networks have demonstrated a frenetic momentum of their own, a pace that is characterized by a staggering rate of change. It is worth considering that within this frenzy of activity there is no Internet structure, agency, or process that is responsible for nurturing or protecting the future of academic projects. The academic projects that exist on the networks are the unplanned children of technopoly.

In this chapter, we relate our experience as sometimes participants and sometimes bewildered observers of aspects of this process. Our particular focus is on the problems that the "technopolistic" character of academic computer networking (as well as some of its other organizational features) has created for our effort to nurture an online center responsive to the preexisting mores of scholars and students in communication-related disciplines. Though we are convinced that computer networking can and will significantly alter the nature of research and education, we have become cautious about the dynamics of cyberspace. Experience supports the value of long range planning and managed growth and a national commitment to a carefully articulated plan of network implementation and support. Lurching about in an environment of high speed technological change can be exhilarating but such environments add substantially to the cost of sustaining high quality academic services.

Comserve and the Culture of Communication Scholarship

Communication is a diverse multi-discipline that straddles departments of journalism, speech, rhetoric, and mass communication, and that has strong substantive as well as historical ties to departments of social linguistics, composition, theatre, and speech disorders. For the most part, the discipline is not technophilic and, for the most part, its practitioners command a modest position within the scale of wages in the American professoriate. Thus, the field presents a reasonably tough challenge for an experiment in high tech communication since its membership is neither inherently attracted to technology nor easily able to afford equipment and software.

In fact it is arguable that, as a discipline, communication scholars are unlikely to be in the vanguard of computer technology. Communication scholars traditionally embrace abstractions and celebrate ambiguity (they like to remind beginning communication students that meanings are in people and "reality" a social production, an outcome of public discourse), and they eschew contexts of scholarship such as those in many sciences that trade in fixed or rule governed systems of representation. This traditional characteristic of the discipline suggests that while the culture of the communication scholar may be poised to take advantage of media that facilitate processes of discourse, it is not a culture that will find attractive a medium where participation requires considerable technical knowledge or the memorization of myriad arbitrary but rigid operational procedures. Communication scholars avidly pursue understanding and insight into the impacts on culture of complex communication technologies, but communication scholars are often disinterested in the technical procedures required to operate the technologies themselves.

It was with this in mind that we launched Comserve in 1986 on the Bitnet network. At that time Bitnet represented the dawn of widespread access to inter-university electronic communication. Virtually all schools had either an IBM mainframe system, a DEC VAX system, or a UNIX system and could simply and cheaply connect all users of such machines to Bitnet. Bitnet was built by enabling a technology that was an inherent component in IBM mainframe systems and by deploying emulation systems for UNIX and VAX computers. Universities rented a dedicated phone line to connect their machines to one other machine on the network, forming a huge tree structure. Messages sent over Bitnet are embedded in files that are transferred automatically by the network from node to node until they arrive at their destination computer, which in turn places the file in the in-box of the appropriate recipient. By Internet standards, this technology is unsophisticated and, until the system was enhanced in the late 1980s, it was relatively slow and prone to bottlenecks, especially in the central or trunk sections of the Bitnet tree structure.

However, Bitnet had several advantages. In the first place, because Bitnet was built using a simple and static technology it is relatively easy to make sense of its operation to users, regardless of their level of background in information technology. Simply put, Bitnet works like a bucket brigade at a fire. Internet's technology, on the other hand, is inexplicable to those who have not been trained as software engineers.

In an ideal world, this would not matter, because effective use of computer networks would not require an appreciation of the technology used to construct and operate the network, just as use of a television does not require knowledge of broadcast technologies. But the Internet is nowhere near that point in its evolution. Very frequently, users are forced to confront the Internet's underlying technology head on in attempts to install, debug, or make use of primitive but complex software systems, and frequently it proves daunting.

Secondly, because Bitnet connects large, multi-user machines, the campus computer center usually takes responsibility for installing, documenting, and maintaining the network connection and for educating the campus in its capabilities and use. Campus personnel were already available to answer questions about other software systems provided on the central mainframe or mini-computer (statistical analysis packages, text formatting systems, etc.), so adding the network communications systems to the list of consultants' responsibilities was natural, at least in principle.

Bitnet has now lost ground to Internet. This has resulted in part because it has become fashionable to replace large capacity multi-user mainframe and minicomputer systems with networks of small computers (workstations and personal computers), and, for technical reasons, it is more difficult to provide Bitnet in such an environment. At many schools the change from centralized computing to distributed systems may appear to achieve real savings in the university's information technology budget; however, reduced expenditures in that budget are often offset by compensatory increases in spending by other departments and by students and faculty (who may have to purchase outright CPU, software, communications gear, network connections, disk drives, etc.). Moreover, though the expense of hardware and software may be diffused, there is often no corresponding plan to sustain high quality support services in the distributed environment. This type of downsizing represents a degree of abdication of administrative support for the deployment of information technology in support of research and education, since not all departments, faculty, and students can afford to purchase necessary technology, training, or support.

Thirdly, because Bitnet is a network representing academic and research institutions, as it grew it spawned a governance structure — the Corporation for Research and Educational Networking (CREN)— that could watch out for the unique interests of the academic community, at least in principle. Though born of it, Internet no longer belongs to the research and education community—commercialization is a fait accompli. Academic projects on the Internet share a medium that appears to be slowly evolving into a kind of hybrid that combines elements of interactive home shopping with the Minitel-style masked encounter. This aspect of the Internet network environment is attracting new businesses, proliferating points of public access, and proving popular with the general public.

Only a few years ago, academic projects that were placed online in publicly available systems were relatively protected from distraction because the public that used the networks was principally an academic public with the interests of scholarship and education firmly in mind. Thus, discussion venues could remain open access. One consequence of this was that network discussion tended to encourage cross-disciplinary dialogue, as scholars from disparate disciplines dropped in on discussions focused outside their own fields of specialization. This process was certainly evident on Comserve. However, like other sites for academically focused dialogue, Comserve is now in some danger of being overwhelmed by network tourists and passersby who do not have a scholarly orientation or sufficient training to participate productively in scholarly discourse. Thus, though there is certainly something to be said in favor of "town/gown" interaction, the kind of dialogue that nurtures progress in scholarship or that is appropriate for advanced education simply cannot be sustained in an open access, mass venue. For this reason the Comserve project has gradually begun to phase in access barriers to its discussion services. Though necessary, this is a regrettable turn of events. Where network visionaries once wrote about the power of computer networks to overcome the progressive narrowing of disciplinary specializations and tear down the walls of universities, new electronic barriers to participation are being erected of necessity.

CREN's failure to position Bitnet as a uniquely academic network has been a standing subject of complaint by Bitnet's own usership and, predictably, Bitnet is today losing membership. It is doing so because it has failed to demonstrate to university computing administrators, whose outlook is characteristically technological, any technical value unavailable on Internet. Scholars do not mourn its passing because Bitnet has never provided any particular academic services—it is just another network. However, it is the opinion of the university computing administrators that generally weighs in this matter, as scholars have never been systematically included in network decision making processes.

By conceptualizing networking from the perspective of technology instead of from the perspective of what technology might provide to researchers and educators, Bitnet indeed provides little additional value. However, CREN could and ought to step in to establish Bitnet

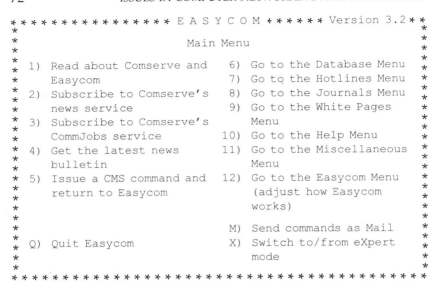

Fig. 1. EasyCom Interface Program

(or perhaps some aspect of the Internet) as a protected venue—an electronic preserve exclusively for scholarship and education that enables, protects, and sustains dialogic processes that are essential to the activities of research and education. CREN should function as the organization that places technology in the service of the mission of the academy. In the movement to the Internet, technology is indeed running away with our culture. There is a clear need for leadership from an agency that represents the interests of the academy.

Thus, in several important respects, in the early years our project benefited by being mounted on Bitnet. Bitnet was simple, stable, explicable, centrally managed, and maintained an academic focus. The range of makes and models of interconnected machines was small, so that it was possible to create and distribute an interface program ("EasyCom") that made Comserve access merely a matter of selecting from menus (see Figure 1). Three versions of Easycom were sufficient to provide simplified interactive Comserve access to over seventy percent of Bitnet's users. All others, as well as all those from other networks, were able to make use of Comserve by sending commands in e-mail.

E-mail, it should be pointed out, though now regarded as somewhat passé by technopolists, remains the single universal mode of internetwork communication. It is the only network mechanism that lends support to the claim that the electronic environment is evolving into a truly international, global venue. Only e-mail provides interconnection among those who use university systems throughout the world. Innovative systems such as Mosaic and Gopher that are currently receiving so much media attention are actually moving network services away from universal access because their use requires substantially more sophisticated and costly software and hardware. The added expense and infrastructure requirements eliminates the possibility of participation in services built around these products for a substantial number of scholars and students in less advantaged nations, not to mention those here in the United States where effective use requires an account on a machine with a direct Internet connection, to which one either has local access or a remote connection via a high speed modem link.

Comserve's parent organization, the Communication Institute for Online Scholarship (CIOS), nevertheless felt pressure to support the newer Internet technologies and has recently completed an effort to provide Gopher access to many Comserve services (see figure 2). The resulting system principally benefits those who can make use of Gopher but are not able to make use of the Bitnet EasyCom interface. Implementation of the Gopher interface has provided a lesson in some of the hidden problems in mounting academic services on Internet. Before

```
┌─────────────────────────────────────────────────────────────────────────┐
│              Communication Institute for Online Scholarship               │
│   Gopher Client                                        cios.llc.rpi.edu   │
│                                                        128.113.33.17      │
│                            Main Menu                                      │
│                  — Background and Orientational Information —             │
│   <document>     Orientation to the CIOS/Comserve gopher service          │
│   <menu>         Info about the Communication Institute for Online Scholarship │
│   <menu>         Info about the CIOS/Comserve service                     │
│                                                                           │
│                   — CIOS/Comserve Principal Services —                    │
│   <menu>         CIOS/Comserve hotline system (electronic conferences)    │
│   <menu>         CIOS/Comserve resource library & full text research service │
│   <menu>         Electronic white pages for the communication discipline  │
│   <menu>         CIOS/Comserve electronic indexes to communication serials │
│   <menu>         Communication Citation Index                             │
│                                                                           │
│              — CIOS Newsletters, Journals, & Current Information —         │
│   <menu>         Recent issues of InterCom—the CIOS/Comserve              │
│   <menu>         The Electronic Journal of Communication—EJC/REC          │
│   <menu>         Current information (new books, job listings, current scholarship) │
│                                                                           │
│                          — Miscellaneous —                                │
│   <menu>         Test your knowledge of human communication               │
└─────────────────────────────────────────────────────────────────────────┘
```

Fig. 2. CIOS Gopher Client Program

discussing these problems, however, it will be useful to provide an overview of Comserve's principal services.

Comserve

Originally, Comserve provided two primary services: file retrieval from an archive of scholarly and educational materials, and a self-service disciplinary "white pages" to which users could add themselves or with which they could locate others (for further detail on Comserve's services, see Harrison and Stephen (1992) and Stephen and Harrison (in press, 1991, 1993a, 1993b)). Over the years, several other services have been added. Principal among these is the "hotline" service, which supports twenty-five public discussion channels representing traditional divisions of communication scholarship, four news channels (for book announcements, job announcements, announcements of general interest, and distribution of abstracts of new and forthcoming scholarship), and fourteen private hotlines that are used in rotation by small groups of students and scholars to support time-limited scholarly projects (e.g., one such hotline was used to support the Sudweeks and Rafaeli project described in this volume; another was used by a group of authors preparing an edited volume on computer-mediated communication (Harasim 1993), and several have been used to support online seminars and courses combining instructors and students from different universities).

Comserve also provides an electronic index to the key periodical literature of the communication discipline, offering better coverage than that available from commercial vendors such as ISI and DIALOG. In addition, Comserve now hosts "Communication Citation Index," which can be used to track citation patterns in communication serials. Comserve features online help and uses a kind of artificial intelligence to offer users suggestions when they send commands to the service that are in error. Comserve can communicate with users in English, Portuguese, Spanish, and French for a majority of its responses to commands, and has the ability to support other language interfaces.

Throughout the course of Comserve's evolution, our desire has been to identify and implement software capabilities that provide value to Comserve's intended audience of communication students and scholars. An alternative approach would have been to build our online center using an existing, general purpose software system that enabled a particular set of technological functions, hoping that our audience would value the kinds of services such an existing system would be capable of providing. This kind of approach is possible using Listserv, which is designed to enable e-mail based conferencing and file retrieval, or using Mosaic and Gopher, which are designed to enable file retrieval, certain kinds of searches, and dynamic display of hyperlinked menus and text.

Though it would have been possible to implement some Comserve functions using these software systems, we would not have been successful in implementing all the functions that we support currently. Moreover, it seems likely that had we started with Listserv, Gopher, or Mosaic, we might not have developed the suite of functions we now support, if only because once one adopts such a system, it may be difficult to imagine providing functions that are not inherent in the system one has adopted. Thus, our preference has been to subordinate issues in software design and selection to our overriding goal of providing services of value to our audience. This is the difference between examining the contents of one's tool box and building whatever house one's tools allow versus designing a house that meets one's functional and esthetic requirements and then appropriating the resources, tools, and technologies to build it. In result, Comserve has evolved into a set of services of particular relevance to the communication field that are delivered within a system that is designed to interact with its users in a framework of sensibility appropriate for an international community of communication students and professionals.

It is difficult to say which approach is more expensive. There are immediate development costs associated with a customized system such as Comserve. However, as Comserve has matured, it is increasingly supplying services of recognizable value to its audience, and in consequence it is becoming steadily easier to obtain donations of support. Although one can initiate services under Listserv, Gopher, and Mosaic without incurring any immediate software expenses, most of the expense in sustaining a full service online scholarly center is not in software development but in the unavoidable costs of overhead associated with any professional service organization. It is not clear if services that depend principally on software packages such as Listserv, Gopher, and Mosaic will have an easier or more difficult time becoming self-supporting. However, it is clear to us that the ability to become self-supporting rests ultimately on users' perceptions of the value a service provides, and without our customized software it is not easy to see how we would have been able to deliver much of the value that inheres currently in our service.

In 1990, in order to help insure Comserve's future, we created an organizational umbrella for our activities in the form of the non-profit Communication Institute for Online Scholarship (CIOS). The CIOS provides a structure for handling Comserve-related expenses, and an organizational identity for our online activities. By 1991, the CIOS began accepting individual and institutional memberships, and embarked on other software projects in support of communication scholarship and education. Principal among these is the publication, beginning in 1990, of *The Electronic Journal of Communication / La Revue Electronique de Communication*, a quarterly peer-reviewed scholarly journal published (in English with French abstracts) through the facilities of the Comserve service itself (Harrison and Stephen 1994; Harrison, Stephen, and Winter 1991). Hence, as the project has progressed it has evolved some of the surrounding structure of a traditional scholarly society.

At least two thorny problems—one technical and the other socio-economic—face those interested in moving from a universal public access model (exemplified by Listserv, Gopher, and Mosaic) to a system capable of recovering costs and protecting resources by limiting access to qualified users. In the first instance, the Internet provides no built-in procedure for identifying who is using a resource. When a service such as Gopher is contacted by a remote user, the network provides a way to readily identify the machine from which the contact originated (e.g., athena.mit.edu); however, there is no way to determine which user on that host originated the contact. This is not the case for e-mail based services or for services that are contacted over Bitnet. However, in the rush to Internet and interactive client/server systems like Gopher and Mosaic, user identification has largely been left behind. This limitation forces service providers to one of several courses of action: (1) to build their own client programs that provide user identification, (2) to provide access on a host-by-host basis rather than a user-by-user basis, or (3) to issue passwords to users and require local logon to the service to users accessing it through telnet. None of these solutions are ideal.

The second problem in imposing a model of regulated access follows from the international character of the networks and the profound difference in the ability of users and institutions to contribute support. We assume that most services that are aligned toward academic audiences define their target constituencies with reference to disciplinary rather than political or economic boundaries. Such services are also likely to view international inclusiveness as one of the real revolutionary benefits of academic computer networks. For the first time in history, it is practical to engage in scholarly enterprises that weave together perspectives from scholars throughout the world. Unfortunately, the imposition of fee-based access regulation mechanisms in an online scholarly service will impact with dramatically different force within the international community of scholars. A $20.00/year access fee for a U.S.

scholar may constitute a trivial expense; however, it may be an impossible sum for those in some regions of the world. Thus, it may be desirable for the service provider to be able to *differentially* regulate access for users from various countries or regions.

The CIOS has implemented several strategies to cope with these problems as the desire to maintain a high quality environment for scholarship has met the exigencies resulting from the deepening and broadening of the Internet's population of users. Our software systems are now cognizant of the point of origin of each contact, and access is regulated in such a way as to assure a minimal basis of support for our services without excluding economically disadvantaged users. No software system will provide a perfect solution to these problems, but it is possible to do a reasonable job within the present network environment.

It should be clear from the foregoing discussion that while we remain enthusiastic advocates of the exploitation of the electronic medium in the service of scholarship and education, due to our commitment to sustaining CIOS services, we tend to look with a different eye on those aspects of the network environment that subordinate the requirements of scholarship and scholarly services to technological adventurism. Until now, information technologists have supplied the only hand on the reins of scholarly networking, and the result has been an environment that is only marginally suitable for stable high quality services, that is technically forbidding, and that has a rate of evolutionary change that is practically viral. In addition, it is difficult to discern the organizational responsibilities of network agencies (to whom does one turn for recourse when university X deploys an e-mail system that does not comply with network standards and the information technology agency at X refuses to answer complaints?), it is virtually impossible to detect the value that is returned for network connection fees paid to organizations such as CREN, and there is no enforcement mechanism or even a common code that might serve as a basis for regulating individual or organizational behavior on the networks. Considered technologically, the networks represent an astonishing achievement; considered from the perspective of social organization, they are practically anarchic. Such has been the product of operating the networks as technopolies.

We believe that the present anarchic state of affairs, often celebrated as having fueled the development of network applications by engendering a spirit of grass roots volunteerism, now threatens to become an impediment to the successful evolution of valuable scholarly services. For some this will seem a harsh assessment since, unquestionably, much has been gained by the selfless enterprise of many visionary volunteers whose labors have been unrecognized except in the aggregate and never appropriately compensated. However, the time has come to reassess the primacy of the frenetic, technopolistic process of invention, and to take steps to assure that the networks will evolve in a way that will support the foundational requirements of high quality academic network services.

With all due humility, we cautiously propose a general course of action: We suggest that universities and colleges join together in the creation of a national organization to provide oversight with respect to academic computer networking. This organization should have a governance structure inclusive of all sectors of the academy, not just information technology. It should be constituted of qualified individuals in areas such as library science, academic publishing, the scholarly societies, and the rank and file of the disciplines. It should be charged with responsibility for creating conditions facilitative of the academy's principal mission of knowledge generation and knowledge dissemination. This organization should work with information technologists to design and implement network policies and technologies that provide a stable, nurturant environment for the construction and deployment of high quality academic services.

To fail to take some action soon will be to place at risk a good deal of what has been accomplished and to invite the possibility of decreasing interest in the application of network technologies in higher education. Why, after all, should such a large portion of higher education budgets continue to be directed toward a developing information infrastructure over which they have little control? Indeed, why should individual scholars invest in an environment in which the ground shifts quickly and without warning, and in which the principal tectonic forces increasingly are political and economic rather than academic? As we indicated at the outset of this chapter, a substantial portion of the best scholarly and educational applications mounted on the networks thus far are the offspring of innovative individuals meeting up with fortuitous circumstances. We believe that much more can be accomplished following a national dialogue establishing goals for academic computer networking and strategies for meeting those goals.

References

Harasim, Linda, ed. (1993). *Global networks: Computers and international communication*. Cambridge: MIT Press.

Harrison, T. and Stephen, T. (1994). The case of EJC/REC: A model for producing, consuming, and delivering electronic journals electronically. In

Paul Fortier (Ed.) *Proceedings of the 1993 University of Manitoba International Conference on Refereed Electronic Journals* (7.1–7.13). Winnepeg: University of Manitoba Libraries.

Harrison, T. M. and Stephen, T. (1992). On-line disciplines: Computer-mediated scholarship in the humanities and social sciences. *Computers and the Humanities 26*:181–193.

Harrison, T., Stephen, T., and Winter, J. (1991). Online journals: Disciplinary designs for electronic scholarship. *Public Access Computer Review* 2(1):25–38.

Postman, Neil (1993). *Technopoly: The surrender of culture to technology.* NY: Vintage Books.

Stephen, T. and Harrison, T. (1991). *Comserve User's Guide. 3rd. ed.* Rotterdam Junction, N.Y.: Communication Institute for Online Scholarship.

Stephen, T. and Harrison, T. (1993a). Comserve: An electronic community for communication scholars. In Ann Okerson (Ed.). *Scholarly publishing on the electronic networks: Proceedings of the second symposium.* Washington, D.C., Association of Research Libraries and Association of American University Presses, 53–58.

Stephen, T. and Harrison, T. (1993b). Online disciplines: Building electronic scholarly communities. *Media Information Australia 67*:71–76.

Stephen, T. and Harrison, T. (in press). Comserve: Moving the communication discipline online. Journal of the American Society for Information Science.

Part III

COMPUTER NETWORKING, RESEARCH, AND ACADEMIC DISCIPLINES

Computer Networking and Textual Sources in the Humanities

Susan Hockey

Humanities Scholarship and Electronic Texts

Much scholarly work in the humanities is based on searches for words, phrases, and other features within textual sources. These sources may be literary works, historical documents, manuscripts, papyri, inscriptions, transcriptions of spoken texts, or dictionaries, and may be in any natural language. Typically, the product of the research process is a journal article or monograph containing an individual scholar's interpretation of the source material. In that interpretation, the scholar may make reference to other articles and monographs that discuss the same material, and may well disagree with the views expounded by other scholars. Other tools of scholarship include reference works and dictionaries, as well as, of course, the library catalogs that help scholars locate the materials.

Another form of textual scholarship is the publication or republication of primary source material in the form of a scholarly or critical edition, which also contains notes, annotations, and other supplementary material intended to help other scholars and students use that source effectively. The supplementary material can take the form of textual variants where several versions of the text exist, notes to clarify the meaning of certain words or expressions, indexes of names or places, or bibliographic references to related material. Traditionally, the notes and annotations appear as footnotes at the bottom of the printed page and indexes or bibliographies as appendices at the end of a volume.

For the past forty years or so, humanities scholars have used electronic versions of textual sources for many scholarly applications, including concordances, word frequency indexes, analyses of style, the production of historical dictionaries, and, more recently, even to model the narrative structures of literature. Hockey (1980) gives an overview of applications, many of which are still current. Butler (1992) includes essays surveying the use of computers for the analysis of written texts. Such projects have been aided by the speed of computer-based searching and indexing and by the computer's ability to file and organize material. For the most part, the texts used for these projects have been created for use by individual research projects or research institutes, and have not often been made available for other applications. Lancashire (1991) is the most useful source of information in print about humanities computing resources. At the time when many of these resources were created, the possibility of delivering them over the network to scholars and students anywhere in the world was not considered. A body of expertise in creating, maintaining, and using electronic texts has thus been developed, but until recently its focus has been more from the point of view of the individual project than for the creation of network-based multi-purpose resources.

However, the availability of international computer networking opens up many more possibilities for the development of electronic texts in the humanities. We are only beginning to understand the full potential of this new medium, but we can build on the experience gained in the use of electronic texts for specific projects to identify some issues that need to be considered in achieving the vision of the global electronic library that will serve the needs of humanities scholarship in the next century. The aim is to make these texts accessible to any scholar or institution in the library environment in a standard or recognized form, that will supplement and enhance the traditional modes of humanities scholarship. The rest of this chapter examines some steps toward achieving this goal. It is mostly concerned with transcriptions of texts, as opposed to digital images of manuscripts, in which there has recently been an upsurge of interest, but the possibility of bringing the two together will be highlighted.

Markup Schemes: The Text Encoding Initiative

Experience with electronic texts has shown that they become much more useful when additional information, such as author, title, chapter, or features such as quotations, proper names, and parts of speech are marked in some way (Coombs, Renear, and DeRose 1987). This enables subsets of a text to be searched, for example, dialogue as opposed to narrative, speeches by certain characters in drama, or certain types of verse. It also provides a means of identifying items that have been retrieved so that their location within the text can be pinpointed. A text that does not have any identification or marking of these items can be used for only minimal purposes. It can be likened to a bibliographic record in which the fields are not delimited. At least thirty different ways of encoding such features now exist, most of which are incompatible. They have also been found to be poorly documented, oriented towards one particular application, and difficult to extend. Much time has therefore been wasted in converting from one format to another.

A new common format is now emerging called the Text Encoding Initiative (TEI). The TEI is a major international project sponsored by the Association for Computers and the Humanities, the Association for Computational Linguistics, and the Association for Literary and Linguistic Computing. The TEI was established in late 1987 in order to address the problems of incompatible encoding schemes and to provide guidelines for new projects. With support from the National Endowment for the Humanities, the Commission of the European Union, the Andrew W. Mellon Foundation, and the Social Sciences and Humanities Research Council of Canada, and aided by the volunteer labor of many scholars who have worked with electronic texts in the humanities, it has defined an encoding format for interchange and for encoding new texts in the humanities and the language industries.

The TEI uses the Standard Generalized Markup Language (SGML). SGML is not itself an encoding scheme, but it provides a framework for an encoding scheme that is flexible and satisfies many scholarly needs. The principle of SGML is "descriptive" rather than "prescriptive," which means that it is independent of any particular application program. A prescriptive scheme defines what function is to be performed on any part of the text, for example, to indicate that a title is in italic. In a descriptive scheme the title is identified as a title. One computer program may then print the title in italic, but another program for searching all titles could operate on the same text.

SGML views a text as a collection of objects or elements, each of which is identified by a tag name. The set of tags that is permissible in a text, and their relationship to each other, are defined in a document type definition (DTD) which a program can use to validate the tags in a text. The tags may also have additional information in the form of attribute values, for example, to denote the language if the tag is for a foreign word, or to provide cross-referencing to information that is elsewhere in the text or external to it. Tags are conventionally enclosed in angle brackets, although these delimiters can be redefined if necessary. Each instance of an element has a start tag, for example, <title>, and an end tag, for example, </title>. In some circumstances, the end tag can be omitted in order to reduce the amount of encoding in a text.

One of the many strengths of SGML is that texts encoded in it are ASCII files. They can thus be moved easily from one hardware and software platform to another. Non-standard characters are normally handled by entity references, which reduces them to the 7-bit character set (a subset of ISO 646), which is currently safe for transmission across all networks. For example, the letter e with an acute accent appears as é, although of course the receiving software would normally translate this into é, which is more readable for the human. SGML thus provides an archival format of the data that is not restricted to any particular hardware or software, and that assures its longevity.

SGML allows multiple, and possibly conflicting, views to be encoded in the same text. It can therefore serve as the foundation for the multi-purpose, multi-functional electronic text. It is sufficiently flexible to provide a means of representing the complex structures and features of humanities texts in such a way that many scholarly needs are satisfied. The use of SGML is not restricted to describing text. It can be used to describe anything, and it is likely that it will increasingly play a role in describing non-textual material such as images, sound, and video, since all of these need textual information of some kind to indicate what they are.

From the outset, the philosophy of the TEI has been to define sets of tags that characterize particular types of text, but to make their use optional. The TEI's Committee on Text Documentation produced the recommendations for an electronic text file header that are discussed further below. The Committee on Text Representation dealt with the logical structure of the text, character sets, and features common to most or all texts, e.g. quotations, lists, names, abbreviations, bibliographic citation, etc. The Committee on Text Analysis and Interpretation developed a number of mechanisms for encoding linguistic and other interpretive material (literary and historical), which permit more than one analysis to be given. The Committee on Metalanguage and Syntax Issues produced recommendations on how SGML might best be used for the TEI, in effect defining a kind of SGML house style for the project.

The first draft version of the TEI Guidelines was published in July 1990 (Sperberg-McQueen and Burnard 1990), and a mechanism was set up for receiving public comment on this draft. In the second phase of the TEI project, specific work groups addressed the topics of character sets, hypermedia, formulae and tables, literary prose, performance texts, verse, critical apparatus, transcription of primary sources, language corpora, spoken texts, dictionaries, terminological data, historical studies, and general linguistics. Individual chapters of the second draft, incorporating the work of these groups, have been made available in electronic form on the fileserver of the TEI's listserv (tei-l@uicvm) and also from several FTP sites. A new print version was published in mid-May (Sperberg-McQueen and Burnard 1994), and forms the first stable set of TEI recommendations that provide a firm basis for the future encoding of electronic texts.

The TEI Guidelines are built on the assumption that all texts share some common core of features to which may be added features specific to a particular discipline area. A user of the Guidelines selects one or more base tag sets, the current choices being prose, verse, drama, transcriptions of speech, print dictionaries, spoken texts, and terminological databases. To this are automatically added tags for features common to all texts and those needed for documenting the text. If appropriate, additional tag sets may also be incorporated. These include segmentation and alignment, simple analytic mechanisms, feature structures, certainty and responsibility, transcription of primary sources, critical apparatus, names and dates, graphs and trees, formulae and graphics, and language corpora. The TEI DTD is thus built up using a model that has been likened to the preparation of a pizza.

The Hypertext Markup Language (HTML), which is most familiar to network users through the World Wide Web and Mosaic, is another implementation of SGML. In its current implementation (most recently documented in Summer 1993), it is more limited in scope than the TEI and is oriented towards the structural representation of prose text. It has something over fifty possible tags, whereas the TEI has about four hundred possible ones, although very few indeed of the TEI tags are mandatory. HTML provides a means of encoding prose texts for presentation on the network and has been very successful in that. The Association of American Publishers also has an SGML application for electronic manuscripts that is now an ANSI standard. It, too, is more limited than the TEI, since its focus is on the preparation of authors' manuscripts for publication rather than on the encoding of existing material.

Documenting and Cataloging Electronic Texts

Adequate documentation and description of each text is also a vital component of network access to electronic texts. Any piece of work is only as good as the data on which it is based, and scholarship carried out on data of dubious origin immediately lays itself open to criticism.

As yet, we do not have any universal equivalent of the information found in a fairly standard form at the beginning of a book. Many of the electronic texts available from different sources on the network at present do not have any documentation associated with them, so the user has no means of knowing where they came from, who created them, and what changes have been made to them since they were originally created. In general, those who have been responsible for compiling electronic texts have not had much experience managing and organizing information in such a way that other scholars can find and use it effectively. Since no other ground rules exist, they have developed their own ad hoc procedures for documenting the texts, or not provided any documentation at all. The result has been a general lack of documentation, and incompatibility between existing systems. This is another area that the TEI has sought to address with its proposals for an electronic file header.

The TEI header consists of a set of SGML elements that provide meta-information about the text. Some of them form the very few TEI tags that are mandatory. The header is divided into four sections. The file description provides bibliographic information about the electronic text and the source from which it was transcribed. Some of the elements within this section map directly onto the fields of a MARC (MAchine Readable Cataloging) record. The encoding description documents the principles that governed the transcription of the text, including treatment of hyphens, quotations, editorial emendations, and the like. The profile description brings together a variety of information not treated elsewhere in the header, for example, information about the natural languages used in the text or demographic information about the participants in the conversation, if it is a spoken text. The revision history documents any changes made to the text much in the same way as the change log found at the beginning of a computer program. The TEI header is believed to be the first systematic attempt to document an electronic text file, and it was designed by a group representing librarians, archivists, and scholars who compile and use electronic texts. Provision is also made for the exchange of TEI headers without the accompanying text, and a chapter of the TEI Guidelines highlights those elements which are recommended for use in these independent headers.

At present, the only catalog of existing electronic texts in the humanities is the Rutgers Inventory of Machine-Readable Texts in the Humanities, which is stored on the Research Libraries Group network RLIN (Hoogcarspel 1994a). The Inventory was established at Rutgers University in 1983 and was taken over by the Center for Electronic Texts in the Humanities (CETH) in 1991. At present it contains some

1700 entries, over half of which are from the Oxford Text Archive (OTA). The OTA was established at Oxford University Computing Services in 1976 to offer scholars a facility for long-term deposit of their electronic texts once they have finished with the text. It contains over a gigabyte of texts in about thirty languages. Some texts are accessible via FTP to ota.ox.ac.uk/pub/ota and many of these now have TEI headers. Many other texts are available for use by permission of their depositors. The OTA represents the only serious attempt to bring together and archive electronic texts that might otherwise be lost.

The texts at Rutgers are cataloged according to the rules in Chapter 9 of the Anglo-American Cataloging Rules (AACR2), which deals with computer files. However, these rules deal mostly with numeric data files and computer programs, and are not especially suitable for electronic text files that are representations of something that already exists in another medium, or where, for example, the user needs to know whether the text can only be accessed by specific software. The rules are also rather specific about the physical format of the file and the medium on which it is stored, although this information is not so relevant in a networked environment. CETH has now prepared guidelines for cataloging monographic electronic texts in the humanities, which provide a basis on which the Inventory can move forward (Hoogcarspel 1994b).

Electronic Texts and Libraries

We have seen that until recently the purpose of almost all electronic text projects in the humanities was to facilitate processes that are very time consuming or difficult to do with print, for example word counts and searches. Once a text is in electronic form, these operations are almost instantaneous and can save many hours or even weeks of tedious research. Most existing electronic texts were created with these functions in mind and the compilers of the texts were also the ones who used them. The library, which in other ways is the main resource for humanities scholarship, was only very rarely involved. It is only recently that the library has begun to play a more substantial role in the provision and use of electronic texts.

At present, the electronic texts most usually seen in libraries are commercially available products distributed on CD—ROM together with searching software. Since these are physical objects, they are more convenient to handle in some ways, and procedures for dealing with them can be modeled in part at least on those for handling print materials. These products can be purchased from recognized sources that offer some assurance of quality and reliability. Several of them, for example the CETEDOC Library of Christian Latin texts,[1] are the by-products of other computer-aided scholarly projects. However, as more of these resources become available, their limitations are beginning to be realized. In general, they are closed systems. The software that comes with them supports only certain functions and does not fully realize the potential of the electronic medium for scholarly applications in the humanities. Most usually, the texts are pre-indexed, and responses to any search requests are only as good as what has been indexed. As more texts become available in electronic form, the size of a CD-ROM is limiting and collections of material spread over several CD-ROMs are awkward to use. Furthermore, almost all these products have different user interfaces and functionality, and, as more and more of them become available, librarians are beginning to appreciate the costs involved in supporting them.

However, librarians soon realized the potential of the electronic medium for the roles that libraries have undertaken for a long time, particularly for access and preservation. The network can offer a solution to many access issues, provided that an adequate system is set up. The availability of so many online catalogs on the Internet is beginning to have an effect. Scholars no longer need to travel to another library to determine whether that library has an item they need to consult. They can find this out by consulting that library's catalog over the Internet. The delivery of the item itself over the Internet is the obvious next stage. This is beginning to happen in a few experimental cases, but further research needs to be done to determine how best to deliver that item.

Digital imaging is also beginning to take the place of microfilm as a way of preservation, and the objective of several current projects is to make electronic representations of textual sources, to ensure that these sources continue to be readable (Robinson 1993). In some cases, print copies made from the digital images are provided as the main means for their use. The digital images themselves are saved as an archival form for the future. From the point of view of preservation, the main advantage of digital images is that they do not degrade during storage or when copied, provided that the storage unit on which they reside continues to be in use. Network access can, of course, also be provided for digital images that have been made for preservation purposes. Again, we need to consider how best that might be done. Textual information needs to be associated with images so that the images can be retrieved from a database. SGML provides a much more flexible way of doing this than a database structure with fixed fields.

Since digital images appear to be so popular at present it is perhaps worth noting here also that digital imaging will not be the solution for the preservation of material that only exists in electronic form, whether as electronic records or examples of hypertext fiction or other genres of literature and art that exploit the electronic medium and can thus only exist in that form. In most cases, textual scholars who have worked with both images and transcriptions of text prefer to use the transcriptions.

A Future for Textual Sources on the Network

Given the time and expense involved in creating an electronic resource, it makes sense for that resource to be useful to as many people as possible. Can the same electronic text satisfy the purposes of access and preservation, yet also serve the needs of scholars who want to use it for retrieval, word counts, and other analytic purposes. What would that text look like and how would it be used?

There is now a very strong case for SGML's being the route to this text. One can envisage an SGML-encoded transcription of the text together with a digital image of the source, if the source is appropriate for imaging. The text would have header information similar to that proposed by the TEI but also including information that would aid the processing of the image. The layered approach of the TEI means that, at one level, there would be a reliable text, perhaps authenticated by a mechanism like the timestamp developed at Bellcore (Haber and Stornetta 1991), but also leaving scholars free to add their own annotations to the text.

Network access is the most effective way for texts to reach as wide an audience as possible. It allows many more texts to be delivered, with the potential for using a broad range of software essential for dealing with the complex intellectual problems of scholarly texts. It also allows access to selective parts of texts from different sources. With a common underlying encoding scheme, sections of different texts can be merged or linked together.

The network is already beginning to transform textual scholarship in some areas. Experimental projects are already being planned in scholarly editing. One can envisage a base text, stored somewhere on the network, to which annotations are made and stored in other places. Each annotation includes SGML elements that identify its source and its intellectual justification, and there may be several annotations, giving different viewpoints, associated with a particular section of text. When several versions of a text exist, there will no longer be the need to privilege any one of them, as occurs in the printed edition. All versions could be made available as transcriptions and digitized images, and scholars will be able to make links and annotations across versions and renditions. This is providing a way forward to the electronic publication of the future, in which these analyses and interpretations are included as layers above the text in such a way that they can be used or discarded as the reader or user of the text wishes.

As more electronic texts become available and searches are performed across a broader collection of texts, there will be a need for better retrieval techniques. Boolean operators and simple collocations provide limited facilities when the text base is very large and when there are many instances of homographs. Word class tags, embedded in a text or associated with it, can help to separate ambiguous forms. Retrieval can also be assisted by a machine-readable dictionary from which a program can derive some semantic information about a word, for example, to disambiguate the money bank from the river bank. We can envisage such dictionaries for many natural languages accessible on the network and linked together through standard structures. For humanities texts, they will need to be very sophisticated, in order to be able to handle material in several languages, variant spellings, variations in names and dates, notes and annotations.

All the issues discussed in this chapter are needed to plan the network-based digital library of the future. The potential offered by this new medium is still barely realized. SGML has provided a route to creating multi-purpose reusable electronic texts whose longevity is assured, but we still have only limited understanding of the potential offered by the network for the use of these textual sources. Further research is needed on access methodologies, and the outcome of this research will be much more successful if the needs and requirements of humanities scholars are taken into account as these mechanisms are developed and tested.

Note

1. CETEDOC is the Centre de Traitement Électronique des Documents. It is located at the Univérsité Catholique de Louvain-la-Neuve in Belgium.

References

Butler, C. (1992). *Computers and written texts*. Oxford: Blackwell.

Coombs, J.H., Renear, A.H., and DeRose, S.J. (1987). Markup systems and the future of scholarly text processing. *Communications of the ACM 30*:933–997.

Haber, S. and Stornetta, W. S. (1991). How to time-stamp a digital document. *Journal of Cryptology 3*:99–111.

Hockey, S. (1980). *A guide to computer applications in the humanities*. London: Duckworth, and Baltimore: Johns Hopkins.

Hoogcarspel, A. (1994a). The Rutgers inventory of machine-readable texts in the humanities. *Information Technology and Libraries 13*:27–34.

Hoogcarspel, A. (1994b). *Guidelines for cataloging monographic electronic texts at the Center for Electronic Texts in the Humanities*. (Technical Report No. 1). Center for Electronic Texts in the Humanities.

Lancashire, I. (Ed.). (1991). *The humanities computing yearbook 2*. Oxford: Oxford University Press.

Robinson, P. (I 993). *The digitization of primary textual sources*. (Publication No. 4). Oxford University Computing Services: Office for Humanities Communication.

Sperberg-McQueen, C.M. and Burnard, L. (Eds.) (1990). *Guidelines for the encoding and interchange of machine-readable texts, draft version 1.1*. (TEI document No. P1). Chicago and Oxford: ACH-ACL-ALLC.

Sperberg-McQueen, C.M. and Burnard, L. (Eds.). (1994). *Guidelines for Electronic Text Encoding and Interchange*. (TEI document No. P3). Chicago and Oxford: ACH-ACL-ALLC.

Cooperative and Collaborative Mediated Research

Duncan Sanderson

In this last decade of the twentieth century, two mutually reinforcing trends can be observed with respect to the way in which research is carried out: institutional emphasis on cooperative and collaborative research, and the development of technological applications that may facilitate this. However, I propose that the role of technologies in collaborative research is likely to be less significant than that which is suggested by some commentators. Following the discussion by Kling (1992) of the literary genres that are associated with social analyses of computing, I attempt to thread a narrow intellectual needle. A perspective is adopted that is neither utopic nor resolutely pessimistic.

I begin the discussion by noting what appears to be an increased institutional emphasis on cooperative and collaborative research. This is followed by a closer examination of these forms of research, as well as of the role that network applications currently play in it. Next, I summarize the results of research projects that have attempted to use interactive videoconference technologies to facilitate their own project management and communication. An overview is also presented of a field study of a distributed research group, their collaboration, and their use of the Internet[1] and a desktop videoconference application. Finally, in the conclusion I note that, although network-based information management technologies may facilitate cooperative research, it is impossible to predict with confidence what role advanced communication applications may play, particularly with respect to collaborative research.

The discussion has implications for researchers, research administrators, network planners, and sociologists of science. I would argue that scientists have a responsibility not only to imagine how technologies could be used in collaborative research, but also to provide analysis

---

*The author gratefully acknowledges the financial support of the Centre for Information Technology Innovation, the cordial cooperation of the atmospheric physics research group, and helpful comments by David Tippin, Teresa Harrison, and Tim Stephen. The opinions expressed here are solely those of the author.

of the limitations, variety of costs, and the benefits of using them. For research administrators and network planners, the discussion suggests the ongoing need to closely examine: 1) the rationale for collaborative research, 2) the possible role and limitations of network technologies for this, and 3) the actual use made of the technologies. For sociologists of science, I point to practices that represent altered modes in the social production of scientific knowledge.

The Trend Towards Cooperative and Collaborative Research

Large-scale multi-party research has existed in the U.S. at least since the Second World War effort to create the atom bomb. Nevertheless, in the last decade, there has been a noticeable increase in institutional emphasis on the need to conduct small and medium size joint research projects. Government grant agencies have begun to offer collaborative research grants with the express objective of creating significant research programs in strategic areas. For example, in Canada, a special Centres of Excellence program was initiated in the late 1980s. A 240 million dollar budget was allocated to the competitive grant program, and applicants had to demonstrate not only that they were leading researchers in their field, but also that a managed, collaborative approach would be taken to conducting the research. Industrial liaison and technology transfer mechanisms were to be instituted, in order to stimulate and insure the rapid economic exploitation of new ideas and research results. The belief that underpins these programs is that joint research projects will lead to relatively higher quality research with more positive socio-economic impacts.

Government, university, and private sector research institutions are all attempting to include other partners in research projects. In the case of government laboratories, the goals are twofold: to increase the public visibility of government-sponsored research, and to use research as an economic lever to help private companies spin off new products and services. For private companies, the offer of private or government participation in applied research activities is a welcome addition to increasingly limited resources for research. In the university, the stagnation of government research grants and a desire to maintain relevant curricula lead university personnel to create joint projects with the private sector. University-industry liaison is becoming a critical facet of university research, and it would appear that increasing energy is being given to the identification and creation of research partnerships.

Thus, there appears to be a new emphasis on the institutional facilitation of joint research, compared to some thirty to fifty years ago. However, one could ask whether or not this has impacted on the day to day work practices of researchers, and what the impact may be. What percentage of researchers still tend to pursue relatively isolated forms of research? Is there a greater tendency for research questions to be influenced by institutional agendas rather than being formulated by the researcher him- or herself? Does the researcher tend to interact with more people, from more varied backgrounds? Are joint projects effective and efficient ways for carrying out research? And finally, are the results of the research of better quality (however this may be determined)?[2]

Although I have few answers to these questions, I raise them here to suggest that, although an institutional emphasis on cooperative and collaborative research can be identified, relatively little appears to be known about the ways in which interpersonal communication between researchers may or may not be changing. Moreover, these issues become still more complex as one attempts to identify the role of network applications in cooperative and collaborative research.

Cooperative and Collaborative Research

Before pursuing the discussion of the role of network applications, it is first useful to characterize and distinguish between cooperative and collaborative research. Some commentators appear to implicitly consider almost any form of scientific communication as collaborative research, although this appears to lump together significantly different situations and practices. The discussion here draws heavily on observations concerning the nature of collaboration, particularly as found in the field of computer supported cooperative work (for example, Kraut, Galeher, and Egido, 1987–1988, 1990; Schmidt and Bannon 1992; Schrage 1990; Suchman and Trigg 1986). Still, I should note that the distinction between cooperation and collaboration is my own and not an axiom of this field of research.

A typical example of collaborative research is a group of researchers with various backgrounds and interests, who jointly identify a common research theme or scientific problem, and carry out coordinated actions in order to create new knowledge in relation to the research question. On the other hand, cooperative research could designate situations in which an individual or group provides another with useful information or data, although little other discussion is held in relation to the data. For example, a cooperative situation would occur if a research group provides another one with medical data, or if a researcher places data on a server in order that others may access it. There may or may not be expectations of reciprocal exchange, and there may be no further action as a result of this exchange.

A number of other characteristics could be noted that help to distinguish between these two ideal types (in the Weberian sense). In the case of collaboration, there generally appear to be more significant demands on the participants, in terms of time commitments, and social and intellectual adaptations to the other participants (Schrage 1990; Kraut, Egido, and Galegher 1990). For example, group members in a collaborative research project will likely expect that others will attempt to understand their particular theoretical viewpoints or interpretations. This results in what several authors have identified as the development of common understandings (Schrage 1990; Suchman and Trigg 1986), although the extent of this may be variable. Extensive coordination of activities is also observed, in part because the work of participants is dependent on that of others. Participants also appear to expect that others will make significant and equitable contributions, and to do so as opportunities may arise. As well, it could be argued that singular objectives and outputs are produced in collaborative research. Finally, some authors note that "social harmony" is not necessarily a defining characteristic, as various forms of conflict may also be observed (Kling 1991; Star 1993).

In cooperative research, many of the criteria noted above are relaxed. Interaction may be punctual, ad hoc, and opportunistic. Varying opinions and theoretical assumptions can remain unchallenged and intact. Actions are more or less coordinated, and this is likely to require less time relative to collaborative research. At one extreme, cooperation could occur simply by not interfering with the work of someone else. But it might also entail informal monitoring for situations in which one could contribute observations or resources that would further someone else's work. Altruistic types of contributions may also take place, although it is possible that the contributor may feel that a visible contribution to a participant in the scientific community may someday make him- or herself more eligible for a return favor. Multiple and heterogeneous objectives and results may be observed, compared with the more unitary ones found in collaborative research.

The characteristics noted above help to circumscribe and differentiate certain sets of behavior that in turn can be observed in relation to the use of communication technologies. Although several research administrators and network planners tend to only use the expression of collaboration, I submit that both cooperation and collaboration are needed in order to more accurately designate a wide range of practices taking place via the academic networks.

The Role of Common Network Applications

Given these background trends and characterization of cooperative and collaborative research, what then is the current role of network applications? Some two decades after the first experimentation with network applications over ARPAnet, general use of Internet currently centers on electronic mail, file transfer, and various forms of remote log-on. In a quantitative analysis of network traffic over the NSFNet portion of Internet[3], the breakdown of data flow was as follows (as measured by the quantity of bytes transferred between all nodes): 48 percent was for file exchange, 28 percent for networked mail applications, 6 percent for interactive applications (it was not clear whether this included both synchronous computer conferencing such as CHAT, and remote log-on to other computers), and 23 percent for other services (such as name look-up and housekeeping). Although newer applications are tending to blur the distinctions between electronic mail, file transfer, and remote log-on (for example, World Wide Web [WWW]), let us retain these categories for the moment as a convenient starting point.

Several empirical studies have also been conducted into the dynamics and use of communication technologies in the scientific community, (for example, Gurd and Picot 1987; Hiltz 1984; Koch 1991; McCreary and Brochet 1991; Rice and Case 1983; Schatz 1991). Other researchers have investigated the use of communication technologies in order to facilitate collaborative research (Abel 1990; Carley and Wendt 1991; Harasim and Winkelmans 1990; Tombaugh 1984). This literature consists mainly of studies of the use of electronic mail, as well as some observations of how data bases may eventually be used in the scientific community. Drawing on these studies, 1 will briefly discuss e-mail, file transfer, and log-on in relation to their role in cooperative and collaborative research.

In the case of electronic mail, distinctions can be made between 1) public forums as found in distribution lists and news groups, 2) particular research project lists, and 3) direct personal correspondence. In the first case, the distribution list consists of people or readers interested in particular questions or practices, and who are for the most part researchers or academics.[4] Even casual observation of these public forums suggests that it is a common practice to ask questions or request assistance and to provide answers, information, or comments in relation to these questions. This sort of discussion can be considered to be a form of cooperative research, in that some of this communication may be useful to someone's research. For example, solutions to problems may be suggested and the names of experts or references may be provided. As well, discussions may be found that stimulate reflection or even become the subject of research projects or scientific publications. However, the key observations here are that these activities depend on voluntary actions of the information provider, the interaction frequently occurs between complete strangers, it is difficult to assess the actual impact of such communication on research, and there may be few instances in which joint research projects or publications result from the interaction. For these reasons, at best, such distribution lists or news groups can only be considered to facilitate cooperative research.

Electronic mail can also be used within a specific project-oriented group, either in the form of a closed distribution list, or through one-to-one correspondence. A good example of this is a quantitative study into the characteristics and content of electronic mail headed by Fay Sudweeks and Sheizaf Rafaeli (see their essay in this volume). Because of its use in project management (formulating and discussing policies) and for the distribution of the data, this particular project could be considered to be an example of collaborative research facilitated by electronic mail. It is unlikely that such a large and diverse number of participants could have participated in a meaningful way without access to e-mail. Most of the participant recruitment, coordination, debate, decision making, encouragement, and data exchange took place through group and private e-mail (there was also some synchronous conferencing between the project leaders and other participants).

However, in some research groups, the content of a distribution list may be little more than an update of the respective research activities of the participants. There is nothing intrinsically collaborative in using e-mail. Recourse to the communication medium in itself does not indicate what the relationship is between those who use it, nor the ends to which the communication may be put. One needs to examine the content of the information being communicated, how the participants are using it, and how the communication is structured. For example, in the Sudweeks and Rafaeli project, the two leaders used e-mail extensively in order to encourage and coordinate the activities of the participants. Harasim and Winkelmans (1990) note that the relative effectiveness of e-mail in a collaborative effort to write a book was mainly due to the small group structure and extensive facilitation that was built into the project structure.

The second major use of Internet is for file transfer, although this is only one phase in a broader information management process of query, storage, and retrieval of information through the use of various server and database technologies. Three forms of scientific use of Internet accessible databases can be identified: 1) searches for certain information (for example, via Archie, Gopher, or search mechanisms integrated into services such as Comserve), 2) the direct transfer of files and software (either through e-mail commands or software that follows FTP, or the File Transfer Protocol), and 3) the "browsing" of linked information (via services and applications such as the World Wide Web [WWW] and Mosaic). With an e-mail request, researchers can retrieve bibliographies, papers, and even data that others have decided to make available on a server (for example, the Mendelian Inheritance in Man project; Lucier 1990). An FTP session can transfer formatted data from someone else's computer. With linked servers (i.e., WWW), the added refinement is that a piece of information can indicate to the user that more related information can be obtained elsewhere (and automatically lead the person to it, even though it is electronically stored on another server).

Still, the observation that needs to be emphasized here is that the information retrieval mechanisms noted above may or may not be pertinent to cooperative and collaborative research. The information or data may be restricted to a limited group, or to only those who take the time to find it. Few common research interests may exist between the file provider and user. There may also be no indication of who provided the file or who used it.

To illustrate this further, I will suggest an analogy based on an imaginary university library. Most academics would consider that a research library (which is essentially a collection of books, articles, and people and mechanisms for finding information), has useful functions of information identification, storage, and dissemination. However, academics generally would not consider that the library has any direct role in relation to cooperative or collaborative research, or any responsibility for the management of data collected by a research group.

However, let's say that, with a research group's permission and help, the library began to store, organize, and make available the researchers' data and project documents. This action could make the research data more accessible to the project participants, increase awareness of what the other participants were doing, and perhaps even allow the researchers to redefine the division of labor. Furthermore, the library could notify other researchers who may have a possible interest in the data, and make it accessible to them. These other researchers could then take the data or documents and do further analyses. In this situation, it would make sense to say that the library had played a useful role in facilitating cooperative research. Similarly, it could be argued that the hypothetical actions taken by the library actually occur via Internet, since work can be publicized, and data can be stored, located, and made accessible.[5]

To extend the analogy further, I could point out that a collaborative research project would not necessarily result from all of this, and the researchers who had gained access to the data managed by the library could do individual analyses and publish their individual papers. The library had facilitated cooperative research, useful in itself, perhaps, but nothing more. On the other hand, researchers who had become aware of the project might indicate to the original group that they could contribute to their monthly discussions, share in the generation of the data, and contribute to writing up the results. The library might then volunteer to furnish plane tickets to allow the researchers to meet and discuss their work. If these working arrangements were agreed to (which may not be a trivial issue in itself), it would be possible to say that the participants had entered into the initial stages of a collaborative research project. The data sharing actions of the library did not necessarily lead to the collaboration (the researchers could have gone off and written their own papers), but given the social processes and initiative of the researchers, it did indirectly facilitate the early stages of the collaboration (by pointing out common interests, managing and disseminating data and information, and allowing the researchers to meet). Again, the same can be said of the Internet. The communication technologies may make it easier to sustain collaboration, but it is the researchers themselves who initiate and create the collaboration.

In a similar but more direct formulation, Star (1993) has noted that "boundary objects," such as common maps or research instruments, help scientists with heterogeneous interests to coordinate and focus their actions. A shared database may play this role. Some research groups may set up a private file server in order to collect or distribute data within the group, in which case the technology becomes a joint work tool. The collection and standardization of information in the database allows comparisons that would otherwise be difficult or impossible. Moreover, by going through the process of defining, collecting, and distributing the information found in the database, the group may be building a social and intellectual foundation for longer-term collaborative research. An example of this will be provided later in a case study.

The third major use of the Internet should also be noted. Remote log-on (telnet) to another computer allows the user to run programs on a distant computer and to receive the results at one's own computer. It can be used to query databases, to run specialized computer software, or to analyze data that is stored at a particular location. It may not be desirable or feasible to allow such software or databases to be transferred to remote sites, since the software may require specialized computing resources (such as a supercomputer or very large database), the remote site may be continually updating the software, or someone may wish to restrict or monitor access to a program.

Once again, this activity may or may not take place in the context of cooperative or collaborative research. If a remote user is carrying out analyses for his own purposes and is being charged for using the remote computer resource (say a Cray computer), then remote log-on simply becomes a means for an institution to recover some of its capital and operating costs. In a collaborative context, though, some software could be a critical and shared tool in the work of several dispersed researchers who are working on a common project. It may not be feasible to replicate the software locally because of extensive data storage or particular computer or operator requirements.

Experiments to Enhance Audio-Visual Communication between Distributed Researchers

Another set of network applications can be identified, some of which are becoming available to the academic community. A number of recent experiments and activities have been undertaken to improve on the communication media that researchers have at their disposal (multimedia mail, decision support systems, distributed multi-author applications, videoconference systems). In this section, l would like to focus on one of these, interactive videoconference systems, and note questions concerning its possible relationship to cooperative and collaborative research. The implicit belief underlying some of the experiments with these systems is that if researchers can see and speak to each other (and show diagrams or graphics), this will help to compensate for their physical separation. Some authors also propose that such systems may allow the direct person-to-person informal communication that often occurs when researchers are co-located (Fish, Kraut, Root, and Rice 1993), and which appears essential in the process of collaborative research (Kraut, Galegher, and Egido 1987–1988).

There are two other reasons that justify a closer examination of this particular application. First, various business organizations have been using conference room videoconference systems, some for several years. The planners and architects of the high-speed academic networks tend to believe that a closely related application, desktop videoconferencing, will become widespread in the scientific community, and be used to facilitate collaborative research. Second, some research organizations have used videoconferencing in the regular conduct of projects (for example, Bell Northern Research), and several research projects have or are exploring its use by distributed researchers (for example, Bellcore, Xerox PARC, the Telepresence Project in Ontario). However, there also appears to be a lack of critical analysis of the implementation process, or of the benefits or problems that may be associated with its use in distributed research (for example, Haythornthwaite, Wellman, and Mantei, in press; Olson and Bly 1991; Fish et al. 1993).

A number of observations can be noted in relation to experiments with videoconference systems in a research setting. In the case of the Xerox PARC project, an existing development group was split between two locations, and a videoconference application was installed (Abel 1990; Olson and Bly 1991). Although communication issues did surface with the technology, such as its limited support for problem resolution and the initiation of social relationships, it also enhanced a certain amount of task-oriented activity. In particular, it appeared that the common visual space facilitated collaborative design.

One of the Bellcore experiments consisted of the use of the Cruiser desktop videoconference system by eleven summer students and their mentors, all in a single building (Fish et al. 1993). Two particular observations need to be made in relation to this experiment. The first is that only twenty-five percent of the calls lasted more than three minutes, suggesting that the system was used infrequently for detailed discussion of research issues. The second observation is that the article does not indicate whether the technology had any particular role in the way in which the students' research was conducted. Also, the question still remains as to whether or not a distributed collaborative research group would use the technology in a more substantive way, since such a group may not be able to easily organize face-to-face meetings.

The Ontario Telepresence project was also created to explore the possible role of desktop videoconference and other technologies, and researchers in this project began initial testing of various technological concepts within the group of participating scientists. In a study of their use of communication technologies (Haythornthwaite et al., in press), a questionnaire was used to probe the relative use of telephone, e-mail, fax, and a desktop videoconference system. In the case of the videoconference system, of the eighty-eight potential pairs who had access to this system, it was only used an average of twelve times per year by the various pairs. This represented only a very small portion of the total work-oriented communications (telephone and fax were also used infrequently, whereas e-mail was used extensively). One possible explanation for the low use was that, just as with the Bellcore experiment, respondents were co-located and could easily organize face-to-face communications.

A Field Study of a Naturally Distributed Research Group

In order to further characterize the nature of collaborative research, and the way in which both conventional and videoconference technologies may be used in this context, I would like to report briefly on a field study that was carried out in 1992 and 1993. The objectives of the study were to explore the nature of an existing collaborative research project, to observe the use and significance of common network technologies by the researchers, and to assess the ease of introduction and utility of desktop videoconferencing for this group.

A variety of data-gathering methods were employed. Three of the working meetings were observed over a nine-month period, and informal conversations were held with several of the researchers at these meetings. On-site visits were made to four of the five geographically dispersed Canadian sites that hosted project participants. Repeated telephone interviews were conducted with most of the participants at various points in the nine-month period. A logbook was kept of events, dates, and discussions. Although a questionnaire was also distributed that explored the collaborative aspects of the project, the discussion here is mainly based on the qualitative observations.

An Overview of the Atmospheric Physics Research Project

The atmospheric physics research project began in the mid-1980s with a request for proposals by NASA. Canadian as well as scientists from another country submitted project proposals. An arrangement was eventually adopted whereby both groups of scientists would make joint contributions to the project, but the participants indicated that significant disagreements between the two groups occurred in the early years of the project. With the participation of over one hundred scientists and contract personnel, the research instrument was specified, built, and launched on a satellite, and began transmitting data in the fall of 1991. I began my observations a year later, when the group of about twenty researchers and graduate students, from five Canadian sites, one American site, and two sites in another country, indicated that they were at a stage of validating the data captured from the satellite instrument.

The researchers' short-term objective was to create a single set of data and data analysis tools, and to correct and transform the data into a format that a variety of project and other scientists could use. This consisted of various initial analyses in order to "check and understand what the data is telling us," before large-scale analysis began. One of the key elements of this validation process was the specification and coding of software that would transform the raw data into a more usable form (thousands of lines of Fortran computer code were written by several programmers in the foreign country). Near-monthly face-to-face meetings, alternating between Canada and the other major national partner, punctuated this work. Various communication and computer network technologies were used, and this will be described in more detail.

The Use of Conventional Network Technologies

All the researchers participating in the atmospheric physics project had Internet mail addresses, and most of the researchers indicated that they sent several e-mail messages per week to other participants. There was no general distribution list for the group, although the project leader had created his own private list to enable him to send out project announcements to all participants. This medium was used for a variety of purposes: sending out summaries of meetings, scheduling meetings, asking colleagues for information, and distributing sections of drafts of papers or asking for comments on these. Participants would also use e-mail to send requests for certain instrument filters to a time allocation committee. E-mail was also a key medium through which project researchers received requests to synchronize data gathering with other researchers who used ground-based instruments.

The telephone was infrequently used, even among the Canadian researchers, and e-mail had become the standard means of communication. There were a number of reasons for this: 1) several participants traveled extensively and this was the easiest way to communicate,

2) all participants had e-mail accounts and used them, 3) the foreign scientists occasionally had difficulties understanding oral English and considered text to be preferable, 4) time differences between participants could range up to six hours, and 5) some participants noted that, with a written message, they could think about the message or look for some needed information before replying.

Some of the researchers also had access to and used a synchronous computer-mediated dialog feature. NASA had provided 56 kbps (kilo bits per second) data lines between three Vax computers in Canada, the U.S., and the other country. By using the Vax "phone" command, a researcher could check whether or not a researcher in another country had logged on to a computer, and then engage him in a textual conversation through the computer. The participants who had access to this, who were mainly responsible for operational activities and software testing, noted that this communication medium allowed them to obtain quick answers to relatively urgent questions. The scientists for whom English was not their mother language also noted that it was easier to dialog in written English, and preferred this means of communication to a telephone call.

The other network application that was used intensively was FTP and remote log-on. Subsets of data from the primary data-base (located at the NASA center) were often transferred to Canada or to the other country (the sheer size of this data prevented it from being completely replicated at the other sites). Researchers at other Canadian sites would then log-on to the central Canadian computer and remotely carry out further analysis of these data subsets, or transfer the data to their own local computer. Eventually, once the data transformation algorithms had been coded and verified, they would be used by a high-speed computer at NASA in order to carry out a major transformation of the backlog of data, and the transformed files would then be available for further transfer and analysis.

Although it is risky to speculate on how the project activities and structure might have been different without the electronic infrastructure noted above (electronic mail, medium speed data lines, FTP, remote log-on, Vax phone), the project would likely still have existed, although more use would undoubtedly have been made of the telephone and fax machine. Additional personnel may have been needed at the central sites for the data analysis. As well, the division of work in which the software development was mainly the responsibility of the group of participants in the distant country, would have been much more cumbersome without this electronic infrastructure, and more significant tensions might have appeared without it.

Still, a number of problems were apparent in the communication structures. One was that the transformation software was continually being updated, and the researchers were not always certain which version they had used for certain analyses, nor which assumptions or parameters were in force for a given version. Another problem that surfaced was that some of the researchers were not sure how to invoke, or which general sub-routines provided by NASA were needed to read, the data stored in the U.S. As well, the researchers desired local copies of the data transformation software, but the group working on this was concerned that if old versions were used (instead of a centralized updated one), this would introduce confusion and errors. Finally, several Canadian researchers felt that the electronic access that they did have to the data was not sufficiently rapid. Some sites experienced significant delays with both remote access and file transfer because of the single 56 kbps Canadian backbone that was available in Canada. The eventual response to this problem was a plan to distribute the data on CD-ROM disks.[6] Also, in order to minimize confusion in relation to what each version of the transformation software did, the software group began to produce and distribute paper and electronic documentation related to the software.

Face-to-Face Meetings

In order to more accurately assess the role of computer and communication technologies in the activities of this group, one also needs to take into account the frequency and functions of the face-to-face meetings. Most of the senior researchers met on a near-monthly basis, and several of the research assistants also attended. During the validation period, presentations and discussions centered on what work had been carried out, what new or persistent questions had emerged from this work, how to interpret the data, what follow-up activities were needed and who would do them, and what algorithms needed to be encoded into the transformation software. The meetings also constituted a deadline for informal progress reports, an opportunity to interactively discuss and orient the work of the other participants, a way of remaining informed of the activities and progress of others, a means of collectively deciding which issues were important, and an opportunity to informally verify that key tasks had been assigned or completed.

It was also possible to observe conflict and disagreement during the meetings. For example, differences of opinion existed in relation to whether or not the validation process was sufficiently complete to allow researchers to begin the scientific analysis. There was even dis-agreement about the "significant similarities or differences" of various graphs that were presented at the meetings! The meetings were also the time at which the three project management committees would usually meet, note the work that had been accomplished, acknowl-edge requests for resources or support, and attempt to resolve any outstanding issues. These committees were the result of expressed and tacit desires of various senior scientists to have visibility and control over the project activities.

To summarize, effective functioning of the project committees and the give-and-take of the discussions appeared to require face-to-face interaction. Nor had there been any serious attempt to redirect the discussions through electronic media, even though the senior researchers indicated that they were tired of traveling and that they were quite at ease with electronic mail. Instead, it appears that the meetings created a public forum where work activities could be easily reported and discussed, and where scientific and project "personae" could be readily created, negotiated, and maintained.

The Implementation of the Desktop Videoconferencing Application

In order to test some of the claims noted previously in relation to the presumed utility of desktop videoconferencing for collaborative research, I indicated to the researchers that a trial of this technology could be arranged with no direct cost to them. There was initial enthu-siasm for the project, and several researchers indicated interest in using the system to present and compare graphics (a shared screen function was part of the system). A few of the senior researchers also hoped that some of the face-to-face meetings could be replaced by videoconferences.

The installation and troubleshooting of the system took several months, but eventually, all of the Canadian sites had a functional unit. A few tests were conducted in which researchers at one site presented and discussed some graphics. Initial reactions to the application were generally positive. However, a few months after these tests, none of the sites had yet used the system to conduct any work-oriented dis-cussions. The research group had not adopted the technology, in spite of their early interest in it and our best efforts to create favorable, although near-realistic, circumstances. Some aid was provided in terms of network and application installation, a "critical mass" of terminals appeared to be attained so that each participant had a number of other potential communication partners, most sites had at least three months of use of a functional terminal, and there were no direct or indirect financial costs for using the system.

Several possible reasons were identified that help to explain why the system was not adopted. Certain characteristics of the desktop videoconference technology limited its usefulness to the researchers, such as the difficulty of using the system to show or transfer images that were on Vax computers, and the impossibility, at the time, of including several persons in a conference. Limited installation support by the manufacturer and busy schedules of local technicians prolonged the implementation period and led to some disinterest in the project. As well, the characteristics and attitudes of the researchers were a factor, in that several were satisfied with existing communication technologies, particularly e-mail, and most did not appear to take sufficient time to become fully proficient with the new technology.

Still, in my opinion, there were other more deeply rooted factors that discouraged adoption of the technology, such as the project structure and the apparent rivalries between some of the scientists. The work that was carried out between meetings was divided up and specified in such a way that it could be carried out by largely autonomous groups at the various sites. The near-monthly meetings were frequent enough to provide the necessary opportunities for high-level verification and discussion of the work. They also provided a public stage on which the scientists could demonstrate and promote their expertise. As well, it is possible that some of the scientists preferred to avoid direct one-to-one discussions with some of their colleagues, as would have been required by the videoconference system.

Conclusion

Two recent, mutually reinforcing trends can be observed with respect to the way in which research is carried out. An increasing number of organizations and research institutions are encouraging or participating in cooperative and collaborative research projects, and this is likely to continue into the twenty-first century. As well, these projects are occasionally facilitated by current network applications, although the conditions and extent of this appears to be largely unknown. All of these trends represent shifts in the way in which knowledge is created. I have highlighted these trends, pointed out significant differences between cooperative and collaborative research, and provided examples of situations and projects in which network technologies may or may not contribute to cooperative and collaborative research.

Several general conclusions can be drawn from the discussion here. First, in the future, many researchers and research institutions will still want to exchange information. More and more pieces of information are exchanged daily over the Internet, although it is difficult to assess the significance of this for research practices or efficiency.

Second, under certain conditions, network technologies are facilitating a process by which a single research project can be divided up among geographically dispersed groups, or by which individuals or groups who desire to more closely coordinate their research activities can do so.

Third, care should be taken to not overestimate the role of network technologies in collaborative research. Collaborative research is often a complex, fluid, and political process. Researchers want to retain a significant degree of independence and autonomy, while recognizing that effective structures are also needed in order to coordinate action. The face-to-face discussion among the atmospheric physics researchers underlines the significant work, social, and intellectual functions of the meetings. Face-to-face meetings and private discussions appeared to be the only effective way of creating project structures, voicing and resolving disagreements, demonstrating expertise, and allowing intellectual synergy to occur. An outstanding question is whether or not current and future applications (particularly those that seek to simulate a face-to-face situation such as a videoconference or decision support system) will effectively support these essential social and communication processes.

Finally, I would also like to comment on current efforts to implement high speed network applications. I do not dispute that many of the technologies related to data and information management and dissemination are likely to be welcomed by the academic community. The university library (and the related academic publishing industry) has been essential to scholarly activity, and network technologies that simulate or extend its functions will undoubtedly find a useful niche. Still, the organization and distribution of information does not necessarily lead to collaboration. It is likely that information and communication technologies will make it easier to engage in cooperative actions, but it is impossible to predict whether or not the technologies will be of much significance in relation to collaboration.

Indeed, the scientific literature provides a limited assessment of the role of potential network applications in cooperative and collaborative research. This has not prevented the promoters of various national high speed networks[7] from claiming that the exponential improvement of current network capabilities and the future availability of currently experimental applications will help support these practices. These promoters often mistake the pioneer testing of an application, usually under highly favorable conditions, for proof of its eventual wide scale utility. More critical assessment and empirical in situ observation is needed before any realistic vision can be projected of the ways in which new network applications may or may not contribute to cooperative and collaborative research.

Notes

1. I use the term Internet since it is a well-known expression that refers to the academic networks, but I implicitly include any of these: Bitnet, NSFnet, CA*Net, and so on.

2. In an empirical assessment of the quality of articles in the field of psychology, Kraut, Egido, and Galegher (1990) found that authors rated their solo articles higher than co-authored articles. Also, both types of articles received equivalent citation by other authors.

3. These statistics pertain to NSFnet, October 1991, and were compiled by Meric Network Inc. A later analysis reported by Eric Aupperle in the Internet Society News, 1994, vol. 2, no. 4, p. 14, although not as clear in its breakdown, suggests that an "other category" of TCP/UDP is increasing in volume as new applications are being used.

4. Non-academics are increasingly gaining access to the Internet, although for the moment, most participants in the distribution lists and newsgroups tend to be academics, researchers, students, or technology developers.

5. However, I would suggest that current tools to locate and access data are primitive, and that learning to locate, store, or transfer the data is not easy.

6. It was ironic that although the researchers were working in a networked environment, they proposed this more static mechanism for data distribution. Proponents of the high-speed networks will see here a further reason to upgrade the networks. Still, the CD-ROM mechanism would have allowed the various sites to create an off-line data library that was immediately feasible and accessible, more convenient than a tape reader, and minimized the use of local hard disk storage capacity.

7. Some of the national high speed network initiatives are: NREN (U.S.), CANARIE (Canada), RENATER (France), SUPERJANET (Great Britain), and AARNET (Australia). Academics and researchers are one of the major user groups targeted by all of the network planners. One of the assumptions behind these initiatives is that high data-transfer capacity is required in order to allow academics to use multimedia applications. It is difficult to predict the extent to which these initiatives will remain distinct from other related but more universal electronic highway initiatives.

References

Abel, M. (1990). Experiences in an Exploratory Distributed Organization. In J. Galegher, R. Kraut, and C. Egido (Eds.), *Intellectual teamwork: Social and technological foundations of cooperative work* (489–510). Hillsdale: Lawrence Erlbaum Associates.

Aupperle, E. (1994). NSFNET backbone trends. *Internet Society News* 2(4): 13–14.

Carley, K. and Wendt, K. (1991). Electronic mail and scientific communication. *Knowledge: Creation, Diffusion, Utilization*, 12(4):406–440.

Fish, R., Kraut, R., Root, R., and Rice, R. (1993). Video as a technology for informal communication. *Communications of the ACM* 36(1):48–61.

Gurd, G. and Picot, J. (1987). *A study of Atlantic Canadian user reactions to inter-university electronic networks*. Laval, Quebec: Canadian Workplace Automation Research Centre.

Harasim, L. and Winkelmans, T. (1990). Computer-mediated scholarly collaboration: A case study of an international educational research workshop. *Knowledge: Creation, Diffusion, Utilization* 11(4):382–409.

Haythornthwaite, C., Wellman, B., and Mantei, M. (in press). Media use and work relationships in a research group. To appear in *Proceedings of the 27th Hawaii International Conference on Systems Science*, Maui.

Hiltz, S. (1984). *Online communities: A case study of the office of the future*. Norwood: Ablex Publishing Corporation.

Kling, R. (1991). Cooperation, coordination and control in computer-supported work. *Communications of the ACM* 34(12):83–88.

Kling, R. (1992). L'étude de l'informatisation dans la vie sociale: comment les conventions de genre construisent nos discours. *Technologies de l'information et société* 4(2):205–237.

Koch, S. (1991). Electronic networks and science. In C. McClure et al. (Eds.), *The National Research and Education Network (NREN): Research and policy perspectives* (69–86). Norwood: Ablex Publishing Corporation.

Kraut, R., Galegher, J., and Egido, C. (1987–1988). Relationships and tasks in scientific collaboration. *Human-Computer Interaction* 3(1):31–58.

Kraut, R., Egido, C., and Galegher, J. (1990). Patterns of contact and communication in scientific research collaborations. In J. Galegher, R. Kraut, and C. Egido (Eds.), *Intellectual teamwork: Social and technological foundations of cooperative work* (149–171). Hillsdale: Lawrence Erlbaum Associates.

Lucier, R. (1990). Knowledge management: Refining roles in scientific communication. *Educom Review*, 21–27.

McClure, C. et al. (Eds.). (1991). *The National Research and Education Network (NREN): Research and policy perspectives*. Norwood: Ablex Publishing Corporation.

McCreary, E. and Brochet, M. (1991). Collaboration in international online teams. In A. Kaye (Ed.), *Collaborative learning through computer conferencing: The Najaden papers* (69–85). NATO ASI Series F: Computer and Systems Sciences, vol. 90. Berlin: Springer-Verlag.

Olson, M.H. and Bly, S.A. (1991). The Portland experience: A report on a distributed research group. In S. Greenberg (Ed.), *Computer-supported cooperative work and groupware* (81–98). London: Academic Press.

Rice, R. and Case, D. (1983). Electronic message systems in the university: A description of use and utility. *Journal of Communication* 33(1):131–152.

Schatz, B. (1991). Building an electronic scientific community. *Proceedings of IEEE* (739–748).

Schmidt, K. and Bannon, L. (1992). Taking CSCW seriously: Supporting articulation work. *Computer-Supported Cooperative Work* 1(1–2):7–40.

Schrage, M. (1990). *Shared minds: The new technologies of collaboration.* New York: Random House.

Star, S. (1993). Cooperation without consensus in scientific problem solving: Dynamics of closure in open systems. In S. Easterbrook (Ed.), *CSCW: Cooperation or Conflict?* (93–106). London: Springer-Verlag.

Suchman, L. and Trigg, R. (1986). A framework for studying research collaboration. In *Proceedings of CSCW '86* (221–228), Austin.

Tombaugh, J. (1984). Evaluation of an international scientific computer-based conference, *Journal of Social Issues* 40(3):129–144.

How Do You Get a Hundred Strangers to Agree?

Computer-Mediated Communication and Collaboration

Fay Sudweeks
Sheizaf Rafaeli

Two heads are better than one, but what about a dozen? Or a hundred? The notion of group brainstorming is an appealing technique, but most studies have failed to support Osborn's (1953) claim that interacting groups generate more ideas than individuals working separately and pooling ideas (McGrath 1984). Empirical evidence from laboratory studies of computer-mediated brainstorming (electronic brainstorming) appears to be more encouraging (e.g. Nunamaker, Vogel, and Konsynski 1991; Valacich, Paranka, George, and Nunamaker 1993; Valacich, Dennis, and Connolly 1994). Does the effect differ outside the laboratory when interacting participants are strangers, widely dispersed and disparate in skills, knowledge, status, and culture? Does the computer-mediated environment also enhance consensus formation? These are crucial questions as computer-mediated collaborative work becomes both feasible and desirable in academia and industry.

In this chapter, the experiences of an ongoing computer-mediated collaboration of more than a hundred researchers who shared ideas and created a database of a representative sample of international, public group, asynchronous computer-mediated communication (CMC) is described. The goal of the chapter is twofold:

*This project could not have been completed without the enthusiasm and expertise of all ProjectH members. Special thanks are due to Joe Konstan, University of Minnesota, who developed all the programs used throughout the project and had a finger on almost every pulse, and to Ed Mabry, University of Wisconsin-Milwaukee, who advised and supported coders as the "Commish." Thanks also to Duncan Sanderson and Ron Rice for comments on early drafts.

The ProjectH research was supported by Comserve, CompuServe, Recanati Fund, and the Key Center of Design Computing, University of Sydney.

1. to focus on product: describe the promises and pitfalls of carrying out research on group CMC; and

2. to focus on process: provide an introspective examination of our own group CMC.

This chapter is about the cobbler not walking about barefoot: studying CMC, using CMC.

Text-Based Computer-Mediated Communication

We need to know more about the changing nature of communication in a population-exploded cyberspace. Corporate and private use of electronic mail (e-mail) systems such as MCI mail, CompuServe and Fido continue to expand, and traditional forms of communication are substituted or complemented. E-mail is both instantaneous and asynchronous, as it bridges spatial, temporal, and societal gaps like no other medium prior to it (Rogers and Rafaeli 1985).

In the networked organization, the informality and interactive features of e-mail encourage employees to cross social and organizational boundaries to share opinions and ideas (Sproull and Kiesler 1991). The very boundaries of organizations are being redrawn or called into question. An interactive communication medium is of little value, however, unless there is a critical mass to communicate. Network use is approaching the saturation point at which the sheer mass of existing and potential users makes it economically and socially attractive to the remaining population (Gurbaxani 1990).

Text-based CMC is commonly compared unfavorably with face-to-face interpersonal communication, because we can't hear intonation that signals a joke, or see puzzled expressions that convey confusion. Face-to-face communication is hailed as the communication standard against which all others are found inferior. The ideal of face-to-face conversation, though, is precisely that: an ideal (Schudson 1978). Is the stereotypical conversation that passes between a long-married couple at the breakfast table a standard, or the phatic communication that is typical when two strangers meet? In reality, face-to-face communication is not always a universal ideal nor universally idyllic.

The prescribed panacea for network ills is usually greater bandwidth to add more social cues and to approximate face-to-face communication. Adding video, audio, and graphics is somehow expected to make the medium more "real." Mabry (1993a) challenges the implication that single-channel (text only) communication is less real:

regardless of the medium—or media mixture—elected for transmitting messages, communicating IS vocabulary-language-and some form of "structure" of symbolic impressions derived from the active use of symbolic expressiveness. A "picture is worth a thousand words" only to those with a thousand words to appropriate for construing the pictorial image. It might only be worth ten words to some people or ten thousand words to some others. A message can only be text+sound+visualization+? because a message encoder can rationalize (a decidedly linguistic task) the assembly of its components into an explanation of planned message effects.

Granted, McLuhan [1964] was at least half right in asserting that the medium is the message in that without a medium there isn't going to be a message. But, a more compelling stance argues that meaning resides in people. In other words, the "reality" of a message is a matter of receiver perception and attribution and not sender encoding complexity. The ultimate reality of any phenomenon is its existence.

It may be, then, that more bandwith does not necessarily mean more effective interaction. A presence, or even an awareness of a presence, may not be a mandatory ingredient of a stimulating and satisfying conversation. The concept of social presence has been discussed by various researchers (Rice and Associates 1984; Short, Williams, and Christie 1976; Walther 1992). The fewer channels or codes available within a medium, it is claimed, the less each participant is aware of others using the same medium. Social presence is regarded as a property of the communication medium. CMC, with its lack of nonverbal and paucity of non-textual cues, is low in social presence and preferred for tasks low in interpersonal involvement. Social presence, a subjective measure of the presence of others, is both intriguing and weakly defined. There is evidence that a high proportion of socio-emotional communication can be conveyed in CMC (Rice 1987; Rice and Love 1987). Interactivity itself proves to be a both measurable and meaningful quality of communication contexts (Rafaeli 1988). In computer-mediated discussion groups, there is the potential for much interactivity. This should lead to high involvement, but does it lead to longer, more complicated processes?

Computer-Mediated Group Activity

Much has been reported about computer-mediated group behavior, most of it relying on data from organizational case studies (Sproull and Kiesler 1986; Zuboff 1988), laboratory experiments (Dennis and Valacich 1993; Dubrovsky, Kiesler, and Sethna 1991; Hill 1982; Poole,

Holmes, Watson, and DeSanctis 1993; Siegel, Dubrovsky, Kiesler, and McGuire 1986; Valacich, Paranka, George, and Nunamaker 1993; Valacich, Dennis, and Connolly 1994), surveys (Kiesler and Sproull 1986; Schmitz and Fulk 1991; Sproull, Kiesler, and Zubrow 1984) and educational settings (McInerney 1994; Sudweeks et al. 1993). Other reports of computer-mediated collaborative work derive from groups formed for a specific task, such as the CommonLISP development program (Steele 1984), teams working on development projects (McCreary and Brochet 1992), and a large group using a computer conferencing system (Hiltz 1983). Less is known, however, about how spontaneous and heterogeneous electronic groups perform, how conflicts are resolved, and how consensus is achieved.

ProjectH, the research group described in this chapter, is grounded in common membership of a computer-networked discussion group and a common desire to understand more clearly the nature of communication, culture, and community on the network. The research, from conception to consummation, has been entirely computer-mediated, "on stage," and public. Records of all discussions, decisions, actions, tools, and policies were (and are) available. This reflects the tradition of hard-sciences' laboratory manuals, and addresses one of the most poorly recorded aspects of group work: the early stages of planning. We describe the CMC counterpart of an initial concept emerging from, say, a hastily drawn sketch in a cafe, or a serendipitous conversation in a bar.

A characteristic of CMC groups is the democratic nature of the mode in which people interact. In the process of collecting a large representative database of CMC, a blend of democracy and "restrained" leadership evolved as an organizational structure. We qualify "leadership" because the coordinators should be regarded as "facilitators" rather than leaders. The only restriction on people's participating equally in generating ideas and developing policies and methodologies were self-imposed restraints such as time limitations, conflicting schedules, and degree of motivation. The coordinators (the authors of this chapter) were merely instrumental in facilitating a productive working environment. Collaboration, at times, appeared to be painstakingly slow, but the progress can be assessed by the efficacy of the process in devising and attaining a common goal.

The ProjectH Study

"Wouldn't this kind of study be relatively simple," said Jim Thomas (1992a). "It's something . . . maybe a few of us could do by dividing up a few randomly chosen groups, whipping into SPSS format, and writing something up." Two years, and more than three thousand coordinating work hours later, we are "writing something up."

It began with an enthusiastic discussion on a Comserve hotline (see the chapter by Stephen and Harrison in this volume) of the dynamics of group CMC, which eventually focused on the nature and longevity of threads. A "straw man" outline of a quantitative study was proposed (Rafaeli 1992a) and a small group of about thirty agreed to participate and code batches of messages. An interim distribution facility was provided by the University of Sydney, and then the group moved to ProjectH, a specially created Comserve-sponsored conference.

News of the study circulated on the network and more than three hundred people contacted the coordinators. The initial ProjectH group quadrupled and eventually stabilized at about one hundred members. Current participants represent fifteen countries, and numerous universities and commercial firms. Participants represent a wide range of age groups (early twenties to late sixties), academic positions (graduate students to professors), and disciplines (approximately 40 percent from the social sciences, 35 percent from the humanities and 25 percent from applied sciences). The study has been a novel approach to groupwork, and the process itself is a rich source of data, as the participants, and the coordinators, had never met. (For a detailed description of the methodology of the study, see Rafaeli, Sudweeks, Konstan, and Mabry, 1994.)

What are we studying?

Decades ago, McLuhan (1964) foresaw a global network creating a global village. It turns out that the "global village" is neither global nor village. The organizing principle is a loosely coupled entity or discussion group, which we will call "list." Each list is a virtual neighborhood, defined by common interest not geography.

The depth of interactivity among discussion groups varies widely. Some groups are like cocktail parties with many conversations (threads) competing, rather like CB radio; some focus around specific topics ranging from postcard collecting to yacht design; some are like notice boards in the local grocery store where messages are pinned and left for others to read and comment on; and some groups merely function as newspapers, disseminating electronic journals or computer programs, and advertising conferences or job vacancies (Sudweeks, Collins, and December 1995).

What do we know about the social dynamics, the patterns of communication, the emergence, longevity, and survival of topics and threads on lists? Where, when and why does "flaming" occur? What is the role of emoticons (graphic icons created from punctuation marks to indicate an emotion)? These questions about the communication qualities of lists and their participants shaped the rationale and design of the study.

The alternatives in studying group CMC are numerous. One can use quantitative or qualitative methods; one may study societies, organizations, groups, coalitions in groups, individuals, or single messages; one may study cross-sectionally, or across time. In our case, we perceived that the greatest opportunity resided in three facts: (i) we are a large group of qualified researchers; (ii) one-shot, one-list studies have been done numerous times; and (iii) introspective reports of discussion groups still need validation from less obtrusive studies of the content. The aims of the study were:

1. to randomly sample a sizeable chunk of publicly available, archived computer-mediated group discussion,

2. to analyze the content of messages contained in the sample,

3. to focus on the single message, authors, aggregate thread, and the lists as units of analysis,

4. to empirically test hypotheses of interest to participants,

5. to collect descriptive data to document the state of the medium and the communication over it,

6. to create a shared database to serve future cross-method, cross-media, or historical analyses, and

7. to conduct research with a group of people diverse in interests, status, age, time, and location.

Conceptualization

During the embryonic, conceptual stage of the study, we found electronic brainstorming to be particularly useful. Many ideas were generated about units of analyses, methodology, hypotheses, and coding. Learning from the diverse experiences and skills of the large number of participants, we chose the following:

1. a quantitative methodology, because we viewed it as dovetailing the large number of experimental, laboratory-based studies of CMC, and the plethora of nongeneralizable surveys of single groups (Fulk and Steinfield 1989; Sproull and Kiesler 1991);

2. an empirical content analysis method that is less sensitive to self-report;

3. a cross-list, cross-time account; and

4. an unlimited range of research questions and hypotheses that can be accommodated within the study.

Research questions of interest were many and varied, and included: what are the characteristics of longer and lasting threads? Are "communities" formed on CMC lists? Can social "density" be measured? How do "free" or "subsidized" lists compare with costly lists? How does metacommunication affect CMC? When and where does "flaming" occur? Are there repeating patterns in the "life" of a group or thread? How is the expression of emotion handled?

Many of us chose one or more variables and described a method for measuring features of interest. The variables, with accompanying definition, extreme case examples, and measurement scale, were collated. A draft codebook was pretested, assessed for reliability of measures and ambiguity of definitions, and revised accordingly.

Ethical Issues

A quantitative analysis of the aggregate of publicly available, archived content of large group discussions that occurred voluntarily is subject to fewer ethical concerns than other types of analyses. Nevertheless, ethical issues were raised: is there an ethical obligation to inform list owners and/or subscribers prior to sampling? Is public discourse on CMC public? Does the principle of "expectation of privacy" apply? Questions were also raised about intellectual ownership and copyright: Who owns the messages that are sent to a discussion list? Who holds the copyright?

Ethical guidelines for the study were proposed:

> We do NOT view the quantitative analysis of publicly posted or archived messages as a violation of anyone's privacy. We will respect any request by list owners or participants to be excluded from the study. However, we will not seek permission. We view public discourse on CMC as just that: public. Analysis of such content, where individuals', institutions', and lists' identities are shielded, is not subject to "Human Subject" restraints. Such study is more akin to the study of tombstone epitaphs, graffiti, or letters to the editor. Personal?—yes. Private?—no (Rafaeli 1992b)

The implications of the proposed guidelines were hotly debated in a prolonged, scholarly discussion. The discussion revolved around three major issues:

1. Is public discourse on CMC public? Some firmly believed that public posts should be treated like private letters. Regardless of widespread distribution and public access of the posts, there is an expec-

tation of privacy. A post is sent to a list in the expectation that the audience is limited, definable, and identifiable, and that the content is not redistributed and quantified. Some regarded public discourse as public domain, and supported the proposed guidelines.

2. Do authors of posts have any legal, ethical, or moral rights? Again, opinions were divergent. Some considered author permissions and citations should not even be optional—authors must be acknowledged and permission obtained if quotations are used. Some questioned the right to intrude in the lives and activities of others, regarding such intrusion as exploitation, particularly if listowners and/or subscribers are not consulted prior to browsing. Some expected that if copyright of public posts is surrendered on joining a list, then this should be made clear to subscribers at the time of joining. Some considered that use of posts should be governed by professional and academic guidelines, i.e., short excerpts can be quoted without author permission.

3. To what extent do the issues of informed consent, privacy, and intellectual property apply to a quantitative study? The need for different guidelines for qualitative and quantitative research became obvious. In the quantitative study proposed, the object of analysis is the communication that is openly posted and distributed, not the personalities involved. The purpose in using quotes is to illustrate a representative example from a randomly chosen sample of discourse, so it is not necessary to include attribution or seek author permission. Some expressed concern about the implications of restrictive use and censorship on scientific enquiry: "If we reify ethical rules/principles (rather than adhere to the spirit and intent of those principles), we risk empirical catatonia" (Thomas 1992b).

The group invested extraordinary effort in June and July 1992 to compromise on a policy that all could accept as a framework for ethical and scholarly research. There were moments of light banter:

AF: As stupid as Jim Thomas is (and he knows it), I think he is right in this case. (Futrell 1992)
JT: As usual, Al's right (I know it), so shortly after this post, I firebombed his Porsche. (Thomas 1992b)

But the discussion turned hostile when rumors of the study spread to subscribers of a popular discussion list. One subscriber, confused about the nature and process of the quantitative research proposed, and fearful of being sampled and scrutinized, attacked the integrity of the study:

> Unless these academo-dweebs get down and dirty with us . . . ,
> the study is bound to be bogus from the start . . . I'm highly
> unimpressed. They remind me of Masters and Johnson. All
> observation, no participation. (No author, cross-posted by
> Maynor 1992)

The prolonged discussion was having an effect on tone. Exchanges became irate:

KW: I should warn you, if you already haven't figured it out based on the agitation your study has caused: there are indeed people here. (Wolman 1992a)

JD: We've figured it out. It is holding up work on the study . . . as it should until we get these issued resolved. . . . If you have objections, express them in the context of the group . . . working with us not pointing your damn finger, saying shame on us (me). (Downey 1992)

KW: I thought that's what I was doing . . . I was partially sympathetic to what I understood about the project. I'm no longer comfortable with it. And if I want to point my finger at you, sir, I will do so, and there isn't much you can do about it, is there? (Wolman 1992b)

and contrite when informed:

KW: First . . . I waded in here over the weekend, got into a barroom fight or two . . . left, and was persuaded by Jim Thomas that I was not dealing with a crew of ogres, unemployed CIA operatives, and voyeurs. In the process of getting that peace made, I learned a great deal about the genesis of the PROJECTH study, discovered . . . that I too might be able to derive some additional knowledge from what happens here. (Wolman 1992c)

In the heat of the debate, people's credentials were questioned and some responded by posting vitas and listing degrees. The issues remained unresolved but the flames were doused with a humorous post:

> Hi (or as they say around here: shalom—which also means peace):
> I think it's back to business time. . . . Am a bit offended that my
> credentials were not disputed. So, just in case anyone is interested:
> I have the longest, reddest, and prettiest beard in cyberspace. . . .
> Any challenges? (Rafaeli 1992c)

Early in 1993, the issues were confronted again. The coordinators drafted an ethics policy and submitted it to the group for approval. Objections were raised. A second draft of the policy was submitted. And a third, and a fourth. The repeated iterations were straining the groups' patience. Some, earlier on, had suggested a voting mechanism while others, including the coordinators, favored persevering in reaching consensus. When it appeared that consensus was unlikely and that the group would vote on holding a vote, the coordinators called for votes on the fourth draft. In summary, the policy states:

> Members of ProjectH acknowledge and affirm the individual rights of informed consent, privacy, and intellectual property. Members are committed to reducing censorship and prior restraint, and believe the issue of informed consent of authors, moderators and/ or archiving institutions does not apply to a quantitative content analysis in which only publicly available text is analysed. Public posts are public and their use is governed by professional and academic guidelines. All necessary measures are taken to separate names of authors and groups from the database. Individual authors and groups are identified by a number and members using the database must outline their procedure for maintaining confidentiality of authors and groups.

The policy (ProjectH 1993) was ratified with a vote of 38:3 in favor. Not all participants voted. Some abstained, and asked that the abstention vote be recorded. With that hurdle overcome, the "field" work began.

Sampling

Selecting a random representative sample of discussion groups was an important phase of the study. Simple and straightforward? Not at all. It was a complicated task that involved reaching agreement on a rigorous empirical stance. We wanted to sample a wide range of groups to be able to draw conclusions about a wide range of CMC, but how is the universe of groups, so diverse in nature and purpose, defined? Do we weight groups by number of subscribers or volume of activity? How do we know which variables need to be controlled and which should be studied? Should we define samples by number of messages, length of messages, time period?

Initial discussions revealed divergent opinions on the virtues of random and stratified sampling. A committee, representing the spectrum of sampling persuasions within the group, considered two extreme proposals:

1. Complete random sampling—pooling all groups from all networks and randomly selecting a sample;

2. Heavy stratification—selecting a set of strata and sampling from within each stratum.

Given limited human resources and availability of accurate information on list characteristics, membership, authorship, and readership, we decided to stratify by network and randomly sample over a restricted domain, excluding foreign language groups, groups on local networks, announcement groups, help/support groups for specific products, test and control groups, groups whose contents are only excerpts of other groups selected by moderators, and extremely low volume groups. An equal number of lists were randomly selected from Bitnet, Usenet, and CompuServe populations. If selected groups did not meet the set criteria, we dipped into the population hat again (and again).

List traffic is dynamic. Some groups are highly active, generating in excess of two hundred messages a day; other groups are almost dormant, generating fewer than two hundred messages a year; some groups maintain a consistent volume of traffic; other groups experience high peaks and low troughs. Sampling an equal number of messages from selected groups has the advantage of capturing threads. Sampling over an equal time period has the advantage of typifying group activity. Rather than risk having to reject a high percentage of groups because we happened to sample during a quiet period, we sampled one hundred messages, beginning on a randomly selected Monday.

Coding

Numerous universal systems for coding were considered and rejected, as coders varied in technical expertise, access to technology and Internet resources, and working style. One member, using the catch phrase "if we build it will you come?", headed a subgroup to develop standard coding formats for different platforms—Hypercard stack for Macintosh, FileExpress database for DOS, and templates for text editors and wordprocessors.

Each batch of one hundred messages downloaded from selected groups was prepared for coders. Programs were written to precode the first six of forty-six variables and to compile a cumulative database of authors across all lists. Coders took, modally, twenty hours to code a batch of one hundred messages. After coding, the data was e-mailed to an account which was set up for automatic processing. The processor checked for errors and completeness, transferred accurate data to a database, and reported error and completion status to the coder and a coordinator.

Reliability

Reliability assesses the degree to which variations in data represent real phenomena, rather than variations in the measurement process (Krippendorff 1980). We considered two reliability measures:

1. Test-standard: This involves training all coders to a standard set by expert coders, and accepting only those who code to the preset level of accuracy.
2. Test-retest: This involves using at least two coders for the same data, to establish the reproducibility of results.

Given the unprecedented nature of the project, the unavailability of an established standard, and the number of coders involved, we adopted a test-retest design and assigned each list to two coders. Due to time constraints which prevented some from completing coding, one-third of thirty-two lists (batches of one hundred messages) were double coded. List assignment was confidential and allocation was random to avoid individual bias.

To eliminate a possible source of invalid (inflated) reliability, coders were discouraged from discussing coding problems among themselves or within the group. Coder queries were directed, instead, to an advisory committee of twelve members. Each advisor ("oracle"), fielded questions on a section of the codebook, responding in a non-directive, analytical manner. The more complicated questions were discussed among the oracles and the "Commissioner of Oracles" (the oracle coordinator, or the "Commish") summarized the discussions, responded to the enquirer, and posted recommendations on potentially universal problems to the group.

Who Owns the Processed Data Set?

The processed data, compiled from archived group discussions, is the result of considerable effort, particularly from those who contributed substantially to the development of the codebook, to policy formation, and to actual coding. Given the public nature of the data, we are committed to conducting the study publicly and making the data available to all. The processed data is the intellectual property of those who participated in the work, and the ProjectH Research Group holds the copyright. Access to and use of the data set is on a staggered basis according to contribution rates. After a two-year exclusive access period by ProjectH members, the data set will be released to the public.

Working Together

The project began with the perception of an opportunity, and a few researchers' agreement to share efforts to produce a body of data. As the scope of the project expanded, invitations to participate were periodically circulated to lists and newsgroups. Our membership quadrupled, and a large-scale project became viable.

Time differences were a problem, but a problem that was turned to an asset. Given that participants are from fifteen countries and five continents, and the coordinators are impaired with an eight hour time difference, and another eight hours are between each of them and the major contingent of participants in North America, we like to think that the sun always sets on at least one part of ProjectH but work never ceases.

Working with a large group of strangers is not easy; working with a large group of strangers, with whom continued contact depends on mutual (and at times unfounded) understanding and the whims of temperamental networked machines, can be frustrating. In most instances, an e-mail address is the only available means of contacting other participants. There are few cues to signify whether nonresponse is due to illness, travel, work commitments, disinterest, or simply network problems. Many weeks were wasted waiting for reactions to open-ended suggestions and proposals. This process was eventually improved by setting a time limit to respond, e.g., "If there is no response within three days, we'll assume you agree and we'll go ahead with the proposed action."

Online group decisions, claim Sproull and Kiesler (1991), are unpredictable, unconventional, democratic, and less constrained by high-status members. In the absence of modifying nonverbal and nonvocal cues, individual influences on group processes are more equitable. Our experience supported this claim. One participant, for example, had no hesitation in expressing disapproval:

CM: Sorry, Sheizaf, I consider this to be a flame. Maybe these questions are irrelevant to you, and maybe they're not the main focus of study right now on ProjectH, but they're pretty relevant to me, and evidently of some interest to others on this list. (Marmell 1993a)

SR: So why are your opinions a 'qualitative discussion,' even if they involve me personally and critically, while my opinions, naming no names, are a flame? (Rafaeli 1993)

CM: It's not my opinion that's qualitative per se, it was the discussion generated on the list . . . I had a real visceral reaction to your comments, and thought you needed to hear what they sounded like. (Marmell 1993b)

There is less emotional and social cost when face-to-face confrontation is remote or nonexistent. The consequence of uninhibited behavior is not necessarily negative; in fact, we found the equalizing effect beneficial:

> There is a sense of cohesiveness with ProjectH exchanges that I don't apprehend on lists. A primary difference comes in not feeling the need to engage in self-credentialing (this-is-who-I-am) statements. . . . ProjectH's goals clarify members' purposiveness and contribute structure (vis-a-vis expectations, ongoing tasks, etc.) to their relationship in ways that less well defined groups may not achieve. (Mabry 1993b)
>   . . . our interactions have created a group culture, complete with norms and values. As a group, we seem to value collegiality, mutual respect, and a sense of humor, while devaluing flaming and argumentativeness. For me, at least, that makes ProjectH a very comfortable place to pursue some interesting questions. (Penkoff 1993)

Perceived social presence of other members did not appear to have diminished with restricted bandwidth. One response to a proposal for a face-to-face workshop to meet colleagues was revealing:

> Fay, I understand the curiosity, but doesn't it strike you as significant that you want to "meet the people (you) will have been working with for two years . . . ?" Haven't we already met? Is there something unreal or artificial about the lack of F2F contact? (Mills 1993)

The absence of social presence is almost an assumed quality of CMC. To compensate, many people engage in speculating about perceived and real differences between in-person and online impressions. However, the relative poverty of bandwidth afforded by CMC will be the first characteristic of CMC to disappear. Technological advances, virtual reality, and even current in-use technology (voice-mail, picture phones, videoconferencing) are rendering moot the bandwidth issue.

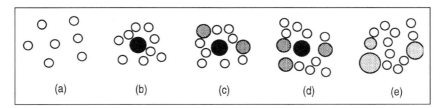

Fig. 1. ProjectH collaborative process. (a) an amorphous group of individuals; (b) a small group of people, led by the coordinators (dark grey), share ideas; (c) the group expands and small committees (light grey) representing diverse persuasions draft proposals for the group; (d) more committees are formed for different phases; (e) individuals and small groups work on different projects using the shared database.

More interesting and relevant questions are: Who do we get to meet or stay in touch with now that we wouldn't have otherwise? What is missing from CMC interactions apart from the fact that we are apart? What can we do to improve such interactions?

The protracted and heated debate on ethics was stimulating but inefficient. The discussions generated more than three hundred messages over a period of eight months, yet consensus still eluded us. From this we learned an essential lesson, and developed a process for improving group consensus.

A political metaphor can be used to categorize collaborative systems (Condon 1993): the "fascist" system in which one person is in control; the "communist" system in which the system itself is in control; and the "anarchist" system in which there is no control. Our collaborative process has a blend of democracy and restrained anarchy (see Figure 1). The coordinators facilitate, volunteer committee members recommend, but no individual or group has control, so in that sense there is more structure than an anarchist system.

Blending democracy and anarchy worked like this: Each phase of the project began with preliminary discussions among the group. Many and varied opinions were expressed and, if necessary, the coordinators focused and summarized the issues. If it was obvious that all issues had been raised and consensus unlikely, a committee of 3–10 volunteers, representing divergent opinions of the group, drafted a compromise proposal for the group. Committee proposals, summarizing the advantages and disadvantages of options considered and the rationale for choosing one over others, were posted to the group for further discussion or fine-tuning. Finally, a time frame (usually a week) was specified for further objections and if there were none the policy was adopted. Using this method, committee consensus took 20–100 messages and list traffic was reduced to a minimum.

In an environment in which the coordinators and most participants had never met before, either on or off the net, different modes of communication for brainstorming were employed with varying degrees of success, e.g., synchronous media (Unix Talk and Internet Relay Chat), specially tailored distribution lists, telephone, regular mail, and some face to face. The coordinators used the Talk program extensively, as it was the most conducive medium for stimulating novel ideas and overcoming thorny obstacles.

Conclusion

The goal of this chapter has been to highlight the products and processes of group CMC by describing the experiences of our own collaboration. The results can be summarized as follows.

Products

The data set compiled by ProjectH, a cross-sectional, representative account of computer-mediated discussions, is being used for research as varied as the ProjectH constituency. The results from these studies are encouraging and enlightening despite the obvious limitations of the unidimensional nature of the data.

The focus of one study is an attempt to measure interactivity, the degree to which communication transcends reaction. Rafaeli and Sudweeks (1996) demonstrate that those messages defined as "interactive" are more opinionated, more humorous, more self-disclosing, more personal, and more likely to express agreement than non-interactive or reactive messages. In contrast to statistical analyses of interactivity, Berthold, Sudweeks, Newton, and Coyne (1996) use an autoassociative neural network to construct sets of features that are typical of messages that initiate or contribute to longer lasting threads. Some of the distinguishing features identified in "referenced" messages are that they are medium length, factual, contain no questions or requests or emoticons, and address another person(s).

Subsets of the data have been used for various studies. Penkoff and Katzman (1996), for example, explore the use of graphic accents (emotional, artistic, and directional devices) as indicators of author gender. The authors found that only a small proportion of network communicators include graphic accents to express emotion in their discourse, but that the users of these devices are primarily women. Focusing on the effects of flames on electronic conversations, Mabry (1996) found support for a consistent relationship between strategic structuring (techniques and tactics such as quoting or recounting) and conciliatory and emotional content: as emotional involvement increases, message structure declines. Zenhausern and Wong (1996) use ProjectH data from Bitnet lists to examine the personality of lists. Three dimensions—activity, participation, and dissemination—were found capable of distinguishing individual list differences.

These eclectic research papers, among others, will be published as a comprehensive book (Rafaeli, Sudweeks, and McLaughlin 1996). Our study supports, if only in case study form, the effectiveness of electronic brainstorming. In addition to the collective book, ProjectH is providing the wider network community with a shared annotated bibliography of more than three hundred entries on CMC, and a questionnaire survey of coders. ProjectH also was a catalyst in the development of an electronic journal edited by McLaughlin and Rafaeli, JCMC (the *Journal of Computer-Mediated Communication*). JCMC is a refereed journal, based on World Wide Web distribution. It carries scientific papers, online and interactive bibliographies, and book reviews. It is available as http://shum.huji.ac.il/jcmc/jcmc.html from the Hebrew University of Jerusalem, or as http://cwis.usc.edu/dept/annenberg/announce.html from the University of Southern California.

Some factors contributing to productivity in the ProjectH experience are:

— a common interest in mediated communication
— effective structuring mechanisms, e.g., oracles, committees, time limits on discussions
— a democratic structure facilitated by the coordinators
— the ability to manipulate social awareness of others, e.g., suppressing awareness to focus on work needs and raising awareness to fulfil social needs.

Processes

Are there any misconceptions about group CMC that we can contradict or discount?

The culture of online groups is typified, particularly in the popular press and magazines, as young, elitist, deviant, and preoccupied with introspective and self-disclosing conversations. As a mature, eclectic, normative, and task-oriented group, we suggest that the popular conception of group CMC culture is by no means universal.

Does the volume and frequency of messages inhibit online collaborative work?

The early stages of the project certainly demonstrated that excessive traffic can create difficulties; however, the organizational structure that evolved reduced traffic to approximately one-tenth of the initial volume. Given that our group CMC is asynchronous and can be processed at each participant's convenience, the time commitment for the later stages is comparable, if not less, than that required for a similar-sized group relying solely on face-to-face communication.

Can a large computer-mediated group of strangers agree?

The ethics discussion illuminated the tenuous concept of consensus. Despite diverging opinions expressed emphatically over a lengthy period, only one-third of the group recorded a vote in favor of the proposed ethics policy. What of the remaining two-thirds? Were they persuaded? Were they unmotivated? Complete consensus is elusive and not even desirable in a group that values each others' expertise and experience. We feel that the approximate consensus adopted is a reasonable solution for a large online group working toward a common goal.

Further Research

Communication technologies and common research interests facilitated the formation of a new community that cut across social, cultural, and geographic boundaries. We believe that the subjective, non-scientific results of the case study reported in this chapter can be replicated. Future studies will benefit from the knowledge that researchers are willing to engage voluntarily in collaborative groupwork. However, we remind those intending to embark on similar studies that an extensive coordinating overhead is necessary to resolve conflict and foster cooperation. Our experience and the ongoing results of our collaboration have shown that strangers are able to work together apart.

References

Berthold, M., Sudweeks, F., Newton, S., and Coyne, R. D. (1996). "It makes sense": Using an autoassociative neural network to explore typicality in computer-mediated communication. In S. Rafaeli, F. Sudweeks, and M.

McLaughlin (Eds.), Network and Netplay: Virtual Groups on the Internet. Menlo Park, Cal.: AAAI/MIT Press (to appear).

Condon, C. (1993). The computer won't let me: Cooperation, conflict and the ownership of information. In S. Easterbrook (Ed.), *CSCW: Cooperation or Conflict*, CSCW Series, London: Springer-Verlag.

Dennis, A. R. and Valacich, J. S. (1993). Computer brainstorms: more heads are better than one. *Journal of Applied Psychology* 78:531–537.

Downey, J. (1992, Jun 21, 7:04 p.m.). Some questions and concerns about "The Study." Available from ftp.arch.su.edu.au/pub/projectH/logs.

Dubrovsky, V. J., Kiesler, S., and Sethna, B. N. (1991). The equalization phenomenon: Status effects in computer-mediated and face-to-face decision-making groups. *Human-Computer Interaction* 6:119–146.

Fulk, J. and Steinfield, C. W. (1989). *Organizations and communication theory*. Newbury Park, Cal.: Sage.

Futrell, A. (1992, Jun 11, 10:08 p.m.). Violation of trust. Available from ftp.arch.su.edu.au/pub/projectH/logs.

Gurbaxani, V. (1990). Diffusion in computing networks: The case of BitNet. *Communications of the ACM* 33(12):65–75.

Hill, G. W. (1982). Group versus individual performance: Are N+1 heads better than one? *Psychological Bulletin* 91:517–539.

Hiltz, S. R. (1983). *Online communities: A case study of the office of the future*. Norwood, N.J.: Ablex.

Kiesler, S. and Sproull, L. (1986). Response effects in the electronic survey. *Public Opinion Quarterly* 50:402–413.

Krippendorff, K. (1980). *Content analysis*. Beverly Hills: Sage.

Mabry, E. (1993a, Nov. 18, 7:23 p.m.). Proliferation of E-publications. In: Interpersonal Computing and Technology [electronic mail system]. Available from ipct-l@guvm.ccf.georgetown.edu.

Mabry, E. (1993b, Aug. 28, 11:02 a.m.) Deleting files and responses. Available from ftp.arch.su.edu.au/pub/projectH/logs.

Mabry, E. (1996). Frames and flames: The structure of argumentative messages on the 'net. In S. Rafaeli, F. Sudweeks, and M. McLaughlin (Eds.), *Network and Netplay: Virtual Groups on the Internet*. Menlo Park, Cal.: AAAI/MIT Press (to appear).

Marmell, C. (1993a, Apr. 7, 11:51 p.m.). Apart from being apart? Available from ftp.arch.su.edu.au/pub/projectH/logs.

Marmell, C. (1993b, Apr 8, 5:10 p.m.). [No subject]. Available from ftp.arch.su.edu.au/pub/projectH/logs.

Maynor, N. (1992, Jun 19, 9:30 p.m.). Qualitative and quantitative studies, Available from ftp.arch.su.edu.au/pub/projectH/logs.

McCreary, E. and Brochet, M. (1992). Collaboration in international online teams. In A. R. Kaye (Ed.), *Collaborative learning through computer conferencing* (69–85). Berlin: Springer-Verlag.

McGrath, J. E. (1984). *Groups: Interaction and performance*. Englewood Cliffs: Prentice Hall.

McInerney, C. (1995). CMC in distance education at the College of St. Catherine: A case study. In Z. Berge and M. Collins (Eds.), *Computer mediated communications and the online classroom.* Volume III: Distance learning (149–163). Cresskill, N.J.: Hampton Press.

McLuhan, M. (1964). *Understanding media.* New York: McGraw-Hill.

Mills, T. (1993, Jun 7, 7:15 a.m.). Private e-mail communication to F. Sudweeks.

Nunamaker, J. F., Vogel, D. R., and Konsynski, B. (1989). Interaction of task and technology to support large groups. *Decision Support Systems* 5(2): 139–152.

Osborn, A. F. (1953). *Applied imagination.* New York: Scribners.

Penkoff, D. (1993, Aug. 28, 9:35 a.m.). Deleting files and responses. Available from ftp.arch.su.edu.au/pub/projectH/logs.

Penkoff, D. (1996). Smile when you say that: Graphic accents as gender markers in computer-mediated communication. In S. Rafaeli, F. Sudweeks, and M. McLaughlin (Eds.), *Network and Netplay: Virtual Groups on the Internet.* Menlo Park, Cal.: AAAI/ MIT Press (to appear).

Poole, M. S., Holmes, M., Watson, R., and De Sanctis, G. (1993). Group decision support systems and group communication. *Communication Research* 20:176–213.

ProjectH Research Group (1993). Ethics policy. Available from ftp.arch.su.edu.au/pub/projectH/policies/ethics.policy.

Rafaeli, S. (1988). Interactivity: From new media to communication, *Sage annual review of communication research: Advancing communication science Vol. 16* (110–134). Beverly Hills: Sage.

Rafaeli, S. (1992a, May 29, 12:27 a.m.). THINGS TO DO—"straw man" outline. In: Computer Mediated Communication [electronic mail system]. Available from comserve@vm.its.rpi.edu.

Rafaeli, S. (1992b, Jun 12, 2:21 a.m.). In lieu of summary: ethics, ownership, technics, and next. Available from ftp.arch.su.edu.au/pub/projectH/logs.

Rafaeli, S. (1992c, Jun 26, 10:52 a.m.). BACK TO BUSINESS—STATUS REPORT. Available from ftp.arch.su.edu.au/pub/projectH/logs.

Rafaeli, S. (1993, Apr 8, 4:01 a.m.). [No subject]. Available from ftp.arch.su.edu.au/pub/projectH/logs.

Rafaeli, S. and Sudweeks, F. (1996). Interactivity on the nets. In S. Rafaeli, F. Sudweeks, and M. McLaughlin (Eds.), *Network and Netplay: Virtual Groups on the Internet.* Menlo Park, Cal.: AAAI/MIT Press (to appear).

Rafaeli, S., Sudweeks, F., Konstan, J., and Mabry, E. (1994). ProjectH Overview: A Quantitative Study of Computer-Mediated Communication, Technical Report, University of Minnesota, and available by ftp from ftp.arch.su.edu.au/pub/projectH/papers/techreport.txt.

Rafaeli, S., Sudweeks, F., and McLaughlin, M. (Eds.) (1995). *Network and netplay: Virtual groups on the Internet.* Menlo Park, Cal.: MA: AAAI/ MIT Press.

Rice, R. E. and Associates (1984). *The new media: Communication, research, and technology.* Newbury Park, Cal.: Sage.

Rice, R. E. (1987). Computer-mediated communication and organizational innovation. *Journal of Communication* 37(4):65–94.

Rice, R. E. and Love, G. (1987). Electronic emotion: Socioemotional content in a computer-mediated communication network. *Communication Research* 14:85–108.

Rogers, E. M. and Rafaeli, S. (1985). Computers and communication. *Information and Behavior* 1:95–112.

Schmitz, J., and Fulk, J. (1991). Organizational colleagues, media richness and electronic mail: a test of the social influence model of technology use. *Communication Research* 18:487–523.

Schudson, M. (1978). The ideal of conversation in the study of mass media. *Communication Research* 5:320–329.

Short, J., Williams, E., and Christie, B. (1976). *The social psychology of telecommunication*. London: John Wiley.

Siegel, J., Dubrovsky, V., Kiesler, S., and McGuire, T. W. (1986). Group processes in computer-mediated communication. *Organizational Behavior and Human Decision Processes* 37:157–187.

Sproull, L. and Kiesler, S. (1986). Reducing social context cues: Electronic mail in organizational communication. *Management Science* 32:1492–1512.

Sproull, L. and Kiesler, S. (1991). *Connections: New ways of working in the networked organization*. Cambridge: MIT Press.

Sproull, L. S., Kiesler, S., and Zubrow, D. (1984). Encountering an alien culture. *Journal of Social Issues* 40(3):31–48.

Steele, G. (1984). *Common LISP, the language*. Bedford, Mass.: Digital Press.

Steinfield, C. W. (1986). Computer mediated communication systems. *Annual Review of Information Science and Technology* 21:167–202.

Sudweeks, F., Lambert, S., Beaumont, A., Bonney, J., Lee, S., and Nicholas, G. (1993). Computer mediated collaboration and design: A pilot project. In S. Hayman (Ed.), *Architectural science: Past, present and future* (299–309). Sydney: ANZAScA.

Sudweeks, F., Collins, M., and December, J. (1995). Internetwork resources. In Z. Berge and M. Collins (Eds.), *Computer mediated communication and the online classroom:*. Volume I: Overview and perspectives (193–212). Cresskill, N.J.: Hampton Press.

Thomas, J. (1992a, May 25, 4:31 p.m.). Bad e-mail posters drive out good. In: Computer Mediated Communication [electronic mail system]. Available from comserve@vm.its.rpi.edu.

Thomas, J. (1992b, Jun 13, 12:17 p.m.). More on ethics and cmc research. Available from ftp.arch.su.edu.au/pub/projectH/logs.

Valacich, J. S., Dennis, A. R., and Connolly, T. (1994). Idea generation in computer-based groups: A new ending to an old story. *Organizational Behavior and Human Decision Processes* 57:448–467.

Valacich, J. S., Paranka, D., George, J. F., and Nunamaker, J. F. (1993). Communication concurrency and the new media. *Communication Research* 20:249–276.

Walther, J. B. (1992). Interpersonal effects in computer-mediated interaction: A relational perspective. *Communication Research* 19:52–90.

Wolman, K. (1992a, Jun 21, 5:37 p.m.). Some questions and concerns about "The Study." Available from ftp.arch.su.edu.au/pub/projectH/logs.

Wolman, K. (1992b, Jun 21, 7:57 p.m.). Some questions and concerns about "The Study." Available from ftp.arch.su.edu.au/pub/projectH/logs.

Wolman, K. (1992c, Jun 26, 9:26 a.m.). Can we talk? Available from ftp.arch.su.edu.au/pub/projectH/logs.

Zenhausern, B. and Wong, F. (1995). A preliminary examination of the demography of Bitnet lists. In S. Rafaeli, F. Sudweeks, and M. McLaughlin (Eds.), *Network and Netplay: Virtual Groups on the Internet*. Menlo Park, Cal.: AAAI/MIT Press.

Zuboff, S. (1988). *In the age of the smart machine*. New York: Basic Books.

Living Inside the (Operating) System:

Community in Virtual Reality

John Unsworth

Machines speak to machines before speaking to
man, and the ontological domains that they
reveal and secrete are, at each occurrence,
singular and precarious.
    —Félix Guattari, *Machinic Heterogenesis*[1]

We live by the mode of referendum precisely
because there is no longer any referential.
    —Jean Baudrillard, *Simulations*[2]

I think a lot of the common assumptions
we make are actually built in to the MOO
apparatus. . . . The elements of the MOO are
constructed for the most part to simulate a real
physical community. Ideas like "privacy" and
"ownership" are constantly implied by the
descriptions and properties if not the actual
programming of every object.
    —Ogre, in *MOO.Terrorism*[3]

This essay is an attempt to describe and explain the way that an unusual (but by no means anomalous) culture has developed under the
aegis of PMC-MOO (Postmodern Culture—MUD-Object-Oriented), a
text-based virtual reality program that runs on a networked Unix
workstation. It is also an attempt to describe the scholarly and pedagogical trajectory of this program, by identifying the conceptual coordinates of its origin.

MOOs belong to a class of programs known as MUDs, and MUDs
are ably defined by Pavel Curtis, the inventor of MOOs, as follows:

> A MUD (Multi-User Dungeon or, sometimes, Multi-User Dimen-
> sion) is a network-accessible, multi-participant, user-extensible
> virtual reality whose user interface is entirely textual. Participants
> (usually called players) have the appearance of being situated in
> an artificially-constructed place that also contains those other

players who are connected at the same time. Players can communicate easily with each other in real time.[4] This virtual gathering place has many of the social attributes of other places, and many of the usual social mechanisms operate there. Certain attributes of this virtual place, however, tend to have significant effects on social phenomena, leading to new mechanisms and modes of behavior not usually seen 'IRL' (in real life).[5]

I will substantially disagree with that last point in the course of this essay, but suffice it to say, for now, that in practical terms, the experience of participating in a MOO is that one sits at a keyboard, in front of a screen, and projects oneself over a global computer network into an entirely textual world, and into an entirely virtual community. Community is generally a function of shared location, shared interests, and sometimes shared government and shared property; in order to deserve the name, a community needs more than one, though not necessarily all, of those attributes.

In the case of PMC-MOO, the community that I will discuss here, all those attributes are present in some sense or in some measure. However, it would be a mistake to see this community, or the larger archipelago civilization of MOOs to which it belongs, as entirely communitarian, or as entirely self-determining. Rather, I will argue, PMC-MOO and MOOs in general take shape under twin forces not unlike fate and free will, where free will is what we have always understood it to be, but where the role of fate is played by the operating system in which the MOO is embedded. The aporia in this analogy, and it is an important one for my argument, is that unlike transcendental fate, computer operating systems are historically and culturally determined.

Unix and Monopoly Capital

To understand the cultural moment that is expressed in the operating system in question, Unix, and to understand the effects of Unix on the formation of MOO code and MOO culture, we must isolate and understand a few concepts and a little history as well. For our purposes, the concepts that matter most are expressed in their most basic form in the Unix filesystem, as hierarchy, user groups, and ownership. The Unix filesystem is hierarchical in its organization, and the particular kind of hierarchy is, in essence, dendritic: file systems have a tree-like structure, with a "root" directory containing files and other directories, or branches, of the filesystem, which in turn can contain other files and directories. In Unix, every file (and indeed, every process) has an individual owner, and the hierarchy of owners explicitly mirrors the hierarchy of the filesystem itself, with the superuser of all users and user groups called "root." Every individual user, then, belongs to one or more user groups, and the permission to read, write, delete, search, or execute a particular file is precisely defined for owner, group, and other. It is difficult to exaggerate the importance of these basic concepts in Unix: in fact, the filesystem organization is itself a kind of first cause for Unix, inasmuch as its origins lie in the dim prehistory of Unix, in Multics. Multics was a multi-user mainframe operating system developed jointly in the late 1960s by Bell Labs, MIT, and General Electric and intended to permit time-sharing on large, expensive, centralized computer resources. Not surprisingly, the developers of Multics, and, after them, the developers of Unix, reasoned that if an operating system will permit many users to look at and manipulate the same files at the same time, it is necessary to establish which users are associated with which files, and what permissions are granted them.

AT&T began developing Multics in 1964, eight years after the 1956 Consent Decree which settled the last anti-trust suit against the company. Although the 1956 decision said nothing about software (because the concept wasn't available), AT&T interpreted the decision cautiously, and when Unix came along, the company decided to distribute its operating system on non-profit terms—licensed at very low cost to universities, and priced prohibitively high for commercial clients, expressly so as to avoid developing a software business. In fact, what was distributed was the source code, which meant that university researchers could tinker with the system, offer improvements, and make modifications to suit their needs. However, since Bell Labs was distributing the software at or near cost, it wasn't particularly interested in providing user support. This fostered two things—a kind of priesthood of the code, manifested as a hierarchy of arcane knowledge about the complex and often cryptically documented system, and a self-supporting user community, which became incarnate in the late 1970s and early 1980s as Usenet. Usenet was (and is) an independent mail network that allowed users to post questions and receive answers about specific features of Unix, or about applications that run under Unix. Usenet still flourishes, and still fulfills its original function, but it has expanded to include discussion of many topics that have nothing to do with operating systems, and it has become an asynchronous culture in its own right.[6]

In the largest context, then, Unix developed as a byproduct of research at a corporate laboratory, under the constraints imposed by anti-trust legislation, which helped to force it out of the channels in which proprietary inventions usually travel in a capitalist economy, and into the freely exchanged economy of academic research and invention. It should also be noted, though, that Bell Labs itself, at least in its research divisions, was and may still be a more fertile environment for technological creativity than many universities. The nature of pure research is that one doesn't know what will ultimately "pay off": therefore, it's necessary to invest in a diversified portfolio of research activities. According to Samuel P. Morgan, a member of the Bell Labs Research Area beginning in 1947 and, during the early seventies, Director of the Computing Science Research Center,

> If there aren't a certain number of things taken up in the organization every year that don't work out, we're not being sufficiently aggressive, or innovative, or we are not gambling enough. . . . We work on percentages, and of course this is true throughout any research organization. We've got to have a certain number of failures. . .[7]

In fact, it is only a very large accumulation of wealth that makes it practical to gamble in this way, investing resources in doing research with no immediately obvious economic benefit. Moreover, the kind of research environment that produces these unpredictable benefits, especially in the area of computer hardware and software, has proven to be decentralized and voluntaristic. This is true even outside of the area of pure research, in the application of computer technology to business operations. According to V. M. Wolontis, Executive Director of the Operations Research Division at Bell labs during the early days of Unix,

> Things in the computer applications field have developed because individual people at the working level have had ideas and have pursued them. Things have grown from the working level up, rather than by some major management figure sitting at his desk saying this shall be computerized, and bingo, a hundred people march in the direction of computerizing a big segment of the operation. There is a tendency for the computer as a tool to inject itself into the operation through the efforts of interested specialists who enjoy it and who want to make the contribution. Management approval is a subsequent step.[8]

Although the kind of intellectual freedom to "play around" with problems and "contribute" solutions does depend on the kind of corporate security that comes only under the auspices of monopoly capital or government, individual projects still have to at least attempt to justify themselves with respect to some cost-benefit analysis, however putative: even when gambling, there are better and worse bets. Within the atmosphere of free invention, the time-sharing and resource-coupling nature of the Unix operating system was driven, paradoxically, by the prohibitive cost of mainframes, which dictated that each machine should have more than one user and, if possible, more than one user at a time. One of the original developers of Unix recalls that, when their group faced the decline of Multics, their requests for new computer equipment on which to write a new operating system were repeatedly rebuffed: "[I]t is perfectly obvious in retrospect (and should have been at the time) that we were asking the Labs to spend too much money on too few people with too vague a plan."[9]

The fact that the operating system developed in the context of a corporate entity whose primary business was telecommunications, and whose primary interests were communications and connectivity, helped to enshrine within it the principles of modularity and inter-operability. But at another level, one extremely relevant to the effects that Unix has had in the world, communication was a motivating factor in the design of this operating system:

> Even though Multics could not then support many users, it could support us, albeit at exorbitant cost. We didn't want to lose the pleasant niche we occupied, because no similar ones were available; even the time-sharing service that would later be offered under GE's operating system did not exist. What we wanted to preserve was not just a good environment in which to do programming, but a system around which a fellowship could form. We knew from experience that the essence of communal computing, as supplied by remote-access, time-shared machines, is not just to type programs into a terminal instead of a keypunch, but to encourage close communication.[10]

The fact that the software these researchers produced was easy to modify, good at accepting instructions from remote users, and unsupported by its corporate parent, helped to ensure that one of the first uses to which it would be put, once it reached the outside world, was the networking of users into a community, originally a user-support community, but later something much more diverse.

If we consider all these factors together, the paradoxes are striking. On the one hand, as a mental representation of the universe of information, Unix is deeply indebted to culturally determined notions such as private property, class membership, and hierarchies of power and effectivity. Most of these ideas are older than the modern Western culture that produced Unix, but the constellation of cultural elements gathered together in Unix's basic operating principles seems particularly Western and capitalist—not surprisingly, given that its creators were human extensions of one of the largest accumulations of capital in the Western world. On the other hand, this tool, shaped though it was by the notions of ownership and exclusivity, spawned a culture of cooperation, of homemade code, of user-contributed modifications and improvements (viz. the canonical/contrib/bin in Unix filesystems, where user-contributed programs are stored)—in short, of "fellowship." And finally, in some sense it is true, as Guattari suggests, that the entire assemblage of causes for Unix is an instance of machines speaking to machines, or needing to speak to machines, with humans as the midwife at this precarious and unlikely birth. In order to explicate this paradox, though, it might help us to consider a set of relevant insights from an early and expert analyst of capitalism, Karl Marx.

MOOs and Marx

In writing about the French Revolution, Karl Marx observed that the civil (or bourgeois) society that was established for the first time by that revolution understands itself to be based on the "natural and imprescriptible rights" declared in the Constitution of 1793, namely "equality, liberty, security, property." According to that document, liberty "consists in the right to do anything which does not harm others"; the right of property "is the right vested in every citizen to enjoy and dispose of his goods, his revenues, the fruit of his labour and of his industry according to his will"; equality "consists in the fact that the same law applies to all, whether that law protects or punishes"; and security "consists in the protection which society offers to each of its members for the preservation of his person, his rights, and his property." It is worth pointing out that each of these rights has its equivalent in the world of Unix: users, the equivalent of citizens, are permitted actions that do not harm the data of others—unless those others have, of their own free will, disposed of that data so that permission is granted to others to overwrite it; the same rights apply to all (within a given user class, at least. All bets are off when it comes to root—but even in Enlightenment democracies, equality has always been the most problematic right, especially when it comes to conflicts of interest between an individual and the state . . . and arguably, since all rights are granted, ultimately, by root, root is the Unix equivalent of the State). Security, in Unix terms, is called exactly the same thing, and providing systems security, so as to protect the accumulated labor of legitimate users, is considered the paramount duty of the Unix systems administrator.[11]

Marx finds these "so-called rights of man" to be the defining characteristics of bourgeois society because none of them

> goes beyond the egoistic man, beyond man as a member of civil society, as man separated from life in the community and withdrawn into himself, into his private interest and his private arbitrary will. These rights are far from conceiving man as a species-being. They see, rather, the life of the species itself, society, as a frame external to individuals, as a limitation of their original independence. The only bond that keeps men together is natural necessity, need and private interest, the preservation of property and of their egoistic person.[12]

Because I am arguing that the MOO draws out and enacts some of the contradictions inherent not only in Unix and Unix culture, but also in capitalism and Western culture, it is important to stop here and concentrate for a moment on the term that Marx opposes to bourgeois monadic egotism. Marx defines "species-being" elsewhere, in manuscripts written during the same period, in terms that cast an interesting light on my earlier assertion that Unix, and in its own turn, the MOO, are mental representations of a world:

> His creation, in practice, of an objective world, his working upon inorganic nature, is the proof that man is a conscious species-being, that is a being which is related to the species as its own essence or to itself as a species being. To be sure, animals also produce. They build themselves nests, dwelling places, as the bees, beavers, ants, etc. do. But the animal produces what it needs directly for itself or its young. It produces one-sidedly, while man produces universally. It produces under the domination of direct physical need while man produces even when he is free from physical need and produces truly, indeed, only in freedom from such need. The animal produces only itself, while man reproduces the whole of nature. . . . It is precisely in his working over of the objective world, therefore, that man proves himself to be really a species being. This production is his active species-life. In and through such production, nature appears as his work and his reality. The object of labor, therefore, is the objectification of the species-life of man: for man duplicates himself not only intellectually, as in consciousness, but also actively, in reality, and therefore contemplates himself in a world that he has created.[13]

Once again, the paradox I have in view is that the material conditions and conceptual rubrics out of which Unix developed are the epitome of capitalist endeavor, and yet Unix itself was circulated on quite anti-capitalist terms, and answers fairly well to Marx's description of universal production (or production that doesn't answer to an immediate need).

The tension between these two concepts—civil (or bourgeois) society as incarnated in the French Revolution's "Declaration of the Rights of Man," and the "species-being" that (Marx says) these rights ignore—is precisely the enabling condition of capitalism:

> In so far as alienated labor tears the object of his production away from man, therefore, it tears away from him his species-life, his actual objectivity as a member of the species and transforms his advantage over the animal into the disadvantage that his inorganic body, nature, is taken away from him. . . . A direct consequence of man's alienation from the product of his labor, from his life activity, from his species-being, is the alienation of man from man. When man confronts himself, he confronts another man. . . . Generally, the proposition that man's species-being is alienated from him means that one man is alienated from another, just as each of them is alienated from human nature.[14]

The second level of our paradox is that, when the MOO arises, it answers, better than Unix or even capitalism itself, to Marx's description of alienation: within the MOO, when one confronts oneself, one literally confronts the representation of a representation of a person— a player, a character, a projection of (alienated) personality. And yet, again, the labor that goes into creation in the MOO is labor which answers exactly to the call of species-life: it is creation in the absence of need, the creation of a supremely useless object, an object world, an objectification of life in the world.

This brings me to the second chapter of this history, which begins about ten years after the invention of Unix, but still in the corporate neighborhood of AT&T, when Pavel Curtis and others at Xerox PARC invented MOOcode. MOOs are not intended to replace Unix in any sense, but they do mimic some of the functions of an operating system, and they mirror many of the features of Unix. In the MOO, which is really just a large database, the world is made up of objects: objects always have a particular location within the database and the fictive landscape of the MOO, and objects are in turn composed of properties and verbs. The universe itself is an object (object \#0), as are all players. Players own themselves, and they belong to one or more classes of players.

The basic classes of MOO-character are player, programmer, and wizard. Many refinements and elaborations of that tripartite scheme have been implemented, but the basic distinctions remain significant: players can move around and communicate, but they cannot build or create things; programmers are players who can also create, program, and recycle their own objects, and they can bestow owned objects on others; wizards are programmers who can also program or recycle other programmers' objects and players themselves. To this extent, then, the MOO adopts the notion of a "root" user, expressing it more fancifully in the term "wizard"—the superuser of all MOO users. In keeping with the dendritic hierarchy of files (and processes) in Unix, the MOO has its own (anthropomorphized) hierarchy of parents and children. Every object and player inherits the verbs and properties of its parent, and commands are always executed along a search path that includes one's entire parentage. In the MOO, things can be readable, writable, and executable by wizards only, by the owner, or by anyone, and the system of parentage, in its effect, mimics the functionality of user groups—for example, the average player on PMC-MOO belongs to the programmer class, which in turn is a child of the basic builder class, which in turn is a child of Frand's player class, which in turn is a child of the basic player class. Such a player has permission to execute any verb associated with any group or class that appears in that family tree.

Unix and MOOcode share the following characteristics, then: both emerged from large corporate research labs (Bell and Xerox, respectively); both are hierarchical, multi-user, time-sharing environments for the creation, storage, and retrieval of information; both systems are predicated on the notion that every object (or file) has both an owner and a location, and perhaps most importantly, both Unix and MOO function as command interpreters and as programming environments. It is this last thing, more than any other single feature, that unites MOOcode with Unix and distinguishes it from other forms of gaming and/or virtual-reality environments. The "OO" in MOO stands for Object Oriented, and it means that programmers can easily have access to the individual building blocks of the MOO, and can use the tools within the MOO to alter or add to those building blocks.

The important difference between a MOO and the Unix operating system, though, is that while both may be considered to be mental representations, or self-representations, of information processing—models, if you will, of collective memory, of communal libraries, even of collective intelligence—the MOO is the world it models, as well as the model of that world. In other words, if capitalism is a first-order model of the way labor and value and power circulate in the world,

Unix is a second-order simulacrum of the way that a particular kind of capital, namely information, works in the world, and the MOO—an inhabitable model of Unix—is then a third-order simulacrum of the world, in which information is not only a representation of labor, and a source of power, and a form of value, but is also quite literally the form that the species-being takes, "not unreal, but a simulacrum, never again exchanging for what is real, but exchanging in itself, in an uninterrupted circuit without reference or circumference."[15]

PMC-MOO: A Virtual Community

It's time now to discuss the way in which one such simulacrum has actually developed, and to think about the future of MOOs in general. PMC-MOO is the MOO with which I am most familiar, since I have been (with the help of many others) running it for the last couple of years, and since it has, at various times, taken up a good deal of my time. It is not the first MOO I started—the NCSU Virtual Campus has that dubious distinction[16]—nor is it the newest (IATH-MOO, the virtual conference center for the Institute for Advanced Technology in the Humanities is the most recent), but it has become the largest and longest lasting of the MOO experiments with which I've been involved. PMC-MOO is an offshoot of the electronic journal *Postmodern Culture*, and it was established to serve two principal functions. First and foremost, it was intended to provide a text-based conferencing facility for journal-related activities, a kind of real-time supplement to PMC-Talk, the Listserv-based discussion group that has always run alongside the peer-reviewed journal. Second, because the object-oriented nature of the MOO made this feasible, it was to provide an opportunity for interested users to produce interactive programs that would demonstrate or interrogate concepts of relevance to the study of postmodernism—object-lessons, if you will. In other words, from the outset, PMC-MOO had that Disney schizophrenia that characterizes Epcot Center—a conference hall surrounded by a theme park, work embedded in play.

For a time, quite a time, it seemed that work might never surface at all in this environment, and early visitors to the MOO would have been justified in doubting that this would ever develop into an environment in which anything useful could ever be done. MOOs are naturally somewhat chaotic, since the program allows everyone in a room to speak and be heard in sequence, with no possibility of interrupting another speaker and with little in the way of etiquette that encourages orderly, single-topic, limited-participation conversations.

Users who have spent some time in MOOs do learn to use some common tools, such as the stage-talk feature, to identify the topic to which they are speaking or the speaker to whom they are responding, and (more importantly) they seem to develop a certain ability to do conversational multi-tasking, but the MOO tends to be a noisy place when there's anything happening at all.

Beyond the noise factor, there is the issue of identity and accountability. Professional life and professional credit depends, to a large extent, on being able to identify the sources of intellectual contributions, and on attributing borrowed ideas to their originators. The MOO, by contrast, encourages the borrowing of code, by making it easy to copy objects and verbs (or pieces of objects and verbs that seem useful) without attribution. The flip side of attribution is accountability: since most MOOs, including PMC-MOO (but not IATH-MOO) allow users to create fictitious names for their players, and since it is generally the case that only wizards can locate a player's home site, anti-social behavior including theft, harassment, impersonation, and even "virtual rape," are common problems in these virtual environments. PMC-MOO's most famous episode of anti-social behavior came to be described as MOO Terrorism, and is described elsewhere in a kind of MOO documentary.[17] After our rocky infancy, though, the community has stabilized a good deal, and it has begun to develop some of the familiar features of civic life—it has a zoning board, a board that reviews requests for quota (the permission to create things), regular public events including poetry slams and other performance events, social hours, and special seminars and events. It also has spawned a number of internal discussion groups on various topics, some of them theoretical, some of them social, some organizational. It is worth noting that, although postmodernism is steeped in the kind of theory that even educated non-specialists find difficult to penetrate, PMC-MOO has succeeded in drawing a broad range of non-specialists into the discussion of theoretical issues, and those non-specialists have frequently challenged and in other ways affected the conversation on those issues. High school students, college students, graduate students, professors, librarians, as well as non-academics, government workers, professionals: the population of PMC-MOO is diverse, if not by comparison to the general public, certainly by comparison to the usual audience for literary and critical theory. Furthermore, people whose background was non-technical have become interested in programming through the experience of inhabiting a shared programming environment, and especially (I think) as a result of being able to see and immediately share the results of their efforts from within the same environment in which they are produced. Some programming that demonstrates postmodern theoretical concepts has, in fact, been done, and efforts are underway to foreground that programming in the landscape of the MOO.

What this factual history suggests is that, like its parent, Unix, the MOO has the capacity to turn play into something useful (though it isn't always easy to predict what kinds of play will prove useful, or in what ways), and it certainly fulfills the desire of the early Unix developers for a communal programming environment in which fellowship could come about. The MOO is also clearly an environment in which, independent of need, one can pursue creative activities with tangible, communal, and perhaps even economic results.[18] As with pure research at Bell labs, it seems clear that in the MOO, innovation comes from the ground up: in fact, the same thing could be said of the Internet itself—that it was born from a monopoly (in this case, the military), and that due to certain external constraints (the threat of nuclear war, which dictated its decentralized design) it has developed into a chaotic, voluntarist, and unpredictably fertile world in which individuals invest large amounts of time and energy "playing" in ways that sometimes produce enormously useful innovations. As far as teaching and research go, the MOO (and the same could be said of the Internet itself) is demonstrably useful for some kinds of pedagogical and conferencing purposes, particularly those which rely heavily on verbal information (as opposed to graphics or sound), and particularly when the community of users has developed a set of consensual rules of behavior that downplay the potential for communicational chaos and anti-social behavior, and that play up the potential for cooperation and collaboration.

In closing, I'd like to recall for a moment a recent advertising campaign for AT&T, in which lots of "ordinary" (but very professional-looking) people are shown using technology in futuristic ways. The tag-line of the campaign is "have you ever . . . You will": "Have you ever gone to a meeting in your bathrobe?" asks the voice-over, while a man lounges at the breakfast table while video-conferencing, "Or sent a fax from the beach?" while the man lounges in his beach-chair, sending a fax from his (apparently sand-proof) laptop: "You will." I'm sure that AT&T intends this campaign to present a happy vision of the future, in which work somehow is less work-like; I'm equally certain, though, that it's possible to view the campaign in exactly the opposite light, to hear an imperative tone in that "You Will," and to consider that, without that handy laptop, the man on the beach might not have to be working. It is, in some sense, the essence of professional occupation that it crosses the line into our personal lives: no profession is truly 9–5. If technology, born from useful play, becomes an environment in which work can be carried on in the guise of play, then either we will never really work, or we will never really play, after this. It remains to be seen which of these—or both, or neither—proves to be the case.

Notes

1. Félix Guattari, "Machinic Heterogenesis" in *Rethinking Technologies*, ed. Verena Andermatt Conley (Minneapolis, Minn.: University of Minnesota Press, 1993), 22.

2. Jean Baudrillard, *Simulations* (New York: Semiotext(e), 1983), 116.

3. "Moo.Terrorism" is the name of an ASCII text file available by anonymous FTP from jefferson.village.virginia.edu, as pub/pmc/pmc-moo/ MOO.Terrorism. It consists of material collected from the MOO database, its mail system, and its player logs, and edited (or "ruthlessly pillaged") by Troy Whitlock.

4. For a suggestive, if somewhat hysterical, discussion of the term "real time," see Paul Virilio, "The Third Interval: A Critical Transition" in *Rethinking Technologies*.

5. The quotation is available electronically through anonymous FTP from parcftp.xerox.com in the directory pub/MOO/papers in the file DIAC92.txt.

6. For an extensive treatment of the history of Usenet, see *Netizens*, an anthology of essays collected by Ronda and Michael Hauben, available by anonymous FTP from umcc.umich.edu, in pub/users/ronda, or from jefferson.village.virginia.edu, in pub/projects/netizens.

7. Malcolm G. Stevenson, "Bell Labs: A Pioneer in Computing Technology" (Part III. Computers in Technology—Today and Tomorrow). *Bell Labs Record* (February 1974): 57.

8. Malcolm G. Stevenson, "Bell Labs: A Pioneer in Computing Technology" (Part II. Helping Man Use the Computing Machine). *Bell Labs Record* (January 1974): 18.

9. D. M. Ritchie, "The Evolution of the UNIX Time-sharing System," *AT&T Bell Laboratories Technical Journal 63.8* (October 1984): 2.

10. Ritchie: 3.

11. It is a somewhat bitter irony that, on the very day I wrote this sentence, PMC-MOO crashed and—because of somewhat shoddy systems administration practices on my part—two weeks worth of changes to the database were lost.

12. Karl Marx, "Writings of the Young Marx on Philosophy and Society." Edited and translated by Loyd D. Easton and Kurt H. Guddat. (New York: Anchor-Doubleday, 1967), 236–37.

13. Karl Marx, 294–295.

14. Karl Marx, 295–296.

15. Baudrillard, 11.

16. A paper describing my experience teaching on the Virtual Campus is available by gopher from the Institute for Advanced Technology in the Humanities: Gopher: jefferson.village.virginia.edu/00/pubs/publications/Virtual.Campus.txt; FTP: pub/pubs/publications/Virtual.Campus.txt; WWW: gopher://jefferson.village.virginia.edu/00/pubs/publications/Virtual.Campus.txt

17. See Troy Whitlock's "Fuck Art: Let's Kill! Towards a Post-Modern Community." Available from the Institute for Advanced Technology in the Humanities via Gopher: jefferson.village.virginia.edu/00/pubs/pmc/pmc-moo/Moo.Terrorism; FTP: jefferson.village.virginia.edu/pub/pubs/pmc/pmc-moo/Moo.Terrorism; WWW: Gopher://jefferson.village.virginia.edu/00/pub/pubs/pmc/pmc-moo/Moo.Terrorism.

18. The National Institute of Standards and Technology, for example, in June 1994 issued a call for proposals on the use of MUDs for manufacturing—a virtual shop floor, if you will. This brings my argument full circle, and perhaps raises the specter of virtual Taylorism . . .

The Multifaceted and Novel Nature of Using Cyber-Texts as Research Data

Laura J. Gurak

As access to the Internet and other global computer networks continues to increase, computer-mediated communication (CMC) presents exciting research opportunities for many scholars. In terms of publication, research, and collaboration, computer networks have the potential to significantly change traditional approaches. Online journals and conferences, for example, speed up the distribution of new research and allow researchers to correspond quickly and efficiently. Information databases and FTP (File Transfer Protocol) sites provide easy access to information, and the speed and interconnectedness of networks provides for collaboration among researchers.

New issues for scholars include not only the use of CMC as a forum for research, but also the study of the communication artifacts, such as e-mail texts or newsgroup/conference postings, produced by this new medium. Communication and language scholars are increasingly researching the social, political, and organizational features of online conferences and electronic mail.

Yet for those wishing to study the discourse of this latest communication technology, unresolved issues arise about how to handle the "cyber-texts" produced on computer networks. Who owns the files and how much of a text can be fairly quoted? Should one get permission to cite a posting even if the author posted a note to a public computer conference? What is the correct bibliographic style for citing such postings?

This chapter looks at the challenges encountered when using computer-generated discourse as research data, drawing on my recent case study, an analysis of the net-based protest against Lotus

*The author expresses her thanks to the following people for their assistance with the legal sections of this paper: Edward Cavazos (Andres & Kurth, L.L.P.); Marc Rotenberg (Electronic Privacy Information Center); Pamela Samuelson (University of Pittsburgh Law School); Mary M. Wood (Albany Law School Library).

MarketPlace. The issues I faced while working with my data, the texts of Usenet newsgroups and other online conferences, illustrate the complex nature of performing such research. While many of these issues have their roots in traditional research concerns, the novel nature of the CMC medium required me to carefully analyze my choices with a fresh eye.

In this chapter, I offer a close look at the challenges of my project and discuss how initial questioning led me to research the ethical, legal, and citation style issues involved in using net-based texts from the Lotus protest. This chapter provides a summary of my research to date and indicates choices that I and other CMC researchers face regarding copyright, fair use, and bibliographic styles.

Within a short time after this collection is published, many of the questions raised in this chapter will begin to have answers, either through legal cases or scholarly standards. For example, as I wrote this chapter, the Modern Language Association (MLA) was drafting standards on citation of electronic texts for its next edition of the *MLA Handbook for Writers of Research Papers*. Yet, hopefully, this chapter will serve not only to illustrate the current situation, but also to stand as future evidence of how communication technologies impact many of our scholarly traditions.

Background

On April 10, 1990, Lotus Development Corporation announced a "desktop information product" called Lotus MarketPlace: Households. The product, a CD-ROM direct mail marketing database, was designed so small businesses could create mailing lists using Macintosh personal computers. MarketPlace: Households contained information on 120 million individual American consumers from eighty million different households and was a joint effort of Lotus and Equifax Credit Corporation.

In the months that followed the announcement, MarketPlace: Households was the subject of intense debate concerning its implications for personal privacy. More than 30,000 people contacted Lotus and asked that their names be removed from the database. The product, originally scheduled for release during the third quarter of 1990, was never released. In January 1991, Lotus announced it would cancel MarketPlace: Households due in large part to public concerns about privacy.

From Lotus's first announcement until months after it canceled the product, the Internet, other networks, and e-mail were a-buzz with discussions and debates about the privacy implications of MarketPlace. People posted Lotus's address and phone number and gave information about how to get names removed from the database. Some posted "form letters" that could be sent to Lotus; others distributed the e-mail address of Lotus's CEO. Notices were forwarded around the net, re-posted to other newsgroups, and sent off as e-mail messages. In the end, corporations and network activists acknowledged the role that networks played in stopping the product's release.

Research Dilemmas: Working in the Electronic Archive

For a rhetorician interested in rhetoric of technology, the Lotus case presented an important set of questions about communities on networks. But the case also raised immediate questions about how to handle the research data, questions that bore a resemblance to those asked by any researcher using archived material, but which took a unique cast because of the "electronic archive" where CMC texts reside.

After months of interviews and phone calls, I had a sense of which newsgroups played a part in the Lotus protest. I then began the process of seeking out any existing archived records of these discussions. Working two years after the protest had taken place, I found it difficult to track down any remaining evidence of the Lotus protest.[1] Yet after long hours hunting through archived files,[2] and after corresponding with moderators and participants in the protest, I found a reasonably extensive set of files from the time period of the Lotus protest.

Once I began the early analysis of my data, however, I faced many questions about its use. Did I need permission from the author of a Usenet posting in order to cite it? How much could I cite? And what citation style should I use, since existing style guides did not adequately cover these texts? The rest of this chapter will describe how I came to answer these questions.

Initial Questioning: Should I Cite These Texts with Real Names?

My first question was whether I needed permission from the authors of the Usenet postings. Although I generally work with texts, I had worked with human subjects and had always sought permission and been candid about the project. Yet I was unsure what analogy was most appropriate for network postings: were they like a conversation or a published text? Computer conferences are often talked about in terms of both of these forms. But which one applied here?

If these postings were like a conversation, then I felt obligated to reveal myself and ask permission to use participants' words in my study. I would want to get permission from all participants, and I might want to use pseudonyms, since people in a group conversation do not expect their words to become public.[3] Yet, if these postings were like a publication, I would not need to ask permission, and I could use their real names (or whatever name appeared in the "from" line)[4] in my study, since people who post to an online forum seem in essence to be "publishing" (albeit informally) in a public place.

To help think through my dilemma, I considered two factors: the nature of the medium and the author's expectations. The nature of newsgroup postings seemed in fact closer to published documents than conversations. Electronic "discussions" have one obvious feature that distinguishes them from face-to-face discussions and makes them more like a publication: like paper manuscripts, online postings are written down in a fixed medium and are made available in a public "space." Furthermore, it seemed clear that authors on computer conferences, unlike people in group conversations, actually seem to expect their texts to be redistributed. Many of the Lotus postings contained phrases such as "pass it on," implying that readers should electronically re-post and re-circulate the message. It is in fact common on the net for people to excerpt from another person's message, insert this excerpt into their own message (sometimes, although not always, with an attached line giving credit to the original author), and post this new message.[5]

Based on the above reasoning, I decided not to ask permission to cite a conference posting. I would simply cite the posting, using the author's real name, as I would cite a journal article or book excerpt. On the other hand, I would treat e-mail as a personal letter, since although it too is inscribed in a fixed medium, e-mail tends to be less fixed than conferences (which are often archived), and, furthermore, authors of e-mail expect their message to be read by the receiver and not by the larger public. When wishing to cite directly from a private e-mail message, then, I would ask permission of the author.

Yet I knew that not all network participants would agree with my rule. In interviews with some of the more active members of the Lotus protest, I learned that at least one person was not entirely comfortable with my using his newsgroup postings as data in my study. Although this same person probably did not mind when others cut and pasted his electronic postings from newsgroup to conference to e-mail message, the thought of taking his words out of the context of the Internet caused him concern.[6]

I later learned of a case where a CMC researcher faced a similar question when studying the discourse from a gay and lesbian hotline. This researcher decided to reveal herself to the hotline and ask how people felt about her using their online texts in her research paper. Many of these participants were angry at the idea of their words being taken out of the context of the hotline. In this case, participants did not view their conference as published text. They saw their hotline as a semi-private conversation; in fact, this hotline had strict requirements about who could and could not join (Addison 1993).

Ultimately, I realized that each researcher would have to decide for him-or herself as to the most ethical way to approach the research situation. In the Lotus case, I did not feel unethical using real names, since the people posting notes did not have any expectations of privacy and were usually aware of their notes being re-posted. Yet I also realized that ethics is not the only consideration. Legal issues, such as copyright and fair use, would also be relevant to my dilemma.

I then turned to legal research to determine if I was making a sound decision. I corresponded with lawyers who specialize in computer law, read case law at a local law school library, and followed ongoing discussions about computerized data and the law. I needed to learn about copyright law and fair use, especially as these concepts apply to both scholarly research and electronic texts. In the next section, I will summarize the results of my investigations. Again, these findings will continue to change over the next years, especially as the Internet is restructured and as the legal system begins to process these issues.

Legal Considerations in Citing Conference Postings

My thinking was confirmed by early legal checking. According to one attorney who specializes in electronic privacy, my "rule of thumb [was] correct. With personal email you should get the permission of the . . . person who gave you the message. With public postings, you are generally free to reprint . . . " (Rotenberg 1993). However, he and other experts were the first to admit that this area of the law is still speculative. One can only make a reasonable guess based on existing laws and cases. Until "cyber-law" is tested out in the courts, no one will know for certain.

Yet some work has been done toward developing standards for network scholarship. Brian Kahin of the Science, Technology, and Public Policy Program at Harvard's John F. Kennedy School of Government has published a set of proposed principles for scholarship on the networks (1993) (see also Brian Kahin's chapter in this volume). These principles were developed based on a widely reviewed initial draft document,[7] and though they are not law, they do provide a starting point for creating guidelines for researchers using network material. They similarly suggest that newsgroup postings should be seen as published material, which could be cited without permission from the author except in cases where list owners indicate specified rules. On the subject of re-posting, one proposed principle suggests that

> Original material contributed to a publicly advertised open list carries an implicit license to re-post or quote provided that attribution is retained and the material is not presented out of context. Material contributed to a list which is not both publicly advertised and open without application does not carry a license to re-post.

The intent of this principle, according to the document, is to "clarify the public/private characteristics of group discussions." In the Lotus case, all newsgroups cited were "public" in the sense that they did not require an application to join. In the case of the lesbian and gay hotline, however, the list would be considered private according to these principles, since the hotline had an application process for membership.

Copyright and Fair Use

In all cases, however, public or private, citations must give appropriate attribution to the author, since the author is the owner of the material and holds the copyright. Existing copyright law, according to one lawyer who specializes in cyberspace law, "seems to hold up rather well in this new digital world" (Cavazos, forthcoming). According to the 1976 Copyright Act, authors no longer need to file a copyright notice with the federal government. The Act removed this "legal hurdle" by providing "automatic protection for just about any original expression which can be fixed in tangible form, as soon as [this form] has been expressed" (Cavazos, forthcoming). Therefore, there appears to be no question that authors of conference or newsgroup postings own the copyright to their work.

Any duplication without permission is technically a violation of copyright. However, the doctrine of fair use has established that under certain conditions, it is not a violation to quote passages of a copyrighted work. Whether a use is fair is based on four factors (Patry 1985, vii):

— What is the purpose of the use? Commercial? Educational?
— What is the nature of the copyrighted material? Published? Unpublished?
— What is the amount or substantiality of the portion used?
— What will the effect of the use be on the value of the copyrighted work?

The safest use is one that is non-commercial, based on published material, does not use too much of the most significant parts of the original material, and does not impact the value of the original. Obviously, these are broad and subjective terms, and, as many have pointed out, courts interpret their importance differently (Cavazos, forthcoming; LeFevre 1992). For example, Karen LeFevre (1992) has shown how scholars' uses of unpublished material can be problematic, for although the use is educational, the nature of the material as unpublished often persuades courts to decide against the researcher.

Therefore, the question of whether computer conference postings are published or not will no doubt be important if and when a court decides on the use of these texts as research material. I was told the following by another attorney:

> Because you are working on a dissertation and presumably any excerpting you might do would be in furtherance of this project, I would expect your uses to be regarded as fair. This is especially true given that the postings are not themselves for commercial purposes and consequently you will not be displacing sales by the authors.

However, given that my dissertation was being reviewed by book publishers, this same lawyer also noted that

> if you contemplate the possibility that your work might eventually be published by a commercial firm, you might decide to err on the side of caution and get permission particularly as to the republication of whole messages instead of just excerpts. (Samuelson 1993)

I decided to do just that. I used excerpts without permission, but obtained written permission where I used entire texts. I also placed these complete texts in an appendix, rather than within my analysis chapters, so that I could easily "shear off" the appendix and integrate excerpts in the published book if necessary.

Cascades: Multiple Authors?

Yet in some cases, it was unclear as to who the true author actually was. On computer conferences and with e-mail, it is a fairly common occurrence to take passages from another person's note and insert these passages into a new note. The resulting note is called a "cascade." Often, the excerpted passages will themselves contain excerpts of other people's notes. Will the real author please stand up? According to one expert, "[a]lthough it is a fairly common occurrence, reposting [a] message to another forum is almost always a copyright violation" (Cavazos, forthcoming). Yet if I wish to cite a cascaded note, am I obligated to get permission or give credit to all the authors?

In the Lotus case, a rather lengthy protest letter made the rounds, beginning with a Boston-based computer consultant and traveling across the country. In my research, I found this letter on three different public newsgroups and one internal company bulletin board. I also found evidence of it's having traveled widely through the use of e-mail. But each time the letter surfaced, it contained some additional added commentary and some changes. So who was the actual author: the original author (the computer consultant) or the original author plus the individuals who re-posted the letter with comments?

In my study, I chose to show good faith by getting written permission from the letter's original author. Based on my understanding of copyright, this person still holds the copyright, since the words are still his own, even though they have been re-posted. Yet in other computer conferences, where cascades can contain the contents of many authors, this scenario still presents questions for researchers.

License: Implied and Stated

There are two other circumstances where a researcher must be careful about citing conferences. First, if the conference or network has a published policy on citing material, you probably should heed this policy. The same lawyer who confirmed my rule of thumb also noted that one source of my data, the Whole Earth 'Lectronic Link (the WELL) has a policy that authors of postings "own their own words." He suggested that "[t]echnically speaking, that means that if you reprint a Well posting you should probably get permission from the person who posted the message" (Rotenberg 1993). Yet this was still confusing to me: the phrase "you own your own words" seemed nothing more than a re-statement of United States copyright law, and did not seem to imply anything special about WELL postings. A more explicit statement might have given me more cause for notice.

Another proposed principle from the policy document does suggest that list owners actively determine and explicitly state the re-posting rules for their conference, list, or newsgroup:

> List owners should give notice of specific rules on re-posting or quotation to all new subscribers. Any rules so announced super-sede general principles.

Researchers working with CMC texts should therefore pay attention to any stated rules about citing or re-posting material from a conference or newsgroup.

The second circumstance requiring special attention is the case where the conference or newsgroup may not have a notice, but where the author attaches a statement regarding reprints directly to his or her posting. Any kind of statement, such as "do not reproduce or distribute without written permission of the author," should probably be taken seriously, and the researcher should get written permission from the author. The draft principles also suggest this approach:

> Notices on individual messages of special restrictions or allow-ances normally override general rules, except that such notices cannot affect the customary archiving, access, and republishing practices of the list as the whole.

If an author attaches such a notice, one lawyer has argued, he or she could be seen as "attempting to establish a licensing agreement with those who circulate a post," since the notice passes the legal test for what constitutes a license" (Cavazos, forthcoming). So it would be wise for researchers to get permission from any author who attaches a notice about citation or re-posting.

Compilation Copyright

One final copyright issue of importance to CMC researchers is that of compilation copyright. In a published collection of essays, the individual authors retain individual copyrights to their specific essays, but the collection editors retain copyright to the work as a whole. This analogy has been suggested as valid for collections of electronic texts, not just electronic journals, but also collections such as archived newsgroups or conferences. A "collective work copyright" exists for those forums "where someone actively serves as moderator or otherwise controls or edits the content of the collection" (Cavazos forthcoming). For example, many commercial online services, such as Compuserve, state their copyright claim to all user messages. What this means for researchers is that

> capturing an entire discussion off of Compuserve or another system and re-posting it somewhere else violates the host system's copyright. Remember, this right is separate from the author's individual copyright in a particular message. (Cavazos, forthcoming)

In my study, I read through entire newsgroups and forums, but I did not use discussions in full. However, compilation copyright is another issue of which CMC researchers should be aware.

Citation Style

Once I felt ethically comfortable, and determined I was on reasonable legal grounds, I was ready to begin citing my data. I quickly discovered, however, that the *MLA Handbook for Writers of Research Papers*, which I was required to use, did not have appropriate citation styles for my data. A quick glance through the other major style manuals revealed the same problem. Although the manuals all had citation styles for data retrieved from online database services, they had no guidelines for e-mail, newsgroup, or conference postings.

I looked for the closest match, as I had done with other research data in the past. An e-mail message, for example, is very much like a personal letter, so the citation style for personal letters might suffice. But a few other fields of information might also be required for clarity. And what about newsgroup postings? What were they like? As with my earlier questions, I found myself looking for an analogy that would help.

At an academic meeting that year, I heard a paper given by a scholar whose primary data is obscure medieval texts on rhetoric. She indicated that her material could not always be cited by conventional standards and that authorship was sometimes unclear. These and other issues sounded strikingly familiar. I realized my data was similar to any unusual non-standard data source. When I asked how she approached this issue, this archivist suggested providing enough information to adequately credit the source and to allow another scholar to find the material (Woods 1993).

This suggestion was confirmed by librarians during my investigation into the development of bibliographic styles. Although noting that "[t]here can be no one standard or universal rule to determine which data elements are just enough in a citation," one text on bibliographic methods notes that

> [a]n entry is adequate when it ensures that the user can unambiguously identify the one intended document, and is given sufficient information for the purposes for which the list was consulted. (Hagler and Simmons 1982, 87)

During the course of my investigation, some of the major style guides began expanding their sections on bibliographic styles for electronic texts. The fourteenth edition of the *Chicago Manual of Style* provides a limited section on "computer documents," and also refers the reader to the ISO standards on electronic document citation (1993, 632–635). These ISO standards, to be published as ISO 10956 ("Information and documentation: Bibliographic references—Electronic documents or parts thereof") is as of this writing still in draft form and could be available late in 1994 (Thacker 1993). *The MLA Handbook for Writers of Research Papers* is as of this writing also adding sections on electronic texts.

While these sections do not give examples of every possible electronic forum, they can provide a basic framework for the researcher. One could use the style guide suggestion as a foundation, and then, in keeping with the spirit of the above bibliography rule, add to it any necessary information to properly credit the source and to give another person the ability to find the same information.

Yet because of the limitations in the major style guides, some CMC researchers have turned to a technical bibliography manual. This manual, the *National Library of Medicine Recommended Formats for Bibliographic Citation* reference, contains (in Chapter 12) extensive field-by-field explanations not only for electronic documents and journals, but also for bulletin boards and electronic mail (Patrias 1991). In fact, the Patrias text was used as a basis for the upcoming ISO standard, 10956, mentioned earlier (Thacker 1993).[8]

Although the major style guides do not give enough information, a catalog librarian's reference such as the National Library of Medicine guide may be too technical for students or researchers. Recognizing the gap between the major style guides and the technical cataloger references, two librarians from the University of Vermont recently published an entire manual devoted to citation styles for electronic texts (Li and Crane 1993). This book is based on the author-date citation system and provides guidelines for every imaginable kind of electronic discourse. The guide contains a wide selection of electronic text styles, and is a good beginning.

The biggest problem with standard citations for electronic texts, one not addressed by any manual, is that the texts are not standard across sites. Unique fields such as message number may vary from system to system. E-mail headers may differ across platforms. Conferences and Usenet newsgroups use slightly different headers and posting formats. This problem complicates not only the bibliographic reference but also the style of in-text citations.

In the Lotus case, for example, I came across many instances where a posting was created by the same author on the same date using the same subject line. This left me with the need for a unique identifier, for use in both the bibliographic reference and the in-text citation. Since message number was not a reliable field, I finally decided on the time of the posting.

MLA style presented me with an additional problem here. In traditional MLA style, two works by the same author are usually distinguished in the in-text citation by using the author's name and a portion of the article title. Since conference postings do not have "titles" and since the subject line is often the same, the only unique identifiers I could find were the date and time. Li and Crane (1993, x) have also noted that date is "of paramount importance in electronic sources" and chose to model their electronic citation guide after the author-date system (used in American Psychological Association [APA] style and offered as an alternative style in the MLA manual). My final choice was to use traditional MLA style for non-electronic citations, but use a version of author-date style for electronic texts.

So, for example, my bibliography might look like this:

WORKS CITED
    Brown, Amelia S. "The Scope of Privacy in a Computer Age." *Journal of Electronic Privacy* 10.1 (1993): 1–18.
    Brown, Amelia S. "Networks and the Right to Privacy." *Computer Law Quarterly* 12.3 (1993): 10–20.
    Green, Oscar A. "Whose privacy, anyway?" Electronic message to Usenet newsgroup alt.privacy. 16 Nov. 1993. 09:53:47 PST.
    Green, Oscar A. "Whose privacy, anyway?" Electronic message to Usenet newsgroup alt.privacy. 16 Nov. 1993. 10:21:42 PST.

And my in-text citations like this:

> According to one person, "It doesn't seem clear whether the Lotus product actually violates anyone's privacy" (Green, "Whose Privacy..." 09:53:47 PST). But later, the same person indicated that "[He was] ready to send a protest notice to Lotus" (Green, "Whose Privacy..." 10:21:42 PST). This mixed response has been noted by other network observers. (Brown, "The Scope of Privacy")

Total use of an author-date system, such as the APA or MLA alternative style, is probably best for extensive work with network postings, since the in-text citations would become less cumbersome:

> According to one person, "It doesn't seem clear whether the Lotus product actually violates anyone's privacy" (Green 1993a). But later, the same person indicated that "[He was] ready to send a protest notice to Lotus" (Green 1993b). This mixed response has been noted by other network observers. (Brown 1993a)

Yet some disciplines may object to author-date, in which case a modified approach may be the best answer. These issues will surely be resolved as the major style manuals incorporate more specifics into their guidelines. Yet for now, it appears up to the researcher to determine the best citation style for his or her data.

Summary: Developing Standards for CMC Research

Many network observers contacted for this chapter agree that the growth of the Internet and other online services has fast outpaced the creation of any standards for using the texts created on these forums. For communication researchers using the cyber-texts created in these forums, this lack of standards adds another level of work and investigation to the research project. In some ways, it is a confusing time to be a CMC researcher. We need to stay in touch with on-going legal cases, new laws and policies, and new approaches to citing data. Yet it is also an exciting time. My study, for example, illustrates the new kinds of communities and social action taking place on the net, but it also provides a hands-on example of the difficulties of working with these texts. During my study, I spoke with editors of style guides, librarians, and lawyers. CMC researchers can play a role in the development of standards by bringing their experiences into the ongoing conversation about research and network texts, and thus contribute to the research environment for communication scholars of the next century.

Notes

1. This experience illustrates a problem with research involving more temporary network texts: non-moderated Usenet newsgroups (where no one is in charge of keeping archived texts and where there is no one to contact for information), poorly organized bulletin boards/conferences, and electronic mail. It can be difficult to reconstruct a network event such as the Lotus case, which spans this range of conferences and networks.

2. I was fortunate to have a background in computer systems, so I was not intimidated by the technical tasks required to access data. Yet my experience raises an interesting question: will research about CMC only take place by those with computer skills? Perhaps new incarnations of the Internet will be more accessible to a wider range of people.

3. People on networks often use "handles" or pseudonyms.

4. As long as I gave proper credit and did not violate fair use, considerations that are appropriate for any kind of citation, paper or otherwise. See next section for more discussion about copyright and fair use.

5. This process is often called "cascading" and is done to establish context for commenting on someone else's posting. See next section for more discussion of cascades.

6. This attitude is related to the overall notion of community that emerged in my study. Conference participants felt comfortable with their words' being redistributed in their own cyber-community, but did not feel comfortable when an "outsider" wished to use their words.

7. This draft document is available by anonymous FTP: ftp.cni.org, under /CNI/projects/Harvard.scp/kahin.txt.

8. The ISO/TC 46/SC 9 secretariat, Jane Thacker, was kind enough to send me the draft document of the ISO standards for electronic citations. I was asked not to reproduce the contents of this document, since it is still in draft form. But I can report that the standards appear very comprehensive and will probably provide a thorough basis for most style manuals.

References

Addison, Joanne. (1993). "Group Identity in Academic and Nonacademic Electronic Forums: Conventions, Constraints and Negotiation?" Penn State Conference on Rhetoric and Composition State College, Pa.

Cavazos, Edward A. (forthcoming). "Intellectual Property in Cyberspace: Copyright Law in a New World." *Cyberspace and the Law: Your Rights and Duties in the OnLine World.* Cavazos, Edward A. and Gavino Morin (Eds.). Cambridge: MIT Press.

Chicago Manual of Style. (1993). 14th ed. Chicago: U. of Chicago Press.

Hagler, Ronald and Simmons, Peter. (1982). *The Bibliographic Record and Information Technology.* Chicago: ALA.

Kahin, Brian. (1993). *Scholarly Communication in the Network Environment: Proposed Principles for Research Communications.* Cambridge: John F. Kennedy School of Government, Harvard.

LeFevre, Karen Burke. (1992). "The Tell-Tale 'Heart': Determining 'Fair' Use of Unpublished Texts." *Law and Contemporary Problems* 55.2: 153–83.

Li, Xia and Crane, Nancy B. (1993). *Electronic Style: A Guide to Citing Electronic Information.* Westport: Meckler.

MLA Handbook for Writers of Research Papers. (1988). 3rd ed. Gibaldi, Joseph and Walter S. Achtert (Eds.). New York: Modern Language Association.

Patrias, Karen. (1991). *National Library of Medicine Recommended Formats for Bibliographic Citation.* Bethesda: U.S. Department of Health and Human Services.

Patry, William F. (1985). *The Fair Use Privilege in Copyright Law.* Washington, DC: Bureau of National Affairs.

Rotenberg, Marc. (1993). Electronic mail message to author. 22 Feb. 1993. 22:22:38 EST.

Samuelson, Pamela. (1993). Electronic mail message to author. 6 May 1993. 07:37:53: EST.

Thacker, Jane. (1993). Letter to author. 6 Dec. 1993.

Woods, Majorie Curry. (1993). Telephone interview with author. April 1993.

Computer Networking in Ornithology

Jack P. Hailman

Ornithology is properly the science of avian biology, as distinct from recreational pursuits of birds, but the media are so fond of labeling bird watchers as ornithologists that the distinction has blurred. Indeed, most professional ornithologists readily admit to enjoying nature as a hobby, and a few recreationalists make serious contributions to the science. Here, I suggest how networking is beginning to manifest itself across the spectrum of ornithology taken broadly, with special analysis of a small, specialized, scholarly network.

Four Manifestations

Ornithology is arguably one of the oldest sciences and probably the most information-productive discipline in all of science. Every major country in the world has a national ornithological society that publishes its own journal, there being four principal national societies in the United States alone. In addition, nearly every state has its own ornithological society with its own journal, many of these miming national journals in terms of strict peer review of all manuscripts and general quality of publication within the framework of local focus. There also exist international journals as well as some regional (multistate) and other local (within state) and specialized outlets, not to mention manifestly recreational periodicals about birds. With this immense outpouring of information about a single class of biological subjects, one might expect ornithology to have paved the way in computer-oriented means of communication. In fact, nothing approaching this has happened; those concerned with the study of birds are only beginning to explore the advantages of networking, as evidenced by four manifestations.

Electronic Mail Capacity

The aforementioned principal ornithological societies in the United States publish a joint membership directory (*The Flock*), which has for the last several issues included electronic mail (hereafter "e-mail") addresses. Sample counts from the 1993 directory revealed zero to four e-mail addresses for every block of ten entries inspected, with roughly fifteen percent of entries providing such information. This count may, however, be low; my own e-mail addresses, although submitted repeatedly, are omitted, and I find numerous instances of such missing information among colleagues with whom I correspond on e-mail. If the count were restricted to those persons listing an academic institution for their mailing address, the percentage on e-mail would be higher. Even if that latter proportion approaches or exceeds one-third, however, the conclusion must be drawn that ornithologists have been sluggish to adopt e-mail communication.

Recreational Bird Networks

The approbation "birdwatcher" is not as appropriate as "bird-lister" for (especially American) recreationalists, whose principal objective is to see as many different avian species as possible. This objective is fed by the immense mobility of birds, coupled with their wandering or being blown off usual migratory courses by weather, so that an individual may show up well outside of its species' stipulated geographic range. Hobbyists achieve personal satisfaction and stature among peers by discovering such waifs and showing them to other bird-listers for independent confirmation. News of rare birds once proceeded mainly by word of mouth, but the availability of telephone answering machines potentiated the establishment of dial-a-bird "hotlines" by local bird clubs. Such electronic dissemination is now so widespread that even cities of less than 100,000 inhabitants commonly have rarity hotlines, and in places such as Florida, organized telephoning networks flash the news from one city to the next. It is, therefore, not surprising that hobbyists were well ahead of professional ornithologists in moving to computer networks for rapid dissemination of information.

A network (Rare Bird Alert) serving the whole of North America north of Mexico, was established by an enthusiastic birder. It may seem unlikely to those unfamiliar with the recreational endeavor that anyone living in, say, the Midwest could possibly be interested in a bird sighted on the coast of New England. But when a rare Arctic gull was found in Massachusetts a few years ago whole groups of birdwatchers from Wisconsin flew east to see the bird. The national rarity hotline was subsequently decomposed into regional networks (e.g, BirdEast) to which anyone could subscribe, and an unedited, listserved, spinoff network (BirdChat) was established for general discussion. BirdChat remains, insofar as I have been able to learn, the sole general ornithological network in existence, and despite an enormous dose of naive chatting, the net does occasionally have a serious exchange about avian biology. There is a rare bird network in Finland (Lintuverkko, which means bird net) that also has occasional serious traffic on avian ecology and other subjects. Perhaps other such nets exist as well.

Large Professional Networks

The first large professional network dealing primarily with birds was established in 1992 as AOUnet-L, the name deriving from the initials of the American Ornithologists' Union. AOUnet-L is a passive, listserved network that posts information concerning upcoming legislation regarding research funding and conservation. The net is thus new and (at the time of writing) unique in ornithology.

Two related networks, dealing partly with birds but not restricted to them, suggest directions in which ornithological nets may develop. Both are devoted to ethology, the study of animal behavior. ABSnet, established as a personal endeavor and later sponsored by the Animal Behavior Society (serving primarily the United States and Canada), has two main types of postings: a directory of subscribers and an aperiodic newsletter. The edited newsletter section contains information about legislation, as in AOUnet-L, but also information about employment opportunities, requests for information, and similar material. The related network, called Ethonet, is very different: it is a listserved, interactive net with no general postings. Ethonet is international in scope and devoted almost entirely to requests for information, which run the spectrum from attempts to locate particular colleagues, through requests for help in writing animal-care protocols, to seeking references on a particular research topic. Some disadvantages of an unedited, interactive network are clear to subscribers: an enormous volume of traffic is sometimes generated, nearly daily, and persons respond carelessly using reply functions so that their answers, even if of a personal nature, are disseminated throughout the world.

Small, Specialized Professional Network

Apparently the only small, specialized professional network yet established in ornithology is Titnet, which is devoted mainly to a particular family of birds (the Paridae): tits, titmice, and chickadees. Titnet is international in scope and considered in detail below.

Analyses

It is an instructive case in the emergence of electronic communication to ask why ornithology has been remarkably sluggish in adopting the new technology. It is also relevant to ask why there exists no outlet whatever for the electronic publication of scientific results, and why only one small, specialized network (Titnet) posts research abstracts. There are a number of candidate answers, not mutually exclusive.

Simple Conservatism

Ornithology's formal institutions are venerable; the American Ornithologists' Union, for example, was established and publishing its journal (the *Auk*) in the nineteenth century. This is not the place to dissect the nature of such institutions, but it suffices to say that those of us who are members of diverse scientific societies can point to many usual "conservatisms" in ornithology. Whether those who study birds are inherently conservative and so structure their institutions, or the conservatism of the institutions influences their members, is difficult to decide.

Lack of Accessibility

Even the most scientific of ornithological societies have large numbers of amateurs among their members, so one might argue that professionals have been reluctant to establish modes of contact that would disenfranchise these amateurs. Such an argument is unconvincing because professional ornithologists have an established track record in the opposite direction (special, limited-privilege membership classes for amateurs), and because the recreational birding networks are principally amateur-driven endeavors. Nor can one argue cogently that professionals lack accessibility. Every major institution of higher learning in the United States provides e-mail capacities for its faculty and staff, and many for its graduate students, if a graduate program exists; and undergraduates are rapidly becoming empowered with electronic mail as well. Nonetheless, perhaps only fifteen percent or so of the serious ornithological community has a published e-mail address, so there may be a natural reluctance to restrict communication with the electronic elite.

Lack of Perceived Need

The principal advantage touted for electronic communication is speed. It is no accident that ornithological networking has developed principally in those specific areas where more conventional dissemination of information would be too slow to be effective: the sightings of rare birds, and pending legislation. Unlike biomedical fields where literature more than a few years old is of limited usefulness, ornithology must contend with the biology of about nine-thousand species and so in many ways is an inherently slow-moving science. The last important paper on a given topic could be more than a half-century old, and there is little perceived need to rush new results into print. As a consequence, avian biologists do not seem to have been strongly attracted to rapid, electronic dissemination of scientific results.

Limited Format

The networking medium is restrictive in format, particularly for the publication of scientific results. In those areas of the humanities and social sciences where the information content of scholarship is encoded primarily in words, e-mail is eminently suitable. Science, by contrast, relies heavily on equations, plots, and graphic materials including diagrams and photographs, all of which are difficult to adopt to current network formats. Ornithologists in particular will be reluctant to give up hardcopy journals, for even the most scientific examples of the genre often run a full-color frontispiece in every issue.

Questionable Acceptability

In the fiercely competitive climate of academe, quality of publication matters. Even the highest quality, fully refereed electronic examples, such as the psychological journal *Psycoloquy*, have yet to gain equal footing with traditional hardcopy journals in the eyes of older faculty making tenure decisions about younger colleagues. And there are attendant problems involving citation format, archiving, accessibility, copyright protection, and so on.

Although no claim for completeness can be made for the foregoing list, the factors identified seem sufficient to account for those areas that have adopted networking (rare-bird alerts, pending legislation, employment opportunities, requests for information) and those that have not (dissemination of scientific results). Nevertheless, a peculiar anomaly remains, namely the lack of research abstracts in all ornithological networks save Titnet. Researchers are fully prepared for this genre through a long history of writing one-paragraph abstracts that are duplicated and distributed at professional meetings. None of the problems associated with ersatz journal publication applies to abstracts, and electronic dissemination would reach far more and far more diverse colleagues than do meeting abstracts. The crystal ball would therefore seem to show e-mail abstracts on the horizon for ornithological networking.

TITNET

As mentioned, Titnet is currently unique in ornithology in several respects. It appears to be the only specialized scholarly network in the field, and the only network in ornithology (including as well the sister discipline ethology) to post research abstracts. It is therefore of some interest, as an example of how scholarly networks originate, first to recount briefly the history behind Titnet. Then I explain its three types of postings, followed by results of a survey of subscribers as to the usefulness of the network.

The History of Titnet

International ornithological congresses are held every fourth year, and a small group of researchers at the 1986 meeting in Ottawa, Canada met informally to exchange information on the biology of tits, called titmice and chickadees in North America. A consensus was reached that colleagues should stay in touch by means of a (hardcopy) news-letter, subsequently dubbed *Parus International*, which continues to be published twice a year at no cost to subscribers. Two years later, a major symposium on tit biology was sponsored by the Wilson Ornithological Society as part of its centennial meeting, held in Philadelphia, and parid researchers from all over the world again met informally to discuss research problems and to expand the activities of the as yet unnamed group, which was subsequently called The International Tit Society (T.I.T.S.). At the third meeting—in conjunction with the International Ornithological Congress at Christchurch, New Zealand, in 1990—those attending decided to initiate an electronic mail network, with yours truly volunteering to found and then manage the endeavor for an unspecified period. It was natural to call the new network Titnet. The scope of T.I.T.S. was also broadened to include cavity-nesting birds of other families, such as woodpeckers and nuthatches, as they share with tits various biological problems.

Titnet is still evolving in terms of both its number of subscribers and the nature of its content. As of 1993, just over sixty subscribers were sprinkled across the globe: Belgium, Canada, Estonia, Finland, France, Hungary, Netherlands, New Zealand, Norway, Sweden, United Kingdom, and United States. Tits themselves are widely distributed but not universally so: they occur through Eurasia and in Africa and North America, but not South America or Australia. E-mail capabilities are rare or absent in several countries having prominent parid biologists, most conspicuously Germany and Japan. The subscribers to Titnet are almost wholly professional ornithologists (faculty, post-doctoral associates, or graduate students). Inquiries about the net are answered with an informational message about its nature and purpose, which discourages amateurs for whom subscription would serve no purpose. However, a few amateurs or others (e.g., a wildlife librarian) do subscribe, and are welcome.

Titnet currently has three series of formal postings: TITNET (full caps, in distinction from the network name), TITNEWS, and *TITNOTES*. Each series is numbered separately, and all postings are archived and available on request, but not, currently, via anonymous FTP or similar means. All postings in Titnet are in English (but see below concerning abstracts in *TITNOTES*). Although Titnet will surely continue to grow, it seems likely that its asymptote distribution list and volume of postings will not necessitate listserver and allied functions.

TITNET: The Subscriber List

TITNET (full caps) was the initial focus of Titnet (the network), and consists of the names of subscribers and their e-mail addresses, home institutions (but not full postal addresses or telephone/FAX numbers), research species, and research topics. TITNET is updated about twice yearly. The aim of TITNET is to facilitate initial contact among researchers having common interests; they can exchange postal addresses and telephone numbers by e-mail if they want to move to a traditional medium.

TITNEWS: The Newsletter

The initiation of TITNEWS was precipitated by the proposal that a database be established for bibliographic material on hole-nesting birds. As the subset of T.I.T.S. members who were on e-mail were the principal concerned parties, Titnet was the natural means for exploring the idea. Therefore, TITNEWS was established as an edited newsletter in which Titnet subscribers could propose actions or comment on those proposed. The original proposal for a database was eventually dropped as expensive and overlapping with broader databases. But TITNEWS persisted as a means of announcing upcoming international meetings and similar newsletter material, with care being given to prevent overlap with any wider networks furnishing more general information.

TITNOTES: The Semi-Journal

The third series of postings to be established is the closest thing Titnet has to an e-mail journal. *TITNOTES* is devoted to original and second-hand material on the biology of tits and other hole-nesting birds. For example, when a new world list of avian species was published, the material on the Paridae was extracted and posted in *TITNOTES*.

In late 1992, it was decided to inaugurate the posting of research abstracts, and the first set appeared in early 1993. In order to develop abstracts gradually, the initial call was specifically for e-mail-formatted abstracts that originally had been prepared for professional meetings. A second posted series of abstracts included one of a manuscript accepted by a hardcopy journal. Also acceptable are abstracts from grant proposals and research summaries prepared for any other purpose, such as progress reports to funding agencies, faculty annual activity reports, and so on. Abstracts in *TITNOTES* must be in English but may be followed by a translation in any language that can be written in the e-mail format.

Is Titnet Useful?

In an attempt to obtain a first assessment of the usefulness of Titnet, a brief survey of mainly yes/no questions was sent to all subscribers in the summer of 1993. Several persons felt they were too new to the network to have formed opinions, others replied that the network itself was too new to assess its effects, and of course several persons did not reply. (They have my sympathy; I do not do windows or surveys.) Based on the two dozen persons who agreed to play this game, the results were as follows.

TITNET, the list of e-mail addresses with research interests, was deemed useful by all respondents (100 percent). Most (83 percent) said that TITNET has helped locate someone with whom they were seeking contact, and half (50 percent) said that TITNET was responsible for making a new professional contact. TITNEWS was reported to have been useful to three-quarters (75 percent) and *TITNOTES* to even more (88 percent) of the respondents. However, only a little over half (58 percent) could point to a specific positive effect that Titnet had had on their research. Only a third (33 percent) said that Titnet had caused a change in the way in which they communicated with fellow scientists, and a very small group (17 percent) reported that Titnet had caused a change in the way in which they did research. Finally, only five persons reported ever having subscribed to a related network (four of them BirdChat), and two of those had dropped their subscriptions because the material was too amateur-oriented to bother with. Even those who did answer the questions posed often echoed the sentiments of the others who said that the entire endeavor was too new for accurate assessment.

Summary and Conclusions

Ornithological networking is currently manifest mainly as rare-bird hotlines for amateurs and legislative alerts for professionals. At least two amateur-driven discussion nets exist (United States and Finland), but only one small, scholarly network has yet been established. Development has been sluggish because of inherent conservatism, lack of accessibility, lack of perceived need, limitations of e-mail format (especially the difficulty of presenting mathematical and graphic materials), and lack of status as a publication outlet for academicians. Users of the scholarly network (Titnet), however, are very positive not only about its future development but also its already manifested usefulness in the scientific endeavor. Only about fifteen percent of North American ornithologists currently list e-mail addresses, but that number grows annually, as does the number of subscribers to networks such as Titnet. The obvious general conclusion is that ornithological networking is still in its infancy, with indications that it is poised on the threshold of an accelerated growth phase.

Roadmap to Scholarly Electronic Communication and Publishing at The American Mathematical Society*

David L. Rodgers
Kevin W. Curnow
Drury R. Burton
Greg S. Ullmann
William B. Woolf

"You have no choice but to jump into this technology, if you plan to live for five or ten years."

—Al Thaler, Program Director
National Science Foundation

"I feel like a deer caught in the headlights of an on-rushing truck."

—Susan Keiser
Oxford University Press

The American Mathematical Society (AMS) is a medium-sized scholarly society, with about 30,000 members, a broader community of approximately 60,000 research mathematicians in North America, and perhaps 150,000 research mathematicians worldwide. The AMS is a membership organization, publisher, and database producer, delivering both print and electronic products and services. Approximately seventy-five percent of revenues are derived from publishing-related activities. The Society publishes six primary research journals, a secondary bibliographic journal (in print, CD-ROM, online, and site-load format), monographs, and special publications. It provides sale of

*Adapted from the final report submitted to the National Science Foundation (May 1994).

177

services to other organizations. Electronic submissions, based on widely publicized guidelines, account for 15–20 percent of the total, but a steadily growing fraction. The Society has made a significant aggregate investment in technology, and has more than a decade of experience using electronic tools for journal and book production, and library support.

Since 1990, the AMS has been engaged in developing a program of initiatives in scholarly electronic communication and publishing. These efforts have been generously supported by grants from the National Science Foundation (NSF).

The purpose of this paper is to outline the framework of activity as a means for better understanding issues. It is part history, part reflection, and part analysis. It is an attempt to understand issues from the perspective of community and culture, and to place them in the context of events and outcomes.

Getting Started

In 1990, Gopher and WAIS were gleams in the eye of their developers. So were World Wide Web and Mosaic. Client-server architecture was still largely a concept, and certainly not an applied practice. Use of electronic mail was on the rise, largely for informal communication or, in some cases, for transport of preprint information. Listserv was a popular distribution method at some sites but was not ubiquitous. VT100 dial-up was the most popular form of connectivity, whether from terminals or personal computers. Modem speeds above 1200 baud were uncommon. Internet connectivity was available in selected settings.

Mathematicians were just beginning to recognize the value of personal computers for the purpose of scholarly activity. Electronic mail was beginning to be widely used. TeX had evolved to a point where it was a language of both communication and transport in the mathematical research community. Preprints, long the preferred means for communicating preliminary results, were starting to be widely circulated by electronic mail. A small number of bulletin boards and Listserv applications were in use.

In January 1990, three representatives from the AMS met with a representative from the NSF to talk about providing electronic services to mathematicians. A proposal was encouraged, which led to a three-year grant to develop electronic services tailored to the special requirements of mathematicians. The grant was awarded in May 1990, and the umbrella system, called e-MATH, went into operation in October 1990.

Generalizations, Goals, and Strategic Direction

As early as 1990, it was clear that the seeds for explosive growth and change were in the air, as barriers to electronic access and connectivity continued to fall or were being driven back. Computers seemed destined to become information appliances used mainly for intelligent, selective retrieval and display of information. Scholarly, legal, and economic issues seemed likely to pose more significant barriers than technology issues before the end of the decade. Ownership of information, peer review, archiving, and cost recovery—all significant barriers—seemed likely, in time, to give way to adaptive solutions.

The goal of the AMS initiative has been to design experiments that are inexpensive, that match solutions to the complexity of problems, and that provide hands-on experience with new technology. We sought to define an architecture for distributed electronic services that is based on standards, and one that can be implemented incrementally. We wanted to improve both quality and timeliness of informal and formal scholarly communication, and to encourage wide-access collaboration in the worldwide community of mathematicians.

In the long run, the goal is to bring modern tools of scholarship to the scholar's desk. In this way, the scholarly process is modeled as a continuum that begins with knowledge creation, and works its way through stages to formal publishing, distribution, and archiving; and not as a sequence of discrete, unrelated activities. We sought to explore uses of technology by scholars, librarians, and publishers. We sought to experiment with new forms of scholarly electronic communication and publishing. We wanted to use partnered efforts as a means of navigating steep development costs, learning curves, and staffing requirements necessary for viable solutions.

The AMS is in a good position to take some risks because of its prior investment in technology. TeX is a typesetting language that has been widely adopted by the scientific community, in particular by mathematicians, even though it has not achieved popular market acceptance. TeX source files are editable, manipulable, and retrievable; in this regard they are more useful than more popular, image-based solutions. By developing electronic services, the AMS gained direct experience in matters that involve ownership of information and cost recovery.

Added-Value of and Barriers to Electronic Communication and Publishing

Electronic media offers opportunity to add value:

— Timeliness
— Convenience
— Expanded Opportunities for Information-Sharing
— Expanded Opportunities for Collaboration
— Expanded Opportunities for Interdisciplinary Activity
— Reduced Production and Distribution Costs
— Reduced Archival Costs

At the same time, it offers barriers that must be navigated:

— Economics (who will pay and how much?)
— Ownership of Information (authors, institutions, publishers)
— Ease of Use and Convenience (the "fun" index)
— Community and Culture (access and reward)
— Technology (connectivity and interoperability)

The e-MATH system has provided insights and experience with all of these issues.

The e-MATH System

The e-MATH system is a node on the Internet:

Gopher e-math.ams.org (130.44.1.100)

or

URL: http://e-math.ams.org/web/index.html

or

telnet e-math.ams.org
login: e-math
password: e-math

The initial e-MATH release was based on use of telnet and access through a semi-public login for which the password was widely publicized to mathematicians. This provided at least one level of indirection from casual intruders, if not much of a barrier to determined hackers. In June 1993, the entire e-MATH system was reorganized around an integrated Gopher/WAIS/Listserv/FTP platform. In April 1994, an AMS home page for World Wide Web was released. ALL e-MATH applications can be reached by any of the three access paths.

From the outset, a distinction between:

— electronic communication—informal sharing of research and professional information by electronic mail, file transfer, searchable databases, software components, and conferencing, and
— electronic publishing—formal reporting of research results that were peer-reviewed and archived by information providers

was made in the way applications were organized and presented. Over its three-year lifetime, a variety of applications have been developed, and new applications are added on a regular basis.

Usage in the first full year of operation was about 50,000 accesses. In 1992, usage jumped to over 100,000 accesses. In 1993, usage broke the 350,000 access barrier. In 1994, usage is projected at 750,000 accesses and the 1,000,000 barrier is not out of the question. The e-MATH system has established itself as a general-purpose platform for delivering a variety of electronic services.

Lessons Learned

The raw materials required to build effective information services are community and data. They need to be cemented together by an infrastructure that takes into account culture, organization, and technology.

First and foremost, we have learned that building electronic communities is a difficult and painstaking undertaking. Even for the favorable case of the AMS, where there was a natural consituency, an average level of computer literacy, and above average level of connectivity, it was just plain hard. It is vastly easier to get activities started than it is to sustain the initial enthusiasm and momentum, and then build upon it. And if you are successful, you need to be prepared to change your ways as both the culture and technology evolve.

Two general strategies are possible. In the first, you develop consensus and do the inside-selling job to the community before anything is built, so there is shared vision. In the second, you survey community resources, identify a kernel set of applications, build them, and then ride the resulting waves. Both approaches have advantages and drawbacks. For a balance of reasons, we selected the latter approach: (1) the NSF was a willing co-investor; (2) AMS management wanted something sooner rather than later; and (3) developers had identified a set of starter applications that would fit into *any* model for comprehensive electronic services that would be the outcome of a more deliberative process.

AMS data required by the kernel set of applications was already captured in digital format, some of it in database format. The problem we encountered once we got by the initial hurdle was that a significant portion of AMS data, while in digital format, was not in any easily reuseable format. The organization and coding of files, designed for production of print materials, were not well suited to electronic dissemination or display. New applications usually required labor-intensive file editing. For applications where data was volatile, updating information was an arduous task. We did not want to imitate organizations we observed making broad announcements of intent, only to discover six months later that they had fallen victim to stale data. Our approach, and our advice to others, is to place a very high priority on quality of information and quality of service.

Retooling production processes is expensive. People resist changing what works, particularly when the payoff is unclear. Our reluctance to do throw-away work, to develop applications that would mire staff down in maintenance activities until changes could be made to production formats and clean solutions implemented, has produced its share of critics. For the long run, however, one of the accomplishments for which the e-MATH system can take some credit is that it underscored for the organization the importance of treating all AMS data as a corporate asset and a candidate for electronic display and/ or dissemination.

Three levels of infrastructure are required for long-term success:

1. the community needs to perceive what you are doing as a coherent program of activity and not integration by stapling together a hodgepodge of resources,

2. the technology platform needs to be widely available, robust, and extensible, and

3. the professional and personal agendas of influential members of the community need to be addressed.

Coherent Program of Activity

From the outset, the e-MATH system has been perceived as a coherent program. It has maintained that image through its three years of operation, regardless of whether various people wanted more of this or less of that. By the end of the first year, whispers could be heard in the corridors of influence that this or that problem could be solved with an e-MATH application. By the third year, the umbrella concept was firmly established and the e-MATH system, whatever its form, was viewed as *the* delivery system for AMS electronic products and services.

The toughest issue that needed to be confronted was how best to strike a balance between those applications that provide access to professional information and those that provide access to scholarly information. We started with applications that provided professional information (e.g., database of mathematicians, employment information, subject classifications for mathematics). People asked for them. They required modest development effort. They required modest levels of support. On the other hand, applications that had scholarly content had *much* longer incubation times. It proved difficult to find volunteers to lead them. A number of obvious candidates (e.g., primary and secondary research literature, preprints) raised thorny questions about ownership of information, access control, imprimatur, and cost recovery.

There was also an interesting dichotomy of interest. The online suggestion box produced a steady stream of suggestions for changes and improvements, almost all of them for more professional information. However, volunteer members of standing committees and executive management at the AMS wanted more applications with scholarly content.

Attempts to interest volunteers in moderating bulletin boards or conferences were largely unsuccessful. After numerous attempts, over a period of almost three years, e-MATH supports about a half dozen Listserv applications devoted to mathematics. Only one bulletin board, on calculus reform, has shown steady growth in subscribers and level of activity. It took Andrew Wiles's announcement of a proof of Fermat's Last Theorem, a 350-year-old problem in mathematics, to trigger a high level of interest in a bulletin board in a short period of time. In that case, over a five month period, about 7,000 accesses to the Gopher selection were recorded and the Listserv subscriber list is about 275 individuals. The remaining four applications have subscriber lists that don't exceed fifty individuals and have track records of low levels of activity.

Technology Platform

We decided early on that the initial platform needed to be based on lowest common denominator technology. We based the platform on terminal emulation. On the other hand, we decided to base network connectivity on TCP/IP (Internet). It allowed us to reach the largest possible audience for the minimum overall investment. We opted for a semi-public login configuration, where the login account and password were published in places mathematicians were likely to encounter them, but where disinterested parties would likely not. Since the e-MATH machine was attached to the AMS network, there were concerns expressed by some AMS staff about the security of the arrangement. One of the design goals of the original user view was to make it hacker resistant. We ran a contest and offered a $100 prize to anyone who could succeed in breaking through the user view and get to the native machine. Expert hackers could penetrate the operating system through known holes. One person succeeded in getting through a loophole and was awarded the $100 prize. That loophole was closed and there have been no subsequent security breaches.

The login facility served us well, certainly before the days when network tools like Gopher/WAIS/WWW were available. We did some early experiments with these network tools. While they showed promise, we had various concerns, and did not join the group of early adopters. We misread the tea leaves, and ignored the adage that ninety percent of user friendliness is doing what everybody else is doing. We had discovered from VT100 that things equal to the same things are not necessarily equal to each other, at least with terminal emulations. We had experienced about six months' difficulty getting e-MATH to work with various VT100 emulations, and it had not been fun. For every complaint we received about not moving to higher ground, we had twenty-five from people for whom VT100 was a hurdle of one sort or another. And, like everybody, *we* resisted changing what seemed to be working, and we did not see the train coming.

In June 1993, we did reorganize the e-MATH system around an integrated Gopher/WAIS/Listserv/FTP platform that we spent six months developing. In April 1994, the AMS home page for World Wide Web was released. e-MATH applications are available from each access path. In conjunction with some unrelated development work done for AMS applications, the payoff has been large, but mostly transparent to outsiders. We have a suite of scripts and programs that allow us to manage a number of important operations automatically. For example, we were able to convert AMS catalog information as it is coded for production of the paper version to a fully configured Gopher application, entirely under software control. The same approach is being used to launch an AMS Preprint Service. It will be cloned for other applications scheduled for development. Nevertheless, our preference for investing in robustness and scalability, rather than jumping on the latest bandwagon, has produced its share of critics.

Professional and Personal Agendas

Clearly, some of the controversial issues are:

— low-technology vs. high-technology applications
— early adoption vs. staged adoption
— inside selling vs. presentation
— short-term vs. long-term development
— professional vs. scholarly information
— infrastructure vs. application development

The central thread through all of this, and the toughest challenge, was to try to manage change in a community that supports a variety of viewpoints, representing different levels of interest, influence, access to technology, and technical intuition. Woven into all of this are issues of governance and oversight.

During the planning phase and for the first year of operation, e-MATH was guided by a very loose mandate, largely in the form of the funding proposal that was submitted to the National Science Foundation. e-MATH was viewed by many as a curiosity or interesting experiment. Progress reports were submitted to AMS and NSF officials, but not much care or attention was taken towards positioning e-MATH in the AMS organization for the longterm. We made the mistake of assuming that usage statistics would carry the day in any discussion. By that yardstick, e-MATH was certainly successful.

Well into the second year, AMS officials were beginning to see that e-MATH was having an impact on Society behavior. Increasingly, e-MATH was proposed as a solution, first for this and then for that problem or concern. e-MATH was starting to show up in minutes of committee meetings, in formal discussions, and so on. The AMS then did what it normally does in such situations. It appointed an oversight committee, or rather made e-MATH report to an existing standing committee. By the beginning of the third year, that standing committee was dissolved. During Fall 1992, a Committee on Electronic Products and Services was formed. The Committee met for the first time in January 1993, and made a report to the Board of Trustees of the Society in May 1993.

In May 1993, the Board of Trustees took two quite remarkable actions. First, it created a division of Electronic Products and Services.

Second, the Board of Trustees approved a pricing model that changed the subscription basis for its secondary bibliographic publication, *Mathematical Reviews*, in ways that position various deliveries of the product (e.g., paper, CD-ROM, site load tapes) to operate by anticipated rules of the future rather than by rules of the past. By these actions, the Society said to itself and others that its future was in electronic media.

The Electronic Products and Services division absorbed the e-MATH system and positions it as a general purpose platform for delivering AMS electronic products and services. Electronic Products and Services has a development group and a delivery and services group. It consolidates a number of staff and the initial group size is about nine full-time-equivalents.

e-MATH funding has always been controversial. It remains tricky. The e-MATH system was developed as a free service, with hooks that make it feasible to offer access to some applications on a fee-for-service or subscription basis. Some AMS officials did not see NSF funding as a co-investment opportunity that would allow the Society to develop capabilities and a knowledge base that was in the organization's interest. Rather, they saw it as a resource sink and an obligation to be assumed when the NSF contract expired. Few saw opportunities to build cost recovery mechanisms for the e-MATH system into various electronic product and service fees, or the possibility for contracted development. For 1995, the AMS is planning to make the early awareness bibliographic publication, *Current Mathematical Publications* (*CMP*), and the secondary bibliographic publication, *Mathematical Reviews* (*MR*), available through the e-MATH system. These applications will be offered on a subscription basis, and a portion of e-MATH operating costs will be factored into the subscription fees. The AMS has also responded to a number of Requests for Proposal (RFP) for contracted development work.

A second, perhaps more instructive example, is the preprint situation. At the end of 1991, our program director at NSF lobbied for a preprint repository. The Foundation had placed some limits on supplementary material that could be submitted in support of certain kinds of funding proposals. This action angered some mathematicians. If e-MATH had a preprint repository, preprint papers could be posted there and retrieved by referees (and others). Early in 1992, we went to Yale to talk with them about the Instant Math Preprint (IMP) service they were developing. Yale expressed eagerness for the AMS to take over this service. We talked about various aspects of the problem, including legal concerns raised by their University Counsel's Office about exposure to lawsuits from publishers. In the end, the technology platform upon which IMP was based was deemed unsuitable, and we set about developing an alternative solution.

Just before we were going to announce a preprint service, a number of people raised concerns. It was one thing for an individual, department, or institution to post preprints. It was viewed as quite another thing for the Society to do so, thereby exposing itself to the danger that it indirectly lent its imprimatur to research results not peer-reviewed. Some people were worried that papers left posted after they were published exposed the Society to the possibility of lawsuit by publishers. Some people worried that if preprints were posted in such a public, systematic way, it would damage the authors' chances of getting those papers accepted with publishers. And so on.

So, in May 1992, in cooperation with the Association of Research Libraries (ARL), a one-day meeting was convened. About twenty interested individuals were invited to attend, representing a variety of organizations, points of view, and expertise. An expert in copyright was invited. We walked through a number of scenarios and the legal expert was able to help the group work through potential problems and recommend paths and remedies. The group appointed a subcommittee to investigate possibilities for discipline-based preprint initiatives. As is sometimes the case, promises were made, the organizers got overcommitted, and something that had had initial momentum lost it. Fall turned into winter. A couple of initiatives drew their roots from the meeting, but no concerted effort materialized.

In Fall 1992, the Committee on Electronic Products and Services was formed and the preprint issue was put on the agenda of its January 1993, meeting. It proved very controversial. One committee member expressed extreme reservation. Some people known to be in favor of moving forward were silent. No resolution or firm plan of action surfaced. In June, when the e-MATH system was reorganized, it was done with an AMS preprint service in mind. In Fall 1993, management decided that it was important to get a formal review of procedures from the Committee on Electronic Products and Services before moving forward, since science policy issues were involved. Preprints were again put on the agenda for the next scheduled meeting of the committee, in January 1994. It was also put on the agenda of the Council of the AMS, the body charged to advise the Board of Trustees on matters of science policy. Both groups voted to move ahead, subject to the proviso that a clear distinction be preserved between preprints and peer-reviewed, archived publications. Editors for *Mathematical Reviews* were involved in scanning items to make certain they have

SOME mathematical content, are nominally classified, and contain no objectionable (e.g., racist) material. The AMS preprint server went into operation in April 1994.

In the area of developing a good organizational infrastructure, then, our efforts were seriously flawed. We did not see the long-term importance of this early enough, or work on it hard enough when it surfaced. We should have undertaken the process of inside-selling the e-MATH program by the beginning of the second year.

Scholarship in the 21st Century University

The lessons learned from the e-MATH initiative are steps on the ladder to scholarship in the twenty-first century university. Many of them seem destined to be repeated as scholarly communities inch forward, pushed and pulled by the confluence of forces around them. Sooner or later, a critical mass of experience will surface, as common wisdom and current patterns of scholarly activity will be transformed.

No one can predict the future, but we feel confident in making two predictions for the *LONG TERM*:

— Scholarly publishing, and not just scholarship, will be based on a process that begins with knowledge creation, and which then advances through status changes that reflect preprint preparation, formal submission, selection, peer review, editorial processing, production, dissemination, and archiving; and not a collection of discrete events.
— Structured information, in retrievable, editable, manipulable format, delivered to the scholar's workstation, will supplant image representation as the authoritative version of choice, with image representation fulfilling the role of derived version of choice.

To achieve these outcomes, *ACCESS* and *REUSE OF INFORMATION* have to become strategic tools, not tactical maneuvers, for scholars, libraries, and publishers.

Access

Technology will make it possible for scholars remote to the author to share in many of the activities that lead up to scholarly publishing. Scholarly publishing will more closely imitate the scholarly process. Knowledge dissemination will move closer to the point of knowledge creation. Point of knowledge will be replaced by a knowledge union.

Scholarly resources will be document databases, available electronically, anywhere, anytime.

The effect of this will be to force information providers (e.g., publishers) to adapt existing mechanisms by which they add traditional components of value (e.g., selection, peer-review, editorial expertise, archiving), and to find new ways of adding value.

Reuse of Information

Digital libraries will be capable of storing vast amounts of information. However, they will need to be supported by an organizational framework that allows content to be intelligently located and quickly retrieved.

Organizational frameworks connect islands of information. Online card catalogues provide the required organizational framework when the unit of inquiry is the topic. Structured information will provide the framework required for retrieval of material of finer granularity. Digital libraries offer the promise of being able to effectively bridge artificial barriers that stand between the source of an idea and its application to any particular purpose.

Conclusions

Timing *DOES* count. It is important to be patient, to watch for deer, to read tea leaves, and to listen for oncoming trains. Being in the right place at the right time is important. It is important not to get too enamoured of the technology of the day. People don't appreciate what they can't see. Don't bet the farm on any particular outcome. It is just as important to move on at the right time as it is to get started at the right time.

The e-MATH system is positioned in a way that allows access and reuse of information to be strategic tools for building an electronic community for mathematicians. We believe that history will eventually judge this initiative to have been a good investment.

The Labyrinth

An Electronic Information Network for Medieval Studies

Deborah Everhart

In describing the process of contemporary critical analysis, J. Hillis Miller explains that the critic gets "so far or so much out of a little piece of language, context after context widening out from these few phrases to include as their necessary milieu all the family of Indo-European languages, all the literature and conceptual thought within these languages, and all the permutations of our social structures."[1] In this vision of the radical intertextuality of even the slightest phrase, Miller describes not only the project of theory, but also the current status of information technology. Data available to us electronically presents itself in a form extraordinarily different from that of the printed book; rather than following the strict linear order of lines on a page and pages in a book, electronic information communicates the intricate links between and within texts, the constantly shifting meanings of words and other bits of information as they appear in different contexts. Hypertext, the technological method whereby context after context can expand out from a single word, provides us with a new way of maneuvering and visualizing information, offering us an opportunity to rewrite not only our understanding of textuality, but also our concepts of authorship, pedagogy, and, ultimately, theory itself.

Global hypertext networks provide the technological basis for these changes, as more and more information becomes available through highly interconnected servers, creating a web of data access and transfer. Hypertext networks expanding around the world offer increasingly sophisticated means of organizing and using information, causing profound changes in academic scholarship. The Labyrinth, a global information network that organizes resources in medieval studies, has been developed to address these changes and to make use of emerging hypertext technology.

The recent, rapid development of electronic resources has outpaced the means of organizing and coordinating these resources. We find that development has followed no clear paths, and the sheer volume of information available on the Internet (and through private and commercial sources) is overwhelming. Consequently, academics

191

are experiencing not only the positive effects of these technological changes, but also the inevitable effects of any major transition: confusion, e-phobia, and a disconcerting division between those who have entered the world of electronic explorations and those who have not. Those of us who enter this world find a vast array of valuable projects constructed in different, sometimes conflicting formats. Many databases operate according to their own ad hoc systems of access, often without providing connections to other databases. Therefore, finding and utilizing electronic resources for medieval studies (as in most other fields) has required considerable telecommunication skills, and users have often been discouraged by the time and energy involved in acquiring these skills. Electronic resources scattered across the Internet are like books in an uncatalogued library, and therefore, they are not used to their greatest potential, because they are not easily found.

Disciplinary servers like the Labyrinth aim to alleviate some of these transitional difficulties by providing organized, easy-to-use interfaces for centralized access to resources in particular fields of study. The Labyrinth provides a useful starting point for research in medieval studies, allowing users to access a vast range of resources from one "home page." The Labyrinth's carefully organized menu structure and the transparency of its connections to remote databases and texts are key features for new and inexperienced users. The entire system is organized according to the way we as scholars think, and online search programs, configurable browsers, and other tools accommodate the different research strategies (and indeed the different thought patterns) of users. But even more, the Labyrinth facilitates new ways of using information, allowing teachers, scholars, and students to make connections relationally across many sources and to use this connected information right on their desktops.

World Wide Web Technology and Hypertext Capability

All of this is made possible by recent technological advances. We now have the technology to construct not only organizational structures for electronic resources, but also infinitely expandable webs of hypertext links among resources. The World Wide Web, one of the most sophisticated networking systems now available, is rapidly expanding on servers around the world. The World Wide Web was developed at the European Particle Physics Laboratory in Geneva, and this networking technology was designed to be a fast and easy way for the physics community to share information and work collaboratively. From this origin, it has quickly grown to include a full range of data from diverse disciplines. The goal of the World Wide Web is no less than the global organization of all information on the Internet, and its potential for continued expansion is extraordinary.

Web networking technology has many advantages that set it apart from other ways of organizing Internet resources. The most distinctive of these advantages, and the characteristic that potentially could have the most profound effect on academic scholarship, is the Web's hypertext capacity, its ability to link documents, databases, indices, and other forms of electronic media through keywords or tags. Hypertext links can provide connections within texts (for example, a reference to another section of the document can take the reader to that section), between texts (taking the reader to a relevant passage in another text), and even between different parts of the Web (taking the reader to another database or another relevant menu structure). These links can be both "hardwired" into the system, so that all users encounter the same choice of links in their exploration of the system, and user-constructed, so that users can create their own preferred sets of links stored on their own computers.

The networking capabilities and advantages of the Web have been gaining recognition in academic communities over the past several years. Researchers in many disciplines have already adapted the Web technology to their needs and have set up their own disciplinary servers. The Labyrinth is one of a growing number of World Wide Web disciplinary servers. Developed by Co-Directors Deborah Everhart and Martin Irvine at Georgetown University in Washington D.C., it provides free, organized access to electronic resources in medieval studies. Easy-to-use menus provide automatic connections to online databases, services, and electronic texts on other servers around the world. In addition, the Labyrinth includes a full range of new in-house resources: an electronic library, online forums, directories, an archive of pedagogical tools, and a reference center for conference news, job bulletins, professional society membership lists, and academic newsletters.

This project not only provides an organizational structure for medieval studies, but also serves as a potential model for similar, collaborative projects in other fields of study, thus opening up new possibilities for the academic communities of the twenty-first century. The Labyrinth is already intricately interconnected with existing disciplinary servers. Since there is no "top" to the Web, no hierarchy of primary and secondary servers, the beginning of the Web is wherever one chooses to enter. For medievalists, the Labyrinth's main menu is a logical starting point, but the Labyrinth's reciprocal connections with other disciplinary servers allow medievalists to branch out into other fields of study and allow researchers in other fields to find relevant medieval studies data. The Labyrinth, therefore, not only organizes and connects resources within the field of medieval studies, but also connects medievalists to the rest of the global Web community.

Accessing Electronic Resources through the Labyrinth

World Wide Web networking technology allows access to an unlimited selection of materials without necessitating that these materials be stored in one location. Consequently, the amount of data available through the Labyrinth can be expanded ad infinitum. An enormous amount of data is already freely available—though sometimes very difficult to find—on the Internet. The Labyrinth provides transparent connections to text and image archives, bibliographies, discussion list archives, library catalogues, and other Internet resources. These connections do not intrude upon the autonomy of existing projects. For example, we offer a connection to the Dartmouth Dante Database (DDD), a public-access database of Dante criticism. The Labyrinth's connection to the DDD does not interfere with the DDD's independent operations. The Dante files remain on their server at Dartmouth, and users are still able to access them directly rather than through the Labyrinth. One advantage of having the Dante project and others like it connected to the Labyrinth is that potential users do not need to know how to make their own connections to these remote databases; in fact, they need not know in advance that the databases exist. The Labyrinth, acting as a heuristic system, allows users to make new discoveries in previously unknown or inaccessible resources.

The Labyrinth not only facilitates connections to outside databases, but also coordinates a full range of in-house resources. One of the largest of these projects is the development of an online library of electronic texts. Our first series of texts will be adopted from the Oxford Text Archive (OTA), a repository for e-texts from around the world. We will be coordinating our efforts with others, to provide standardized markup and add to the Labyrinth library approximately one hundred OTA titles from Old English, Middle English, Old French, Old Norse, Old High German, and Latin, including a number of collections such as the Old French Corpus and the Old Norse Corpus.

The Co-Directors will ensure that electronic texts in the Labyrinth library include an electronic text file header that describes the bibliographic source of the text, the encoding used within it, and the revision history of the file (according to the precedent set by CETH, the Center for Electronic Texts in the Humanities, with reference to Text Encoding Initiative Guidelines and the Anglo-American Cataloguing Rules for computer files). The standardized format of file headers will allow for traditional "card catalogue" searches within the Labyrinth library. It will also provide users with an immediate summary of the size, structure, history of corrections, and encoding format of a particular file. This information will allow immediate verification of file status and thereby ensure the integrity of data.

Thanks to the efforts of those involved in the Text Encoding Initiative (TEI) (see the chapter by Susan Hockey in this volume), we now have a coherent system of Guidelines for the Encoding and Interchange of Machine-Readable Texts in the Humanities. Consistent application of the TEI Guidelines will produce a body of compatible electronic texts that will be immediately useful for scholarly research and teaching and easily transferable into new technological formats. The main advantages of TEI-compliant texts are: 1) all texts have a consistent encoding scheme that applies to all aspects of the texts; 2) the encoding is formally verifiable with SGML-aware software; 3) the encoding scheme has been designed by a community of potential users; and 4) the encoded texts are usable by any software system developed for e-texts now or in the future. This last point provides assurance that as better text-browsing and indexing software is developed for SGML texts, Labyrinth texts will be usable with this new software, and the Labyrinth library as a whole will be able to migrate into new technological platforms. Furthermore, by using the TEI Guidelines to mark up texts before including them in the Labyrinth, we hope to encourage the production and dissemination of TEI-compliant texts, thereby facilitating the development of reciprocal connections between the Labyrinth library and other electronic libraries.

As the Labyrinth grows and expands, we will provide access to an increasing number of digitized images, including digital images of manuscript illustrations and text, medieval art, architecture, maps, and objects from daily life and material culture. Researchers, technicians, and library conservators agree that using digital enhancement software on high resolution manuscript images will soon be an important component of manuscript analysis. The Labyrinth will stay at the forefront of these changes, providing access to images and links to texts pertaining to these images, thus utilizing not only hypertext but also hypermedia technology.

The Co-Directors will develop new in-house resources in response to the needs and interests of users. Our initial configuration includes a directory of medieval studies discussion lists, newsletters of professional associations, a job list, a conference news directory, works-in-progress forums, topical and perhaps temporary forums relating to joint projects (i.e., texts with multiple editors, or the organization of international conferences), bibliographies, and the tables of contents of professional hardcopy journals. All of these resources are interconnected with hypertext links, and they are also searchable.

Scholarly Discussion and Publication

The development of one component of the in-house resources began in the summer of 1993, when Deborah Everhart, Martin Irvine, Patrick Conner, and William Schipper founded Interscripta, a topical online forum. The opening discussion on Interscripta, the topic of which was the nature and purposes of this new venture, took place in June 1993, involving more than three hundred scholars (medievalists and also scholars from other fields who are interested in this forum and its possible application to other areas of study). Since then, Interscripta discussions have focused on a series of cutting edge topics, bringing together scholars from all over the world to address current issues in medieval studies.

Each six-week discussion on Interscripta focuses on a specific topic in a forum much like a round table discussion. Topics are proposed by scholars, then the advisory board of Interscripta reviews and chooses topics, schedules discussions, and oversees the general operations of the forum. Each topical discussion is moderated by an individual scholar, and at the close of the discussion, the moderator shapes the material into an article which is distributed to all participants for review and commentary before its final revision. Finished articles are then submitted to the online journal *Interscripta* for expeditious publication. Traditional print journals often have a two-year backlog of articles, and a scholar's work may take even three years from writing to publication; *Interscripta* publishes new, innovative work immediately. Our aim is to provide a forum for focusing electronic discussions into organized bodies of information representative of current work in our field. The collaborative nature of these discussions, and the range of possibilities for innovative publication of results, make *Interscripta* unlike anything available in print medium.

Pedagogical Resources

The Co-Directors of the Labyrinth are developing research forums like Interscripta hand-in-hand with pedagogical resources. The Labyrinth's text and image databases provide a strong foundation for our archives of student resources and pedagogical tools. Our archive of pedagogical tools makes a full range of teaching resources freely available, complete with hypertext links to the Labyrinth library and the rest of the Web. We offer sample syllabi and course outlines, study questions and writing assignments, e-anthologies, bibliographies, aids for learning medieval languages, even multimedia teaching platforms. The pedagogical archive of the Labyrinth is based on contributions from users, representing the widely differing strategies, agendas, and teaching tools of faculty from around the world. Through the Labyrinth, an instructor teaching Dante for the first time in a remote area far from a major university has access to the teaching experience and resources of specialists in the field, as well as the Dartmouth Dante Database, specialized discussion lists, and many other resources.

Cross-Disciplinary Exchange

All data developed as part of the Labyrinth is freely and publicly accessible on the Internet. Users can access this data by using any Web browser, either locally (on their own computers) or remotely (by telneting to the server at Georgetown and using a Web browser there). The URL (Uniform Resource Locator) for the Labyrinth main menu is

http://www.georgetown.edu/labyrinth/labyrinth-home.html

No passwords or access codes are required, and all information needed for navigating the system is integrated into the Web browser. Furthermore, anyone who wishes to use Labyrinth resources can access them not only through the Labyrinth main menu, but also through other databases and disciplinary servers. We are working closely with the developers of other projects, coordinating our efforts to ensure reciprocal connectivity. For example, users of the History Network can access medieval studies resources on the Labyrinth, and Labyrinth users can connect to the History Network to find more general history resources. The sharing of information through these mutual connections not only benefits the users of both networks, but also encourages collaborative and cross-disciplinary projects.

The Co-Directors will personally facilitate cross-disciplinary exchange by providing on-site demos, seminars, and consulting services at institutions that are considering the development of similar projects in other fields. Furthermore, documentation outlining the stages of development of a web server is available through the Labyrinth, as are how-to guidelines and the history of the Labyrinth. The Labyrinth is an open-ended project, and will grow and change with new developments in technology and in medieval studies. We welcome suggestions for expansion, and we encourage potential developers to contact the Co-Directors of the Labyrinth for further information by sending e-mail to labyrinth@ gusun.georgetown.edu. The sharing of such information will facilitate the coordination of disciplinary servers in the humanities, such that we may avoid duplicated efforts and incompatible systems. We hope that our experience in developing the Labyrinth will be of use to others as our profession navigates the transition from traditional forms of research and pedagogy to the technological possibilities of the coming decades.

The Changing Face of Scholarship and Academia

The Labyrinth provides an example of the networking possibilities afforded by Web technology. The Labyrinth's combination of in-house resources, organized connections to outside databases, and powerful indexing tools to search these resources provides teachers and scholars with a new world of data and ways to use it. This project and others like it have the potential to enhance research and pedagogy by making an enormous amount of data universally available, easy to access, and convenient to use. The practical implications of such uses of Internet technologies are manifold. The Internet is already fostering unprecedented communication, flooding the lines with mail from a rapidly growing number of discussion lists. The Internet democratizes the process of sharing ideas and information.

In the midst of this rapid expansion of online discussions, the organization of diverse resources in Web hypertext networks has the potential to revolutionize the ways in which we and our students gather information and conduct research. Web technology allows searches across databases and facilitates customized manipulation of data. Files residing on servers around the world thus become part of one's desktop resources. Fast, powerful indexing programs allow users to process massive amounts of data with a single command. These tools for sorting and analyzing data not only save time, but also allow users to perform searches and make connections that would not have been possible before. In fact, users can request searches that encompass databases they may not have known existed. The Web's interconnectedness encourages users to discover new resources and establish new relationships among sources of information. Hypertext links among texts and databases provide new ways of conceiving and representing information.

Speed is a central factor in these changes. In a world of information overload, the ability to maneuver and sort through massive amounts of data becomes more relevant than an attempt to digest and understand all of the current work in one's field. The sheer volume of information available, not only on the Internet but also in the recent explosion in print publications, necessitates a new methodology, or at least a deconstruction of traditional methodology. Scholars may no longer operate under the illusion that they have mastered all relevant information in their field; and once the expectation of mastery is deconstructed, we can adopt a new metaphor, that of the skillful navigator, the explorer, the user of sophisticated tools. The next generation of scholars will know how to navigate incredibly complex webs of knowledge and how to manipulate information in ways inconceivable with previous methodologies. Knowing how to gain access to desired information could replace the ideal of mastery of specialized knowledge.

The Web both metaphorically and practically deconstructs the illusion of the academic master and the authority of the author. Because the manipulation of information in the Web is user-centered, the new scholar does not follow the author's guidelines, does not read texts chronologically or entirely. The Web scholar makes decisions and maneuvers data in ways directly relevant to his or her own research and intentions, decentering the traditional concept of authorship by producing a new hypertext of connections among fragments of authors' works. As George Landow points out in his astute analysis of how hypertext reconfigures the author, hypertext "narrow[s] the phenomenological distance that separates individual documents from one another in the worlds of print and manuscript. In reducing the autonomy of the text, hypertext reduces the autonomy of the author."[2] And the concept of authorship is further decentered by group practices, as new forums like Interscripta facilitate collaborative writing and blur the distinctions of identity and intellectual property.

These changes reflect the nature of our postmodern world, a world of radical interconnectedness and rapid transitions. The technological innovations shaping the late twentieth century are currently changing not only the practical tools of our educational institutions, but also the organizational structures of the institutions themselves. Our research and pedagogical practices in the twenty-first century university will be inextricably linked to changes in technology, and our ability to adapt traditional educational practices to technological and ideological changes could largely determine the future of academics.

While the accelerated pace of change is intimidating, the vastness of new territories to explore is invigorating. Hypertext global networks, the Labyrinth among them, could reconstruct the twenty-first century university as a global web of universities with tremendous potential for international influence. As J. Hillis Miller points out, "one important aspect of these new technologies of expression and research is political. These technologies are inherently democratic and transnational. They will help create new and hitherto unimagined forms of democracy, political involvement, obligation, and power."[3] As we develop global hypertext communities, we will be shaping not only the future of academics, but also, potentially, the organization and intellectual activity of our highly interconnected world.

Notes

1. Miller, J. Hillis (1979). "The Critic as Host." *Deconstruction and Criticism*. Harold Bloom, Paul de Man, Jacques Derrida, Geoffrey Hartman, and J. Hillis Miller (Eds.). London: Routledge and Kegan Paul, p. 223.

2. Landow, George P. (1992). *Hypertext: The Convergence of Contemporary Critical Theory and Technology*. Baltimore: Johns Hopkins University Press, p. 71–72.

3. Miller, J. Hillis (1990). "Literary Theory, Telecommunications, and the Making of History." *Conference Papers from the International Conference on Scholarship and Technology in the Humanities*. Elvetham Hall, England, p. 20.

*Part IV*_____

USING COMPUTER NETWORKS FOR TEACHING AND LEARNING

Online Education
The Future

Linda Harasim

Human communication over distributed computer networks, developed in the early 1970s (Quarterman 1993), has within its short history contributed to launching a new environment for educational delivery and interaction: Online Education. Since the mid-1970s, e-mail and computer conferencing have been adopted by educators and adapted into educational environments that radically alter the relationship of the learner to the teacher and to the content of the curriculum. Traditional boundaries (geographic, temporal, and pedagogic) have been crossed in ways hitherto unimaginable, and the result is unprecedented new forms of intellectual and social interaction.

Computer networking and conferencing have found important practical application in education with such innovative developments as online delivery of courses, networked classrooms, and knowledge networks linking peers and experts. The benefits have been powerful and compelling, and have contributed to a paradigm shift in education. This shift is especially evident in higher education.

This chapter examines key dimensions of the online educational paradigm shift and explores the implications for the future of educational computer networking.

What is Online Education?

Educational applications of computer networking systems (electronic mail, bulletin boards, and computer conferencing systems), while a relatively recent phenomenon, are becoming a major area of growth, innovation, and change affecting all levels and modes of education. In less than two decades, educational opportunities and futures have been dramatically reconfigured with the advent of computer networking. Despite its educational impact, there is, as yet, no universally adopted term for this new field. Some of the terms which have been coined refer to specific applications of educational computer networking. Hiltz (1993) coined the term "virtual classroom" to refer to online delivery of post-secondary courses and the software specially designed to support this application; the "networked classroom" typically refers to place-based classrooms that employ computer conferencing or networking to link classrooms in different locations (Teles and Duxbury 1991, 1992). Related terms such as the virtual schoolhouse, campus, or university, similarly serve as metaphors, evoking online equivalencies to the familiar place-based entities.

The term "online education" is intended as generic, referring not to specific applications but to the field of educational computer networking, regardless of educational level, pedagogy, or design (Harasim 1990). For the purposes of this chapter, the term online education is used in this generic way.

Online education thus covers a variety of applications, from formal course activities to informal peer networking and interaction. (Harasim, Hiltz, Teles, and Turoff 1995). Here we will consider especially applications related to course activity. Currently, the predominant applications of computer networks are as curriculum enhancements: networks serve as a supplement or adjunct to regular instruction to complement regular classroom or distance education activities. This approach, adjunct mode, is also the most common in university and distance education networking activities. However, the totally online mode is also gaining popularity for delivery of courses and degree programs. In totally online mode, the network serves as the primary environment for all course-related interactions (class discussions, individual and group work, etc.).

Online education shares certain fundamental characteristics with the face-to-face educational environment: interactive group communication. However, the attributes of anytime, anyplace communication make group interaction and collaboration in online media distinctive. People can interact with one another in such formats as dyads, seminars, group projects, or role plays, take part in e-lectures, or contact the instructor, tutors, or subject experts all online. However, they are communicating with one another at different times and from different locations. Online education can also enable group communication over an increasingly wide selection of media (text, audio, video, graphics, animation, and virtual reality).The unique combination of place-independent, asynchronous interaction among groups of people linked by networks enables new educational approaches and sets of learning outcomes.

A New Paradigm

Computer networks are having a major impact on enhancing and transforming teaching and learning relationships, opportunities, and outcomes. Traditional educational structures are being dramatically altered by new communication and information technologies. Networking, the convergence and maturation of computing and telecommunications, has become a force for a new form of education, creating a paradigm shift: a change to a new model and set of expectations and rules for how to function successfully within a new learning environment. The following sections outline the themes or threads that are the key elements of online education that underlie the new educational paradigm.

Shifting the Focus from Knowledge Transmission to Knowledge Building

Until recently, theories of learning and cognition (both behavioral and cognitive information processing) have been characterized by a communication metaphor based on a transmission model (Cunningham, Duffy, and Knuth 1993). In this model, a body of knowledge external to the learner (such as information in a lecture or a textbook) is transmitted to the learner, and the responsibility for optimal transmission is on either the message, the message source, the transmission conduit, or the receiver. This communication metaphor reflects the broadcast model, in which one source transmits to many receivers. In education, learning approaches such as lectures and presentations, whether in face-to-face lecture halls, or transmitted by television or radio, are based on this model. The view of the learner is one of the passive recipient. The transmission metaphor is also echoed in the transportation metaphor. The concept of the "Information Super-Highway" may be viewed as an extension of this line of thought: information being transmitted along the networking conduit.

More recent theoretical developments have provided alternative views of the learning process, focusing more on knowledge constructing or knowledge building than on transmission. In this view, knowledge is actively constructed by learners interacting with one another to better understand the world in which they live. In this model, the view of the learner is one of active participation and engagement.

This model is also found among scientific research teams, illustrating the organization of work in knowledge-intensive industries and service organizations. The "knowledge-creating corporation" ceases to be a figure of speech and becomes a literal characterization of a wide range of organizations that flourish through the continual production of new intellectual property (Scardamalia and Bereiter 1993). There is a sound psychological basis for regarding learning as a constructive process not fundamentally different from the creation of new knowledge. There is potential for computer networks to support efforts to reform education so that it, too, takes on the dynamic character of a knowledge-creating organization. It can be forcefully argued that the successful societies in the next century will be those that find ways to convert educational institutions into knowledge-building institutions.

Designs for Maximizing Inclusion

There is growing evidence that asynchronous network communications tend to equalize participation, offering less opportunity to dominate and a greater opportunity for people who are reluctant to speak up in face-to face communication (Harasim 1993). The next four sections outline design characteristics inherent in network learning that contribute to increased participation and inclusion in online courses.

Expanded Educational Access.   Computer networking has enabled interactive education without borders. Students can link with other students or access experts or resources, regardless of where they are located. Learners in remote areas are no longer denied access to the kind of education that they want or need, simply because of their location. Nor are people who are housebound (whether due to age, physical ability, or family responsibilities) out of bounds for education. Networking also promises the augmentation of personal/professional networks into a global community. Expanded access empowers the learner and enriches her/his resource base. Online education is not only courses, credit, and curricula—but the opportunity to engage with others, to share and create knowledge together.

Restrictions of time are also dissolved by networks. Asynchronous interaction facilitates communication across time zones as well as increased control by the user over the time and pace of participation. Learners who require additional time to present their ideas are not interrupted by more assertive individuals; each user can access the system at the time of her/his choice; and each user can access the system as frequently and for as long as required. Learning online thus enables participants to engage at their best learning-readiness time, and also supports thoughtful consideration of the interaction—for messages received and sent.

Networks enable linkages between school and work. Experiments with professional development courses offered entirely online have demonstrated networking to be a tremendously powerful agent for enhancing educational effectiveness for all involved. Adults with full-time jobs who took courses online report that online courses helped to dissolve the dichotomy between theory and practice, a disjuncture so common to professional development courses and training programs

(Harasim and Smith 1994). There was an increased continuity between learning and professional life. Networks can help to make those connections, and learning becomes integrated into life.

Collaborative Learning and Teamwork. Networks are group communication environments that augment social connectivity. Learning online enables unprecedented forms of collaboration, based on shared interest rather than shared geography.

Networking enables learners to work together to support one another in problem-solving, information-sharing, knowledge-building, and social communication. Collaboration is among the most effective approaches to cognitive and social learning. Writing skills are improved through writing to real audiences; mathematics learning is enhanced through group approaches; scientific collaboration reflects real world practice. Working collaboratively introduces multiple perspectives on an issue or topic. Moreover, working together can be a lot more enjoyable than working alone.

The literature on peer collaboration indicates that as ideas are presented, there is a need to actively build linkages and associations and to organize the ideas. Interaction among peers is important to internalizing attitude change. Information is processed, weighed, reorganized, and structured in this process, both by each individual and also by the group. The online environment is an effective medium for collaborative learning and supporting a "collective intelligence."

Networking enables global collaborations, an essential preparation for life in the twenty-first century. The opportunity for cross-cultural global contact can help to build mutual respect, trust, and the ability to work together. Through online education, the interconnectivity among learners of the world can contribute to developing approaches for addressing today's problems: global, political, social, and environmental. Moreover, in addition to enhancing global understanding, global communication can enhance local understanding.

Active Participation. The network encourages, even requires, active rather than passive learning. Active participation is required because, in a text-based environment, it is necessary to make a comment in order to be "seen" as "present." Once an idea is articulated and presented to the group forum, it becomes part of an ongoing interaction in which it may be challenged or expanded on by peers in the process of knowledge building.

Online education is perhaps unique in the ability to support active learning by all participants, because the online classroom is open seven days a week, twenty-four hours a day. Air time is not limited and thus not as easily controlled by a few individuals. In the traditional classroom, even in cases where instructors favor active student interaction, class sizes of fifty or even fifteen students preclude input by some or most students. There is simply not enough time. Online education, based on asynchronous communication, offers unique opportunities for active participation. Students in online courses have access to the air time they want or need, enabling everyone to participate. Network environments such as educational computer conferencing do not entirely eliminate domination by a few more vocal participants. What is new and different is that conferencing ensures that dominance by a few does not exclude the ability of others to have their say.

The quality of participation can also be enhanced online. Asynchronicity provides each user time to formulate ideas and contribute responses. Students who characterize themselves as timid, passive, or unable to think quickly "on their feet" in face-to-face situations report that asynchronicity enabled them to participate more actively and effectively. Asynchronous communication provides participants the opportunity to comment immediately or to reflect and compose a response. Together with the opportunities for composing (and editing) a response in the text-based medium, asynchronicity can contribute to improving the quality of student interaction, enhancing opportunities for thoughtful and reflective participation.

Student-Centeredness/Fluid Roles. Today it is possible for anyone to become an information provider for others, thereby both democratizing information access and enabling new roles for network users. In the most successful online courses, students assume some of the roles that traditionally belong to the instructor. Individually or in groups, they develop expertise on a topic, and present their new knowledge to the rest of their learning community.

The text-based nature of networking also offers a social "equalizing" effect. Text-based communication lacks mechanisms for displaying or enforcing social differentiation by gender, or physical handicap, for example, which in other communication contexts interfere with group interaction. Online learners report that text-based interactions diminish the stereotyping associated with high external social status or physical appearance, thereby removing a significant barrier to equal participation (Harasim 1987).

Learning Networks as Online Learning Communities

Computer-mediated communication is capable of supporting socio-emotional communication as well as task-oriented communication; in fact, without personal, emotional communication, the group will not be nurtured (Rice and Love 1987; Hiltz and Johnson 1990). There should be places to "play" and socialize online, as well as places to work.

Those who are not experienced with online communication will need guidance about appropriate and inappropriate behavior, and there will need to be some "meta-discussions" about netiquette and possible misunderstandings. Personal socializing should be confined mainly to private messages and to conferences or spaces set up specifically for "extracurricular" activities. But it needs to encouraged, as a way for learners to build a supportive peer community online that ideally will extend beyond a single course, to create a kind of "cohort" that takes many courses together as part of a program.

Lifelong Learning. Online education offers a framework for lifelong learning. There is a tremendous need for ongoing educational opportunities. Life in the twenty-first century promises to be increasingly demanding in terms of the pace of technological changes, and need for relevant information and skills in group problem-solving to deal with global and local challenges of economic, political, social, professional, and environmental problems. Online educational activities will facilitate our access to the best resources when we need them. The online system may well be designed so as to support not only a variety of communication media but a range of instructional designs, ranging from online course delivery based on group learning approaches to various forms of "learning on demand," integrated into a learning model in which education and training occur in a variety of environments (school, home, workplace) throughout a person's life.

Finally, boundaries between academic disciplines will be challenged by the demands of life in the twenty-first century. New interdisciplinary, problem-solving approaches to the curriculum will become common, and online education will be both a catalyst and a response to that need.

Implications for the Future

Computer networks both require and enable new forms of teaching and learning. This fact creates the basis for changes in how education will be conceptualized and practiced. One of the basic requirements for education in the twenty-first century will be to prepare students for participation in a knowledge-based economy in which knowledge will be the single most critical resource for social and economic development. Students need new and different information resources, skills, roles, and relationships. The traditional model of the school as separate from society, and the concept of education as internal to the school, is being recognized as outdated, inappropriate, and incorrect. This shift extends as well to the model of the learner. The concept of education is changing from one based on individualism and competition (where collaboration and exchange among students is viewed as disruptive or cheating), to one in which teamwork and networking are valued—mirroring changes in society and the work force.

One of the ways to understand the importance of online education is to examine the changes it could bring about in educational practices and institutions. The members of this community who experience the changes most immediately are the instructors. The average instructor has a certain number of fixed hours during the week when he or she engages students in a classroom setting. For a college or university educator there may also be a set number of "office hours" during which the instructor is available to the students. Whatever this amount of time is, instructors know that there is a finite and predictable period of time during which they might be approached by students.

The learning network environment is available to the students and instructors on a 24-hour-a-day basis. As a result, the students expect regular and ongoing interaction with the instructor. In a college environment, for example, the turnaround time to respond to students can be reduced from a week to a day. For a public school teacher, this might go from a day to hours. While the student might feel good about this improved flow of communications, it is not clear that all instructors will welcome this change in the ability to regulate and control the interaction rate with students.

Networking technology not only affects the pattern of communication between the students and the instructor, it also expands opportunities for students to communicate among themselves. It allows the students to "collaborate" with one another as a part of the learning process. It enables students to work in small groups to exchange information on assignments and to collaborate on their lessons. In fact, one of the most effective forms of assignments is giving the students responsibility for providing some of the lesson material for the course. Individual students or small groups of students go out and explore topics that they deliver to the rest of the class. Will this be viewed by administrators as the instructor shirking his or her duties? Will students feel that this is more work than what is traditionally expected and resist or complain? In a classroom one can always be quiet, but in a learning network the student is forced into participation. How will this affect various types of learners? Will the student tolerate the added effort that equal and active participation implies? Finally, what will the accreditation institutions say about students doing some of the teaching?

There are thus many challenges confronting educational administrators. For example, team-teaching courses becomes very easy within the context of a learning network. How do we evaluate and compensate educators in a team-teaching environment? The same effect can be had by mixing courses, that is, two different courses can meet together in a learning network to explore the same topic area from different academic perspectives.

While the network learning process brings impressive benefits to those involved, there is an investment of effort and of learning to be made by students, educators, and administrators to both incorporate and master this approach to learning. It represents a significant change in current approaches and practices at all levels in the educational process.

It is no longer possible for the instructor to dominate the students by the commanding nature of his or her presence in a face-to-face environment. In the electronic environment, the instructor can only earn respect by exhibiting expertise and command of the subject matter. Students may show more of a tendency to challenge instructors in the electronic environment. If students are given the ability to enter anonymous or pen-name comments, this tendency can be even more pronounced. Instructors face a reduced ability to control the students online, as opposed to face-to-face.

On the other hand, students may not appreciate exposing their own performance to fellow students. It is one thing to expose cognitive shortcomings to an instructor, but quite another to expose them to fellow students. In a classroom one can always be quiet, but in a learning network the student is forced into participation. How will this affect various types of learners? Will the student tolerate the added effort that equal and active participation implies?

While the network learning process brings impressive benefits to those involved, there is an investment of effort and learning to be made by students, educators, and administrators to both incorporate and master this approach to learning. It represents a significant change in current approaches and practices at all levels in the educational process.

Network technologies provide the means whereby learners can interact with peers, resources, and experts to build knowledge and develop skills. Networks enable the teacher to become a facilitator, providing educational structures and guiding the learner in accessing the data and organizing the information into knowledge. Teachers need no longer serve as the font of information and knowledge. Networks also enable education to become inter-institutional, tremendously extending the access of the student and the teacher to information resources and expertise around the world, at the best facilities available.

Many aspects of online education are new, and have not been available in the traditional classroom. The opportunity for each member of a group to participate actively and frequently is not possible in the time-dependent, face-to-face classroom, nor is it always possible to reflect and compose a response to a discussion, or for students to work at their best learning readiness times. These new opportunities, which characterize network learning, promise improvements in cognition and social interaction. Moreover, as the technologies that support online education improve, the opportunities to further augment educational collaboration will increase. The nature of online education is still being shaped; nonetheless, the outlines of a new way of teaching and learning are already visible.

The use of networking technologies in education alters the relationship of the learner and the teacher to educational resources and processes. The online learner has more options and more control over the nature of interaction. Access is expanded across time, place, and subject. Online learners of the future will have access to formal and informal education of their choice, wherever they are located, whenever they are able to participate—early morning, during the day, or late at night. The online learner will be an active participant in the learning process, rather than a passive recipient. The online learner will learn from experts and peers wherever they are located; the learning process will not be limited to certain places or times, nor will learning be a phenomenon for certain age groups or professions. The curriculum will be more interdisciplinary and integrated, with links between theory and practice becoming common. Moreover, the concept of who is a teacher and who is a learner will become more fluid.

Conclusions

Networks are social spaces with the potential to be more egalitarian than other media for social interaction. The nature of networking technologies tends to democratize participation and enable increased interaction among learners and between learners and their facilitators/teachers. But the democratic potential of networks is not guaranteed. A tremendous investment in infrastructure will be required if this potential is to be realized. The information highways, in the form of fiber-optic or other backbones that can give free or reasonably priced connectivity to anyone, anywhere, need to be built. Equipment will need to be available to students, their families, and teachers. Online education requires that policies be established in relation to such issues as cost and access, so that it does become accessible to all who can benefit, regardless of their ability to pay, just as universal free public school education has been provided to all children.

Moreover, online education requires that cultural and organizational structures be developed to support collaboration, and that participants, especially teachers, be trained in how to design and implement online education approaches. These steps must be taken in order to realize the potential that networking systems provide.

Global changes at all levels of society and technology have both enabled and required new educational responses. Based on global interactivity, collaborative learning, and lifelong access to educational activities and resources, online education is part of an educational paradigm shift and provides an approach that emphasizes international connectivities and engenders new ways of working, studying, and problem-solving. Online education provides a model and approach to meet the challenges of the twenty-first century, enriching educational processes and resources beyond what has hitherto been possible.

References

Cunningham, D. J., Duffy, T. M., and R. A. Knuth. (1993). The textbook of the future. In C. McKnight, A. Dillon, and J. Richardson (Eds.), *Hypertext: A psychological perspective*. New York: Ellis Horwood.

Harasim, L. (1987). Teaching and learning online: Issues in designing computer-mediated graduate courses. *Canadian Journal of Educational Communications 16*(2):117–135.

Harasim, L. (Ed.) (1990). *Online education: Perspectives on a new environment*. New York: Praeger Publishers.

Harasim, L. (1993). Collaborating in cyberspace. *Interactive Learning Environments 3*(2):119–130.

Harasim, L., Hiltz, R., Teles, L., and Turoff, M. (1995). Learning networks: A field guide to teaching and learning online. Cambridge, Mass.: MIT Press.

Harasim, L. and Smith, D. E. (1994). Making connections, thinking change together: Women teachers and computer networks. In P. Bourne, P. Masters, M. Gonick, N. Amin, and L. Gribowski (Eds.), *Feminism and education: A Canadian view*, Vol ll. Toronto: Centre for Women's Studies in Education, OISE.

Hiltz, S. R. (1993). *The virtual classroom: A new option for teaming via computer networking*. Norwood, N.J.: Ablex.

Hiltz, S. R. and Johnson, K. (1990). User satisfaction with computer mediated communication systems, *Management Science 36*(6):739–764.

Quarterman, J. S. (1993). The global matrix of minds. In L. M. Harasim (Ed.), *Global networks: Computers and international communication.* Cambridge: MIT Press.

Rice, R. E. and Love, G. (1987). Electronic emotion: Socio emotional content in a computer-mediated communication network, *Communication Research* 14:85-108.

Scardamalia, M. and Bereiter, C. (1993). Technologies for knowledge-building and discourse. *Communications of the ACM* 36(5):37–41.

Teles, L. and Duxbury, N. (1991). *The networked classroom: An assessment of the Southern Interior Telecommunications Project (SITP) Report of Phase 1.* Burnaby, B.C.: Faculty of Education, Simon Fraser University.

Teles, L. and Duxbury, N. (1992). *The networked classroom: Creating an online environment for K-12 education.* Burnaby, B.C.: Faculty of Education, Simon Fraser University (ERIC ED348 988).

Hypermedia and Higher Education

J.L. Lemke

Why Hypermedia?

Hypertext and hypermedia (its logical extension when non-text, mainly visual, media are included) are not as revolutionary as they are sometimes made out to be. They embody powerful, traditional scholarly principles of cross-reference among diverse sources; what is revolutionary about them is the ease with which computers will allow us to put these principles into practice.

This simple quantitative change in ease of operation, however, can lead to profound changes in scholarly communication, interactions between teachers and students, the skills of authorship, and the very paradigm of learning itself. These are the matters I want to discuss in this essay. In particular, I want to consider some possible futures for scholarly hypermedia literacy and for educational practice. What are the skills and frames of reference that scholars and students of the future are likely to need in order to create and creatively use hypermedia works in the context of pervasive online access to information and to one another? How can education take advantage of information technologies to help students develop the skills of independent learning and problem-solving? If we choose to make use of the new technologies in these ways, what additional capabilities would we want them to provide?

The concept of hypertext was originated by Ted Nelson in the late 1960s as a vision of what computers could allow us to do with the written word (Nelson 1974). He realized that, so far as its computer implementation was concerned, a text was simply a form of data, and could be treated as a data structure, or database, as easily as it could be scrolled across a screen in the traditional way. It would be possible to "dip into" a large text at any point, using search algorithms to locate what we were looking for. And, for the computer, two texts in the same file, or in linked files, were essentially part of the same

*This article first appeared in substantially the form presented here in *IPCT, Interpersonal Communication and Technology: An Electronic Journal* [IPCT-L@GUVM.BITNET], April 1993.

database. Cross-reference between these texts could be seamless, with the reader or user seeing only a single, composite text. Nelson imagined all the libraries of the world as one integrated textual database, and each particular "text" as a hypertext: a selective guide to information that would actually be located in many other texts. (This vision has antecedents in Vannevar Bush's famous "Memex" concept, e.g., Bush 1945.)

The vision has not yet come to pass, but computer programs are now available (e.g., Hypercard and later developments such as Storyspace; e.g., Bolter, Joyce, and Smith 1990; Bolter 1991) in which it is possible to create linkages between particular points in one text, including the one you are currently writing or reading, and points (and the associated text) in several other works. There are also commercial software programs (authoring systems, e.g., Toolbook, Hypercard and Supercard, Macromind Director, Authorware Professional) that enable an author to design not simply a sequence of words that can be read as a user wishes, but a branching system of textual and non-textual elements, with both internal and external links, that a user can interact with, in effect creating a different instance-text each time the system is used.

The *technology* is revolutionary. Its *principles* have been the foundation of scholarship in our culture and many others almost forever. Scholarship weaves a fabric that ties together information from diverse sources. Scholarly works cite their sources and refer the reader either to specific portions of them, or to the whole. Scholarly readers, especially in technical disciplines, but frequently in the humanities and social sciences as well, do not invariably read a work from first word to last in exact linear order. We dip into works at various points, reading conclusions first, skipping back and forth between main text, footnotes, endnotes and references, figures, legends, and captions. We read often enough with more than one book open before us: the focal text, a key cited reference, a specialist dictionary or handbook, our own evolving manuscript. Books have been designed to be used as databases (reference works) for just as long (perhaps longer) as they have been written for sequential reading.

Why do books have indexes that make them infinitely more valuable to scholars? and why do tables of contents list not just the included topics and their order, but the page numbers where they can be found? Simply because it is just not true that these books were ever meant to be read only in the strict linear order in which the text appears on the pages.

The classic literary text, which builds its narrative, character development, and aesthetic effects on the assumption that the reader starts at the beginning and proceeds linearly and continuously, is not the paradigm of texts in general. There have always also been catalogues and archives, handbooks and dictionaries, reference compendia and concordances, edited volumes, bibliographies, anthologies, etc., which assumed readers would use them just as we now consult databases. Even literary texts have often experimented with encouraging (or requiring) nonlinear readings (cf. Landow and Delaney 1991; Landow 1992; Burnett 1993).

Scholarly texts in general, and technical and scientific works in particular, also rely heavily on non-text media: diagrams, tables, graphs, charts, maps, photographs, drawings, etc. Until costs of including such material in print began to grow prohibitive in very recent times, most scholarly works made rich use of visual and figural communication.

Hypermedia is the scholar's and the scientist's dream. It is instant intertextuality (cf. Lemke 1985; 1993a) without unnecessary efforts by author or reader; it is immediate inclusion of reference material in any medium, with the freedom for the reader to follow any thread as far (even beyond the author's pointing) as wished.

Of course this is going to be the medium of choice for scholarly communication, as soon as it becomes familiar and widely available. And since it will be preeminently a medium of *communication*, we will want it to be an "online" medium, that is, we will transmit and receive hypermedia works (and access the textual and non-textual databases they make use of) over wide-area networks, like the present Internet (cf. NAS 1989; Crowley 1991; Pierce 1991; Kahin 1992).

Libraries and computer centers will integrate their functions. There will be seamless connections of local-area networks and wide-area ones, so that we will as readily use this medium to share instructional materials with our students (as they will share their projects with us) as to share professional work with our colleagues. And this in turn will revolutionize the paradigm of education and learning itself, as I will argue below. (If this were a hypertext, you could "click" here and go directly to that argument.)

In the sections that follow, I want, first, to share with you two visions of higher education in the near future, when online hypermedia has become the normal working routine of faculty and students. Then, I want to discuss the implications for education and learning arrangements. And finally, I will turn to questions of what we need to learn, and what we need to design to get the most out of hypermedia technology in our work. All assuming that you read this text linearly.

Two Visions of Hypermedia in Higher Education

A student sits down at a workstation somewhere on campus, or dials in by modem from a terminal at home. She searches the network of databases on campus, and its links through NREN (National Research and Education Network) and the Internet to databases world-wide, for text information on poverty in Korean cities, for statistical data from independent sources, for video documentaries and still photographs. She explores an unfamiliar database on popular music traditions, and discovers folk songs of the urban poor, whose lyrics and harmonies become an organizing focus for her hypermedia report. Downloading the information she needs, the student calls up a hypermedia authoring program environment, selects video clips, photos, and music, cites textual and statistical material, placing it in the context of the immediacy of her subjects' lives, writes an analysis of the song lyrics and a critique of the bias of the video reporting in both its voice-over and its visual editing, synthesizes the information, cross-references it for the user by hypermedia tags (which also lead to source citations), provides several alternative pathways through the emerging work, and writes, using an auxiliary music synthesizer program, a new, hopeful final verse to one of the folk songs of poverty. She animates the title and visual map-guide to the hyperstructure of the work and logs the report into the university database.

She sends an e-mail message to her Media and Fine Arts instructor and asks if he will examine it and evaluate its effectiveness and aesthetics. She also notifies her Urban Issues instructor that Version 1 of her report is ready for evaluation. When Version 3 is later released for wider access, several other students and faculty members incorporate portions of it into ongoing works of their own. A copy is logged into a public database, and, in the next two years, is accessed by 117 people worldwide.

A faculty member is doing research on vorticity in superfluids. She engages a session-logging program to record her work as she searches a remote database on the Internet for the report of a colleague's research, recently logged in an index she often uses. The report contains a video of the apparatus and the real-time computer graphic representation of the pattern of fluid flow during a critical experiment. Noting a significant innovation in the time-lag between two phases of the experiment, she activates a 3D graphics simulation program for her own apparatus and introduces the modification. No significant new result appears. She then activates the link to her lab, splits the screen to see real-time video and the computer representation of actual new data simultaneously, and directs the robotic control systems to begin a new experimental run with the time-lag innovation. Amazingly, she sees the same result as in the colleague's report, runs a detailed comparison of his video and computer results with her own, verifies the replication of results, and programs a series of variations to be run as further actual experiments during the night.

She then studies the simulation program to see why it could not predict this new phenomenon, and writes out several possible changes to it. Which one will be incorporated will depend on the results of the night's experiments. Three weeks later, she logs a hypermedia report of this new work into the special Internet interest group on superfluids, and uses the session log of that first night to prepare a separate hypermedia teaching module which will take students at various levels of sophistication, from undergraduates with an interest in the processes of scientific work, to her own new graduate students, along pathways that will enable them to see, almost through her own eyes, what she did and how she did it, with commentary added later. A copy of this is also logged to a database on scientific activities, where it is later used by a sociologist of science to make a point in a presentation about the effects of immediate vs. delayed posting of results on patterns of scientific collaboration.

A Distributed Model of Academic Communication and Instruction

There are, at present, two rather different and somewhat conflicting models for academic communication. On the one hand, we like to think of ourselves as a multitude of true communities, holding continuing and evolving conversations through publications, conferences, and private exchanges. Scholarly communication conforms to a "distributed" model of communication: many voices are speaking and contributing to the conversation, it is essentially "dialogical."

Within this model, each contribution is seen, however, as a monologue (a book, a paper, a letter, a statement), but a monologue that is still implicitly dialogical (citing sources, replying to critics, anticipating objections, contrasting theories, etc.), because the community we are addressing and the community we are making reference to are, ultimately, the same community.

All this begins to disappear when it is not our peers that we are addressing, but our students or a wider public. They are not fully participants in the conversation. Indeed, there no longer is a true conversation in the best sense. We pass over into a second, "centralized" model of communication: one voice speaking, perhaps with a multiplicity of messages, but in each class there is only one teacher, in each lecture hall only one speaker. Perhaps it would be healthy to have two or three instructors simultaneously presenting to create a more authentic conversational space in the classroom, but the present economics of higher education forbid it. Students can turn to the text-book, or the reading list, or the library, for other points of view, but they cannot truly dialogue with them as they can with a teacher. They can and do frequently turn to each other, which has advantages and disadvantages.

The distributed model, which is, I think, the preferred model for all of us, has now been extended into the realm of electronic, computer-mediated communication. Nearly every academic discipline has several online electronic discussion conferences and at least one online electronic journal. People, or groups, can publish their work simply by placing it at a computer site (host) where other people's search programs (e.g. Gopher, Archie, Veronica, see Krol 1991; Kehoe 1993) can find it by key words or author names. The distributed model is coming into its glory these days, with truly international communi-ties of scholars in almost constant, and very nearly instant, com-munication. It can, in fact, be a little overwhelming until we begin to filter and select just those issues and subgroups in which we wish to participate at a particular time.

Graduate students, and even some undergraduates, have begun to join these conversations, mostly as auditors. There are special groups just for them, and some where they can dialogue with more experi-enced scholars. In some universities, instructors have set up electronic conference groups for their classes, to promote cooperation and ex-change outside class time, among the students and with the instructor. It has happened, as well, that instructors have pooled their talents to be available online to larger groups of students, and perhaps some have been so farsighted as to invite, say, a reference librarian or other useful specialists to join the online group (see Schriber and Graziadei this volume for some examples).

These local groups can operate over local area networks of per-sonal computers and workstations, or through the campus mainframe computer, with modem telephone line connections to home, dorm, and office. The international groups operate through mainframe links to wide area networks, regional (e.g., NYSERNET in New York State), national (NSFNet, ARPAnet, the future NREN), and global (Bitnet, or the loosely organized global network of networks known as the Internet).

All students should have access, at least, to local area network (LAN)-based discussion groups that include participation by not only specifically assigned course instructors but larger pools of faculty members, reference librarians, and other specialists. In time, universities should seek to include off-campus specialists in these conference groups as well. This would go a long way toward making the distributed model of scholarly communication equally the model for academic instruction and student learning.

Far from increasing everybody's burden of work, this model literally distributes the burden more efficiently. If you have participated in electronic conference groups, you will know that it is easy to get a question answered. The person who answers has not had to spend time finding the answer; in most cases they already had it at hand and needed only to transmit it. In addition, one person's question is often many people's question, and the single public answer serves for all. Indeed, you will often get more than one answer, from more than one point of view (some of which pass on simple misinformation), and sometimes the differences will lead to discussion. This is intellectual community in a way that today's classrooms, however wonderfully they try to mimic real intellectual communities, simply cannot compare to.

Those departments and universities that offer this mode of instruction will have a strong and well-deserved competitive advantage. They will also be able to extend it into their continuing education or distance education divisions, to establish electronic universities, to make alliances to pool resources (library resources, faculty resources) with other universities and indeed with other sorts of institutions, all online, or, as it is more fashionable to say today, in cyberspace.

Independent Learning as a Paradigm for Higher Education

The earlier technologies and economics of higher education led us not only toward a less distributed, more centralized model of instructional communication—they also led us to accept a curricular paradigm, rather than to model education on our own scholarly practice. Scholars learn by seeking out, or creating, whatever knowledge seems relevant to answering questions or pursuing intellectual agendas of their own making. We produce public reports of our work, and they are judged by whether or not they are eventually useful to other scholars, or are lost and forgotten. If we seek out a colleague, or read the work of a specialist, it is to answer our own questions. We learn what we choose to learn and we are judged by our choices, by the value, in the opinion of our community, of what we have learned.

Scholars are not alone in practicing this form of learning, which I will call "independent learning," though of course we learn very much as members of communities. Anyone who visits a museum, explores a library, or peruses a reference text, does the same. And so do all travelers, all thoughtful men and women, who explore life and take from it what they will, which we may then judge as valuable to us or not.

But higher education, and most pre-collegiate education as well, is not at all based on this paradigm. In fact, except for rare cases of "independent study courses" or "research experience" courses, it is almost totally excluded from undergraduate education (and in very few of those exceptions are students truly encouraged to formulate and answer their own questions). Is it so surprising, then, that students come to their first genuine research experience, well into graduate study if not only when they must formulate a dissertation proposal, almost totally unprepared by experience for independent learning and genuine scholarship? Or that they go to non-academic institutions desperate for "independent problem-solvers," with no preparation for what they are expected to be able to do? What sort of apprenticeship in scholarly learning and research have we really given them?

What we have given them is a "curricular" education, which conforms to a totally different paradigm of learning. The questions, problems, issues, and goals are all set long before the students enter the room, and without regard for their personal agendas, interests, experiences. The final examination could usually be written before the course commences. Students are evaluated on the basis of how well they have learned the prescribed curriculum. Nothing could be less like an apprenticeship in scholarly inquiry. The students are not inquiring, they are obeying.

The closest that we come today in higher education to the independent learning model is in allowing students wide latitude to select topics for their papers, and training them to do at least library research on their topic. These papers, however, are not judged by a community for their real usefulness. They are judged by single individuals according to how closely they imitate authentic scholarship.

We do not need to continue to make these compromises with our principles as scholars and researchers. We can create genuine communities, linking teachers, scholars, specialists, and students at particular levels of sophistication. We can help students learn how to explore subject areas, select worthwhile topics, identify and analyze useful sources, synthesize them to create new meanings, and discuss them with others.

Of course, we will continue to guide students by showing them overviews of fields, introducing them to new concepts, demonstrating and practicing methods and techniques with them, modeling for them more sophisticated scholarly and research practices. But we can at least do this within a context where students' goals are to produce valuable work about topics of their own choice, and, hopefully, with criteria of evaluation of the results that are specific to the work produced, rather than to pre-fabricated, all-purpose, universal curricula.

In the visions above, I have tried to show, partly by suggestion, how this process might work, and I hope that they will repay close rereading at this point. We are *not* producing critical, independent scholars, researchers, and problem-solvers today in anything like the numbers our disciplines and our society need. I believe that this is as much because we are not preaching what we practice, not teaching students to do what we do (but only trying to teach them to know what we know), not being true to the meaning of scholarship itself, as for any other reason.

The new technologies of higher education will give us another chance. To use them well, we need to understand the fundamental skills they require of a sophisticated user. These are not, I believe, mainly technical skills. Rather, they are the direct transposition into a new domain of the familiar principles of scholarship and research.

Fundamental Skills for Hypermedia Literacy

We are speaking here of hypermedia literacy in higher education. I have already tried to sketch out, both in the two visions and in my discussion of distributed models for scholarly and instructional communication and independent learning paradigms in higher education, a picture of what we can do with hypermedia and online communication systems. But what specifically, in this new context, do we all, teachers and students alike, have to know how to do in order to use hypermedia in these ways?

I would like to propose a list of fundmental skills for the new hypermedia literacy. Each of them is an extension into a new context of traditional skills of scholarship and research.

Database Exploration

How do we know what's out there? How do we build up a map of the world of knowledge, of information? This is partly a matter of disciplinary traditions (subfields, key questions), partly a problem of representation (see Design below), and mostly a matter of strategies of *exploration*.

We have largely neglected teaching the skills of exploration, because curricular models of education do not require them. But for students to be independent learners, and for ourselves as researchers, we know that it is very important to be able to survey a new area of study and develop a sense of what it contains, what it is likely to contain, how it is organized, and in what ways it might be relevant to our own research concerns. This is especially important before selecting a specialization, when changing fields, or when doing multidisciplinary research. It will be a critical skill in the future, especially outside the academy, where many of our students will frequently be expected to change from one area of work to another and quickly "catch up" with its problems and issues.

How do you find out what collections a library contains? How do you find out what organizing questions have determined the structure of specializations in a field? How can you explore a large electronic, online database, such as for example, the MEDLARS national database of medical information, to find out what kinds of information it contains? Or to construct for yourself a research problem that can be answered by using it? This is not different in principle from a scholar's arriving in a new city and beginning to explore a specialist library collection or archive to see if it contains interesting material for new potential research projects.

Information Search and Retrieval

It is one thing to find out what information exists. It is another to locate and retrieve a specific, identified, bit of information. In between are the general problems of the reference librarian, more or less focused inquiries, starting from questions or problems and in search of relevant information, but not yet seeking a specific work or fact.

Where can I find information on . . . ? Where can I find information of this type (pictures, maps, musical scores, statistics, pamphlets) on . . . ? What information is available on . . . ? How can I actually get hold of this source?

Very soon, all the libraries of the world will be one virtual library, all the databases on every subject will be available through a common interface, and they will contain not just numbers and texts, but every visual and auditory form of information and, someday perhaps, tactile ones as well (see "Design and Development for the Future" below). And not just maps and photographs, but films and videos of every phenomenon and human activity known as well as imagined. Reference librarians will be critical specialists in the global informational era, and all of us will have to learn to be amateur reference librarians to a much greater extent than we already are. Even when expert systems begin to automate some of these functions, we will still have to know how they work and what to ask them to do for us. For further discussion see, for example DiMattia (1991), Peters (1992), Saunders (1992).

Authoring Skills

Academics in some fields have become overly dependent on communicating through verbal text alone. The costs of reproducing diagrams, much less plates, much less color, and the impossibility of incorporating video or animation, sound effects, and other media in printed books and journal articles have led some of us to forget how important visual media were in academic writing in the past, and perhaps to neglect the fact that in all the technical, scientific, and most social science disciplines, the uses of diagrams, tables, graphs, charts, and even photographic stills is common and necessary.

Word processing and desktop publishing systems have raised our awareness of the role of fonts, typefaces, type size, and page layout even for verbal text. Verbal text is itself a visual as well as a linguistic medium, which is why we can readily combine it with other visual media. Computer displays will allow us to add color effects to text itself, and even to animate the text, to have it change before the viewer's eyes.

"Authoring" is coming to be the term for multimedia (and in practice, hypermedia) writing. It does not simply mean writing in the sense of composing verbal text. It includes the skills of skillfully juxtaposing verbal text with other visual media of various kinds in order to create more meaning through the implied and explicit relations of these elements than the elements would have in isolation. Each element contextualizes the others, and the result, potentially, is a multiplication of meaning, and not merely a redundant repetition in an alternative form (cf. Lemke 1993b, 1993c, and below).

Authoring is thus something like graphic arts design, and also something like motion picture production. Imagine being able to incorporate documentary footage in a paper, or a rotating three-dimensional diagram of relationships. It is also a great deal like traditional scholarly writing: making links between one's own text and the texts (and other media) of others. This can be done in such a way (in principle) that the reader/user of your hypermedia creation would have automatic access to the original sources you cite, so that he or she could read as much of the original context as desired, or consult more than simply the data or image you had cited. Your bibliography, in fact your in-text citations, would be gateways to the original sources in their entirety. This last technology is not quite yet available to us, except in experimental form, but the stand-alone productions of hypermedia authoring systems, which carry their textual and multimedia references internally (like quotations, rather than citations), are a pretty good interim substitute.

Authoring also exploits the nonlinear potential of all text. An author-designer of a hypermedia work (and these can be as simple as a student term-paper or as complex as a CD-ROM encyclopedia) must address the question of how the user will interact with the work. You can offer a simple linear sequence with each subsequent presentation activated by "moving on" (turning the page, pressing a key) from the previous one. The user can then skip around by exploring, searching, jumping. You can offer a menu, like an automated table of contents or index, to allow user-guided browsing. You can create a more complex internal architecture for the work, in which you design links, which may be activated or not at the user's option, that tie various portions of the work together in different possible sequences. A treatise on the history of surgical instruments, for example, might show a plate from an early text, and allow the user to "click" on drawings of instruments shown in the plate to move to text about that instrument, or to an animated sequence, partly under user control, that would show the historical sequence of development of instruments of that type, from the one pictured through time to its modern successor. Perhaps one could interrupt the sequence and click on an intermediate form to obtain the date, source, etc. for that exemplar.

User Skills

If authoring is an extended form of writing, then user skills are those of reading hypermedia. Since hypermedia are generally meant to be read within a program environment that is essentially the same as the authoring environment, reading becomes (as for scholars it has always been) a sort of virtual writing (cf. Lemke 1989). We will be able to annotate, customize, and even add to or modify our copy of the work as we please (while always also retaining it in its original form, and many intermediate forms in the history of our interaction with it).

Students will certainly need much more help from us in understanding how to read non-text media and how to interpret text and other media each in the context of the other. They will need to learn strategies for "navigating" in large works (perhaps with the aid of visual maps of the works' content domains and types and their major built-in internal links).

Well-designed hypermedia works will invite users to interact with them, to select individual pathways through their internal architectures, to wander the byways of the work as database, as well as to follow it in its main arguments. We can think of a hypermedia work as a system that, in interaction with the user, presents a different instance-text (or presentation sequence) on each occasion, for each user, with only accidental repetitions. In some ways, it will be the same work for all, in others, a different work for all. Exactly as all texts have always been.

Design and Development for the Future

This picture of what can, and what, I believe, ought to be done with online hypermedia capabilities in higher education provides a context for thinking about further development of the medium.

I have already assumed the first big technological step: that we will very soon be able to transmit and receive multimedia files over the wide-area networks of the Internet, just as we can now do over local-area networks. This will begin with the capability of transmitting graphics along with text, and accessing image databases as easily as textual and numerical ones (see Austin in this volume). This is already possible to some degree, but lack of standardization still stands in the way of its becoming an integral part of normal communication in our new electronic communities.

We have already noted that true hypertext and hypermedia systems should function as interfaces that provide automatic online access to source texts and media cited within them, not merely containing quotations from these, but allowing us to call up the complete source works. (Or access the source databases online. This is not a particularly difficult technological problem, but it does require us to think of all works as parts of a larger web, each connected with many others. We do this already, but only in a very abstract way. It can now be literally true for all readers and writers.)

We have also considered the need to design hypermedia works that invite the reader/user to interact with them and construct, on each occasion of use, an individual trajectory through the resources the work contains (or acts as a gateway to). This principle can be taken further. The hypermedia work could actually generate verbal text and visual elements in response to reader input, rather than simply displaying or accessing pre-existing text and visual elements. In effect the work would mediate between a database and a user, fashioning user-specific versions of itself on demand. This is not far from the notion of an AI Tutor, an expert system that analyzes user input, including questions, searches for appropriate data, and fashions from that data a coherent answer.

Such systems might be called *meta-media* programs, since they would really consist of algorithms for generating hypermedia works. They could range in function from those that merely slightly personalize the text based on user answers to system queries (How old are you? Have you read Freud's *Interpretation of Dreams*? Can you read German?), to those that build complex models of individual users at various times, keep track of the history of the user's interaction with the system, analyze the content and context of user questions, and generate text and images *de novo*.

Natural language text-generation is a major effort of present research in artificial intelligence, as is the "parsing" or syntactic and semantic analysis of user input. But already, researchers have begun to design model systems that can adjust the output to various characteristics of individual readers/users (cf. Hovy's 1987 PAULINE system). It may turn out to be easier to do this in the context of a particular specialized field than to do it in a universal, content-independent way. Any shortcuts that give us practical capabilities sooner than general solutions should find an eager market in education (and many other fields).

A related need is for better searching tools. The bigger and more diverse the information world becomes, the harder it is going to be to find what we want in it, even with a good reference librarian and a subject specialist online. At present we search by key words (controlled vocabulary and synonym tables, author names, etc.) and by simple logical combinations of these (Boolean searches, such as: FREUD and HERMENEUTICS but-not RICOEUR after 1970). In time, we will need to be able to search by *semantic patterns*, such as: X example-of Y influenced-by Z, or X cause-of Y, which will give much more specific results than generic searches for X-and-Y-and-Z.

It is not just better ways to navigate in verbal text space that we will need. We will also need ways to search for, and/or label and characterize, visual images. Suppose we remember seeing a graph that had an inverted-U shape to it, but not what variables it related. We should be able to search on the element type (2D GRAPH) and on some basic characterization of the visual image itself.

Above all, we need to better understand just how, in various genres, we do in fact already conventionally combine verbal text with, particularly, visual media elements to create complex meanings for readers that depend on the elements' relationships to one another. And then go on to explore the new ways in which we can multiply verbal and visual meanings by one another to expand the intellectual and communicative power of hypermedia.

In the further future lies the promise of VR, virtual reality technologies, the true gateway to "cyberspace." With this interface to computational systems for storing and manipulating data, we will be able to build worlds (abstract or realistic, direct representations of first-order reality or works of the imagination), enter them, touch and manipulate their objects, and work magic at will on the fabric of their virtual reality (see, for example, Rheingold 1991; Benedikt 1991). Because many such worlds will be shared online, and because in such worlds we can create virtual libraries and virtual classrooms in endless variety and at almost no marginal cost, they will constitute a cyberspace, a parallel, multiplex reality that will embed ordinary reality intellectually as surely as the reverse will be true physically and materially. These possibilities will loom large in the future of higher education (e.g., Lemke 1992), and perhaps the future of what it means to be fully human.

Conclusion?

Monologically, and in traditional genres, texts follow a linear path and, being finite, come to an end, where a little ritual is performed to commemorate the occasion (a summary, a peroration). Dialogically, and in a hypertext or hypermedia genre, there is no linearity, no definitive end. A summary may be available, and we can consult it whenever we wish, exactly as any sophisticated reader does even with a printed text. (The peroration, on the other hand, seems rather to lose its ceremonial function.)

Dialogically, every text is a moment in a larger conversation, and with even the simple technology of the present Internet, this article (originally distributed through an electronic journal) was (and is) meant to elicit response: queries, further development, diverging arguments, disagreement. The subject of this paper is not a well-defined phenomenon yet; it is an emerging one. It will be, in part, what we make it. I mean this article as a contribution to how we envision information technology's future role in our lives as teachers, scholars, and researchers. I invite you to join me in this very practical work of the imagination.

References

Benedikt, M. (1991). *Cyberspace: First steps.* Cambridge: MIT Press.

Bolter, J. D., Joyce, M., and Smith, J. B. (1990). *Storyspace: Hypertext writing environment for the Macintosh.* [Computer Software]. Cambridge: Eastgate Systems.

Bolter, J. D. (1991). *Writing space: The computer, hypertext, and the history of writing.* Hillsdale, N.J.: Lawrence Erlbaum.

Burnett, K. (1993). Toward a theory of hypertextual design. *Postmodern Culture* 3(2).

Bush, V. (1945). As we may think. *Atlantic Monthly* 176(1):101–108.

Crowley, T., (1991). Scholarly communication: A case study in the use of BITNET. In G. Mckye and D. Trueman (Eds.), *The Twelfth Educational Computing Organization of Ontario Conference and the Eighth International Conference on Technology and Education, Proceedings,* (491–493). Toronto: ECOO.

DiMattia, E. A., Jr. (1991). New technologies and the library: A remote access perspective. *Microcomputers for Information Management* 8(1):45–51.

Hovy, E.H. (1987). Generating natural language under pragmatic constraints. *Journal of Pragmatics* 11(6):689–719.

Kahin, B. (1992). Scholarly communication in the network environment: Issues of principle, policy and practice. *The Electronic Library* 10(5):275–285.

Kehoe, B. (1993). *Zen and the art of the Internet: A beginner's guide.* 2nd ed. Englewood Cliffs, N.J.: Prentice-Hall.

Krol, E. (1992). *The whole Internet user's guide and catalog.* Sebastopol, Cal.: O'Reilly and Associates.

Landow, G. P. (1992). *Hypertext: The convergence of contemporary literary theory and technology.* Baltimore and London: Johns Hopkins.

Landow, G. P. and Delany, P. (Eds.) (1991). *Hypermedia and literary studies.* Cambridge: MIT Press.

Lemke, J. L. (1985). Ideology, intertextuality, and the notion of register. In J.D. Benson and W.S. Greaves (Eds.), *Systemic perspectives on discourse* (275–294). Norwood, N.J.: Ablex Publishing.

Lemke, J. L. (1989). Social semiotics: A new model for literacy education. In D. Bloome (Ed.), *Classrooms and literacy* (289–309). Norwood, N.J.: Ablex Publishing.

Lemke, J. L. (1992). Education, cyberspace, and change. Electronic paper for the Information Technology and Education Electronic Salon, ITED-L@DEAKIN.OZ.AU; published in EJVC: *Electronic Journal on Virtual Culture,* EJVC-L@KENTVM.KENT.EDU, March 1993.

Lemke, J. L. (1993a). Intertextuality and educational research. *Linguistics and Education,* 4(3–4):257–268.

Lemke, J. L. (1993b, July). *Making meaning with language and other semiotic systems.* Paper presented at International Congress of Systemic and Functional Linguistics, Victoria B.C., Canada.

Lemke, J. L. (1993c, December). *Multiplying meaning: literacy in a multimedia world*. Paper presented at the National Reading Conference, Charleston S.C.

National Academy of Sciences. (1989). *Information technology and the conduct of research*. Washington, D.C.: National Academy Press.

Nelson, T. H. (1974). *Dream machines/Computer lib*. Chicago: Nelson/Hugo's Book Service. [republished 1987, Redmond, Wash.: Tempus].

Peters, P. E. (1992). Networked information resources and services: Next steps on the road of the distributed digital libraries of the twenty-first century. In B. Sutton and C. H. Davis (Eds.), *Networks, open access, and virtual libraries: Implications for the research library*. Urbana, Ill.: Graduate School of Library and Information Science, University of Illinois at Urbana-Champaign.

Pierce, J.W., (1991). Computer networking for educational researchers on BITNET. *Educational Researcher* 20(1):21–23.

Rheingold, H. (1991). *Virtual reality*. New York: Simon and Schuster.

Saunders, L. M. (1992). The virtual library revisited. *Computers in Libraries* 12(10):51–54.

Equal Access to Computer Networks for Students and Scholars with Disabilities

Sheryl E. Burgstahler

> The computer is one of the most liberating and empowering technologies to come along in a long time for people with a variety of handicaps.
>
> —N. Coombs, a blind professor who teaches deaf students

A growing number of individuals with disabilities are attending institutions of higher education and pursuing scholarly interests ("Facts You Can Use," 1993). As academic programs become increasingly information-rich, access to computers and networks has become essential to assure equal opportunities. Federal non-discrimination laws (e.g., Section 504 of the Rehabilitation Act of 1973, the Americans with Disabilities Act of 1990) are generally interpreted to mean that educational institutions must provide computer and network access to students and faculty with disabilities whenever it is required to pursue academic studies. In order to meet this requirement, individuals with disabilities must be given access to special adaptive technology. Many adaptive devices are commercially available. Once appropriate adaptive technology is provided on computer systems connected to campus and international networks, students and scholars with disabilities can independently participate in academic collaborations and use online library catalogs, books, journals, dictionaries, encyclopedias, newspapers, and other information resources (Coombs 1991; Eastman and Green 1992; Taylor 1991). Only then can they be fully included in the practice of academic scholarship in the information age, where use of global networks for collaboration and information access is critical.

Network Applications

Applications for which the network can be used as a tool for students and scholars with disabilities include information access, distance learning, and communication.

Information Access

Networks provide new options for accessing information. There has been an explosion of electronic versions of books, periodicals, library catalogs, encyclopedias, dictionaries, newspapers, and other resources that are being made available over international networks. Some suggest that traditional libraries will someday become largely electronic libraries, in which printed materials are available through computers connected to international networks. One project alone, Project Gutenberg, aims to distribute one trillion electronic copies from a collection of 10,000 books through computer networks by 2001.

Online information sources provide opportunities to independently read journals, newspapers, and books on a computer screen for those with disabilities that make it difficult to turn pages of publications. Voice, braille, and large-print output technology allow students and scholars with visual impairments to access online resources. Some people with learning disabilities that affect their reading abilities can benefit from the use of voice output systems that read text as it is presented on the screen. With these tools, individuals with disabilities can access resources that were not specifically developed for them, thereby increasing the quantity of information that is accessible to them. For example, in the past, individuals who were blind had independent access to only those materials produced in braille or recorded using cumbersome, time-consuming processes undertaken by the government, not-for-profit organizations, schools for the blind, and volunteers. For other materials, they relied on human readers. These services provided access to only a small fraction of the material available to readers of publications in standard print. When network access and adaptive technology is made available to those who are blind, they can use materials that have not been specifically created for them. Access to voice output systems and electronic news feeds, for example, allow individuals who are blind to "read" the newspaper each day without the help of other human beings.

Distance Learning

Some colleges and universities are beginning to offer distance learning programs where electronic networks are used to reduce constraints that once limited education to those individuals and resources that could be in the same place at the same time. Students with disabilities who have adaptive technology can benefit from the growth of distance learning programs where students and educators "meet" electronically for instruction and discussion. This educational option challenges the campus-bound model for education and allows full participation of students with disabilities who are not able to come to campus. It also provides flexible teaching options for many faculty members, including those who have disabilities.

Communication

Telecommunication is a powerful communication tool for individuals with disabilities. Individuals who are deaf were once limited to communicating electronically with only those who owned a special TDD communication device for the deaf. Today, those with hearing impairments who have personal computers, modems, appropriate software, and network access can communicate with anyone else who has access to the network. When computer-mediated communications are used to supplement or replace classroom discussions, they allow students and faculty who are deaf or who have speech impairments to communicate on an equal level with hearing and speaking participants. For those with disabilities that tend to limit in-person contacts, electronic communication provides access to individuals with common interests for the purpose of delivering and receiving instruction, sharing information and ideas, and collaborating on research. With adaptive technology that provides independent access to electronic bulletin boards and discussion groups, individuals with disabilities can be equal participants in the global community.

Computer Network Access

Before the benefits of computers and networks can be realized by individuals with disabilities, barriers to their use must be removed through the provision of adaptive technology. Thousands of adaptive hardware and software systems are commercially available to provide functional alternatives to standard operations. They assist individuals with disabilities in controlling input, interpreting output, and reading documentation. The following sections describe basic approaches for making computers and networks accessible for individuals with disabilities, so that they can participate in academic and employment activities with maximum degrees of productivity and independence.

Mobility Impairments

Equipment that provides flexibility in the positioning of monitors, keyboards, documentation, and table tops is useful for many individuals with disabilities. Plugging all computer components into power outlet strips with accessible switches makes it possible for individuals with disabilities to turn equipment on and off independently.

Some adaptive hardware and software assist individuals with little or no use of their hands in using a standard keyboard. Individuals who have use of one finger, a mouth-or head-stick, or some other pointing device, can control the computer by pressing keys with the pointing device. Software utilities can create "sticky keys" that allow sequential keystrokes to input commands that normally require two or more keys to be pressed simultaneously. The key repeat function can be deactivated for those who cannot release a key quickly enough to avoid multiple selections. Keyboard guards (solid templates with holes over each key to assist precise selection) can be used by those who lack fine motor control.

Sometimes, repositioning the keyboard and monitor can enhance accessibility. For example, mounting keyboards perpendicular to tables or wheelchair trays and at head-height can assist individuals with limited mobility who use pointing devices to press keys. Other simple hardware modifications can also assist individuals with mobility impairments. For example, disk guides can assist with inserting and removing diskettes; a dedicated hard disk and/or computer network access can eliminate or reduce the necessity to do so.

Some hardware modifications completely replace the keyboard and/or mouse for individuals who cannot operate these standard devices. Expanded keyboards (larger keys, spaced far apart) can replace standard keyboards for those who lack fine motor control. Mini-keyboards provide access to those who have fine motor control but lack a range of motion great enough to use a standard keyboard. Track balls and specialized input devices can replace mice.

For those with severe mobility impairments, keyboard emulation is available, including scanning and Morse code input. In each case, special switches make use of at least one muscle over which the individual has voluntary control (e.g., head, finger, knee, mouth). In scanning input, lights or cursors scan letters and symbols displayed on computer screens or external devices. To make selections, individuals use switches activated by movement of the head, finger, foot, breath, etc. Hundreds of switches tailor input devices to individual needs. With Morse code input devices, users input Morse code by activating switches (e.g., a sip-and-puff switch registers dot with a sip and dash with a puff). Special adaptive hardware and software translate Morse code into a form that computers understand, so that standard software can be used.

Voice input provides another option for individuals with disabilities. Speech recognition systems allow users to control computers by speaking words and letters. A particular system is "trained" to recognize specific voices.

Special software can further aid those with mobility impairments. Abbreviation expansion (macro) and word prediction software can reduce input demands for commonly used text and keyboard commands. For example, word prediction software that anticipates entire words after several keystrokes can increase input speed. In addition, on-screen help can provide efficient access to user guides for individuals who are unable to turn pages in books.

Visual Impairments

Most individuals who are visually impaired can use standard keyboards, however braille input devices are available as well. Large print or braille key labels assist with keyboard use.

Special equipment for the visually impaired can modify display or printer output. Computer-generated symbols, both text and graphics, can be enlarged on the monitor or printer, thereby allowing individuals with low vision to use standard word processing, spreadsheet, electronic mail, and other software applications.

For individuals with some visual impairments, the ability to adjust the color of the monitor or change the foreground and background colors is also of value. For example, special software can reverse the screen from black on white to white on black for people who are light sensitive. Anti-glare screens can also make screens easier to read.

Voice output systems can read screen text to blind computer users. Special software programs "read" computer screens, and speech synthesizers "speak" the text. The availability of earphones for individuals using voice output systems can reduce the distractions for those working nearby.

Refreshable braille displays allow line-by-line translation of the screen into braille on a display area where vertical pins move into braille configurations as screen text is scanned. Braille displays can be read quickly by those with advanced braille skills, are good for detailed editing (e.g., programming and final editing of papers), and do not disrupt others in work areas because they are quiet. Braille printers provide output for blind users.

Scanners with optical character recognition connected to computers can be used to read printed material and store it electronically on computers, where it can be read using voice synthesis or printed with braille translation software and braille printers. Such systems can provide independent access to journals, syllabi, and homework assignments for blind students and faculty. Some hardware and software vendors also provide braille, large print, or ASCII versions of their documentation to support visually impaired users.

Hearing and/or Speech Impairments

Speech and hearing disorders alone do not generally interfere with typical computer use. However, speech synthesis is critically important to individuals who cannot speak. Advanced speech synthesizers are close enough to human quality to act as substitute voices. They allow students with portable systems to participate in class discussions. Word processing and educational software may also help hearing impaired students develop writing skills.

Although most individuals with hearing impairments can use computer applications without special adaptive technology, alternatives to audio output are available. For example, if the sound volume is turned to zero, one computer system flashes the menu bar when audio output is normally used.

Specific Learning Disabilities

Educational software where the computer provides multi-sensory experiences, interaction, positive reinforcement, individualized instruction, and repetition can be useful in skill building. Some individuals with learning disabilities who have difficulty processing written information can also benefit from completing writing assignments, tutorial lessons, and drill-and-practice work with the aid of computers. For example, a standard word processor can be a valuable tool for individuals with dysgraphia, an inability to produce handwriting reliably.

Individuals with disabilities who have high rates of input errors can benefit from using spell checkers, thesauruses, and grammar checkers. In addition, word prediction programs (software that predicts whole words from fragments) have been used successfully by individuals with learning disabilities. Macro software that expands abbreviations can reduce the necessity to memorize keyboard commands, and can ease the entry of commonly used text.

Some learning disabled individuals find adaptive devices designed for those with visual impairments useful. In particular, large print displays, alternative colors on the computer screen, and voice output are useful for some individuals with visual or reading disabilities. Computer documentation provided in electronic forms can be used by enlarged character and voice synthesis devices to make it accessible to those with reading difficulties. People who have difficulty interpreting visual material can improve comprehension and the ability to identify and correct errors when words are printed in large fonts or spoken.

Computer Network Access on Campuses

As computer and network use increase, post-secondary institutions are beginning to address accessibility issues (Burgstahler 1992; Murphy 1991). However, availability of computing services for students with disabilities varies greatly, and is generally at a lower level than other services for students with disabilities (Horn and Shell 1990). Many campuses have developed no services at all in this area. Colleges and universities are particularly inadequate in providing access to computerized card catalogs and other information resources available over campus and national networks (Wilson 1992).

The results of a campus computing survey (Eastman and Green 1992) suggest that public institutions and two-year colleges have made more progress in developing policies, procedures, and plans for addressing the computing needs of disabled students than private and four-year institutions, respectively. A recent study (Burgstahler 1992) of post-secondary institutions suggests that access to computer and network resources for students with disabilities is very limited, with access more prevalent in public and larger institutions. Evidence suggests that, to comply with federal legislation, institutions must make greater efforts to assure nondiscrimination on the basis of disability with regard to access to computer and network resources.

Post-secondary institutions planning computing and networking services for students and scholars with disabilities should examine the services that are currently provided to others on campus, including computer operating systems supported and resources accessible through the campus network. The legal expectation is that students and faculty with disabilities be provided equal access to the computer and network resources available to others. Working relationships should be developed between central computing services organizations, disabled student services offices, libraries, and other units who provide services on the network or support students and employees with disabilities, in order to set priorities and develop and implement plans to effectively accommodate individuals with disabilities.

By considering access for individuals with disabilities at the same time that colleges and universities wrestle with general computing and networking issues, it may be possible to effectively integrate access for individuals with disabilities into these plans. For example, as the library catalog and other information is made available over the campus network, it should simultaneously be made accessible from computers with adaptive technology. The material should be presented in such a way that it is conveniently accessible by individuals using adaptive technology. For example, if graphical user interfaces are employed, character-based alternatives that are compatible with speech output systems should be made available to students and scholars who are blind (see McNulty this volume). In addition, when new terminals and computers are being considered as campus standards, access issues for individuals with disabilities should enter into the final decision. Campuses that failed to comply with the Architectural Barriers Act incurred expensive retrofitting costs, such as those related to installing elevators in existing buildings, in order to comply with the later Rehabilitation Act of 1973. Institutions can guard against making similar costly mistakes with respect to computer and network access by considering adaptive technology early in the development stage.

Conclusion

Computers and networks are changing the way students and scholars communicate and access information across their campuses and across the country. However, students and faculty with disabilities at many schools are not guaranteed access to these enabling tools. The access needs of individuals with disabilities in higher education will continue to increase as computer and network use spreads into a wider range of academic courses, and as the number of students with disabilities attending colleges and universities increases. Although progress has been made in developing equipment and software that can provide students with disabilities access to computers and networks, much needs to be accomplished before equal access is achieved. Institutions should make efforts to assure nondiscrimination on the basis of disability regarding access to computer and network resources. The goal should be to provide individuals with disabilities equal access to the computer and network technologies that have become indispensable tools in the information age. Programs should be flexible and responsive in order to adjust to the influx of students with disabilities, to changing student needs, and to evolving technologies.

References

Burgstahler, S. E. (1993). Computing services for disabled students in institutions of higher education. *Dissertation Abstracts International* 54:102A. (University Microfilms No. 9312661).

Coombs, N. (1991). Window of equal opportunity—online services and the disabled computer user. *Research and Education Networking* 2(9):15–19.

Eastman, S. and Green, K. C. (1992). *Campus computing 1991—the EDUCOM-USC survey of desktop computing in higher education.* Los Angeles: U.S.C. Center for Scholarly Technology.

Facts you can use. (1993, June/July). *Information from HEATH,* 4–5.

Horn, C. A. and Shell, D. F. (1990). Availability of computer services in postsecondary institutions: Results of a survey of AHSSPPE members. *Journal of Postsecondary Education and Disability* 8:115–124.

Murphy, H. J. (1991). *The impact of exemplary technology-support programs on students with disabilities.* Washington, D. C.: National Council on Disability.

Taylor, M. (1991). Telecommunications: A life skill for persons with disabilities. *Closing the Gap* 10(2):1, 28–29.

Wilson, D. L. (1992, January 29). New federal regulations on rights of the handicapped may force colleges to provide better access to technology. *The Chronicle of Higher Education:* A1, A22–A23.

Medieval Misfits

An Undergraduate Discussion List

Carolyn P. Schriber

When Don Mabry first introduced members of the American Historical Association to the idea of e-mail discussion groups in 1991, relatively few academics realized the potential benefits.[1] The early HISTORY discussion group he described had approximately 140 members. When a plaintive question went out, asking whether anyone in the group was interested in the Middle Ages, only five medieval historians identified themselves. We've come a long way since then. HISTORY itself now has nine subsidiary lists and subscribes over four hundred members. More significantly, its members have spawned dozens of other history-related discussion groups. A listing of discussion groups of interest to professional historians in late 1993 contained 105 listings.[2] A list for those interested in Anglo-Saxon history, language, and literature now boasts over eight hundred members, and a fairly new group for medieval historians added its six hundreth member in September 1993.[3]

The medium has indeed become an international exchange, where faculty members from all over the world can share syllabi, bibliographies, book reviews, research tips, reports on works-in-progress, and announcements of new collections and upcoming conferences. Perhaps even more important, a discussion list becomes an expanded commons room, where old acquaintances are renewed and new friends made, where insider jokes receive an appreciative audience, and where esoteric problems can hope to find a quick solution. A researcher without access to a major library can often find a helpful colleague willing to photocopy a needed passage or supply a page number missing from an essential footnote. A stymied translator can seek suggestions for handling an awkward phrase, and an instructor can quickly determine whether a proposed textbook is still in print. Conference sessions can be filled out, and a traveller can even pick up a tip on where to get a cheap meal near the British Library.

In the early years, this bounty was limited to academics with access to an institutional connection to Bitnet or Internet. A few graduate students contributed to the lists, but they often sent their first postings with abject apologies for intruding on the musings of "real" scholars, expressing the same hesitation they might have felt about entering a faculty commons room without an invitation. Undergraduate participation was almost unheard of and frequently discouraged. A hesitant question about a term paper might well be dismissed with an admonition to "go do your own homework." Several things were wrong with that attitude. Students, whether at the graduate or undergraduate level, have a knack for raising uncomfortable questions, and fresh viewpoints have the potential to shake a whole assembly of stodgy academics out of their self-satisfied assumptions. Good students tend to rise to the challenge of conversing with their elders on a higher intellectual plane than that offered by their contemporaries. Such conversations stimulate their interest and open lines of inquiry that otherwise might never occur to students. As we move toward the twenty-first century, discussion lists offer an untapped resource that universities cannot afford to withhold from budding young scholars.

I first became interested in introducing my undergraduates to the benefits of e-mail after observing the operation of a private list set up for graduate seminars at the University of Kansas. These students submitted periodic reports on their research and readings, soliciting comments from their fellow students, as well as from several faculty members who had been invited to sit in. The resulting discussions were impressive. The students responded well to criticism, defended their positions with scholarly passion, and spurred further debate that ranged freely about the assigned topics. Perhaps because the postings had a specific goal, they tended to be more focused, and therefore more informative, than the often rambling discussions initiated by weary professors procrastinating about grading the latest set of term papers. I wondered whether the same technique would be successful at an undergraduate level.

Preparing for Medieval Misfits

Rhodes College is a small private liberal arts school with a highly motivated and talented student body. The history department, with its nine full-time faculty members, usually has sixty to seventy majors enrolled. That very favorable student/teacher ratio has many advantages; we grow to know our students well and can follow their progress closely throughout their college careers. But there are also drawbacks. Evaluation of learning outcomes in history is by its very nature subjective. We can test for knowledge of facts, but recalling names and dates is only a small part of what we want our students to accomplish. We want them to develop research techniques, critical thinking, and scholarly writing habits. More important, we expect them to approach a historical question from a solid foundation of fact, to evaluate the evidence with an open mind, and to defend their conclusions with intellectual honesty.

In a small department such as that at Rhodes College, where each professor works in a different specialty, students seldom get the chance to have their work examined from a variety of viewpoints. Students in medieval European history courses, for example, echo my approach. While I may approve their views because they reflect my own thinking, I recognize, as perhaps they do not, that other medievalists approach the same topics from different directions. My students thus have little opportunity to test their work against standards other than my own. As a department, we had taken steps to deal with this problem. Majors were required to take a variety of courses spread over European, American, and non-Western fields. We tried to bring to campus each year an assortment of guest historians who could discuss alternate approaches and unfamiliar types of research. Still, at the level of evaluating student efforts, not much had been done to broaden the assessment procedures. When the time came for students to work on historical projects, they continued to write for the professor who would do the grading. That practice did little to foster the intellectual honesty and critical thinking for which we were aiming.

In Spring 1993, I was scheduled to teach a senior seminar for history majors. The class would have fourteen students enrolled, every one of whom I knew and many of whom had taken three or more of my classes. The purpose of this course was to provide what our catalog called a "capstone experience," a forum in which graduating seniors could demonstrate that they had mastered the fundamental skills of their chosen field. They would be required to do a great deal of critical reading, to research a topic in depth, and to submit a well- written term paper. I had chosen the topic "Medieval Misfits," with the following course description:

> This course is designed to focus attention on the people most overlooked in regular medieval history classes. We will spend little time with "those who fight (the traditional armored knights), those who work (the peasants in the field), and those who pray (bishops and priests)." Instead we will look for the misfits and non-conformists of medieval society: those who, precisely because they were somewhat out of step with their world, sought new solutions or brought about change. Students will examine in detail some of the side issues that influenced the social and economic

development of medieval Europe, such as love potions and herbal brews, labor riots, religious fringe groups, and attitudes toward the getting and spending of money. Among the not-so-ordinary people discussed will be heretics, witches, money-lenders, magicians, renegade monks, and holy anorexics.[4]

My greatest concerns were that students would enter the class assuming that they already knew what I expected of them and that they would try very hard to produce the paper they thought I wanted. Instead, I determined to shake them up a bit, both by changing my own historical approach and by forcing them to take other viewpoints into consideration. To broaden the students' exposure to different ideas and evaluative approaches, I needed a network of consultants who could provide diverse and continuing feedback through a computer discussion forum. In October 1992, I began to lay the groundwork by creating a private discussion list that runs on Bitnet. During the initial testing and shake-down period, list membership included a dozen or more Rhodes students, five members of the history faculty, five other Rhodes faculty members from related departments, and four historians and graduate students from the Universities of Kansas and Illinois.

Cooperating students from my History of the Ancient World class were given the option of submitting their papers electronically to this network. To my delight, the first paper submitted to the list kicked off a wide-ranging discussion. The student posted a paper on the causes of the Second Punic War, in which he stated that "the strongest argument is the one for inevitability, since both sides were fully aware of the consequences of their actions."[5] Responses came back almost immediately. A Rhodes French professor was first to question the writer's assumptions:

> Wait a minute here. I think the cart is put before the horse. The first question should be what the author of this piece means by causing a war. Is he speaking of the particular events that launched a particular battle that began a particular war or is he considering why a particular war was fought at all? Obviously the two questions are related; yet they will have, often, different answers.[6]

A more detailed critique from Prof. Lynn Nelson at the University of Kansas followed:

> Generally speaking, historians should avoid use of the concept of "inevitability" when searching for the causes of an historical event. "Inevitability" means that no other outcome was possible, and

such a thing is impossible to prove. To do so, you must be able to demonstrate that every other conceivable outcome was in fact impossible. An historian never has enough data to do such a thing. . . . Lastly, you are in deep waters when you assert that a war was "inevitable." Wars are not subject to physical laws, like earthquakes. They are human actions, and when you say that a human action is inevitable, you are suggesting that humans cannot control their own actions. This leads to a whole series of very basic (and rather depressing) conclusions about the past and the future.[7]

This focus on a single word caught the students by surprise and forced them to think about the assumptions inherent in their use of language. Their ponderings bounced back and forth between the discussion list and the classroom, drawing into the debate other members of the class who had not at first been reading the e-mail messages. I was particularly pleased with a student who raised a question that provided fuel for an additional class session:

How about inevitability in the sense of war being the primary option or solution to settling disputes? Does this make it inevitable? Did any precedent exist for not going to war when two powers such as Rome and Carthage developed a territorial dispute? I don't believe that war in itself is inevitable in the sense there was GOING to be a second Punic War after the defeat of Carthage in the first. But in the case of Rome, I don't see much evidence for diplomacy among rival states.[8]

The discussion continued for several more days and elicited fourteen postings from eight different members of the discussion list. After Thanksgiving, the student whose statement had raised the issue of inevitability voluntarily rewrote the paper, modifying his position in light of the comments he had received. The experiment was enough to convince me that this approach was not only viable but valuable, both to me and to the students.

The Character of Discussion on Medieval Misfits

Running such a list is, of course, time-consuming, and archiving the postings takes up a great amount of computer space. With the help of a local grant, I was able to increase my computer capacity, to provide storage space for archiving list postings, and to hire a student assistant to manage the list.[9] In January 1993, the network went into full operation. Students in my senior seminar were required to submit project proposals, annotated bibliographies, thesis statements, book critiques, and summaries of their research findings to the network. They were also able to ask questions, seek bibliographical assistance, and discuss preliminary findings before they committed themselves to polished paper format. As the word spread, list membership expanded to over forty members. We attracted students and faculty, both locally and from SUNY Buffalo, Colorado State University, and the University of Texas at Austin. During the semester, we were linked via Bitnet to the graduate-level list at the University of Kansas, which by that time had been running successfully for over a year. Their membership of over fifty historians extended our audience to the west coast and to England.

Predictably, some students were reluctant to try the new class structure. One young man declared his scepticism with his introductory posting:

> As regards the seminar's computer format, I don't like it. I have at my house a very weak Mac, one that can do very little but serves my needs. I'm always inert when it comes to learning how to do wonderful new things with computers. Word on the street is that these e-mail lists are addictive; I guess I'll make a good barometer. If I can be hooked, anyone can.[10]

Another was dubious about her computer skills but at least willing to try the new format: "My experience with BITNET and medieval history is limited, so please bear with me for a while. I'm hoping this program will help me get over my computer phobia."[11] Others leaped in eagerly: "I am looking forward to the seminar and to the use of the computer. I am addicted to the e-mail craze, so anyone who would like to converse with me about just about anything is more than welcome."[12]

After introducing themselves to other members of the lists, students were asked to submit a tentative prospectus of their paper projects. They did so hesitantly at first, without any expectation that others would be interested. But responses came with regularity, as members of the list suggested books to be read and questions to be explored. Rhodes faculty members were incredibly generous with offers to discuss topics and share the resources of their personal libraries. The impact of being held accountable to a wide audience became evident early in the semester, when a student proposed a vague topic for her senior paper:

> Well, I have finally settled on a senior paper topic! I will write on Catherine of Siena. I have already found quite a few books on her, but I would appreciate some help finding a few sources that may give me some off-the-wall information on my misfit! Thanks!!![13]

Almost immediately, another history professor responded: "You can't get off so easily! WHY Catherine of Siena? Is it her lifestyle (you medievalists must excuse the modern term)? her visions? her theology? her community? Tell us more!"[14] The student rose to the challenge:

> Alright, Alright, here is some more information!! I have been wanting to learn more about the issue of Holy Anorexia. I am fascinated by the fact that a modern (or so I thought) disease was the cause for many of these medieval women to have visions that were seen as proof of their holy ways and deep beliefs. So, I picked up a book titled *Holy Anorexia* and began to read. Catherine of Siena was so bizarre that I simply could not pass her up.[15]

This time the response came from the English department: "Good answer, Kelley. In which case you will also want to get a look at Caroline Walker Bynum's *Holy Feast and Holy Fast. The Religious Significance of Food to Medieval Women*.[16]

Soon, students were exchanging information and offers of assistance among themselves. One student bookstore employee noted a recommendation to another class member, and sent the following message: "Laura, I think we have a used copy of *Medieval Women's Visionary Literature* in the bookstore. I'll check it out when I'm at work tomorrow."[17] Two roommates planning to purchase a modem asked for advice and received mailing addresses, price lists, and phone numbers.[18] Another picked up on the significance of a book reviewed in class: "Melissa, Do you still have *The Medieval Underworld*? If so, I'd like to take a look at it if you aren't in need of it. Thanks."[19]

An even more exciting breakthrough came when students began to use the list to continue discussions begun in class. During one Tuesday morning class, we had talked about ecclesiastical iconography and its use as a didactic tool for a largely illiterate congregation. Shortly after class one young man posted the following reaction:

> I was just thinking about how the church seemed to dominate/ dictate every aspect of medieval society. "The church, from its legalization until the modern period, has been at odds with the world, and yet in control" (thanks, Jara). What similiar

institutions exist today? I think the power of the media, esp. T.V., has some similiar characteristics on our society today. Take the past election for instance—the media dictates what the populus knows. The media dictates what issues are important. Anyway, I was wondering now that we have completed Little's *Religious Poverty and the Profit Economy in Medieval Europe* if ya'll have any opinions on this matter.[20]

It was an interesting question, but within the formal classroom setting, the student had not raised it. The class did not meet again until Thursday, and chances were good that, if the discussion list had not been available, it would have remained just a random thought, lost in a flurry of other activities. But Charles had raised a question that had also troubled his classmates, and they reacted with surprisingly vehement arguments. That afternoon and evening, fourteen postings from eight different people appeared. The discussion went on until close to midnight:

Nowadays, the media, I think, has become our conscience. As Laura said in class, the world appears to be shifting away from religion. Maybe the media is here to remind us, in some weird way, of the difference between right and wrong by at least forcing us to take a stand one way or the other, a way of forcing us to look at our own morality. Who knows? . . . I think the media is purposely at odds with the world in an attempt to better the world (although it doesn't always seem that way due to their frequent biases), much like the medieval church which remained at odds with the world in order to set a constant example or supposed ideal for the populus to strive for.[21]

The next day saw no lessening of interest in the question; I was especially pleased with the way the students were able to debate current issues without losing sight of the origins of the discussion:

Laura, it seems that you and I agree that the media [gets] its power from the people. But, you said the medieval church was a different story. So, let's turn this discussion back to our time period for a moment as I ask: Where did the medieval church get its power? If not from the people, then from whom or what?[22]

As I read the student postings, I realized that I was witnessing an informal class session without any of the usual barriers of time or space. The discussion offered me a perfect chance to guide students' thinking toward some sort of formal resolution during our next class:

> I have deliberately stayed out of this discussion because you have
> been doing such a marvelous job of self direction. Your comments
> online, like those in class, are becoming more and more perspica-
> cious. However, in the interest of channeling this discussion to-
> ward tomorrow's class, let me raise a couple of questions for you
> to ponder tonight. Who are these "people" you keep talking about?
> When you use that term, do you apply any limitations (socio-
> economic, gendered, generational, intellectual) to it? Can you use
> the same phrasing when talking about medieval "people"? Your
> references to the influence of the medieval church seem to me to
> imply that the "people" are passive—that they have EARS to hear
> a message that is being foisted upon them. Where and how do
> medieval "people" find a VOICE?[23]

In the ensuing class the students were better prepared and more
eager to participate than they had ever been. Understandably so.
They had raised their own questions and thus had an interest in
solving them. Nor did the discussion end there. Postings continued
for another week, bringing in eight new participants and broadening the issues to include cultural relativism, the value of education,
and the nature of truth. Eventually, the last two discussants, Prof.
Lynn Nelson of the University of Kansas and Clay Combs, the young
man who had been sure that he did not like this whole idea, took
their argument off-line and continued a fruitful private computer
correspondence.

By mid-semester, debate on the discussion list had become
almost a way of life for the entire class. Topics sometimes veered
toward the frivolous, as individuals raised questions about such
things as the origin of neckties, the first appearance of the cross-cut
saw, and the plural of virus. Some postings were deliberately provocative. One student stirred up a flurry of activity with his one-
sentence question: "Isn't religion just socially acceptable magic?"[24]
Other topics were emotionally charged. The class was attempting
to wrap up the semester with a definition of the term "misfit" just
at the time that the news concerning David Koresh and the Waco
crisis broke. The seeming coincidence forced the students to rethink
their assumptions once more:

> We have not come to the conclusion that the label "misfit" is any
> sort of justification, disclaimer or excuse. Misfit is a way to look
> at unusual individuals, who may not have anything else in com-
> mon, as a group. By looking at the experience of misfits we can
> learn something about the nature of societies. By looking at a
> specific misfit we can learn about his society.

If in the case of Koresh we refuse to take any of the blame, if we don't look at the media or the government and consider the roles each played in the incident, if we simply write Koresh off as crazy, a radical, another Charles Manson, without trying to determine *why*, we are doing a great disservice to our society and ourselves. . . . Yes, Koresh was responsible. But that responsibility must be shared. This is where the misfit theory is important. If we study the fringe of medieval society in attempt to understand the society as a whole, shouldn't the same be done (or couldn't the same be done) in the 20C.?[25]

Some Direct and Indirect Benefits of Medieval Misfits

When I looked back at the e-mail experiment at the end of the semester, I was delighted with its success. Some students had blossomed into full-fledged scholars. One young woman who had never participated in class discussions discovered her voice at the keyboard. Behind the anonymity of a computer screen, she joined the discussions and revealed a keen intellect. When her classmates reacted favorably to her unique contributions, she began speaking out in class for the first time in four years. Another admitted to one of our computer experts that she was putting much more effort into her writing because it was being "published" among people she didn't know. As individuals saw the quality of work being done by their classmates, they began to reassess their own work. Although not all were aware of the element of competition, their submissions improved noticeably in content and style as the semester progressed.

Student access to resource materials had expanded. Almost every student had explored the holdings of libraries other than our own. We established a common file on the VAX academic volume, where large files of general interest items could be stored and used by all network participants. Materials included extensive bibliographies, instructions for accessing and using other instructional computer software, and directories of databases available on Bitnet. Students themselves were able to share bibliographic material without the added expense of making copies for all their classmates.

I, too, benefited. List discussions gave me a chance to observe the thought processes behind the work students were turning in. As a result, my own comments on drafts and final submissions grew longer, more detailed, and more pertinent. Input from faculty members outside the department and the Rhodes campus suggested a more interdisciplinary approach to broad historical issues. When students received advice and criticism from many different participants, they explored ideas that might never have emerged in our closed-door classroom. Throughout the term, my syllabus expanded to accommodate these fresh and important new topics. Students received peer evaluation at every step of the senior seminar experience and learned from the comments of their classmates during the writing process. Their final papers were models of organization and in-depth research and, therefore, a pleasure to read and grade.

In their class evaluations, students unanimously agreed that the computer list was a valuable addition to the course and that they would enjoy taking other courses run in the same way. While they did not find computer submissions easier than the old hard copy format, they affirmed that they thought they had learned more than they would have in a traditional course. All members of the class agreed that their computer literacy had increased, and six of the fourteen had so enjoyed the e-mail experience that they had joined other academic discussion lists.

Within the history department, both students and faculty had found that e-mail had much to offer. We began using the net for department announcements and for sharing items of general interest. Opening the list to all members of the department increased the amount of communication between students and faculty. Younger students learned what would be expected of them in upper-division courses, and faculty members exchanged ideas. Open-ended discussions contributed to a feeling of community among list members. Because the network list approach proved successful, it served as a model program that could be adapted to courses in other departments. The following semester, Rhodes had four classes being conducted at least partially through network discussion lists, and four members of the Misfits class continued to correspond with the list even though they had graduated. My intention is to continue to offer one course each semester that utilizes the original list.

Conclusion

In the coming years, the e-mail program at Rhodes has the potential to expand geometrically. Participants will increase their computer skills and discover the many sources of data available through computer networking. Once students are comfortable with electronic communication and file retrieval, we can introduce them to other computer-assisted learning activities. Internet resources such as Gopher for sophisticated database searches, MELVYL for access to the California library system, and CARL for worldwide journal article access are only a few of the possibilities that will extend their research opportunities. The long range goal is to provide full computer literacy for all students. If we are to prepare our graduates to function efficiently in the twenty first century, we cannot afford to do anything less.

Notes

1. Donald Mabry (1991, February). Electronic mail and historians. *Perspectives: American Historical Association Newsletter 29*(2): 1, 4, 6.

2. H-Net British and Irish History discussion list. (1993, Nov. 15, 10:32 a.m.). H-Net guide to history lists on Internet & Bitnet 11–12–93. Message to: Multiple recipients of list H-ALBION.

3. ANSAX-L@Wvnvm and Mediev-L@ukanaix.cc.ukans.edu.

4. Description taken from course syllabus.

5. Cifreo, Eric. (1992, Nov. 16, 12:34 a.m.). Rome and Carthage. Message to: Multiple recipients of list MISFITS. Because this is a private discussion list, it has no official archives. Postings are kept only in a file under my personal VAX account and are not available for retrieval.

6. Ledgerwood, Mickle. (1992, Nov. 16, 3:12 p.m.). RE: Rome and Carthage. Message to: Multiple recipients of list MISFITS.

7. Nelson, Lynn H, (1992, Nov. 18, 3:26 a.m.). Rome and Carthage. Message to: Multiple recipients of list MISFITS.

8. Mitchell, Charles. (1992, Nov. 18, 4:28 p.m.). Inevitability. Message to: Multiple recipients of list MISFITS.

9. Funds came from an in-house fund set aside annually to finance faculty-initiated projects that enhance student appraisal and evaluation.

10. Combs, Clay F. (1993, Jan. 19, 3:54 p.m.). Introduction. Message to: Multiple recipients of list MISFITS.

11. Ford, Melissa T. (1993, Jan. 20, 7:07 p.m.). Introduction. Message to: Multiple recipients of list MISFITS.

12. Hill, Jara L. (1993, Jan. 20, 12:10 p.m.). Introduction. Message to: Multiple recipients of list MISFITS.

13. Slagle, Kelley L. (1993, Feb. 1, 9:03 p.m.). Misfit topic. Message to: Multiple recipients of list MISFITS.

14. Murray, Gail. (1993, Feb. 1, 9:18 p.m.). RE: Misfit topic. Message to: Multiple recipients of list MISFITS.

15. Slagle, Kelley L. (1993, Feb. 1, 9:41 p.m.). More on Catherine of Siena. Message to: Multiple recipients of list MISFITS.

16. McEntire, Sandra. (1993, Feb. 2, 9:12 am.). RE: More on Catherine of Siena. Message to: Multiple recipients of list MISFITS.

17. Crabb, Lynn E. (1993, Jan. 27, 8:23 p.m.). RE: Christine de Pisan. Message to: Multiple recipients of list MISFITS.

18. Barker, Ray C. (1993, Jan. 22, 9:43 p.m.). Cheap modems, attn. Sean & Eric. Message to: Multiple recipients of list MISFITS.

19. Mitchell, Charles S. (1993, Feb. 16, 1:28 p.m.). RE: Ford: Critique. Message to: Multiple recipients of list MISFITS.

20. Mitchell, Charles S. (1993, Feb. 9, 11:16 a.m.). Power of church. Message to: Multiple recipients of list MISFITS.

21. Helter, Jackie L. (1993, Feb. 9, 12:52 p.m.). RE: Power of church. Message to: Multiple recipients of list MISFITS.

22. Hill, Jara L. (1993, Feb. 10, 11 :57 a.m.). RE: Laura's message. Message to: Multiple recipients of list MISFITS.

23. Schriber, Carolyn P. (1993, Feb. 10, 3:58 p.m.). "People?" Message to: Multiple recipients of list MISFITS.

24. Cifreo, Eric. P. (1993, Mar. 30, 1:45 p.m.). Magic. Message to: Multiple recipients of list MISFITS.

25. Hill, Jara L. (1993, Apr. 22, 11 :46 a.m.). RE: Questioning comments. Message to: Multiple recipients of list MISFITS.

VICE in REST

Do you have a VICE ? Do you get enough REST ? Well, the answer is yes to both! These are the first two questions I ask students in each of my classes and the subsequent response I give after a brief reflective pause. VICE in REST is a computer-mediated communication, presentation, teaching-learning, and assessment project that I have been developing since the fall semester of 1984 to effect course and curriculum redevelopment, and enhance and extend instructor-student and student-student interaction in the "process" of teaching-learning.

Knowledge of the biological world is based on two important processes: the scientific process, which consists of accessing and assessing information, noting uncertainties, asking questions, establishing a logical experimental design, testing hypotheses, and forming conclusions, and effective communication of the new knowledge and understanding that is gained as a result of using the scientific process. Students should not only experience the excitement of discovery, connecting concepts, and the satisfaction of solving problems but also the excitement of sharing their new knowledge and understanding with peers. As an educator and researcher, I view investigating biology as more than just doing experiments; it is also an approach to collaborative teaching-learning. Various telecommunicating technologies are used to create a Virtual (Instructional) Collaborative Environment (VICE or ViCE) in Research, Education, Service and Teaching (REST). This is part of an academic and services partnership project entitled "The Digital REST Area at SUNY Plattsburgh on the Information Superhighway."

To succeed is to achieve an "understanding" in learning. Hence, one must examine, question, and explore the "best" available information easily and quickly. One of the most important aims in education is to introduce the student to the process of inquiry and contemporary tools used to access people and information. Interaction with colleagues and initiation of experiments are the primary ways scientists have to find out how nature works, and scientific knowledge is only as sophisticated as experiments permit. In the real world of research, half the battle is knowing WHAT QUESTION TO ASK, the other half is FINDING A WAY TO ANSWER IT. New knowledge rarely comes from simply sitting back and thinking. As educators, we also need to constantly assess, plan, create, DO, and re-assess our teaching-learning process.

Computer-mediated communication (CMC) is a highly interactive technology with great potential to impact the shape of education. The lecture has been the most common form of communication in the university between instructor and student. While the computer can be used to deliver instructional material, its inherent interactive power makes it better suited to facilitate dialogue, group discussion, and discovery learning. This makes the learner a participant rather than a spectator. When the computer is connected to high speed data networks, the instructor and student can increasingly access people, libraries, databases, and other information sources instantaneously from almost anywhere. Today's information technology promises an educational revolution that puts the learner, not the instructor, in the center of the process, and that transforms the professor from a dispenser of information into a discussion moderator and skilled resource expert. In this age of information access, the educator needs more than ever to direct the learner in how to find what is relevant and what to do with raw information to turn it into useful knowledge.

The goal of VICE in REST is to use appropriate and inexpensive technology to develop navigation and help resources that allow immediate access to people, science education, and research materials locally and on the Internet; in addition, it is essential that it be simple to update or add new materials. This currently is being done using electronic mail and conferences, Gopher, and several forms of World Wide Web (WWW) multimedia client/server software, such as Mosaic, Netscape, HTTPd (HyperText Transfer Protocol daemon), Timbuktu (a TCP/IP screen-sharing program), HyperCard, and QMark. I have been constructing a set of navigation guides through the Internet with the hope that the materials developed and referenced improve science teaching-learning and/or simplify the process in some way. There are pointers to college, division, and departmental policies, schedules, admissions, advisement and registration information, faculty profiles, courses, lecture and laboratory materials, library information and resources, general reference tools, alumni, employment opportunities, campus and local news and services, catalogs of images, shareware, and discussion groups. Many of these include hypertext documents related to various science disciplines, works-in-progress, journal indices and abstracts, lesson plans and experiments, exhibits, and many others.

The objective of this chapter is not to provide instruction on how to use a specific technology tool, but to show how I use computer and telecommunication technologies to enhance, extend, and supplement a collaborative teaching-learning environment. It assumes that you have at least a passing knowledge of electronic mail and conferences, client/server software, Gopher, Mosaic, Netscape, or other WWW browsers. (See the chapter by John December in this volume for an introduction to these technologies.)

Challenges in Education

Higher education in the United States must undergo its most significant changes in the next decade if we are to regain and surpass the stature we once had globally. We are not producing critical, independent scholars, and problem-solvers today in anything like the numbers our disciplines and our society need (AAC, 1991; Boyer 1987). Perhaps this is because, as J. R. Lemke has argued elsewhere in this volume, we are not preaching what we practice; we are not teaching students to do what we do, but only trying to teach them what we know. Good teaching-learning is intimate with the true meaning of research and scholarship. Today, students across the world can experience the excitement of learning through exploration and discovery. The point is to get students actively involved in their education.

To truly affect teaching-learning, we must adopt strategies with a more long-term focus, i.e., to the needs of science students of the future, to the task of effectively supporting tomorrow's life science educators, to the development of new approaches and curricula, and last but not least, to new ways of planning for life-long learning. But not every challenge can be met in the traditional classroom today (Lewis and Hedegaard 1993).

The convergence of computing, communications, and traditional educational technologies empowers us more than ever to discuss, plan, create, and implement fundamentally unique strategies for providing access to information and facilitating collaborative teaching-learning environments. VICE in REST involves technology-based facilities, technology currently present on campus as well as emerging technologies such as electronic mail and conferences and multimedia client/server and authoring programs, by faculty and students working together in a teaching-learning partnership. This approach facilitates the coming together of a community of learners without the arbitrary barriers of time and space. Mosaic (client) and HyperText Transfer Protocol (HTTP server) integrate access and use of various classroom media (text, images, sound, and video) via the Internet, all with an easy mouse-click and icon-oriented graphical user interface. This will be the university and classroom environment as we move into the twenty-first century. The ultimate goal is to provide instructional materials seamlessly WHERE, WHEN, and HOW users want it.

Technology in Education?

We need to examine the role of technology in education and understand what we want to achieve and whether a given technology or combination of technologies will help us reach specific objectives. Educational goals MUST drive technology, not vice versa! Further, no two learners may learn from the same presentation in the same way or as well. No two instructors may be able to use the same medium in the same way or as well. No two lessons may be suited for delivery by the same style or through the same medium. The point is that technology should be looked upon as an "adjunct" tool in the teaching-learning environment. Connectivity and interaction are paramount to meaningful advances in the life-long teaching-learning process. Hence, the task an instructor faces when considering what pedagogy to use in instruction should include a process that is diagnostic in nature—one where we ask ourselves which channels are appropriate for particular communication and teaching-learning styles, as well as for specific objectives.

Faculty and instructional developers are exploring how instructional strategies and educational technologies can contribute to solving educational problems we face today. There is evidence that the use of collaborative teaching-learning strategies, together with the concomitant development of a supportive environment, can revitalize the classroom process for both instructors and learners (Gamson and Associates 1984; Svinicki 1990). Application of computer technology in education contributes to an infrastructure that allows both instructors and students to collaborate in the teaching-learning process in more democratic and reflective ways (Adams, Carlson, and Hamm 1990; Harasim 1990a, 1990b).

21st-Century-University Teaching: Learning and the Scholarly Environment

The convergence of computing and communication technologies with education creates a world-wide web of people, places, and information. It connects instructor and instructor, instructor and student, student and student, and campus with library, dormitory, other universities, home, schools, and businesses without the barriers of time and space. With technology-based presentation lecterns, libraries, and classrooms, and personal computers in the home, office, and dormitory, the pedagogical and learning potential for both instructor and student is limited only by our imagination.

Over the last five years, the State University of New York (SUNY) at Plattsburgh—a medium-sized institution of approximately six thousand students—like many universities across the world has created a technology environment on campus that provides ubiquitous access to both on- and off-campus information resources for faculty and students. Several public access multi-platform computer laboratories and two computer classrooms primarily for instruction in writing are available; in addition, several technology-based classrooms, as well as presentation lecterns in small-, medium-, and large-sized lecture halls with a strong emphasis on multimedia capabilities, became available during the 1993–94 academic year. The latter include various devices such as computers (IBM compatible and Macintosh), a document camera and computer-controlled CD-ROM drives, laser disc, and VCR players, as well as a slide-to-video projector, a computer, computer video conferencing hardware and software, and video overhead projection system. In addition, a PictureTel 4000 dialup two-way audio and video system with connections currently to five remote sites coupled with previously established telecommunication connections to local, Bitnet, and Internet services, information, and databases was recently installed. These facilities have been created to take advantage of both the technology present on campus now and new technologies that will soon be here. Additional classrooms, public laboratories, and presentation lecterns are also planned for the 1995–96 academic year and beyond. Two data ports and cable were made available in each dormitory room during the fall 1994 semester.

Courses and Structure: How is VICE in REST implemented?

I teach a variety of both moderate and small enrollment courses at SUNY Plattsburgh, and use computer technology in my pedagogy to enhance and extend collaborative teaching-learning. "General Biology" I (four credits) is required for biology majors usually at the freshman level. The course consists of approximately 125 students in the lecture portion who are subsequently divided into groups of twenty-five for laboratory sessions. The emphasis of this course is on the cellular and molecular basis of life processes. "(Tele)Communicating Biology" (three credits) is a required course for biology majors at the junior level (two sections of fifteen students each) that examines how computer technology can help develop and enhance written and oral communication skills. "Immunology" (three credits) is a one semester course for 15–24 junior and senior level students with a focus on the principles of host defense mechanisms. "In Vitro Cell Biology & Biotechnology" (fifteen credits) is a full semester residential course (10–12 hours/day, 5–7 days/week for a total of sixteen weeks or seven hundred hours of hands-on training) in cell biology/culture, molecular biology, and biotechnology. It is taught at the William H. Miner Research Institute, which is a satellite campus approximately fifteen miles from the main campus. Placement of up to eighteen undergraduate, graduate, and continuing education students is competitive and by application.

The technologies used to establish VICE in REST as a companion to traditional classroom meetings are: (1) the use of electronic mail to provide individual instructor contact and assistance seven days a week, twenty-four hours a day; (2) electronic conferences to provide lecture notes and other supporting materials; (3) client/server software (Gopher, Mosaic/Netscape/Lynx) to access Internet resources; (4) Timbuktu (a TCP/IP screen sharing program); (5) PictureTel (dialup two-way interactive video and audio) and CU-SeeMe (TCP/IP two-way video and audio computer conferencing); and (6) multimedia authoring systems such as HyperCard and Question Mark (QMark) to administer multimedia tutorials, practice tests, and final assessments. As part of the curriculum in each course, instruction is provided in the use of personal and mainframe computer hardware and software. Students are automatically registered with an account on the VAX mainframe computer to provide personal access to local, Bitnet, and Internet services, information, and databases.

Telecommunications and Multimedia

Today, teaching and learning occurs in the context of pervasive online access to people and information. Electronic mail and conferences provide for convenient computer-mediated communication with people in different geographical locations who may have quite different schedules and responsibilities. Also, they provide quick access to information and other resources for multimedia presentations and lessons within and among universities, libraries, departments, and programs (Kehoe 1992).

Several Transmission Control Protocol/Internet Protocol (TCP/IP) client/server programs that run over network connections, and the vast majority of various multimedia applications which are standalone programs for desktop computers, are at the heart of interactive multimedia. The use of computer-controlled media is referred to as inter-active because it enables a whole new level of user interaction with, and control over, materials in a number of forms, such as text, image, audio, and video, as well as utilities such as telnet and File Transfer Protocol (FTP). The computer's power to search for and retrieve information can be used to interlink and annotate related topics to create a "web of information." The instructor-learner follows a "uniquely" personal trail through the information, becoming an interactive par-ticipant in the flow of information to learning.

The Challenge: Change, Time, and Budget

As education and technology advance, it becomes increasingly critical to keep up with the growing needs of faculty and students with fund-ing that, unfortunately, gets more and more scarce every year. Today, departments usually consist of too few people responsible for sup-porting large numbers of students at many different sites, many of whom may also happen to be non-traditional students. This is a prob-lem nearly all colleges and universities are facing. Imagine what could happen if we could pool the resources of people and information through technology to address this problem.

"I'm having a problem with 'such and such.' Can you explain and show me what to do? But I can't meet with you now because I have a class and then I have to go to work. Where, when, and how can we get together?" It's impossible to be everywhere, to meet each and every need, and to answer all individual questions. So, we spend a lot of time giving verbal instructions over the telephone and/or in class, group, or private sessions, trying to answer questions effectively.

The time-consuming learning process can prove exceptionally frustrating when the user cannot understand a term or articulate a problem. Initially, the solution appears to be hiring more people, cre-ating new/different materials, and/or providing formal instruction. There are just two problems to this solution: lack of time and lack of money. Are there other options? Yes. There are numerous technologi-cal alternatives that allow instructors to provide information to their students and allow students to discover information themselves.

Electronic Mail and Conferences

Electronic mail is used for instructor to student, student to student, and small group contact, and to elicit class participation and com-ments on an instructor's or student's comment or question. It has the advantage of being personal and individualized. Each of my courses also has a VAX Notes computer conference that enhances, extends, and supplements class meetings. The electronic conferences provide lecture notes and reference materials, as well as asynchronous discussion via a pre-established organization of topic headings. Each electronic conference has an agenda and focus for lecture topics, seminars, and discussions presented in the courses, as well as course information, example tests, and student evaluations. In VAX Notes, agenda items are called TOPICS, and moderator's or participants' comments on these topics are called REPLIES. A piece of electronic mail either introduces a topic or serves as a reply. There can be any number of topics in a conference, and each topic can have any number of replies. A topic and all of its replies is called a DISCUSSION.

For example, the Biological Sciences conference for my university department offers individual topics that provide information about the department, programs of study, advisement, research projects, jobs, graduate school programs, internships, scholarships, and other subjects useful to students or faculty. The Cell Molecular Conference for "General Biology," "Immunology," and "In Vitro Cell Biology & Biotechnology" is organized into topics relevant to the structure of these courses, such as: the evolution of the cell, how cells are studied, immune system and antigens, immunoassays, virology laboratory, and biomedical ethics.

VAX Notes allows participants to use the electronic mail utility to send topics/replies and/or messages to any user without leaving the conference. All conferences are set for public as opposed to private access. Hence, from both a local and remote perspective, these electronic conferences can be accessed by any user from any VMS system where the VAX Notes software has been installed, including any of the seventeen-plus campuses in SUNYNet (Kahn 1992).

Gopher Applications

Of the applications developed in recent years to support teaching-learning and scholarship through resource discovery and information retrieval over the Internet, the University of Minnesota's Internet Gopher is arguably one of the most important developments. Gopher has made the Internet both accessible and usable for large numbers of old and new telecommunication users, many of whom lack the knowledge and training to make extensive use of the resources accessible to them over the Internet. Gopher is a text-based point (with arrow keys) and press (return key) client/server program. Files located on machines in other geographic locations can thus be located, read, saved, and/or printed with a minimum of effort by users.

Gopher systems can be created that provide links to files around the world, thus allowing students to easily access and obtain useful information about a field of study. For example, point your Gopher client to baryon.hawk.plattsburgh.edu/11/Academic Departments/ Biological Sciences 70. Particular items in the menu can be reviewed by pointing to (use down cursor key) or typing the item number and selecting (press return key) the item of interest. As you will see, this menu presents information about the department, and also allows students to begin exploring other resources.

Each item followed by a slash (/) represents an additional directory of information, with menu items that can be selected. If you were to select item "Various BioGophers, Gophers, Libraries, & Search Tools/," as would be indicated by a right arrow in front of that item number, then you would be presented with another menu of items. This menu presents students with the possibility of accessing biological science databases, discussion archives, governmental resources maintained by other Gopher systems, and several other resources.

The World Wide Web, NCSA Mosaic, Netscape, & Lynx

Gopher systems, as well as most other types of Internet information retrieval systems, are also accessible through World Wide Web clients or browsers, such as "Mosaic", developed by the National Center for Supercomputing Applications (NCSA) and Netscape by Netscape Communications, Inc. These browsers or clients can retrieve text, images, sound, and video. Before discussing clients, a few words about the World Wide Web are in order.

The World Wide Web (WWW) works under the popular client-server model. A Web server is a software program running on a computer whose only purpose is to serve documents to other computers when asked. A Web client is a program that interfaces with the user and requests documents from a server as the user asks for them. The phrase "World Wide Web" or "WWW" is often used to refer to the collective network of servers speaking the language that Web clients and servers use to communicate with each other. This is called the HyperText Transmission Protocol (HTTP). All Web clients and servers must be able to speak HTTP in order to send and receive hypermedia documents. For this reason, Web servers are often called HTTP servers.

Based on the World Wide Web (WWW) technologies developed at the European Particle Physics Laboratory (CERN) in Switzerland, "Mosaic" is a distributed hypermedia system designed for information discovery and retrieval over the global Internet. Using the X Window system as its interface, WWW clients unify access to various protocols, data formats, and archives, and provides interfaces to external viewers designed to handle graphics formats other than the X bitmap (e.g., JPEG, TIFF, DVI, MPEG, and PostScript). For example, within the framework provided by a single interface, a user may run a Gopher session, instruct an Archie client to run a search, or retrieve images from The Library of Congress's Vatican exhibit or the Smithsonian's photo catalog. WWW software consists of cross-platform client/server programs. "Lynx," on the other hand, provides a user-friendly hypertext interface for users on UNIX and VMS platforms, and allows information providers to publish information located on any platform that can run a Gopher, HTTP, WAIS, FTP, or NNTP (Usenet News) server. Lynx clients use the WWW hypertext format (HyperText Markup Language), but only provide for the text-based (as opposed to graphical) information.

World Wide Web clients/servers use hypertext and hypermedia to create links within a document that lead users to other documents, lists, multimedia resources, or actions. WWW clients' hypermedia capabilities are derived from the use of the HyperText Markup Language (HTML). HTML uses tags to indicate formatting or structural information. One of the structures HTML tags may specify is a link to another document, which may be situated on the same server or located somewhere else on the network. Based on a single directive known in the context of HTML as an "anchor," the tag points to a specific file and provides the basis for a traversable link between the anchor and the file to which the link points.

The operational significance of the embedded "anchors" is that, at least in principle, files located anywhere on the Internet may be linked, and links may be added or deleted in accord with the requirements of either document designers or users. As a result, the WWW is capable of supporting several modes of asynchronous collaboration, including document annotation, document cross-linking, and document revision control. In addition, NCSA Mosaic can communicate directly with Collage, which is NCSA's synchronous collaboration tool intended mainly for use in scientific data analysis and manipulation, and NCSA's Data Management Facility, which is a relational database system designed especially for scientific data.

The World Wide Web Univeral Resource Locator (URL) http://bio444.beaumont.plattsburgh.edu/ is a pointer to an HTML document that serves as the "home page" for The Digital REST Area at SUNY Plattsburgh, with links to the WWW Biological Sciences resources on the Internet used by students and faculty in SUNY Plattsburgh's Department of Biological Sciences. A home page is an all-purpose directory presenting a master menu of documents related to a particular subject, project, or administrative unit. The URL http://bio444. beaumont.plattsburgh.edu/BiologicalSciences.html is a pointer to the home page for the SUNY Plattsburgh Department of Biological Sciences. The URL http://bio444.beaumont.plattsburgh.edu/Biosciences.html is the pointer to a HTML document for Bio-Sciences resources on the World Wide Web. Items that are underlined are linked to related documents or menus. Students "clicking" on these links will discover other information useful to them about SUNY and about biological resources available through the Internet.

Timbuktu Pro

Farallon's Timbuktu for Macintosh and Windows is a software application that enables users to exchange files, as well as remotely access and control Windows and Macintosh computers across a network, just as if they were at the remote locations. I have found that it is a means for effective teaching-learning since it provides a user the ability to use his/her tactile and visual senses in addition to the audio provided by the telephone or software such as Maven and IPhone.

The screen sharing feature in Timbuktu, which can be used over AppleTalk and TCP/IP networks such as the Internet, is a most valuable tool. With Timbuktu, I can easily connect to a computer at another site, take control, and explain to another instructor or student how to do something while demonstrating the function. It also provides for a more efficient and effective means to send and share files such as a "Help Desk," which is a file containing answers to questions that students ask frequently. When a student is not able to connect to a server, locate a student module, or experiences some other technical problem, the instructor can, from a remote location, find and fix the problem. All that is needed is to connect to the user's screen to see what's happening. Timbuktu saves time by allowing the instructor or another student to quickly assess the situation and help solve the problem.

PictureTel and CU-SeeMe

The dialup PictureTel 4000 and TCP/IP CU-SeeMe real-time video and computer conferencing systems are two-way interactive video and audio communication technologies that are being used for distributed learning courses and training. In addition, such systems also provide delivery for conferences, seminars, lectures, training videotapes for VAX and PC/Mac computers for use in education in technology and technology in education development. The videotapes can be used by faculty, staff, and students for telecommunications training in their offices or dorm rooms, as well as over the campus cable system.

Multimedia Authoring Programs: HyperCard and QMark

HyperCard is an authoring tool used to write tutorial and self-assessment software. This software allows a computer to interface with and control CD-ROM drives and videodisc players. Courseware created using this program can thus incorporate video images and access huge amounts of information that can be stored using CD-ROM and laserdisc technologies. The delivery system can be as simple as a Macintosh Classic equipped with a CD-ROM drive and laser disc player along with HyperCard. A computer station such as this is referred to as Multimedia Scholar's Workstation. Students have access to these workstations in library study preview carrels and departmental computer classrooms, where presentations, tutorials, and assessments are stored on a server. For an example of this, see the URL http://bio444. beaumont.plattsburgh.edu/MMViceInRest.html.

I have created several HyperCard stacks for the courses I teach. In addition to providing an overview of the course content, tutorials, and practice as well as self-assessment tests, these stacks control a laserdisc player which, together with a laserdisc, provide the slide images and graphics I use in lecture. But the stacks can be used with or without the aid of a laserdisc player. This means that the images and graphics I use are no longer available to students "only" during a lecture period for a few seconds. They can be accessed any time, for as long as a user needs. The WWW also serves a similar purpose.

I've used QMark to create, administer, and analyze tutorials, surveys, and objective and free-format self-assessment tests. In fact, one of the first things students must do in each of my courses is to take a QMark-delivered introduction to electronic testing tutorial, as well as a computer user's survey. This introduces students to electronic testing and allows me to assess both their attitude toward and experience(s) with computers. Tutorial and assessment materials include background information, complete with multimedia supporting materials. Questions are one of 8 types—multiple choice (includes yes/ no, true/false), numeric, fill in the blanks, word answer, free format, matching/ranking, multiple response, and explanation. A variety of ways are used to present the assessments: providing students with feedback on answers after each question, after the assessment, or not at all. A range of options, including time limits, hints for wrong answers, and letting students pass over questions, may be invoked, depending on the objective. Students can review the tutorials and answer the tests without needing to be familiar with the use of computers. Delivering tutorials and tests is easy with distribution over the local network. It is secure as well. Test answers are marked immediately and stored on disk for later analysis by the instructor.

Using Telecommunications and Multimedia in Biology Courses

Advances in thinking about telecommunications and multimedia using computers can invigorate the way we teach and the way students learn. I have found that electronic mail, conferences, and interactive multimedia stand-alone and TCP/IP client/server programs and tutorials emerge as media that, if well integrated into a course, can contribute significantly to a better, more student-centered learning climate. Using an innovative blend of computer telecommunications and video hardware and software, instructors can create exciting learning environments that allow students to emulate the process of research and scholarship in their discipline as they move from concept to concept and medium to medium at their own direction and pace. By providing telecommunications and multimedia capabilities in lecture halls as well as in specialized classrooms and public access facilities, the presentation of lectures, lessons, and assessments can be discovered, enriched, made more memorable, and broadened to include resources not previously available easily out of the classroom.

In general, there are three major ways that I use telecommunications and multimedia for instruction: for presentations (lectures), as resource materials (enhancement), and for individual study (lessons and assessments). Telecommunication and multimedia materials provided through the Internet and my own tutorials are used to cover the principal content of a course and to supplement lectures by providing more in-depth explorations of various concepts. The key is that students not only have access to an instructor's presentation and lesson materials in a manner not previously possible, but they are also in control of their own learning to an unprecedented degree. I also use computer-mediated communication (CMC) and multimedia for investigative and collaborative learning in classes; the URL http://bio444.beaumont.plattsburgh.edu/BMTCancer/BMT.html is a pointer to an example of an undergraduate technology research project on "Bone Marrow Transplant & Cancer Treatment," which utilized faculty, librarians, online searches, and the Internet as resources. The following approaches are employed.

Content-Related Information and Discussions Between
Class Meetings

Probably the least demanding approach is to use CMC and multimedia as an extension of the classroom. There is never enough class time when it comes to presenting and discussing all issues related to a given topic. Electronic mail and a computer conference together are ideal ways to continue a class meeting.

All lecture materials and example tests are posted under appropriate topics in the conferences, or are provided via multimedia tutorials and practice assessments. Students can explore any or all of the sections in a conference or stand-alone tutorial. CMC is also used to prepare for class discussions. In this case, the instructor or student(s) post a summary paper in a conference. An electronic survey of opinions or comments on a topic is carried out prior to a class session order, to assess how to discuss it in a more informed and focused way.

From time to time, students are explicitly asked to respond to a short answer question or problem found under a topic in the conference. Students are instructed by electronic mail and/or a note left under a particular topic in a conference or stand-alone tutorial to provide their response(s) by a certain date and time; these instructions also indicate whether they should post their response as a note in the conference (open or hidden), send it as an electronic mail message, and/or provide it as a paper copy to hand in to the instructor.

Students frequently form study groups to review material on upcoming tests. This group format can be used as a model for electronic collaboration that allows test preparation to become a meaningful instructional goal in itself. I use electronic mail, conferences, and multimedia tutorials to pose problems, suggest and discuss approaches to solutions, and publish the products of individuals and groups in preparation for further live discussion. I have tried two versions of this approach. In the first, I enter review questions after each lecture in a conference topic and appoint a number of student groups to discuss and post their answers for the class to review. Different groups take turns throughout the semester. In the second version, students are given electronically protected tutorials in which they must discuss a solution(s) to a problem presented in the lesson.

Seminars and Collaborative Projects

In the seminars "(Tele)Communication Biology" and "Immunology," weekly "seminar papers" based upon recently published journal articles are prepared by students and posted in an electronic conference topic called "Journal Club" about a week before a live class presentation. In some instances, the entire seminar presentation occurs online. Two students serve as moderators for each seminar; after consulting with the class via electronic mail, they respond in writing by commenting on what they have learned and what questions, suggestions, or criticisms they have concerning the seminar subject matter and/or presentation. Other students are also free to leave a response as well. The presenter of the seminar paper then serves as the instructor by responding to these replies, comments, and questions.

Electronic conferencing is also used in "(Tele)Communicating Biology" for students' collaborative preparation and contributions to the publication of a biology newsletter for the department called "Biology Times—Get CoNnEcTeD." The students maintain complete ownership and editorship of the content. The newsletter is published at the beginning of each semester and distributed to all students, alumni, and faculty of the department. In addition, the newsletter is made available electronically via the Department of Biological Sciences' Gopher and Mosaic servers. For examples of the newsletter, see the URLs: http://bio444.beaumont.plattsburgh.edu/PDFiles/Biology/Bio380ATimesMay'95.pdf and Bio380BTimesMay'95.pdf. Other activities involve the preparation by each student of an Electronic Career Portfolio in the BIOCOM VAX Notes Conference. Students are assigned their own topic, in which they place material they prepare, such as an access permission form, cover letter, resume, biography, letter of recommendation for another student, seminar outline, term papers, etc. This material serves as assessment and evaluation material as well.

Using the Five-Minute Electronic Paper to Evaluate Course Content

I also use a five-minute electronic version of the "one-minute paper," advocated by Cross and Angelo (1988), as a quick, simple means of assessing student response to teaching-learning. Richard Light (1990) has suggested that the one-minute paper was the single most successful innovation that instructors in one study had applied in their classrooms. I too have found it to be invaluable, especially doing it via CMC using VAX Notes.

I use communication via the electronic conferences to evaluate course content by asking students to post a weekly "5 minute electronic paper" responding to the following two questions: 1) What was the major point you learned this week? and 2) What was a point you least understood? At the beginning of the first lecture of each week, I review and respond online and in class to each student. This exercise gives students the opportunity to put course content into their words, to tell me what I need to be reviewing in the lecture material for the next week and thus direct course content, and sometimes to follow a train of thought that may not have been fully formed during the class sessions of the previous week. The following comment illustrates this last point:

> My question concerns the experiment discussed in Thursday's class (T-cell differentiation/HLTA/ERFC receptor production). One of the inferences (you) made was that the growth factors (responsible) for HTLA/ERFC (appearance) were produced in the thymus (higher percentage of developed cells on thymus enriched media) and the cells which developed on the spleen enriched media were due to growth factors produced in the thymus but were carried to the spleen by lymph/blood. This seems a poor inference based on the data available. Maybe the growth factors are also produced in the spleen in smaller amounts or in equal amounts except for a few which are not present at all. Why not also add a fourth sample with serum enriched media and see if the growth factors are also present in blood?

Since I thought this quite an astute observation on the part of the student for an important control, I immediately sent an electronic message to the student telling him so, and asked if he would be interested in doing this as an undergraduate research project next semester. He answered affirmatively and later did the experiment. (He found no effect.)

I have also instituted online course evaluations to gain further insight into my teaching-learning. Students are asked to respond both at midterm and at the end of the semester to the following question: "What have you wanted to say that evaluation forms did not permit you to say?" After entering their replies, students can set the note to "hidden," so that only they and the instructor can read it.

Much of the reaction to the use of technology in the classroom has been positive. For example, students appreciate the opportunity to learn about these technologies, and to learn how they can be used in their fields to locate information and resources. They also have found that the writing exercises, facilitated by the technology, improve their understanding of the material. But, of course, the feedback has not been all positive, although it is always constructive. For example, some students have told me that they need more "paper" supplements to the electronic information, and their comments have been useful in assessing the effectiveness of tutorials and online assessments, and redesigning them. The most significant point that I have learned is that students will "say" things to a computer terminal that they will not say in the classroom environment, because of what they think, their colleagues might think or in a one-on-one situation in an instructor's office, where a student often feels intimidated.

Advantages of Telecommunications and Multimedia for Instruction

Why should universities, instructors, and students, turn to telecommunication and multimedia technologies? What are the educational benefits?

Access to CMC, multimedia stand-alone and client/server technologies, TCP/IP screen sharing, and desktop video conferencing in teaching-learning can give us another chance to solve current problems in education. To use them well, we need to apply them in the context of the familiar principles of scholarship and research. This simple change will lead to profound changes in scholarly communication, interactions between instructors and students, the skills of authorship, and the very paradigm of teaching-learning itself.

Telecommunications can easily provide rapid access to documents that can be conveniently updated to reflect new knowledge and incorporate new text, graphics, video, or audio material, without major overhauls in the structure of a presentation or lesson. Also, course materials are more readily available to learners without the arbitrary barriers of time and space.

Further, the judicious use of telecommunications and multimedia make course materials more engaging. Through the provision of high-quality sound, images, and video, multiple senses in the learner are engaged in the learning process. And when course materials are more engaging, they tend to be more "memorable" (Lewis 1993; Multimedia—A Primer for Educators, 1993). This is so because multimedia offers a far more effective way of communicating dynamic concepts than can media such as standard text and illustrations. The use of CMC and multimedia in VICE in REST has demonstrated a variety of advantages over traditional forms of classroom instruction.

Activates Individual and Group Participation

Students have more equal opportunity to participate when accessing information in an asynchronous mode via electronic mail, conferencing, and client server programs such as Gopher and Mosaic. Further, desktop video conferencing provides an "up close and personal" initial engagement which translates to "attention=retention." These are connectivity tools which, when combined with TCP/IP screen-sharing programs such as Timbuktu, offer new approaches for instruction not previously possible. Also, students are no longer restricted by the limited classroom time available in a given lecture or seminar session, and they are no longer restricted by fellow students who are quicker and more eloquent in their oral contributions. Having time to compose a response in a thoughtful fashion is a major condition for educating reflective learners. But the medium goes further and adds an important element—the element of writing for an audience. When everybody in class can read everyone else's comments, the motivation increases to express original ideas rather than parrot those of the instructor (Harasim 1990a, 1990b). Many of today's students lead hectic lives, especially the growing number of non-traditional, older students. Time for a college education is limited increasingly by other obligations. Systematic group work outside of class is not always possible, because class and work schedules (possibly combined with family responsibilities) leave little flexibility for extra activities. The only way to accomplish collaborative work is through a medium that allows people to interact with each other at their convenience, rather than a mutually agreed-upon time and place.

Creates Networks Between Instructors and Students

Most people are willing to use new avenues for making social contacts when they are encouraged and provided with a minimal structure. CMC such as electronic mail and conferencing, desktop videoconferencing, TCP/IP screen-sharing, client/server programs, and multimedia group activities, provide such new avenues. One can intentionally use a topic in the electronic conference as a general class forum on issues designated by students. In this fashion, one can encourage the development of a sense of community, in which class members learn to respect different opinions of others while at the same time arguing their point and developing their own convictions. Further, SUNY's seventeen campuses plus community colleges are largely now networked via SUNYNet (Kahn 1992). Linking student populations throughout the system via electronic mail and conferencing, desktop video conferencing, TCP/IP screen-sharing, and client/server public information access, such as that provided through Gopher and WWW clients, opens up a whole new dimension of the educational process and avenues for learning that no current classroom can provide.

Helps Reevaluate Teaching-Learning and Initiate
Course Redevelopment

Finally, as I incorporate more and more CMC and multimedia client/ server technologies in my teaching, I have come to question my traditional role as a instructor. I recognize more than ever that there is a positive impact on teaching-learning when I entrust students with more influence on the direction a class takes. Electronic mail and conferences, together with development of client/server multimedia information in a partnership, brings learners closer to instructors, learners closer to each other, and creates the opportunity for new contacts more readily.

With these new technologies, the instructor has, first and foremost, to be concerned with students' learning, i.e., with that part of the instructional process that the traditional knowledge-transfer model of teaching takes for granted. This difference in orientation causes considerable alterations in various aspects of the classroom. Thoughtful use of telecommunications and multimedia does improve student involvement in the learning process, reduces the feeling of anonymity that many students have in courses, and also contributes to a sense of community.

Important problems, however, have yet to be addressed if telecommunications and multimedia are to reach their full pedagogical potential (Lewis 1993). Besides issues of access and ease of use of the technology, the traditional structures of university teaching and learning create the biggest hurdles. Instructors will have to rethink their assumptions about teaching, and students will have to confront their entrenched expectations about classroom learning. Hence, the most promising potential of technology-based teaching-learning is that it can help us rethink the current teaching-learning paradigm.

VICE in REST is and always will be a work-in-progress. A long-range goal is that both science instructors and curious students would be able to log on to the server and find supplementary resources to teach and learn about many subjects in the biological sciences. Needless to say, these resources would act only as a map, NOT the actual science. To explore these VICE in REST navigation tools and teaching-learning materials, point your favorite Gopher client at baryon.hawk. plattsburgh.edu/11/Academic Departments/Biological Sciences 70, or WWW client to: http://bio444.beaumont.plattsburgh.edu/, and select the Biological Sciences link.

References

Adams, D., H. Carlson, and Hamm, M. (1990). *Cooperative learning and educational media: Collaborating with technology and each other.* Englewood Cliffs, N.J.: Educational Technology Publications.

Association of American Colleges. (1991). *Liberal learning and the arts and sciences major.* Washington, D.C.

Boyer, E. (1987). College: *The undergraduate experience in America.* New York: Harper & Row.

Cross, K. P. and Angelo, T. A. (1988). *Classroom assessment techniques: A Handbook for Faculty.* Ann Arbor: National Center for Research to Improve Postsecondary Teaching and Learning.

Gamson, Z. F. and Associates. (1984). *Liberating education.* San Francisco: Jossey-Bass.

Harasim, L. M. (Ed). (1990a). *Online education: Perspectives on a new environment.* New York: Praeger.

Harasim, L. M. (1990b). Computer-mediated communication and collaborative learning. Keynote address to the Conference on Collaborative Learning in Higher Education, Oct. 12, Bloomington, Indiana. ERIC Document Reproduction Service, ED 335 984.

Kahn, R. L., (1992). Overview of a statewide academic network SUNYNet. *T.H.E. Journal* 20(4):85.

Kehoe, B. P., (1992). *Zen and the art of the Internet: A beginners guide.* Englewood Cliffs, N.J.: Prentice Hall.

Lewis, C. T. and Hedegaard T. (1993). Online education: Issues and some answers. *T.H.E. Journal* 20(9):68.

Light, R., (1990). *Harvard Assessment Seminars, First Report.* Cambridge: Harvard University School of Graduate Education.

Multimedia—A Primer for Educators. (1993, Jan/Feb). Higher education product companion 2(2):16.

Svinicki, M. (Ed.) (1990). *The new face of college teaching.* San Francisco: Jossey Bass, New Directions in Teaching and Learning Series, No. 42.

The Solidarity Network

Universities, Computer-Mediated Communication, and Labor Studies in Canada

Jeff Taylor

Athabasca University is an open, distance university located in Athabasca, Alberta, Canada. Its mandate is to break down barriers that traditionally restrict access to university-level education. This mandate is interpreted broadly to include constraints of time, space, educational background, and social position. In the latter case, the university offers innovative programs in the areas of women's studies, native studies, and labor studies.

Athabasca University's Labour Studies Program is one of a small number of similar programs in Canada. It is unique in a couple of ways, however. For one thing, like all of Athabasca's programs it is available entirely through distance education, making it the only distance education labor studies program in the country. It is also unique in that the program has a mandate to provide education to its adult constituency, which in the first instance is the Albertan and Canadian labor movements. One of the ways this mandate is achieved is to collaborate with organizations, services, and educators in the labor movement.

In one such collaboration Athabasca University is cooperating with the Canadian Union of Public Employees (CUPE) and the Solidarity Network (SoliNet). CUPE is Canada's largest union, with over 400,000 members in 2200 locals scattered across the country. It represents public sector workers in hospitals, schools, municipalities, and other such work-places. SoliNet is an electronic mail and computer conferencing system owned and operated by CUPE since 1987, and made available to the Canadian labor movement generally. It links over one thousand users from across the country, as well as some subscribers from the USA and other countries, providing a vital information medium that is unconstrained by time and physical space (Belanger 1990a).

In the first part of this chapter, I will discuss SoliNet as an educational medium, highlighting the ways in which the network is currently used to conduct formal union education and to informally educate participants on a variety of issues of importance to the Canadian labor movement and its social partners. Particular attention is paid to the labor education conference that the Athabasca University Labour Studies Program conducted during the fall of 1992. In the latter part of the chapter, I will assess SoliNet's potential as a means of delivering university credit courses in labor studies to adult students in the labor movement. In so doing, I will place this experience in the general context of adult and workers' education. And I will briefly situate the argument in discussions about the social significance of computer-mediated communication (CMC) and the impact of CMC on the labor movement.

SoliNet

For CUPE, the main impetus in developing SoliNet was to provide for the union's own computer needs. A union of its size in a country like Canada, with six time zones, presented significant communication challenges. CMC seemed to offer a solution. After testing various electronic mail services, CUPE chose CoSy—the conferencing system developed at Canada's University of Guelph—because it combined e-mail and conferencing.[1] The latter feature was particularly attractive to an organization such as a union, in which group discussion work plays an important role.

Within CUPE, SoliNet conferences are used to coordinate collective bargaining by supporting contract negotiations and administration, keeping track of grievances throughout the union, providing research support to negotiators, and supporting strike activity. During contract negotiations, for example, geographically dispersed bargaining committee members participate in closed (confidential) conferences. Information for members is put in another closed conference, and members are asked for their response to management offers. This allows the bargaining committee to keep the membership fully informed and involved. During the life of a collective agreement, meanwhile, the filing of grievances is simplified because of the existence of a central grievance conference. Using text-searching procedures, union representatives can find information on specific grievances as they prepare their own grievance applications. In these and other ways, CMC has made CUPE's collective bargaining function more effective (Belanger 1990a).

Equally important, though, is SoliNet's educational potential for CUPE. For example, online short courses on technological change, women in the workplace, occupational health and safety, and union databases have been taught on SoliNet at different times since 1988. Participation has ranged from about thirty to one hundred people in these courses. Normally the courses run for one to two months and are moderated by an expert in the area. The courses are divided into weekly topics, with the moderator leading the discussion and uploading any relevant material into the conference. Participants then add comments at their leisure. As I write this, a month-long course entitled "Workers Controlling Technology" is being offered on SoliNet. It is conducted by Heather Menzies, a Canadian expert in the field.

CUPE also uses SoliNet to provide follow-up support for live courses, to link union education representatives, and to provide information through electronic newsletters. In the latter case, every Monday morning a summary of the previous week's labor news appears on SoliNet. CUPE and non-CUPE members can download the material to their own programs or printers and use it in their own newsletters.

From the beginning, CUPE intended that SoliNet would be made available and would be used by other unions and like-minded organizations and individuals. Some of the above features are used by other organizations. Other unions, for example, support their collective bargaining functions using SoliNet conferences. Furthermore, the weekly news bulletins, and short courses that are not CUPE-specific, are open and available to anyone who is a SoliNet subscriber (Belanger 1992a).

What is of more interest, however, are the topic-based online discussions that exist on SoliNet. From the "Lounge" (a general discussion conference) through "NDPLabour" (a conference discussing the relationship between the social-democratic New Democratic Party and the labor movement) to "ACN" (a conference devoted to the Action Canada Network, an organization originally formed to oppose the Canada-United States and North American free trade agreements), the broader concerns of the labor movement are debated and analyzed. It is in these conferences that the political and activist faces of the labor movement are most clearly revealed. In "NDPLabour," for example, an agonizing debate took place during 1993, as the Canadian labor movement was reassessing its historic relationship with the New Democratic Party (NDP). Many Canadian unions, including CUPE, are formally affiliated with the NDP. But many unionists felt betrayed by the NDP government in the province of Ontario (Canada's most populous province). Early in 1993, this government suspended collective bargaining rights for public sector workers and rolled back their wages. Debate raged as to whether or not the labor movement should withdraw its support for the NDP. This electronic conference provided a cross-section of the more general discussion. Participants from British Columbia (on the Pacific coast and with an NDP government) were able to debate participants from Ontario (a Great Lakes province) about the relative merits of the NDP administrations, for example.

The "NDPLabour" conference, and others like it, allow members of one union to speak with other unionists, and with individuals such as academics from outside the labor movement who are SoliNet participants, about issues of common concern. At its best, SoliNet is contributing to the building of a social movement when it facilitates these discussions and the actions that grow from them. In the "ACN" conference, and other conferences concerned with free trade, for example, resources and information that facilitate the struggle against free trade, and the corporate agenda that labor and others feel is being promoted by free trade, are shared. Furthermore, popular alternatives to this agenda are formulated, debated, and refined. In the process, links are made between individuals in various unions and, more importantly, relationships between the labor movement and kindred movements are nourished.[2]

SoliNet, then, has become a diverse medium which, at one end of the spectrum, serves the immediate collective bargaining needs of CUPE and other unions. At the other end, the network facilitates broader based political and social-movement organizing that sustains the labor movement and its vision.

Athabasca University and SoliNet

It is apparent both to SoliNet and to Athabasca University that collaboration is mutually beneficial. It is in SoliNet's interest to expand its educational offerings. Indeed, one of SoliNet's educational ideals always has been to offer an online university labor program. Similarly, the Athabasca University Labour Studies program is able to fulfill its mandate in a new and exciting way by adapting its offerings for electronic delivery on a union-based network. The labor studies program is able to provide an alternative method of course delivery to its core constituency and, in the process, raise its national profile.

The first example of Athabasca University—SoliNet collaboration is the Labour Education conference, which took place on SoliNet between October and December of 1992, and which was moderated by the Athabasca University Labour Studies Program. A total of sixty-eight individuals registered for the conference. Since CUPE has established computer facilities in offices across Canada, inevitably it was the majority union represented in the electronic conference. But the conference also attracted representatives from the United Steelworkers, the British Columbia Teachers Federation, the Telecommunications Workers, the Woodworkers, and others. Participants also included university labor educators from across Canada (some working overseas), and two from the USA.

The discussion followed a suggested agenda, with new topics introduced every week or every two weeks. These included the provision of labor education in Canada and abroad, links between internal union education programs and educational providers, the differences between industrial relations and labor studies, and the role of distance education and new communication technologies in labor education. But the discussion also ranged across the implications of post-fordism for labor, the role of intellectuals in the labor movement, and the nature of trade unionism. The agenda proved to be flexible and free-flowing. The conference generated 155 separate messages, a few of which were longer comments split into two shorter messages, while others were little more than participants' introducing themselves or the moderator's asking the contributors for more information on comments made. But the majority of the messages provided information, insights, and opinion on labor education that participants had experienced or offered (Taylor 1993).[3]

As an example of a specific topic, the discussion of new communication technologies revolved around how participants used SoliNet in their day-to-day work, the potential for computer networks in labor education, and the use of CD-ROM technology in labor education. The most interesting part of this section of the conference was Ken Hansen's report from the health and safety project that he runs in Mozambique (Hansen 1992). Hansen is developing a CD-ROM disk to animate the health and safety work in their project. The disk will have a large amount of text on technical and union issues in occupational health and safety, photos, drawings, and floor plans of workplaces and their hazards. It will also have sound (workplace noise, for example) and video images in the program. The users will be allowed to point and click their way through the content in the order they wish. Parts of it will look like a simulation game, while other parts will look like an expert system. The challenge, according to Hansen, will be to make the program truly interactive and popular educationally, rather than a pre-packaged message. In response to this challenge, he says, they will try to write the program so that there is access to a variety of viewpoints.

The role of the program will be to challenge and to question, rather than to dictate.

Athabasca University and SoliNet plan to offer the Athabasca Labour Studies Program online via SoliNet to trade unionists who are interested in pursuing university-level education, but who are unable to attend a traditional university, and for whom print-based distance education is unappealing. Students will be able to study either for the University Certificate in Labour Studies (thirty credits) or for the Bachelor of Arts Major in Labour Studies (120 credits). As a first step in this venture, the introductory labor studies course will be offered on SoliNet during the fall of 1994 to a group of CUPE members who have already completed some internal union education, and to CUPE education officers. Assuming this pilot project is successful, further courses will be offered on SoliNet the following year.

As a distance education university, Athabasca University is well placed to adapt its course for CMC delivery. Nearly all of Athabasca's courses, including all of those in the Labour Studies Program, are in print-based home-study packages. Most courses contain a student manual, which is an extensive outline of the course and a guide to university services; a study guide, which replaces the lectures of a traditional university and consists of questions and commentary built around readings; and textbooks and books of readings. A regular home-study student registering for an Athabasca University course receives the course package in the mail, has six months to complete a self-paced three-credit course, and has access to a telephone tutor to assist with the completion of the course (Van Duren 1989).

The CMC students on SoliNet will receive the regular home-study course package through the mail. (Eventually, all of this material may be available online—for most courses, it is in electronic form now—but for the first few CMC offerings we will use the print-based home-study courses and enhance them with CMC.) As they are registered as Athabasca students, they will be registered as SoliNet users and as members of the course conference. The CMC courses will be group-paced rather than self-paced. Hence, the group of 20–25 students in each class/conference will begin the course on the same day and the course will run for eighteen to twenty weeks. The conference will serve as a virtual seminar room in which various seminar topics will be discussed. Students will take turns leading the discussion in the conference. In the case of the introductory labor studies course, each of the six units in the course will be discussed for about three weeks. Students also will be required to complete three written assignments during the course. These will be sent to the instructor, and returned, using SoliNet's file transfer feature. Students also will be able to communicate with the instructor and with fellow students using electronic mail. For those courses that include a final examination (the introductory labor studies course does not), students will sit an invigilated examination in their home community, according to Athabasca University's regular examination procedures for its home-study students.

Workers' Education

Besides mutual benefit, there are broader reasons why Athabasca University and SoliNet should be cooperating. Historically, adult education and workers' education have been intimately linked. Indeed, in the British and Canadian traditions adult education has been synonymous with the provision and cultivation of critical skills for working people. An important part of this mission has been to provide students with the skills required for democratic citizenship. At its best, this tradition taught a broad curriculum based on the liberal arts, in which a critical perspective was developed and taught (Welton 1987; Friesen 1984).

In a cross-fertilization between teaching and scholarship, adult education teachers have made significant contributions to critical studies during the twentieth century. The lectures of cultural and literary critic Raymond Williams in the British Workers' Education Association and Oxford University's Extramural (adult education) department provided the material for many of his early books, most notably his reinterpretation of English literary history in *The Long Revolution* (Williams 1975; McIlroy 1993). Similarly, the English historian Edward Thompson sketched out his magnificent *The Making of the English Working Class* while he was an extramural tutor at Leeds University (Thompson 1953). And the Canadian economist and historian Clare Pentland, who wrote pioneering studies in Canadian economic and labor history, was a key figure in adult and workers' education in Manitoba between the late 1940s and the 1970s (Friesen 1993).

Primarily because of pressures from business and business supporters in colleges and universities, this critical and liberal arts orientation in adult education has been narrowed in recent years. Increasingly, adult education has come to mean "training" for the labor market, and notions of intellectual enrichment or cultivation of democratic sensibilities have been rendered unimportant, insignificant, or marginal. Worker education has become the training of workers (McIlroy and Spencer 1988; Welton 1987). In the process, the broader and more critical element of adult education as workers' education has become cloistered in labor studies, which has little more than a toehold in Canadian universities.

Furthermore, in Canada, most workers' education is carried on within unions (Swerdlow 1990). Major unions conduct their own educational programs and the national Canadian Labour Congress, the provincial federations of labor, and municipally-based labor councils host special schools for affiliated unions. In these educational programs, unions teach their members collective bargaining skills and how to be union stewards, provide a labor perspective on social and political issues, and give their members critical information on emerging workplace issues such as new managerial strategies. Hence, in contrast to the United States and the United Kingdom, where colleges and universities play a role in educational provision for unions, in Canada unions do their own educational work without relying on post-secondary institutions (Spencer 1994). Indeed, unions often are suspicious of universities and their objectives, which is not surprising given the increasingly business orientation of universities. The narrowing focus of adult education, coupled with the gulf between unions and universities, means that any links between unions and universities are difficult to cultivate and nurture. Many people in these two institutions, however, believe that such links are necessary, both to ensure that post-secondary education is accessible to working people and to counter the negative effects of business on universities.

Labor Studies and CMC

One of the attractions of CMC for distance-learning labor studies, therefore, is that it allows students to interact with one another. The conferencing component, in particular, facilitates group discussion and debate that is an important element in critical adult education and in labor studies. One of the drawbacks of print-based home study is that students learn in isolation. In the Athabasca University model, each student is assigned a telephone tutor, so the student has a learning mentor with whom to interact, but the contact with other students is limited, and group discussion is nonexistent. CMC may allow distance labor studies educators to retrieve this important element of adult education.

Within labor studies and in the labor movement, CMC is being promoted by some as a crucial element in the response of international labor and social solidarity movements to the current phase of capitalist development. Peter Waterman (1992), for example, argues that in the traditional labor movement communication practices were and are seen as means to organizational and institutional ends. They are simply tools to be used in the pursuit of labor organizing, mobilization, and bargaining. In other words, communication is seen as something that is external to the economy and society. As a result, while various media such as print played an innovative and exciting role when they were first used in the labor movement, they quickly became staid transmitters of information as they became institutionalized. This had negative consequences for the labor movement in earlier periods, but it poses a fundamental problem in the current epoch.

The present phase of capitalist development, Waterman maintains, is one in which information plays a significant role, and, in order for labor to mount an effective counter-offensive to capital, it must both develop a theory of communication and appreciate the impact and potential of CMC. This involves a recognition of the central economic and social role of communication, which means, among other things, that the phenomenon cannot be viewed instrumentally. Nor should one view CMC in either utopian or apocalyptic terms. Communication in general, and CMC in particular, will transform the conditions in which the labor movement operates, and will alter the practice of the labor movement regardless of the position unions take in relation to it. Like capitalism itself, communication is transformative.[4]

How, then, to proceed? First, the constraints on CMC have to be noted and analyzed. CMC had its origin in the defense department of the capitalist world's leading military power (Mosco 1989). Furthermore, like other communication media before it, in its early stages CMC is a relatively flexible, open, and accessible medium. It is easy for unions and similar organizations to set up and run their own networks or to gain access to international networks. But how long will this last? If the previous experiences of the press, radio or television are any guide, these spaces soon will be constrained or closed off as corporate control is exerted (Fones–Wolf 1993; Godfried 1993; Pizzigati and Solowey 1992).[5]

Second, what is the potential of CMC for the labor movement and for labor studies? If we accept that communication is more than a tool (Innis 1951; Williams 1975), that it is central to the way in which we interact in contemporary society (Habermas 1979), and that CMC in particular alters our social interactions (Poster 1990), how does this affect the way in which CMC is used? Some positively argue that CMC offers new democratic potentials, providing the basis for a new global civil society (Frederick 1992). Others are more skeptical about computer technology in general, pointing to the authoritarian uses of databases and electronic monitoring (Gandy 1989). While there is truth

in both of these positions, and they should be articulated and analyzed, they may be beside the point. The issue is how do we fit into
a mold the technology and the medium, while remaining conscious,
first, of their determining powers and, second, of their connection to
broader, inegalitarian social forces?

These are substantial theoretical questions that can only be raised
here. What should be noted, though, is that, since CMC is interactive,
there is a degree of social agency in the medium that is not present in
print, radio, television, or cinema, and that is greater than in telephone
voice communication. This is important in unions because the success
of the labor movement, measured by its ability to challenge the control
of business over workers' lives, ultimately depends on a membership
that is prepared to exercise its agency and power to shape its own
future. Of course, the technology cannot create agency, but it can facilitate its operation in a way that previous media could not.

In the case of education, which is the subject here, CMC offers
the opportunity to interact with a wider range of students than either
traditional classroom teaching or broadcast- and print-based distance
education. For labor studies, and other areas such as women's studies
where there is a critical connection between the academic material and
the intended audience, this interaction is crucial. It is not enough, in
other words, to convey information or to present a body of knowledge
for students' reception. Students must engage with the material and
interact with others, in order to understand the material and, more
importantly, to ensure that the material has an impact on their lives.
Furthermore, the experiences of the students are an important gauge
of the material's validity and a key primary source for the discipline
(Green 1992).

Conclusion

Computer-mediated communication is more than a tool for labor
movement activists and labor studies educators. It is a context in which
we are operating and will increasingly operate in the future. The issues we face are how do we move in cyberspace and how much of the
space are we able to claim and use in the face of the constraints that
dominant social and economic forces will surely exert? From an
educator's perspective, CMC offers new opportunities to rekindle the
critical, worker-centered legacy of adult education. It also allows the
Athabasca University Labour Studies Program to reach and serve a
wider and more geographically dispersed constituency than would
otherwise be the case. Furthermore, the medium's features ensure that

the social interaction that is crucial to workers' education can find a place in distance education. For the labor movement, meanwhile, CMC allows unions to communicate more easily and to interact with their members. And the international labor movement is able to coordinate its activities and to facilitate immediate communication among workers in various countries in the face of an avaricious global capitalism.

For worker educators in unions and in universities, CMC offers a potential medium of cooperation. In the face of a hostile social, economic, and political environment, in which labor is under attack and universities are faced with "business plans" in which they are told to do more training and less educating, cyberspace may be a place where alternate links can be sustained. In any event, we have little choice: the electronic mode of information is with us, and how we challenge, shape, and control it will determine our futures.

Notes

1. See Mason (1989) and McCreary (1989) for discussions of CoSy.

2. The three conferences named—ACN, Lounge, and NDPLabour—are all moderated by Marc Belanger, who is the coordinator of SoliNet. These conferences continue indefinitely, with the participation rate varying over time. Please note that these are general references to the conferences, each of which contains hundreds of individual messages: Belanger 1990b, 1992b, 1992c.

3. Again, please note that this is a general reference to the whole conference, which generated 155 separate messages during its two-months duration: Taylor 1992.

4. See Harvey (1989) for a broader theorization of the current phase of capitalist development.

5. For a slightly different experience, in which a radical newspaper adopted the techniques of capitalist marketing in order to survive, see Shore (1988).

References

Belanger, M. (1990a, May). SoliNet: Computer communications by an employees' union. In *Proceedings of the Third Guelph Symposium on Computer Mediated Communication* (233–245). University of Guelph, Guelph, Canada.

*Belanger, M. (Moderator) (1990b). LOUNGE. SoliNet electronic conference. Ottawa: Canadian Union of Public Employees.

Belanger, M. (1992a). Computer communications in the labour movement. *Labour Education* 89(4):3–6.

*Belanger, M. (Moderator) (1992b). ACN. SoliNet electronic conference. Ottawa: Canadian Union of Public Employees.

*Belanger, M. (Moderator (1992c). NDPLABOUR. SoliNet electronic conference. Ottawa: Canadian Union of Public Employees.

Davie, L. (1988). The facilitation of adult learning through computer-mediated distance education. *Journal of Distance Education* 3(2):55–59.

Fones–Wolf, E. (1993, October). *For better listening: Organized labor and radio, 1940–1960.* Paper presented at the Fifteenth Annual North American Labor History Conference, Detroit.

Frederick, H. (1992, September). *North American NGO computer networking against NAFTA: The use of computer communications in cross-border coalition-building.* Paper presented at the XVII International Congress of the Latin American Studies Association, Los Angeles.

Friesen, G. (1993). H. C. Pentland and Continuing Education at the University of Manitoba: Teaching Labour History to Trade Unionists. *Labour/Le travail 31*(Spring):301–313.

Friesen, G. (1994). *Adult education and union education: Aspects of English Canadian cultural history in the 20th century.* Unpublished paper, University of Manitoba.

Gandy, Jr., O. H. (1989). Information privacy and the crisis of control. In M. Raboy and P. A. Bruck (Eds.), *Communication for and against democracy* (37–58). Montreal: Black Rose.

Godfried, N. (1993, October). *Propaganda, education, and alternative broadcasting: Organized labor and radio stations WCFL and WEVD, 1926–1938.* Paper presented at the Fifteenth Annual North American Labor History Conference, Detroit.

Green, J. (1992). Making access to higher education meaningful to unionized workers: A case report. *Labor Studies 17,*(2) (Summer):18–30.

Hansen, K. (1992). Message Number 146. In J. Taylor (Moderator), *Laboureduc/general.* SoliNet electronic conference. Ottawa: Canadian Union of Public Employees.

Habermas, J. (1979). *Communication and the evolution of society.* Boston: Beacon.

Harvey, D. (1989). *The condition of postmodernity.* Oxford: Basil Blackwell.

Innis, H. A. (1951). *The bias of communication.* Toronto: University of Toronto Press.

Mason, R. (1989). An evaluation of CoSy on an Open University course. In R. Mason and A. Kaye (Eds.), *Mindweave: Communication, computers and distance education* (115–145). Oxford: Pergamon.

McCreary, E. (1989). Computer-mediated communication and organizational culture. In R. Mason and A. Kaye (Eds.), *Mindweave: Communication, computers and distance education* (101–112). Oxford: Pergamon.

McIlroy, J. and Spencer, B. (1988). *University adult education in crisis.* Leeds Studies in Adult and Continuing Education, University of Leeds.

McIlroy, J. (1993). Border country: Raymond Williams in adult education. In J. McIlroy and S. Westwood (Eds.), *Border country: Raymond Williams in adult education.* Leicester: National Institute of Adult Continuing Education.

Mosco, V. (1989). Critical thinking about the military information society: How Star Wars *is* working. In M. Raboy and P. A. Bruck (Eds.), *Communication for and against democracy* (37–58). Montreal: Black Rose.

Pizzigati, S. and Solowey, F. J. (Eds.) (1992). *The new labor press: Journalism for a changing union movement.* Ithaca: ILR Press.

Poster, M. (1990). *The mode of information: Poststructuralism and social context.* Cambridge: Polity.

Shore, E. (1988). *Talkin' socialism: J. A. Wayland and the radical press.* Lawrence: University Press of Kansas.

Spencer, B. (1994, June). *Labour education in Canada: What's going on?* Paper presented at the Society for Socialist Studies Annual Meeting, Calgary.

Swerdlow, M. (1990). *Brother Max: Labour organizer and educator.* St. John's: Committee on Canadian Labour History.

Taylor, J. (Moderator). (1992) LABOUREDUC/GENERAL. SoliNet electronic conference. Ottawa: Canada Union of Public Employees.

Taylor, J. (1993, June). *Labour education conference on SoliNet.* Paper presented at the Society for Socialist Studies Annual Conference, Ottawa.

Thompson, E. P. (1963). *The making of the English working class.* London: Victor Gollancz.

Van Duren, J. (1989). CMC at Athabasca University. In R. Mason and A. Kaye (Eds.), *Mindweave: Communication, computers and distance education* (211–214). Oxford: Pergamon.

Waterman, P. (1992). *International labor communication by computer: The Fifth International?* The Hague: Institute of Social Studies.

Welton, M. R. (Ed.) (1987). *Knowledge for the people: The struggle of adult learning in English-speaking Canada 1818–1973.* Toronto: OISE.

Williams, R. (1975). *The long revolution.* London: Pelican.

*These dates refer to the year during which these ongoing electronic conferences commenced.

Creating a Virtual Academic Community

Scholarship and Community
in Wide-Area Multiple-User
Synchronous Discussions[1]

Michael Day
Eric Crump
Rebecca Rickly

Welcome to Cyberspace!

"Now, please, everyone lock your wigs, let the air out of your shoes and prepare for a period of simulated exhilaration! Everybody ready? Let's get in 'sync' for our Flight To The Future!"[2]

The tour guide's scenario might sound a bit Disneylandish, but then many portrayals of cyberspace and virtual reality in the popular media have had fabulous, futuristic, gee-whiz qualities to them. That, or they are sprinkled with fear, with nightmarish invocations of Big Brother. Or both. In our experience, however, cyberspace is neither an eternally approaching technoUtopian future nor a yawning techno-totalitarian pit about to swallow civilization. It is radical and exciting and ordinary. As Amy Bruckman noted during a 1993 CNN feature on virtual reality, "People talk about cyberspace as if it were the future, but cyberspace is here—this is it. People live online in this world and make friends there, and work there, and play there."

And they are learning in it. Widely accessible real-time communication and textually-constructed virtual environments are springing up rapidly, and are providing new prospects for engaging in the on-going learning process. These social spaces—which exist in the intricate web of wires that cuddle the planet—represent the emergence of a new kind of learning environment. What we suspect is a new university is spreading rhizomatically and quite literally beneath the hoary brick and mortar of the ancient academy. As an institution, the university is now faced with hard choices, whether to somehow incorporate these new environments into its time-honored structures (thereby altering the old structures in unpredictable ways), or to resist the insidious encroachment of the Net. Based on our own research and early explorations of real-time communication on the Internet we think the former is the better course.

Professional Communities

As an example of professional community building on the network, we will trace briefly the progress of a group of scholars who have found a new way of productively brainstorming and collaborating in a virtual, text-based real-time environment. The authors and a number of colleagues from MBU-L (MegaByte University, a distributed electronic mail list devoted to teaching writing more effectively using computers) discovered the sometimes wild world of Internet Relay Chat (IRC), a program that allows global real-time communication in writing via networked personal computers. Although the group was already part of an electronically constituted community, accustomed to discussing issues, sharing assignments, and reporting on successes and failures in our various projects, meeting on IRC introduced a new and exciting dynamic to our work together.

Imagine sharing the screen with two, five, or even more colleagues in order to brainstorm as if you were talking around a conference table! Some readers may be familiar with the "talk" feature on the Internet, where two people, even though they are in distant locations, can converse with each other in writing. Others may be familiar with an in-class real-time computer networked writing environment known as ENFI, Electronic Networks for Interaction. This environment was originally developed for deaf students at Gallaudet University by Trent Batson, but writing instructors soon discovered that the activity of writing to each other on a computer network helped even hearing enabled students gain confidence in their writing. At schools around the world, students regularly meet with teachers to discuss issues and write collaboratively on the network, using programs such as Forum or Daedalus InterChange.[3] Teachers report major successes creating communities of writers using programs like these.

Internet Relay Chat

Many of the writing teachers who used these tools with their classes wanted to be able to use the same tools to talk to each other. The only problem for the 480 (as of Nov. 27, 1993) teachers on MBU was their geographic separation. The tools they used in the networked classroom did not allow them to communicate in the same way on the network. Stumbling upon IRC late in 1991 seems to have provided a solution to geographic distance.

A few years ago, other Internet users discovered that they needed a tool they could use to talk with each other in groups in real time. So Jarkko Oikarinen, a Finnish programmer, created IRC to allow real-time multi-user interactions on the network. The software is free, which means that almost anyone with Internet access can download client and server programs and use them to talk with others.

In early 1992, a few members of MBU-L created a virtual academic IRC community, meeting regularly on channel #cw to discuss pedagogy, theory, and practical concerns of writing teachers. Early on, they read and discussed an interesting thesis by Australian researcher Elizabeth Reid, *Electropolis: Communication and Community on Internet Relay Chat*.[4] Reid asserts that IRC is a developing subculture and can be described as a postmodern phenomenon. She also shows how the lack of visibility, voice, and physical presence of the communicating parties could actually help some shy people gain confidence in writing to others, because they cannot be seen. Further, Reid discussed how the use of graphical elements and textually described expressions and emotions helped to build a sense of shared community.

MediaMOO

The biweekly discussions on IRC continued until April 1993, when many of us on MBU saw an intriguing invitation. MIT media researcher Amy Bruckman had set up a special virtual environment called Media-MOO on a computer in her department and made it available to scholars of media studies, composition, and communication. To understand what MediaMOO is, some background may be needed, a brief description of MUDS and MOOs (members of a family of programs often referred to collectively as MU*s) follows.

A MUD is a Multiple-User Dimension (or Dungeon, a name left over from the days when these environments were used purely for sophisticated versions of Dungeons and Dragons-like games.) It is a computer database that allows multiple users to log in by telnet and interact with each other in real time. A few years ago, one of the programmers at Xerox's Palo Alto Research Center, Pavel Curtis, came up with a simplified code for a new kind of MUD, the MOO. MOO means MUD, Object Oriented. In the MOO, users can easily create and manipulate virtual objects (which are themselves functioning programs), as well as move from virtual room to virtual room—all in textual form.

Now, why would writing teachers want to have programmable objects and rooms, instead of just text? Quite simply, to provide divided spaces or channels (the rooms) in which they can work uninterrupted by others, and to allow them to create text-objects, such as working drafts or notes, which they can show to other participants. Just as you might hand around copies of a handout in a conference room, or project it on the wall, so can you share prewritten texts with others in the MOO. With everyone viewing the same piece of writing, you can then discuss it and modify it. Each person can mail the text to him- or herself and have an electronic copy at home, or print it out. The same is true for the discussion itself. All participants can save a copy of the text of the session, print it out, revise it, take ideas from it, and then use it to create a more formal written document, such as one to be published or presented at a conference.

Further, the text-based virtual reality in the objects and rooms of the MOO creates a metaphoric place, a constructed world, a fictional work/playspace that allows teachers and researchers to vicariously experience a textual environment in a manner similar to the way they use the creative imagination in reading and writing good fiction. With the current state of communication on the network—voiceless and disembodied—teachers and researchers use their imaginations and the MOO environment to create a sense of *place* in which productive and creative interaction can occur.

For those who participated in electronic mail exchanges and were accustomed to the semi-formal presentation style of e-mail messages, the new real-time environments of IRC and MOO offered the possibility of rather down-and-dirty brainstorming sessions, which had features of both oral discussion and written argument.

On a continuum between formal publication and casual hallway chat, e-mail discussions such as MBU lie somewhere around the middle, and IRC and MOO a little closer to casual talk. IRC and MOO differ from oral chat in that they occur completely in writing (real-time written conversation), so the interaction can be recorded and saved. In this environment, the words are not evanescent; they have a substance only writing can give them. Anyone can save them, refer back to them, and modify them, just as many members of the professional community have done to prepare chapters and conference presentations.

However, the resemblance of real-time networked communication to oral interaction is strong enough that these real-time environments actually represent a convergence of orality and literacy. Indeed, where Walter Ong (1982, 136) calls telephone, radio, and television, among other media, "secondary orality," Eric Crump sees these text-based real-time exchanges as a kind of "tertiary orality" (Symposium,

1993). Playful repartee and thoughtful exchange naturally mingle in this environment, just as they do in friendly oral exchanges among scholar/teachers.

In the tertiary orality of real-time networked environments, composition teachers and scholars can collaborate on projects in a virtual roundtable to come up with ideas that none of them would have hit upon on their own. It is this process that, following the biological model, we call synergy.

Synergy and "Thought-Coming-Into-Existence"

The exploratory nature of the medium makes it ideal for collaboration and invention, for testing new ideas, for capturing thought as it comes into being—before the critical consciousness has a chance to kick in and censor the statement that might, with further consideration, have seemed too odd to utter. Because of the sheer pressure to enter into the conversation or not be heard, participants must think on the fly, inventing at the edge of consciousness and possibility. In so doing, they may stumble upon truths and ideas they might have cast off in the highly reflective self-consciousness of the "solitary writer crafting sentences" scenario. If they permit these utterances to fly out, others may see in them ideas the original writer had not foreseen, and build upon them. In so doing, the participants collaborate to bring thought-structures into being through writing. As such, the natural heuristic effect of rapid oral interaction can influence the invention process of a conversation that is also a written document.

IRC, MOO, and Community Building

Many researchers have noticed that the real-time environment extends and solidifies the solidarity and community one comes to feel after being part of scholarly e-mail exchanges like MBU for a while. Where the scholars interacting on e-mail are separated by both distance and time, IRC and MOOs bring them together in time, and allow them to quickly exchange feelings and ideas in a sort of "virtual roundtable" discussion that at times seems to have extraordinary power to generate new ideas. The synergy of "thought-coming-into-existence," then, is a communal endeavor, fueled by the interactions that occur.

Invisible Bodies, Graphical Emotions

On IRC and MOOs, writers can put in as much of themselves as they want to; the physical cues of face-to-face conversation (dress, appearance, sex, race) are not at issue, with the result that they feel safer that others will not be judging them on those cues. The emotional cues are generated purely through graphical means, such as the smiley faces, or words like <blushes> that describe actions associated with emotion. These emotional cues—methods of graphically displaying surprise, joy, sadness, interest, or anger on the screen—serve to let participants experience more of each others' virtual personalities, and in so doing build a sense of shared experience and community vital to the collaborative writing environment.

Getting Accustomed

Real-time environments such as IRC and MOOs have been criticized as fancy playthings, a waste of time. Like any medium for communication, they can be used for mindless chat. But they do have possibilities for invention and collaboration when participants actively set up goals for each session and do their best to abide by those goals.

Further, the graphical interface, with comments scrolling by at odd speeds, and questions distant from their answers, can be highly unnerving to some. However, academics *can* get used to it if they give it a chance; it is just as valuable (or more) as a roundtable discussion at a national conference, in terms of the wealth of ideas exchanged and explored. In terms of overcoming the geographic isolation of places such as Rapid City, South Dakota, or Muncie, Indiana, or Columbia, Missouri, the real-time globally networked environment daily provides many of the features of a face-to-face meeting or conference, with none of the associated costs of travel.

Electronic conferences such as these should never completely replace face—to—face meetings. Indeed, nothing can replace the spontaneity and interaction of oral exchange. Amy Bruckman notes that "Embodied experience has features the virtual can not and should not try to replace. It's not a substitute—it's something different" (Roush 1993). Yet virtual environments have features embodied experience cannot match. The real-time networked environment can allow us to stay better connected with colleagues with similar interests around the world, and this feature is especially important to scholars who reside in geographically isolated places. They can stay in touch with the latest developments and collaborate on projects day-by-day instead of waiting for the postal services to deliver correspondence and print journals.

But the value of these environments is not limited to collegial interaction. They are already being used in some schools to connect writing classes across the country for group work.

Some writing teachers hope that students will receive valuable feedback and a sense of purpose to their writing through a combination of real-time and e-mail exchanges with their peers in other locations. These real-time written exchanges have proven their worth on local area networks as invention and dialogic tools for writing classes, but the challenge now is to find ways to allow students from different geographic locations to work together in MOO-like environments. Some researchers have noted that not only does the MOO provide a place for interaction in writing, it also constitutes an environment that can be manipulated only in text. In the hands of capable teachers who set up writing-curriculum oriented goals for their students, interaction on the MOO may indeed help students become more confident and versatile writers. Indeed, as Fred Kemp (1993) and Michael Day (1993) have suggested, we may be able to harness some of the energy young people put into Nintendo, and use their urge to manipulate their environment on the computer screen as a way to get them involved in writing and interacting with others.

Many have claimed that the advent of computer-mediated communication has brought about a paradigm shift in the nature of communication itself. In the workplace, the instantaneous nature of e-mail and the possibility of collaborative projects across great distances has changed the way people work. If communication and work have changed to some degree, and will continue to change, do we not owe it to our students to reflect those changes in what we teach and how we teach it?

We are not arguing that real-time network environments supplant oral and paper-based communications. We wish to provide alternative avenues for our students to succeed, but we will continue to teach using the more familiar oral discussions and paper-based reports, in order to prepare students for a wide range of communicative tasks. In terms of its ability to stimulate invention, feedback, and discovery of audience, we think that real-time networked environments should be added to our list of writing tools.

Student Communities

After our successful collaborative sessions held on IRC, and later on MU*s, it seemed natural to us that writing teachers would want to give their students the same opportunity for successful global collaboration—not such a big leap for many students. Today, networked classroom discussion programs running on a local area network (LAN), like InterChange and Aspects[5], allow students to hold synchronous class discussions electronically. When they first enter college, many students operate more comfortably on an oral plane than on a written one; these electronic forums, then, provide a much-needed bridge between oral and written discourse (Butler 1989; Bump 1990; Langston and Batson 1990; Day and Batson, 1995). While little hard data presently confirm the success of synchronous conferencing programs at improving students' more traditional writing, or how they influence the quality/participation level of students in traditional class discussion, their advocates staunchly support their use.

At one time, networked classrooms were heralded as the great equalizer: their introduction was supposed to provide an egalitarian forum where teachers weren't privileged by their physical presence at the front of the room, where students could not be interrupted, where student to student discourse could take place, where all students could participate in the making of meaning, rather than the more traditional oral "call and response"-type question and answer sessions. The advocates of networked classrooms hoped that the physical anonymity that the students felt would allow the more reticent among them to feel confident stating their views, that groups of people who had been "marginalized" due to race, ability, gender, etc. would be placed on the same level as those in the middle, and that everyone would have the chance to participate equally in the social construction of knowledge. Later, as the field began to look more critically at what it was embracing (prompted by articles like Hawisher and Selfe's (1991) "Rhetoric of Technology"), the *inherent* value of these synchronous conferencing programs has been brought into question, for in many instances, the interaction is NOT egalitarian. Professors often respond more or less frequently to men than women; not all students participate at the same level or as often; and the professor still has the power of surveillance, and can go back and check to see who participates, basing a grade on the amount of participation.

Clearly, the technology of the classroom and its associated power codings cannot be usurped simply by introducing network technology. But network technology also offers access to a vast educational underworld that is not yet marked by the same hierarchies of power. Out on the Internet—where authority is widely dispersed—there's less resistance to egalitarian social and educational relationships. Professors and students may not *be* equals, but they have equal access to the conversation. Computer-network technology is not so radically egalitarian when it is squeezed into the established power structure of the classroom, but outside the classroom, out in the anarchic, diverse melee of the global network, it provides an environment in which authority is distinctly reconfigured.

Internet programs like IRC and MU*s are natural extensions of LAN-based programs like InterChange and Aspects, since they, too, can provide an electronic forum for class discussion using a real-time written medium. In IRC or MU*s, however, the student knows that the participants are not limited to those with access to the LAN, which creates a true sense of anonymity. They know as well (or soon discover) that, while rules of "netiquette" do exist, they are covert and changeable on the Internet. Finally, a conversation held in IRC or MU*s belongs more to the student, for it is more difficult (though not impossible) for a teacher to watch, record, or grade the amount or quality of participation on such a forum.

A sample assignment asking students to explore IRC on their own and then analyze their experience follows:

Analysis of IRC Community

Based on your observations of and reactions to at least five IRC channel discussions, write a paper examining *how* community is formed in this electronic medium. As you write up your essay, remember to blend observation with interpretation: What did you "see" and "hear"? What did it mean? Keep the following points in mind as you observe, participate, and write:

—How well do the participants already seem to know each other? How can you tell when participants are or are not already acquainted?

—How are newcomers received into any particular discussion?

—What kinds of "netiquette" rules are at work in each discussion? In other words, what standards of verbal propriety are at work in each discussion? How are they maintained?

—Do smaller communities exist within larger discussions? What kind of community dynamics exist there?

—Because this is a purely verbal medium, participants rely almost entirely on language to convey their personalities. In what ways do you see individual personalities expressed? How are YOU using language to express your own personality?

—Does anonymity of the participants alter how they react to one another, including yourself and other participants?

—How do you see community formation occurring within the IRC setting?

—How does an IRC community differ from other communities in which face-to-face interaction occurs?

Benefits of Networking

What are the benefits of such a global interaction? To determine this, we first need to assess what we deemed beneficial in our own collaborations, then see if it crossed over to the students' experience. As mentioned before, the interaction in IRC and MU*s is often fast and furious, mimicking an oral exchange, but with a textual base, which allows for more specificity, gives a point of reference, which then allows for synthesis to occur more easily. Students who find themselves more comfortable in an oral medium are often "at home" on these programs due to the similarity to oral utterances. Students often purposely disregard conventions of edited English, spelling phonetically, not using capitalization or other punctuation, often in an effort to create a sort of "voice." Yet they are usually quick to clarify if someone doesn't understand what they meant.

As scholars, we found the synchronous Internet programs beneficial in terms of developing new communities, and in strengthening existing communities. Students found the community-building inherent to these media to be perhaps the most important aspect of using IRC and MU*s. The writing students who used these programs were overwhelmed at the possibility of communicating with people all over the world. They all returned frequently on their own, even after the assignment was finished, to continue conversations with those they'd met before, as well as to meet others with whom they might enjoy engaging in a dialogue. Interestingly, many students who enjoyed the orality of the medium often began to rely on a more text-based form of communication as they became involved in an electronic community. Once comfortable within a community, they taught each other to send e-mail over the Internet, and composed more thoughtful asynchronous exchanges, much as we had done while getting to know one another. Thus, for some the real-time networked environment formed a bridge from casual oral to more sustained written forms of communication.

A secondary benefit, one that the students (and we) didn't count on, was the opportunity this medium gave to examine electronic exchange in the context of more traditional oral and written communication. In our experience, we were often mistaken as to the identity of an electronic speaker, often placing him/her on a much higher level (interestingly, never lower) in the hierarchy of the academic community (for instance, when we began this project, we were all graduate students; yet we each assumed the other two were full professors, based on the ethos they had created over the net). Students who examined responses they got soon became suspicious as to who was telling the "truth" about themselves (as one young woman put it, "I met four men in one evening who were blond, blue-eyed, and 170 pounds—that can't happen, can it?"). As they became more comfortable, they began to experiment with the medium, constructing themselves as "other" in order to see how they would be received. Many students came away from this experience angry or frustrated, recognizing for the first time what it might be like to be marginalized. They conducted informal research on their own, and placed the knowledge they gained into their growing awareness of the conventions operating in the formation and maintenance of community.

Based on observations of the students' reactions, one of us decided to explore the boundaries of discourse by doing a little "gender-bending" of her own—and like her students, was intrigued, angry, and frustrated at the results. Her story follows:

> Identity is easy to manipulate on most MU*s. For instance, when a "guest" logs on many of the MU*s, no description or address is available for that person. Once when I was logged on as a guest on Media MOO, I entered a discussion with three "regular" characters (all young males in their early to mid-twenties, all at respected universities). I attempted to join in, but my statements were discounted until they found out that I was "Paul" from "Indiana University" and a "full professor of English, with a specialization in rhetoric" (I am female, and, at the time, a graduate student in composition).
>
> I was given instant credibility and authority. Suddenly I was being asked my opinion, and it was received with thoughtful consideration—the very same opinion that, only a few moments earlier, had been either ignored scoffed at. Like my students, I was made aware of the conventions that surround the interaction of the community to which I belong.

This account illustrates how electronic, verbal exchange on the net allows both students and professors to discern characteristics (and constraints) of human interaction that too often are practically invisible to us in face-to-face situations.

Negotiating Change

Escape from the classroom! Flourishing egalitarian communities! Freedom to experiment with identity! It is easy to get excited about the possibilities these real-time Internet applications open up for students and teachers—they *are* thrilling; we *are* excited—but as we participate in the technological reshaping of education, enthusiasm is often tempered by the less glorious side of the revolution. We face everything from annoying technical snarls to disturbing incidents involving violations of privacy and individual rights. It is tempting for technophiles and other true believers to dismiss these problems as mere "growing pains." And while there seems to be no evidence that the once-feared "Big Brother"-type surveillance system will come about, we need to heed the disturbing cases of abuse that continually surface, lest they become widespread. How we go about addressing the social and educational problems presented by the Net in general, and its realtime environments in particular, will be acutely affected by a situation that is not so much a specific problem as an eternal quandary. As Nancy Kaplan (1991), Cynthia Selfe (1992), and others have asserted, no technology is free of ideology. Or desire, we would add. Ideology and desire are lenses through which we can apprehend nearly everything humans do, so it is important to keep our eyes open to what they can reveal about relationships as fundamental as the one between technology and (academic) culture. As we consider how IRC/MU*s might contribute to education, we have to keep in mind that in addition to social and technical problems, political and cultural tensions will be produced. Traditions and conventions of all sorts are being buffeted by the winds of change, and whenever that occurs, the adherents of the new and old orders (and the majority with mixed allegiances) often get into ideological wrestling matches. The stakes are high enough. Everyone has some interest—financial, professional, personal—in which particular technologies, which sets of practices and values, and which cultural features surface as dominant.

Currently, digital technologies and their associated features (some of which we've discussed above) are ascending. Print technology and culture are still unquestionably dominant, but the challenge of computer-mediated communication is a serious one, one the Old Order will not avoid. Still, the process through which the technocultural transformation from print to network takes place is not determined and not predictable in any but the broadest terms. The technology that enables real-time communication tends to be extremely flexible. We might say that various real-time computer-mediated communication (CMC) applications inherently promote no particular agenda, but that is not the same as ignoring the ideological implications of these applications. They provide a space in which a tumble of competing agendas can be unleashed to contend for the prize of power and cultural dominance.

Real-time environments can as easily be used to control access to power and protect an establishment status quo as they can to provide open—perhaps egalitarian, perhaps anarchic—power relations. At the extremes, political mayhem, unfettered greed, and sexual predation are already surfacing in these new environments, along with (sometimes within) the utopian democratic environments we prefer to emphasize. Rather than transitory difficulties (i.e., "growing pains"), these problematic aspects of real-time conferencing may be signs of maturity. They indicate that enough people with enough diversity of cultural and ethical interest are interacting within a shared "space": a culture has developed, and with it come the problems that typically befall people coexisting in such diverse cultural space.

As Amy Bruckman suggests, the network world is a thriving and teeming place where people work and play and, well, *live*. And as with life outside the wires, whenever humans come together, complex social relationships develop. We have seen tightly knit, intellectually stimulating communities emerge in the real-time environments we've described. The Netoric Project on MediaMOO is one example. Netoric is a suite of virtual conference rooms and resources for composition teachers created and coordinated by Tari Fanderclai and Greg Siering. Every Tuesday night, Netoric holds an open public meeting in one of their rooms, the Tuesday Cafe, that often attracts twenty or more teachers. There is always a specific and timely topic of professional interest, but the conversation is frequently littered with personal asides, jokes, gossip—all the social "glue" that holds communities together and helps people enjoy what otherwise *could* be just another dreadfully dull working meeting.

Tuesday Cafe may epitomize the exciting, productive, and liberating aspect of real-time network places. But a MOO can just as easily host virtual atrocities. In horrifying detail, Julian Dibble has chronicled the virtual sexual abuse of two MOO players. "A Rape in Cyberspace" tells of an incident on a MOO in which one person manipulated text so that it would seem as if several other characters (inhabited by real people) were committing various humiliating and unspeakable sexual acts. The incident occurred in a public room in full view of others watching in horror on their computer screens, so the effect of the violation was increased. The fact that the whole event occurred as disembodied text, text formed of ephemeral electrons no less, does not mitigate its social and technological implications. The same program that provides teachers and students with a liberating and collegial environment in this case provided a sociopath with the means to humiliate and abuse real people via their virtual personae. Dibble says the story

> asks us to shut our ears momentarily to the techno-utopian ecstasies of West Coast cyberhippies and look without illusion upon

the present possibilities for building, in the online spaces of this world, societies more decent and free than those mapped onto dirt and concrete and capital.

Of course, we would hasten to add that to "look without illusion" (even if possible!) requires that we hold at arms' length not only "techno-utopian ecstacies" but perhaps dystopian neo-Luddite paranoia, as well. Between these extreme tendencies, and between the extremely wonderful and horrific online events that emerge to corroborate both, is a vast middle ground of experience that includes a diverse mix of productivity and destructiveness, of zeal and restraint, of joy and anger. We probably shouldn't find it strange that life on the net is very similar to life in the physical realm.

The process of creating a safe and civilized real-time network world where scholarship can flourish will be quite a challenge, not the least because these environments tend to provoke such acute cultural tensions within the academy. IRC and MU*s foster a certain amount of anarchy. In their "natural" state, they are subversive, at least relative to stable, traditional, institutional formations, in that the activities they facilitate often violate the sensibilities of print-oriented academicians. Print and its attendant culture adhere to principles of depth of thought, originality, efficiency of expression, linearity of form, and— Richard Lanham adds—a fundamental self-denial (1992). Real-time online environments may kindle more resistence and resentment from print-based scholars than other computer-mediated communication forms because they are more dramatically different from print in terms of the style of writing and interaction they foster. Lanham argues that digital media in general are fostering the reassertion of rhetorical sensibilities and approaches, as opposed to the Platonic tradition of dialectic and philosophy which has held sway at least since the sixteenth century and the influence of Peter Ramus. Real-time CMC environments epitomize his claim; they lean even further back toward oral and rhetorical modes than do asynchronous online environments. They favor copiousness, expansiveness (we could even call it "verbal voluptuousness"); a tendency toward superficiality, indulgence, and encompassing inclusivity. In such a way, these environments could even be said to revive something of the "multiplex ratio disputandi" of renaissance humanism; that joy in exploring issues that do not easily resolve into simple binaries.

Real-time CMC environments may simply appear too messy to be valuable from the perspective of those oriented toward print. They incorporate a great deal of "phatic" communication, which on the surface seems pointless and humdrum—mere "noise" to some—but on a deeper level serves to build and maintain the kinds of cooperative relationships scholars need to be able to work together productively. So much of the conversation and interplay may seem pointless (and would be in a print venue), but it does have purpose in constructing a community of scholars, just as cocktail party banter at a major conference can serve to build connections among academics. Collaborative work of the sort we do in these environments may also seem counterproductive to academics for whom the notions of individuality and originality in scholarship are most important. Looking at a transcript of a MU* session, in which ideas build as they are passed from person to person, one might ask, "How do we tell which ideas belong to which people? How do we ascribe ownership?" Contemporary critical theory has problematized the notion of originality, however, and many scholars are becoming more comfortable with assigning authorship or ownership to a group. Still, the speed of network interaction and the mutability of "authoring groups" make it difficult for text produced online to find a neat fit with standard conceptions of authorship/ownership.

We can find several historical moments parallel to the experiences of those pushing for acceptance of real-time CMC environments in the world of mathematics, specifically fractal theory and fuzzy logic. James Gleick tells us how pioneers in chaos studies struggled to be understood prior to the general acceptance of chaos as a legitimate science. Gleick says that at the time Benoit Mandelbrot was first describing the phenomenon of fractional dimensions, the very idea of fractals was "a conceptual high-wire act. For nonmathematicians it required a willing suspension of disbelief" (1987, 98). The reason disbelief required suspending, according to Mandelbrot, was the "total absence of intuition. One had to create an intuition from scratch. The old intuition was misleading" (Gleick 1987, 102). From the perspective of conventional wisdom, even in its best and highest form, fractals were impossible. Scientists were trained to be sophisticated observers of the world, but their training itself blinded them to the possibility of fractional dimensions. Likewise, a lifetime of training and practice in the conventions and values of print make it very difficult for many scholars to apprehend the possible value of real-time textual interaction.

Lofti Zadeh recounts a similar resistance from the scientific community to his fuzzy logical theories of machine control based on degree and imprecision. The artificial intelligence community so deeply "embraced classical logic, classical predicate logic" (Woehr, 47) that they refused to see the value of the new intuition Zadeh had pioneered.

Likewise, scholars in many disciplines today are so immersed by their acculturation in a print-oriented academy that they find it difficult to see real-time network communication as anything but a marginal oddity, a place for immature students to gab but not a place for legitimate inquiry and interaction to thrive. Technophiles and other true believers often exhibit the inverse, finding it difficult to see how print practices and approaches might profitably inform real-time environments. Somewhere between these emotionally charged positions there must be a space in which this technocultural transformation can be productively negotiated.

We count among the assets of IRC and MU* environments the fact that they are opportunities for testing and perhaps breaching the traditional boundaries that segregate academic communities and sensibilities, boundaries such as those beween departments and academic fields. But traditional institutional structure has for so long depended on print as its primary medium, and print underlies the academic hierarchy that these virtual environments explode. The traditional structure does not automatically have a way to account for new media that offer significant departures from the values that have grown up around print technology, industrial economies, and compartmentalized hierarchical structures. Real-time networked environments bring with them the possibility for radically reconfiguring those basic organizational structures, allowing interaction to form more along lines of interest than along traditional institutional and disciplinary boundaries. Students, credentialed scholars, and even people outside the academy may be able to interact more collegially, to the benefit of all groups.

The programs that make real-time CMC environments possible have been developed entirely outside the intellectual and economic structures that typically provide the content and context of education (commercial textbooks and software), by people who were not given prior authority by the academy to devise educational tools. The code for both IRC and MU* environments is written and maintained by volunteer programmers who are, in their "spare" time, creating powerful and potentially liberating environments through which people can attempt to escape the confines of traditional institutional compartments, for better or worse. In terms of the ideological flavor woven into these systems, it matters that they were designed primarily by people we affectionately refer to as nerds, people who are almost always relatively low in the institutional hierarchy, rather than by faculty or administrators. The anarchic behavior we see and hear about is not only a function of the technology but of the rebellious subculture that created the environment.

The physical and pedagogical constructs of our educational system—the classroom, the lecture, the test, the paper, the grade—are suddenly made visible in new ways by the presence of these new modes of communication and the sensibility that typically accompanies them. People who are thoroughly vested and invested in the current system may understandably feel very vulnerable when the veil has been removed. Quite suddenly, the traditional shape of academic learning environments—the proscenium classroom and its various physical and pedagogical features—is no longer the only show in town. Its long-assumed inevitability has been called into question before (Barker and Kemp 1990; Moran 1992), but the presence of virtual learning spaces provides an alternative that adds force to the critique. Forces of social enertia ensure that traditional structures will not succumb quickly to competition from these strange new educational spaces, but the traditional practices and sites will come under increasing scrutiny as a result of the existence of viable alternatives on the networks. For instance, since we started writing this article, at least six new MU*s have come into being (that we know of; very likely there are more that have not been publicly announced), which are learning environments by design. Two of them are not just supplements to established programs, but are attempts to create educational organizations entirely online. The number of IRC channels continues to grow apace. In fact, a new IRC network formed not long ago in response to the overwhelming volume of conversation on the system. Compared to the stable environment of the classroom, these environments may appear chaotic, even anarchic at times, but they provide opportunities for motivated learners (and may in fact help motivate learners) that do not typically exist in higher education. The critique of traditional education structures is certainly overdue and quite possibly will yield some needed changes, but the same freedom that allows new conceptions to emerge also allows new problems to arise. Change, as always, is both exciting and discomfiting.

Or perhaps the radical possibilities will be muted as the academy adopts and appropriates—civilizes—these wild places. In an essay about his attempts to encourage professional interaction on Media-MOO,[6] Wade Roush (1993) sketches out his own rendition of the future university. In his "metaversity,"[7] students and teachers simultaneously inhabit "real" life and a virtual environment that looks very similar to the MU*s scholars are beginning to use now. Roush follows a fictional scholar through a typical day as she jumps back and forth as needed between her physical setting and the virtual world, but her activities in each are functionally the same. She communicates with students and colleagues, does some research and other work. Her daily routine is not very different from ours. This model suggests that the features of convenience offered by these new environments will do far more to bring them into vogue than their revolutionary possibilities. What we do (and within what institutional structure) will not change much, but we'll be able to do it much more easily. Lectures, grading, and text-books can be transplanted to online environments—if that's what educators want. We would argue that such approaches are probably not the best use of the new environments (they are retrograde, to put it baldly), and that the new environments offer opportunities to try productive new approaches to education. Granted, we'll have to sort through some of the confusion and uneasiness these new environ-ments create, and the uncomfortable ethical and pedagogical ques-tions and issues they raise, but the rewards, we think, are worth the work.

We are at a stage common to radical technocultural shifts. The obsolescent technology—print, in this case—still pervades society, but its days *as a dominant force,* as a *shaper* of culture, are clearly numbered (Benedikt 1992; Bolter 1991; Landow 1992; Lanham 1993; McLuhan and McLuhan 1988; Nelson 1987; Perelman 1992). Print's slippage from dominance will be mourned by many, but the process is normal enough. There are any number of analogous situations throughout the history of technology (Marvin 1988; Eisenstein 1979), but one of the most common comparisons looks back to the period straddling the nine-teenth and twentieth centuries, when horses were still common en-gines of transportation, even after the introduction of commercially produced automobiles, but no longer represented the future of mobil-ity in the developed world. The world had already changed. A cen-tury later, although the role of print in society and the economy has changed, most people still study, write, and think in terms established by the university of the print era. They will continue to use print technology, as appropriate, for some time to come, but the "metaversity" already exists in crude form and, though not recognized by all, edu-cation has already changed radically as a result.

The change seems to have come with a lurch, as radical changes—paradigm shifts, if you will—often do, and it seems to be dragging on and on, a slow process of evolution. It may seem paradoxical to claim the co-existence of revolution and evolution, but that's a fair char-acterization of these trying times. We might think of it as a big rock plunked into a calm pond: the splash, in this case, has been made, but the ripples are still traveling across the surface, disturbing its peace and distracting attention from the fact that the rock has become part of the pond's bed. Change, we know, does not come gracefully or without considerable challenges and problems. For all the new possi-bilities opening up with the emergence of real-time CMC network environments, there are as many difficulties to address, not the least of which is how scholarship can simultaneously bend them to its purposes and adapt to their shapes. As Shoshana Zuboff (1988, 5) notes, "There is a world to be lost and a world to be gained." As we explore these new environments for scholarly learning, we will need to develop appropriate criteria for recognizing quality and reliability in sources of information we find and put on the net, a process that involves problematizing the notions of quality and reliability themselves. And we'll need to discover methods of dealing with abuses of new-found freedoms. In short, we will begin the process of civilizing this wild and provocative new environment we've found on the net; however, scholars and scholarship will not remain unchanged by the process. The main requirements for this endeavor are conceptual agility and a spirit of adventure.

Notes

1. This article was conceived on the net (on IRC), created on the net (initially on IRC and e-mail, later on MediaMoo), and discussed and revised on the net (on MediaMoo and e-mail). It serves as an example of the evolving scholarship and academic community available on the Internet.

2. From the play *I Think We're All Bozos on This Bus,* The Firesign Theatre.

3. Forum is a freeware program developed by Robert Boston, Iowa State University. InterChange is part of the Daedalus Integrated Writing Environment, a commercial package produced by the Daedalus Group of Austin, Texas (InterChange is a registered trademark of the Daedalus Group).

4. *Electropolis* can be obtained from Comserve or FTP. See References for address and directory information.

5. Aspects is a program published by Group Logic Inc. that allows real-time, collaborative editing of a single text by a number of co-editors.

6. This essay is unpublished in print but is available online via anonymous FTP. See References for address and directory information.

7. Roush admits to borrowing liberally from an Apple Computer demo called Knowledge Navigator, a fictional system that fully integrates text, video, audio, vocal human-machine interaction and other not-so-farfetched technological promises. He also acknowledges his debt for the term, "metaversity," to Neal Stephenson's version of cyberspace in the novel *Snow Crash,* called the "metaverse." Stephenson's metaverse entailed real-time holographic interaction.

References

Austin, P., Bergman, P., Ossman, D., and Proctor, P. (1972). I think we're all Bozos on this bus. *The Firesign Theatre's big book of plays* (107). San Francisco: Straight Arrow Books.

Barker, T.T. and Kemp, F.O. (1990). Network theory: A postmodern pedagogy for the writing classroom. In C. Handa (Ed.), *Computers and community: Teaching composition in the twenty-first century* (1–27). Portsmouth, N.H.: Boynton-Cook.

Benedikt, M. (1991). *Cyberspace: First steps.* Cambridge: MIT Press.

Bolter, J. D. (1991). *Writing space: The computer, hypertext, and the history of writing.* Hillsdale, N.J.: Lawrence Earlbaum.

Bump, J. (1990). Radical changes in class discussion using networked computers. *Computers and the Humanities 24:*49–65.

Butler, W. (1989, May). *The construction of meaning in an electronic interpretive community.* Paper presented at the Computers and Writing Conference, Minneapolis.

Day, M. (1993, May 9). Message to participants of CW93 FORUM. In CW93 FORUM [electronic discussion group in conjunction with the 9th Computers and Writing Conference]. Ann Arbor: University of Michigan. Message number 41.

Day, M. and Batson, T. (1995). The network-based writing classroom: The ENFI idea. *Computer Mediated Communication and the Online Classroom,* Vol. 2 (25–46). Cresskill, N.J.: Hampton Press.

Dibble, J. (1993, December 21). A rape in cyberspace, or how an evil clown, a Haitian trickster spirit, two wizards, and a cast of dozens turned a database into a society. *The Village Voice:* 36–43.

Eisenstein, E.L. (1979). *The printing press as an agent of change.* Cambridge: Cambridge University Press.

Gleick, J. (1987). *Chaos: Making a new science.* New York: Penguin.

Hawisher, G. and Selfe, C. L. (1991). The rhetoric of technology and the electronic writing class. *College Composition and Communication, 42:*55–65.

Kaplan, N. (1991). Ideology, technology, and the future of writing instruction. In G. E. Hawisher and C. L. Selfe (Eds.), *Evolving perspectives on computers and composition studies: Questions for the 1990s* (11–42). Urbana, Ill.: NCTE.

Kelly, K. and Rheingold, H. (1993, July/August). The dragon ate my homework: MUDS are the latest rage on college campuses all around the world. *Wired,* 68–73.

Kemp, F. (1993, May 6, 9). Message to CW93 FORUM. In CW93 FORUM [electronic discussion group in conjunction with the 9th Computers and Writing Conference]. Ann Arbor: University of Michigan. Message numbers 35 and 41.

Landow, G. P. (1992). *Hypertext: The confergence of contemporary critical theory and technology.* Baltimore: Johns Hopkins UP.

Langston, D. M. and Batson, T. (1991). The social shifts invited by working collaboratively on computer networks: The ENFI project. In C. Handa, *Computers and community: Teaching composition in the twenty-first century* (140–159). Upper Montclair, N.J.: Boynton/Cook.

Lanham, R. A. (1992). Digital rhetoric: Theory, practice, and property. In M. C. Tuman (Ed.), *Literacy online: The promise (and perils) of reading and writing with computers* (221–243). Pittsburgh: University of Pittsburgh Press.

McLuhan, M. and McLuhan, E. (1988). *Laws of media: The new science.* Toronto: University of Toronto Press.

Marvin, C. (1988). *When old technologies were new: Thinking about electric communication in the late nineteenth century.* New York: Oxford University Press.

Moran, C. (1992). Computers and the writing classroom: A look at the future. In G. E. Hawisher and P. Leblanc (Eds.), *Re-imagining computers and composition: Teaching and research in the virtual age.* Portsmouth, N.H.: Boynton-Cook.

Nelson, T. (1987). *Computer lib/Dream machines.* Redmond, Wash.: Microsoft Press.

Ong, W. J. (1982). *Orality and literacy.* New York: Methuen.

Perelman, L.J. (1992). *School's out: Hyperlearning, the new technology, and the end of education.* New York: William Morrow.

Reid, E. M. (1991). *Electropolis: Communication and community on Internet Relay Chat.* Unpublished thesis available via anonymous File Transfer Protocol (FTP) at parcftp.xerox.com in pub/MOO/papers subdirectory.

Roush, W. E. (1993). *The virtual STS centre on Media MOO: Issues and challenges as non-technical users enter social virtual spaces.* Unpublished essay available via anonymous File Transfer Protocol (FTP) at media.mit.edu in pub/MediaMOO/Papers subdirectory.

Selfe, C. L. (1992). Preparing English teachers for the virtual age: The case for technology critics. In G.E. Hawisher and P.J. LeBlanc (Eds.), *Reimagining computers and composition: Teaching and research in the virtual age* (24–42). Portsmouth, N.H.: Boynton/Cook.

Symposium—Deafness and orality: An electronic conversation. (1993). *Oral Tradition* 8(2):413. (published thread from the Listserv list ORTRAD-L.)

Woehr, Jack. (1994). Lofti Visions, Part 1: An Interview with Lofti Zadeh, the father of fuzzy logic. *Dr. Dobb's Journal* (July):44–59.

Zuboff, S. (1988). *In the age of the smart machine: The future of work and power.* New York: Basic Books.

*Part V*_____

USING COMPUTER
NETWORKS TO
DISSEMINATE
KNOWLEDGE

Dimensions of
Electronic Journals

Brian R. Gaines

Some three hundred and thirty years ago, the first two scholarly journals came into being: the *Journal des sçavans,* in January 1665 in France, and the *Philosophical Transactions* of the Royal Society, in March 1665 in England. Now, as we prepare to enter the next millennium, the two have grown to some fifty thousand, and paper journals are becoming perceived as increasingly ineffective means of scholarly communication, and as expensive and outmoded sources of information overload. The growth of knowledge that commenced in the seventeenth century enlightenment has become a major problem, the understanding and control of which, through information sciences and technologies, is now an important knowledge objective in its own right.

However, the transition from paper to electronic journals is not a simple process of technological substitution. Book-sized microcomputers with high-resolution screens and optical disk readers are already available which could support electronic journals that emulated paper journals. However, the use of computers and networks in scholarly discourse has already taken advantage of many new capabilities that go beyond such emulation, and the direct substitution of electronic for paper journals is no longer attractive. The new features include rapid and widespread dissemination through the Internet, content-directed retrieval from a large body of material, multimedia presentation of sound, color pictures, videos, and simulations, and access to data sets and programs. Electronic journals do not emulate paper journals, and are best understood as a major revolution in the media for scholarly discourse.

While much of what is happening in the transition from paper to electronic journals is welcome in terms of enhanced capabilities, it also raises concerns about possible negative side effects, such as breakdowns in the quality assurance associated with journals' editorial and refereeing processes, the universality of access to knowledge, and the

*This work was funded in part by the Natural Sciences and Engineering Research Council of Canada. Further material on related topics is available in the archive ftp.cpsc.ucalgary.ca in the directory pub/KSI.

315

preservation of knowledge through long-term archives. The processes of discourse through paper journals have become embedded in scholarly culture through three hundred years of experience, and there are risks in making a major and rapid transition to a new technology. Since journal publication is a distributed responsibility of the entire scholarly community, it is neither possible nor desirable to control the transition. Individuals and disciplinary communities will use the new resources as they see fit, and all one can do in a book such as this is attempt to provide analysis and advice that may be useful to those responsible for some aspect of electronic journal publication.

The primary objective of this chapter is to provide an overview of the main characteristics of electronic journals in relation to issues of scholarly discourse, particularly those of quality assurance. It provides a check list of significant dimensions along which electronic journals may vary in ways relevant to readers, authors, and publishers. It is not intended to be prescriptive. There is scope for completely different patterns of scholarly publication than those we have developed in the past. These will develop through creative experiments and community evaluation of the utility of the results. Other chapters in this volume provide details of existing experiments, and recommendations based on them.

Technological Aspects of Electronic Journals

The enabling technologies for electronic journals have been the personal workstation, the Internet, the modem, and the laser printer. It is the decreasing cost of, and the resultant ubiquity of access to, these resources that has provided an environment in which electronic publications can reach the majority of the scholarly community. Widespread access has come about through requirements for word processing and electronic mail rather than for journal publication, and it is important to remember that the availability of these technologies for scholarly discourse is a minor side effect of their other applications. The developers of electronic journals have to take advantage of technology trends over which they have little influence.

Early Experiments with Electronic Journals

The transition to a technology able to support electronic journals has been very rapid and is a phenomenon of the 1990s. Technologists such as as Wells (1938), Bernal (1939), and Bush (1945) noted the need for new technologies to replace paper journals in the 1940s and 1950s.

Lancaster (1978) documented the basis of increasing library costs in great detail, and saw "paperless information systems" as providing a solution to the problem. In the late 1970s, an experiment took place with National Science Foundation (NSF) funding, in which a psychological journal on mental workload was developed and operated on the EIES (Electronic Information Exchange System) computer-based conferencing system (Hiltz 1984). The rationale and expectations for the new technology were expressed in the final report on that experiment:

> The traditional journal system has among its strengths a defined subject-matter, a developed body of subscribers, an experienced editorial staff, a group of referees chosen for competence in the subject matter, and a form that is convenient in numerous ways, including, for example, portability. Authors submit articles to the editors; the editors choose referees to review the material; the referees submit their judgements to the editor; and the editor makes a decision whether to accept or reject material. If the decision is to accept the article, it is edited and put into the production pipeline, eventually being included in a volume that is printed, bound, and mailed to the subscribers. On the other hand, the drawbacks of the traditional journal include such problems as the fact that each volume contains material that many subscribers are not interested in; that delays between acceptance of an article and its publication are often long, as much as a year to two years; that library storage is expensive and space consuming; that finding specific material can be difficult and time-consuming; and that the limitations on the size of a volume drive editors and authors toward excessive brevity and limits the publication of raw data. (Sheridan, Senders, Moray, Stoklosa, Guillaume, and Makepeace 1981, 8)

The report remarks that "the results fell short of initial aspirations," and "many of the participants, not themselves experienced with computers, found EIES inconvenient or difficult to use" (1). However, dissatisfaction with the technology is not surprising at a time before the advent of UUCP and Usenet, when access to the system was at 110 or 300 baud, largely through teleprinters, and with no possibility of transmitting anything other than textual material in a discipline that traditionally makes heavy use of graphs and figures.

Such technical limitations still applied at the time of the larger British Library BLEND (Birmingham and Loughborough Electronic Network Development) experiment in the UK from 1981 through 1983 (Oakshott 1985), but the political restrictions were equally significant. BLEND was undertaken in major part because the telecommunications authority in that country, the British Post Office (BPO), had vetoed participation in the NSF experiment because the digital communication involved would infringe its monopoly. In agreeing to BLEND, however, the BPO imposed restrictions on participation that restricted readership of the electronic journal to a small part of the relevant scientific community. Such restrictions on access would not have allowed an electronic journal to have a meaningful role in scientific communication at that time even if the technology had been adequate.

What has happened in the 1990s is that personal computing systems have fallen in cost to become as ubiquitous as the telephone system, and the monopolistic control of telecommunications has been relaxed through deregulation in the majority of Western societies. In addition, the capabilities of the low-cost technology to support high-quality, multimedia publications has greatly increased.

*Problems of Data Interchange Formats for
Journal Material*

The primary residual weakness in the technology for electronic journals is the lack of standardization of the typographic, image, and page layout information that constitute the electronic representation of journal material. Computer typesetting systems use proprietary coding schemes, as do word processing and page layout programs, although Microsoft's Rich Text Format (RTF) (Walden 1987) has become a *de facto* partial interchange standard as a result of commercial needs to offer users ways of migrating from one program to another.

In the academic world TeX (Knuth 1986) has become widely used by mathematicians and computer scientists since its adoption by the American Mathematical Society, and is treated as a standard in related publications. The device independent intermediate output format of TeX, DVI format, has become widely used for archives of papers in computing and mathematics, since it is reasonably compact and readily converted to output on laser printers. The lower level image format of PostScript (Adobe Systems Incorporated, 1986), which is the "machine language" of many laser printers, is also used as a common archiving format, since it is non-proprietary and can be exported from many word processing and page layout programs.

The difficulty with going to as low-level a format as PostScript is that it is not compact, not universally usable as an output standard, and not indexable or editable as a document. The current difficulty with any higher-level standards is that they are substantially less universal, and the more proprietary ones are also not indexable or editable except in the related application software. There are two solutions to this problem on the horizon. One is that the growing need for document interchange between word processor users has encouraged the development of a substantial secondary industry offering data conversion programs. Many such programs are now available at low cost for personal computers, and it is becoming reasonably safe to assume that one will be able to convert a document developed on one mainstream document processing system to be accessible on another mainstream system. In particular, Adobe's Distiller program (Seybold 1993) converts PostScript to a format that may be indexed, cut, and pasted, as if it were a word processor document.

The second solution to the lack of formatting standards is the development of graphic and typographic structuring languages that are designed for document interchange. The Standard Generalized Markup Language (SGML) (Goldfarb 1990) is the major contender. It is a way of embedding a knowledge structure in a document that specifies the roles, within a predefined structure of potential roles, of each component of the text, for example, title, author, first-level heading, and so on. SGML is a very flexible standard, essentially providing a meta-language for defining markup conventions through formal Document Type Definitions (DTDs), and this enables it to be applied to the representation of complex document structures such as those for mathematics, music, chemical formulae, and hypertextual links. SGML does not address issues of image interchange formats, but it supports the markup of images as being files defined in other ISO, or industry, standards. The protocol used in World Wide Web documents is HTML (hypertext markup language), a particular format within the SGML rules.

The major advantage of SGML from a conventional publishing perspective is that different "house styles" can be applied to the same SGML document. An associated disadvantage to an author is that he or she loses the control of layout that comes from supplying "camera-ready" copy. However, authors in this situation can also use an SGML publishing system on their personal computers to apply their own "house styles" to the SGML text. Brailsford and Beach (1989) provide an interesting discussion of these issues in the context of their planning for the journal *Electronic Publishing,* which commenced in 1988 to itself become an electronic publication at a later date, and Alexander and Water (1990) provide a critical commentary on SGML from a publisher's point of view.

The Internet MIME protocol for multipurpose Internet mail extensions (Borenstein and Freed 1993) is not based on any of these standards but rather provides a meta-standard within which plain text, RTF, PostScript, SGML, and other document formats can be used as required. MIME enables a wide range of text, typographic text, fully made up documents, pictures, video, and sounds, to be transmitted over Internet through a well-deflned protocol. Convertors and filters are being developed for MIME, so that material sent in any format can be viewed in systems, or on equipment, that does not fully support that format.

The management of document interchange formats is a major problem for developers of electronic journals. Approaches range from using ASCII text only, by prescribing TeX or PostScript, to allowing a very wide range of formats. It is unlikely that there will ever be a single universal standard, and support for a few common formats is the most common compromise.

Sociological Aspects of Electronic Journals

Advances in technology enable the publication of electronic journals, but a technological perspective alone does not address some major issues, because it does not encompass the social needs motivating the use of the technology. Journals are the major medium for discourse in the scholarly community and, as such, are intrinsically part of the social processes in that community. This section reviews the role of social processes in knowledge production, and emphasizes the significance of journals in ascribing priorities to intellectual innovations as part of a social reward system encouraging knowledge production.

Because the material in journals has become detached from the activities, mental processes, and an existence of its originators, it may be seen as a record of those activities and an external expression of those processes, available for the critical assessment of others independent of the originator. This gives rise to the "objective knowledge" perspective on scholarly materials, as products of human activity that are ultimately, in some sense, independent of it and autonomous in their own right (Popper 1972).

Hence, one role of the journal is to act as a repository of knowledge and to make this widely available. This role involves the nature of knowledge, particularly as it is perceived by the client community who are not so much concerned with critical development of scholarship but with use of "knowledge" as something that is reliable in application and whose sources can be trusted. The philosophical definition of knowledge as "justified, true belief" provides a generative principle for the quality control that is applied to scholarly publication. The objective is *truth*, but this arises from the expression of the *beliefs* of authors, through arguments which *justify* those beliefs. The refereeing processes of current journals have been developed to apply standards of "truth" and "justification" to the material submitted, so that certain minimal levels can be relied on as applying to all material in those journals.

Justifications in the literature are generally not independent of one another, but cross-reference other justifications to form a network of interdependent material. At a coarse level, much of this structure is apparent through the citations between publications, and citation analysis provides a useful overview of the structures of scientific disciplines and their interrelations (Garfield 1979; Bayer, Smart, and McLaughlin 1990). The formal structure of scholarship as objective knowledge may also be modeled as a network of linked theories (Balzer, Moulines, and Sneed 1987), whose dynamics of change may be modeled in terms of the underlying structural dependencies (Stegmuller 1976) which are again reflected in the citation patterns in the literature.

This "objective knowledge" perspective on journals emphasizes the significance of the product, its quality, and the technical linkages between items. There are complementary perspectives that see knowledge production and dissemination as a human social process, and emphasize the producers, their quality, and social linkages between them (Cole 1992). Like all human discourse, the communications of scholars through journals serves many functions and carries many messages other than those overtly communicated. The review process that ensures that material is of adequate quality has the side effect that the successful publication of material in a journal reflects well upon the authors—their statuses are enhanced by that of the journal in which their work is represented. In disciplines where scholarly research is dependent on access to limited resources, whose allocation is itself dependent on estimates of the status of the researchers, the journal publication process becomes part of the economic dynamics of the research program itself. The link between perceived capabilities and access to research resources significant in enhancing those capabilities is a positive feedback loop that gives rise to what has been termed the "Matthew effect" in science (Merton 1968), that "unto every one who hath shall be given."

The intricate involvement of journals in the processes and value systems of scholarship, and particularly the direct impact of journal publication on the allocation of resources to individual scholars, imply that the development of new technologies for scholarly communication is not solely a technical matter. They have to be designed to play an effective role within the social infrastructure of scholarship, and any changes and extensions to the nature of the publication process have to be examined in relation to both that social structure and the underlying dynamics of knowledge itself.

Dimensions of Electronic Journals

We are seeing new patterns of scholarly discourse emerge through use of the Internet, and these are exciting for their innovation but also problematic, because many aspects of scholarly publication, such as quality assurance, archiving, and universality of access, are not being addressed in ways that correspond to models established for paper publication (Gaines 1993). This section provides a framework for analyzing these issues within the new context of electronic publication.

One way of coming to terms with alternative approaches, and their relative merits and roles in scholarship, is to classify them along major dimensions of variation.

D1. Private—Public

Whether material is available to only restricted participants or generally available. E-mail is essentially private and most news groups are public, but many forms of semi-restricted access along this dimension are possible. For public news groups, an interesting subdimension is whether users are registered so that one can tell who has expressed interest, and a subdimension of such registration is whether one can tell which users are active recipients. That is, there are possibilities for instrumenting communities and measuring knowledge flows in ways that are much more difficult to achieve with paper-based media.

D2. Discursive—Archival

Whether the service essentially supports discourse or the storage of materials, or both. E-mail and news are both generally discursive, whereas data repositories are archival. However, again many variations are possible along this dimension, since some news groups are also archived, and archives with sequencing, for example through accession dates, can be used to support the type of "discourse" that is typical in journals where one article specifically comments on a previous one. An important subdimension here is the period of time over which material remains accessible. News is generally accessible for short periods, typically two weeks, unless archived, and archives generally maintain material for some years, but there is often no guarantee of this, and rarely a definite policy for the updating of versions of the "same" material.

D3. Moderated—Unmoderated

Whether material has to pass some checking process before being disseminated or is accepted without question. E-mail is unmoderated, as are many news groups, but checking is also common to support groups that wish to communicate information satisfying certain quality controls such as relevancy. There are many significant subdimensions here concerned with how, by whom, and on what basis the checking is done.

D4. Requested—Sent Automatically

Whether material is sent only on request or transmitted automatically to an individual or group of users. E-mail is sent automatically but news, even though it is sent automatically to sites, is accessed only at the request of users. Archives generally only respond to requests, but mailing list servers send material through e-mail to everyone registered with them. An important subdimension here is the visibility of material not sent automatically. News groups have a high visibility through specialist access programs designed to support browsing, but remote archives may be totally invisible to someone who does not know of their existence. Some archives provide automatic notification of updates and good browsing facilities, while others provide minimal directories to compressed files with non-mnemonic names.

D5. Standard Format—Nonstandard Format

Whether the material is available in one of a number of well-defined and interchangeable formats. As already discussed, it is unreasonable to require a single standard format, but it is possible to operate with a range of formats that can be converted into a locally usable form.

D6. Accessible Content—Inaccessible Content

Whether the full content of the material is available for search, indexing, or reuse, or whether only an image description is available.

D7. Multimedia—Textual

Whether the documentation representation supports fully typographic text, diagrams, pictures, sounds, video, and so on, or only text.

D8. Transient—Permanent

Whether the material is available only for a limited period or indefinitely. Permanent availability is important to the "freezing" of a particular statement of knowledge to make it a well-defined subject of critical commentary.

D9. Mutable—Immutable

Whether the material is fixed, so that the apparent publication is not subject to change, or can be edited without this being apparent except through content. This is, again, important to scholars having access to, and citing, precisely the same statements. Immutability does not imply that later versions of a document cannot be issued, only that these are treated as later descendants, not replacements.

D10. Authenticated—Unauthenticated

Whether the material can be checked to be an authentic, unedited copy of the version issued. This ensures that immutability can be propagated to replicas of documents.

D11. Registered—Unregistered

Whether the material has been registered with some independent authority to establish date of publication. To be useful, this registration has to be of an authenticatable and hence immutable document.

D12. Indexed—Not Indexed

Whether the material is indexed in well known, publicly accessible archives. This is important in supporting awareness of relevant material. The utility of the index may vary, depending on the amount of contextual and classificatory material entered, and on the quality of associated services, but some degree of minimal indexing is essential to the functions of a journal.

D13. Annotatable—Unitary

Whether the material is structured in a way supporting precisely defined internal citation. Page and line numbers have never been very satisfactory, but at least they were functional for paper documents. We need to establish new conventions for electronic publications that can be supported by software. Uniform standards cannot be assumed, and the conventions will need to be fairly pragmatic for each form in which publications might be issued. This is very important to support peer commentary, conceptual and argument form annotation, and hypertext linkages.

D14. Attributed—Anonymous

Whether the author of material is identified. This is primarily relevant to refereeing, where referees are usually anonymous. There are a few publications that do not supply the identities of authors to referees, but this is not usually effective, since they are often obvious and also the publication should be refereed from the perspective of a reader who will have the full information and can interpret statements in terms of knowledge of the author or authors.

In terms of these dimensions and the discussion in this article, publications in an effective electronic journal should be public, archival, moderated, available to be sent automatically, in a standard format, with content fully accessible, supporting multimedia, permanent, immutable, authenticated, registered, indexed, annotatable, and attributed. None of the current applications of Internet satisfy all these requirements, and no past or currently established electronic journals satisfy them either. However, none of them are now technically difficult to satisfy.

An Agenda for Electronic Journals

This section stands alone as a statement of objectives for the development of electronic journals, based on the discussion of the preceding sections, but summarizing it in terms of action points rather than derivations.

A1. To enhance scholarship by systematically improving the creation, dissemination, and utilization of knowledge.

The difficult concept here is "systematic improvement," which may seem impossible, given the anarchy of knowledge creation processes, and undesirable, given that much of that anarchy may be essential to innovation. However, it is the very fact that we recognize these issues that makes it reasonable to attempt to support knowledge processes systematically, including the freedom to innovate without constraints. We can use the capabilities of information technology to allow the media supporting scholarship to evolve from being passive repositories to becoming the life worlds of our nomadic knowledge products, and this means supporting the continuing evolution, and co-evolution with ourselves, of the knowledge worlds that we create.

A2. To improve the productivity of individuals and groups generating and using knowledge.

We should not assume that improvements in the processes of recording and disseminating knowledge will automatically result in improvements in scholarship. It is important to establish the requirement for advances in the technology in terms of support for the knowledge production processes of individual scholars and communities of scholarship. In particular, these processes should be studied in depth, and the impact of new technology on them should be monitored with a view to continuous improvement and enhancement of services.

A3. To reduce the adverse impact of the growth of knowledge by improving access to knowledge sources.

The major problem, currently, is not the lack of opportunities to publish but the information overload created by the growth of knowledge and the freedom to publish. It is the capabilities to organize, index, search, and use knowledge in electronic form that are most important in the design of electronic journals. For example, it would be absurd to design electronic publications in which the user did not have complete freedom to analyze and restructure the published material. Facsimile-style replication of paper publications might speed access to the material, but it would be a short-term expedient that did nothing to alleviate the fundamental problem of information overload.

A4. To increase the speed of knowledge dissemination.

The processing lag between a publication's being available in draft form and being published in journal form is several years in many disciplines, particularly for the most highly regarded journals. Scholars attempt to overcome this by informal dissemination of manuscripts, and this process should be supported through electronic archives.

A5. To increase awareness of relevant material.

All forms of dissemination, and particularly the informal availability of material prior to formal publication, are ineffective unless potential users are aware of the existence and availability of the material. The indexing of archives should be supported through the evolution of increasingly effective information retrieval systems taking advantage of access to the full text of the material.

A6. To maintain openness of access to material.

Concern has been expressed about the development of electronic cliques in which senior scholars maintain a discourse that is not open to others, either because they are unaware of it or because they are not allowed to join. There will always, presumably, be discussions that are appropriately private or confidential for good reasons. However, it is important to support and encourage the open access to knowledge which is already part of the culture of scholarship and of our society's attitude to knowledge. Electronic communications have the advantage of supporting the critical discussions commonly associated with workshops, without the physical restrictions on attendance that limit participation in conventional meetings. Experience with current mailing list servers shows how much can be learned from access to the ongoing discussions of major scholars about critical issues, and it is important that this type of peer commentary be supported and encouraged in the operation of electronic journals.

A7. To improve access to existing knowledge.

A critical mass of material available in electronic form will be most rapidly achieved through incorporation of conventionally published material as soon as possible. In particular, pre-circulation and parallel publication of material to be published in paper journals should be encouraged by establishing public archives in which scholars may deposit their publications, including already published material.

A8. To increase cross-disciplinary access to knowledge.

Much of the compartmentalization of scholarship can be attributed to the need to manage the growth of knowledge and avoid information overload. New developments should not take current disciplinary boundaries for granted, but should question their roles and placement.

In particular, there will be scope, once large amounts of material are available electronically, for new approaches to the structuring of knowledge, and these should not be impeded.

>*A9. To support the development of overt conceptual structures for knowledge.*

Past media have encouraged the linear presentation of material and the implicit embedding of argument structures within the text. Electronic media give scope for major innovations in presentation, such as labelled hypertextual links, and the shadowing of informal arguments by formal and operational ones, using techniques of artificial intelligence. It is probable that few of the experiments to date in hypertext and computer-based knowledge representation will prove to be effective in the long term, and that the major innovations are yet to come, involving approaches that have not yet been developed. Innovation and flexibility in the use of electronic media should be encouraged and explicitly supported, not impeded.

>*A10. To use modern information technology to support the achievement of these objectives.*

This is perhaps a rather obvious presupposition to the preceding objectives, but it is proper to place it late in the sequence as the servant to the other objectives, not their master. We will always have much activity that is "technology-driven," where those who see the elegance and potential of new technologies attempt to deliver it in useful form. However, it is important to balance the technology thrust with thoughtful planning that is "market-led," where those who see the essential needs of scholarship attempt to mobilize appropriate technology.

>*A11. To support existing innovations in scholarly communication.*

Ease of access to existing network services has allowed many scholarly communities to develop new modes of operation on an informal basis. This makes available valuable empirical data that is important to the development of effective electronic journals. In particular, a perspective that sees the electronic journal as a formalization of this network discourse, in the same way that paper journals formalized postal and verbal discourse, is a useful counterbalance to one that sees electronic journals as the emulation of existing paper journals.

*A12. To minimize the disruptive aspects of the
introduction of new technology.*

Much of the "human factor" of the introduction of electronic journals
is subsumed in this statement. Designs that are based on existing usage
of word processors on personal computers and existing access to networks are far more likely to succeed than those that require major
changes in existing technologies or work practice.

*A13. To maintain flexibility, allowing enhancements in
technology and changing requirements to be incorporated
with the minimum of disruption.*

Electronic systems can be designed for change with automatic conversion between standards and continuous enhancement of capabilities,
without disruption of services. Often, however, they are not, and
flexibility should be stated as an explicit requirement.

*A14. To encourage cooperation between those operating
existing media and services and those developing new
approaches.*

Electronic journals not only have close relationships to existing journals,
their editors, refereeing systems, authors, readers, and publishers, but
also to a wide range of associated activities, such as abstracting, indexing, and information retrieval services, and to many aspects of library
services and librarianship. It would be of greatest service to scholarship
to mobilize the knowledge and resources available through these existing institutions to develop electronic journals as expeditiously and effectively as possible. It is possible that some of those potentially involved
may see the new medium as a threat, and not be prepared to cooperate,
but it would be counterproductive to presume lack of cooperation in
advance. There is most to be gained in the short term by sharing information, resources, and opportunities, and attempting to enhance scholarship through open collaboration on a professional basis.

*Al5. To prevent any abuses of monopolistic control or
copyright legislation that restrict developments in
scholarly discourse.*

The community of scholarship at large should be made aware of the
new possibilities for the dissemination of knowledge and mobilized to

protect them from abusive practice if necessary. Ultimately, scholars are the major producers and consumers of knowledge and in a position to regulate the market place to the best advantage of the community at large.

Action Plans

The action points in this section are intended as examples to focus attention on a number of simple initiatives open to the scholarly community that could develop electronic publication services by mobilizing existing resources at a minimum cost and with a high chance of success.

P1. An Electronic Journal Consortium

Establish an electronic journal consortium as a loose confederation of interested parties communicating through Internet with a view to sharing ideas and technology, encouraging necessary developments, and supporting experiments with electronic journals.

This is a typical Internet activity, and has the usual advantages of mobilizing a diverse community without requiring a central power base, and completely transcending national and disciplinary boundaries. This consortium can have fruitful collaboration with those concerned with document standards, multimedia communication, groupware, and so on. It will serve to facilitate change and the evolution of *de facto* standards through experience. The actual operation of particular journals will be through editors, anonymous reviewers, commentators, and so on, as it is now, and it is important that these disciplinary communities have access to reliable, fully functional technology which they can use without responsibility for development and maintenance. It is probable that a printed form of most electronic journals will be required for the foreseeable future, and that support of printed output of a parallel paper publication should be treated as a major initial requirement.

A reference model for an electronic journal emulating paper journals and significantly enhancing their features might be:

1. A community concerned with a sub-discipline founds an electronic journal by defining the publication objectives, establishing a review board of relevant experts, and negotiating a paper-based publication arrangement with a book or journal publisher. It is assumed that the community already operates a list server and a Gopher.

2. Potential contributors routinely put their working articles in their local archives, making the knowledge rapidly available through FTP and Gopher. The appropriate format currently is PostScript, since this supports full typography, diagrams, and pictures, can be generated by virtually all word processors on all platforms, and can be read and printed using public domain programs on all common platforms. It is also annotatable, searchable, and reusable using Adobe's Acrobat technology (Seybold 1993).

3. When a contributor wishes an article to be reviewed for the journal, he or she informs the editor by e-mail of the location of that article.

4. The editor assigns reviewers, and also makes it known to the community at large through the list server that the paper is subject to review, so that anyone may comment on it.

5. When the editor has sufficient commissioned and other reviews, he or she sends them to the author with an editorial decision. It may also be seen as appropriate to make these reviews publicly available in the journal archives.

6. If the editorial decision is to publish without change, then the article is moved into the journal archives. (It might seem reasonable to just put a pointer to the article in the journal directory of the community Gopher, but copying the paper to the archives is intended to create an immutable "published" version.) If revisions are required, the author makes them, and the process loops back to 3.

7. Annually, or by volume, a paper volume of the electronic journal is published. This may become unnecessary in the long term, but currently such parallel publication is essential to make the published material universally available.

P2. Publication Archives

Establish public publication archives in which scholars can place electronic versions of works published in peer-reviewed paper journals.

These archives should support authentication, so that the copies obtained from them can be distributed with the means to check that they have not been edited. Generic archives for all disciplines and publications are suggested, so that they can be put in place rapidly, without dependence on action in particular disciplines. Restriction to published works is suggested, so that the archives do not become overloaded with material, or have to establish their own moderation procedures. This suggestion relies on scholars' having the right to make whatever use of their material they see fit, and is an extension of the existing practice of distributing reprints. It seems unlikely that even publishers who do not explicitly return this right will object to the archives. Most scholars would assume that they have this right anyway, and would not continue to publish in journals whose publishers attempted to claim otherwise. Note that the works would not be placed in the public domain, and that the scholars and publishers would retain their copyrights. The use of material without due acknowledgement is very easy to detect in electronic publishing, and offenses ranging from professional discourtesy to outright plagiarism would be much more visible than they are now.

P3. Public Indexes to Personal Archives

Establish public indexes of personal or institutional archives of material that has not been peer-reviewed.

This is intended to support the current practice of placing submitted manuscripts, draft documents, reports, and data in public archives under local control, but to make the contents more accessible to the community. It balances the restriction of the publication archives above to articles published in peer-reviewed journals, by supporting any amount of publication based on the resources of the author or his or her institution. Permanence, immutability, and authentication should be encouraged in these archives, but these can also be achieved by setting up sub-archives that transfer selected material from the personal archives, probably operated by some disciplinary sub-community.

These three action plans are complementary and together, including also current network activities, they would give an adequate basis for a major acceleration of the progress towards electronic publication. They form a basis for the development of extended services based on content searches, hypertext linkage of peer commentary, knowledge structures for disciplines, and so on. However, before these new developments occur we need a critical mass of material available on the net and a significant community of scholars drawing upon it on a routine basis. That has to be our first practical objective, and it is the one addressed most directly by these three action plans.

Conclusions

Publication in paper journals is still the major system supporting human knowledge processes. If computer-based systems are to have any significant long-term impact on human knowledge processes, the functions of the paper journal have to be subsumed and enhanced. To do so effectively requires deep understanding of the social processes underlying scholarly activities and publication, their support through the existing publication and library systems, and how that support can be emulated and enhanced through computer and communication technology.

References

Adobe Systems Incorporated (1986). *PostScript language reference manual.* Reading, Mass.: Addison-Wesley.

Alexander, G. and Walter, M. (1990). A fresh look at SGML: The conventional wisdom changes. *Seybold Report on Publishing Systems 20*(7):3–16.

Balzer, W., Moulines, C. U., and Sneed, J. D. (1987). *An architectonic for science: The structuralist program.* Dordrecht, Holland: Reidel.

Bayer, A. E., Smart, J. C., and McLaughlin, G. W. (1990). Mapping intellectual structure of a scientific subfield through author cocitations. *Journal of the American Society for Information Science, 41*(6):444–452.

Bernal, J. D. (1939). *The social function of science.* London: Routledge.

Borenstein, N. and Freed, N. (1993). MIME (Multipurpose Internet Mail Extensions) Part One: Mechanisms for specifying and describing the format of internet message bodies. Internet. RFC 1521.

Brailsford, D. F. and Beach, R. J. (1989). Electronic publishing—a journal and its production. *Computer Journal, 32*(6):482–493.

Bush, V. (1945). As we may think. *Atlantic Monthly, 176:*101–108.

Cole, S. (1992). *Making science: Between nature and society.* Cambridge: Harvard University Press.

Gaines, B. R. (1993). An agenda for digital journals: The socio-technical infrastructure of knowledge dissemination. *Journal of Organizational Computing, 3*(2):135–193.

Garfield, E. (1979). *Citation indexing: Its theory and application in science, technology and humanities.* Philadelphia: ISI Press.

Goldfarb, C. F. (1990). *The SGML handbook.* Oxford: Clarendon Press.

Hiltz, S. R. (1984). *Online communities: A case study of the office of the future.* Norwood, N.J.: Ablex.

Knuth, D. E. (1986). *The TEXbook.* Reading, Mass.: Addison-Wesley.

Lancaster, E. W. (1978). *Toward paperless information systems.* New York: Academic Press.

Merton, R. K. (1968). The Matthew effect in science. *Science 159*(3810):56–63.

Oakeshott, P. (1985). The 'BLEND' experiment in electronic publishing. *Scholarly Publishing 17*(1):25–36.

Popper, K. R. (1972). *Objective knowledge: An evolutionary approach.* Oxford: Clarendon Press.

Seybold (1993). Electronic document delivery. *Seybold Special Report 1*(3):3–17.

Sheridan, T., Senders, J., Moray, N., Stoklosa, J., Guillaume, J., and Makepeace, D. (1981). Experimentation with a multi-disciplinary teleconference and electronic journal on mental workload. Massachusetts Institute of Technology.

Stegmuller, W. (1976). *The structure and dynamics of theories.* New York: Springer.

Walden, J. (1987). *More file formats for popular PC software.* New York: Wiley.

Wells, H. G. (1938). *World brain.* New York: Doubleday.

Electronic Academic Journals

From Disciplines to "Seminars"?

Jean-Claude Guédon

Electronic publishing has become a catchword and a fashionable topic. It also meets with a fair amount of resistance, as it threatens to modify working habits and a number of social relations.[1] It has become clear that electronic publishing will not prevail on the ground of technical superiority alone; how the means of communication adapt to the communities that make use of them is also part of the equation.[2]

Electronic texts have recently attracted the attention of a wide variety of academics, ranging from specialists of literary studies to philosophers, from people interested in academic publishing to librarians.[3] Scientists, some very prominent, have also started to pay attention to developments that may deeply transform the conduct of research in the next couple of decades.[4] More than anyone else, perhaps, librarians have been particularly attentive to these new trends that will revolutionize their profession in ways that may be uncontrollable and not necessarily positive. Finally, both commercial and academic publishers also keep a close eye on a variety of trends, when they do not try to set the agenda themselves.[5] In short, electronic publishing is fast becoming a significant sub-specialty within the general concern and interest for the (poorly named) information highway.[6]

This chapter will deal with academic electronic periodicals, and it will place its main focus on the ways in which the digitizing of documents and their diffusion through the Internet may affect the structure of research. In particular, by exploring the relationship between print, electronic publishing, and disciplines, I hope to illustrate a wider phenomenon characterizing the complex positioning of two competing media as one begins to challenge the other's monopoly. A historical detour through the emergence of periodicals within the print medium provides a number of interesting handles on this whole question, and permits one to speculate on the forms academic publishing may take with the appearance of electronic media.

335

A Bit of History[7]

In Europe, the first newspapers appeared early in the seventeenth century, notably with *Nieuwe Tydinghen,* which started in Antwerp in 1605. Learned periodicals did not appear until 1665, when the *Journal des sçavans* saw the light of day in France. The *Philosophical Transactions* of the Royal Society quickly followed in Britain.[8] The French journal was quite broad in its scope, its goal being to spread the news inside the *Republic of Letters.* It mentioned recent books and summarized them, recorded eulogies of recently deceased luminaries with a review of their main achievements, described recent experiments in physics and chemistry, as well as various discoveries in the sciences and the arts. It also gave accounts of the more recent judgments in both secular and Church tribunals, of the censorship exercised within Sorbonne and other universities, in France and abroad. In short, anything of interest to the "Gens de lettres" was to be available in the journal.

The aim of de Sallo, *the Journal's* first editor, was quite clear: in one simple sweep, thanks to the use of the printing press, he wanted to substitute himself for the rich but unsystematic flow of correspondence that had contributed so much to the rise and growth of the *Republic of Letters.* Instead of having many one-to-one messages, with all the attendant problems of misinterpretations, erroneous copying, and chance distribution, de Sallo was proposing a neat, clean, systematic solution. It rested on a novel use of the printing press that, so far, had essentially limited itself to producing whole volumes.

A similar viewpoint presided over the birth of the *Philosophical Transactions.* In his introduction, Henry Oldenburg wrote:

> Whereas there is nothing more necessary for promoting the improvement of Philosophical Matters, than the *communicating*[9] to such, as apply their Studies and Endeavours that way, such things as are discovered or put in practise by others; it is therefore thought fit to employ the *Press*[10], as the most proper way to gratifie those, whose engagement in such Studies, and delight in the advancement of Learning and profitable Discoveries, doth entitle them to the knowledge of what this Kingdom, or other parts of the World, do, from time to time, afford, as well of the progress of the Studies, Labours, and attempts of the Curious and learned in things of this kind, as of their compleat Discoveries and performances . . .[11]

Oldenburg's phrasing forces us to retrieve the truly revolutionary nature of what was achieved when print was first reconceptualized from a diffusion to a communication tool. But to go beyond the periodical as an apparently gentle or innocuous innovation, we must clearly set the functions of the printed periodical against those of the printed book.

Designed initially as a prop for memory, writing came to play a key role in defining and giving existence to doctrinal canons. The Church used writing and the related reading skill as a way to control and transmit the divine message and its holy, but nonetheless human, commentaries to its hierarchy. A large fraction of manuscript production and distribution was closely related to this task.

Print, when it emerged, contributed to solidifying the canon by standardizing the text and by immensely multiplying the number of sites where it could turn up. A printed text is hard to destroy, because rigorously identical replicas are distributed over large enough a territory to ensure the saving of a few copies in the midst of the most difficult situations. The ability of print to support and define a canon is but the flip side of its ability to protect an opinion or idea.

What makes the printed periodical a radical novelty is that it reversed this trend. It did so by mechanically multiplying something that, normally, is singular—namely a handwritten letter. It did so by recording something that, normally, dies out with the last echoes of a spoken voice—namely a debate. Printing a periodical meant recording elements of an unlimited *process of debate* that stalks the meanders of research. Starting with an innate and unique ability to create a doctrinal monument, print suddenly stumbled upon the opposite ability: keeping a live and manifest register of all the successive corrections, revisions, and revolutions that ideas, beliefs, and theories undergo.

Consider the quandary of a librarian at the end of the seventeenth century. What could it have meant for him to store a book-like object that, while offering the appearance of permanence, only contained the transient, conversation-like dialogue of a moment? Up to that point, storing a text in a library had meant consecrating it once again beyond print, as part of some canon, be it that of the Church or the law, for example. The library's initial and main function had been to build a *fixed* memory of definitely accepted products, and not a memory of the *process* through which certain products had temporarily appeared in learned discussions. Until the periodical, the library had had the ambition to offer a collection that strove to approximate an ideal, essentially fixed, set of texts as well as it could. In so doing, it had acted as if it wanted to amass all the elements of a finished palace, with no trace of any scaffolding. With printed periodicals, on the other hand, not only did parts of the scaffolding remain visible, but, in some way, they became more important than the palace itself. The palace could never be completed, and its plan would be subjected to sporadic revisions to the point of becoming unrecognizable. The fixed archive had thus given way to a living and movable *jurispru-dence of the intellect*. The combined machinery of the book plus the library had moved from incarnating the canon to becoming an active, probing, and agile research instrument.[12] A deep cognitive shift had just taken place with the arrival of the printed periodicals.

There is more. The building of a jurisprudence of the intellect was achieved in the context of deep ideological battles. Controversies, often quite heated, underpinned the attempt to produce periodicals, and editors as well as authors often tailored the information to the needs and constraints of the moment and of the surrounding commu-nity. In this context, the social weight of printed documents invariably increased if they appeared to be the product of objective rules rather than the expression of mere opinion. This meant that selection (and exclusion) was recast inside mechanisms designed to improve the le-gitimacy of texts and, as a consequence, their authority as well. Except that in the process, authority became a product of the jurisprudence of the intellect and not obedience to a canon. Meanwhile, as libraries gradually learned to integrate these new, apparently transitory, objects in their collections, the process of legitimation reached completion. Nowadays, research libraries spend more on periodicals than on monographs.

From that point on, acceding to periodical print meant being part of the *legitimate* record of human thought—a human thought well designed to begin its hallowed march toward truth. Periodicals had thus contributed to give room and visibility to the ongoing, collective work of thinkers. Soon they would assemble under the banner of progress, and would even create a collision, often referred to as the Enlightenment, with the venerable and static monuments of institu-tional or ancient truths. It is probably bold, but not too far from the truth, to claim that the arrival of the periodical signaled the coming victory of the Moderns over the Ancients.

Italians, in 1668, and Germans, in 1670, quickly imitated the *Jour-nal des sçavans* and the *Philosophical Transactions*.[13] From then on, the creation of periodicals accelerated, but it was really in the eighteenth century that they multiplied in the hundreds. A. A. Manten mentions that most led a very precarious existence, rarely exceeding a year, with one or two issues coming out.[14] A good many electronic academic journals are already faring better than that.

Manten also reminds his readers that the advent of the periodical did not stop private correspondence overnight. The practice continues to the present, but its meaning and importance have changed. How-ever, if the *Journal des sçavans* had sought to rationalize the epistolary network that had fueled the cultural achievements of the *Republic of Letters,* it was because the system was overburdened.

Inside the web of letter exchange that spanned most of Europe in the seventeenth century, some individuals had come to play a very important role, because they wrote more letters and managed to transfer information in a stimulating way that pushed the debate further on. In the early seventeenth century, Mersenne was such a key figure, and his ability to sustain links between philosophers of all feathers was like maintaining bandwidth. His talent for recasting statements and solutions as further problems was not unlike that of good moderators on a modern "Listserv." However, despite all his skill, good will, and stamina, Mersenne's role as one of the human engines of the *Republic of Letters* was constrained by time and information limits. Even with the help of similar energetic luminaries, the *Republic of Letters* was facing severe restrictions on the amount of communication it could support. At this juncture, print technology looked very promising and perhaps unavoidable.

The emergence of printed periodicals in this fashion shows how dependent on older models they were at first. Intimately tied to epistolary practice, journals tended to favor details and facts over arguments, originality over exhaustivity, fragments over fully deployed texts. Fast food for thought was already the order of the day, so to speak—a concern reflected in the *Journal . . .* when, in the 1670s, it decided to revert to weekly publication after a few years when it had limited itself to an issue every two weeks.[15] Short summaries of all manner of books, as well as news about various cures, inventions, *Curiosa* in short, abounded. Clearly, when pressed for time, various "virtuosos," as the English would have then said,[16] could rely on a quick print fix: instead of writing a whole treatise, with all the attendant difficulties, costs, and delays, it was easier, much faster, and almost as effective to send a letter to the editor of such a journal and have a piece of news printed that way. Thus, distinctive originality became the key to social visibility well before Bourdieu thought about it, three centuries later.[17]

At first, journals did not enjoy the authority of books, but their status received unexpected help from the question of priority claims. Increasingly, these became settled by relying on the published record and not on the evidence of private exchanges. Obviously, the material form of the printed journal offered a fairly reliable handle on the vexing question of how to date a discovery in some unambiguous way. It became clear that the testimony of one or two correspondents could no longer offer the irrefutable support that print automatically provided.

A discovery or invention existed when, and only when, it went public by way of print. Journals became the guarantee of originality and, as a consequence, had to distinguish carefully what belonged to whom. This meticulous accounting stimulated the rise of another writing device: the footnote.

The original designers of journals had certainly not thought about priority questions as a way to promote their new form of publishing; yet they gradually learned to recognize it and make good use of it. For example, the *Mémoires de l'Académie royale des sciences* fell into the habit of printing papers about three years after it heard them. However, its papers retained the date of the reading, to set the paper in its original research context. To complicate things further, the Academy allowed authors to make slight, but not insignificant changes to their papers in the meantime, to keep them abreast of what had intervened. As historians of Lavoisier can testify, he made skillful use of this practice (and of parallel channels) to try to have the better of both worlds, particularly in his priority debates over the discovery of oxygen.[18]

Out of the undisciplined activity, and the effervescent exploitation of print, new forms of cognitive order emerged that could not have been anticipated beforehand. As the eighteenth century progressed, the support for journals shifted from entrepreneurial individuals to established societies or academies and this allowed for greater permanence.[19] Printed periodicals eventually came to depend on institutions, professions, and religious groups. However, in pretending to become a permanent voice for them, they strongly contributed to the emergence of something entirely new in the area of knowledge— namely, the *discipline* as we know it.

An illustration taken from the history of chemistry will help illustrate the point above. The *Annales de chimie,* were founded around the chemical school based on Lavoisier's new ideas. Retrospectively, creating a chemical journal looks quite natural, as chemistry has since evolved into a huge disciplinary structure. At the end of the eighteenth century, however, this was not the case. On an institutional basis, chemistry was barely visible: in France, it had gained the status of a class within the Royal Academy in 1699, and that was its best claim to fame. Chemistry demonstrators performed in the King's Garden and a few medical faculties, particularly Montpellier. Professionally, most people practicing chemistry were either apothecaries or medical doctors. In print, a few treatises competed for a limited market of apothecaries. In short, chemistry was a hybrid domain, half practical, half theoretical, with a low degree of theorization, a marginal role in universities and academies, an uncertain relationship with physics, and a somewhat questionable reputation in the eyes of the public because of popular associations with alchemy, on the one hand, and poisons, on the other. Its only redeemable value was that it had also managed to attract the attention of a class of well-to-do, forward-looking noblemen and high bourgeois. Guillaume-François Rouelle, who taught some chemistry to Lavoisier, also counted among his disciples Diderot, Turgot, and Jean-Jacques Rousseau. At its best, chemistry in late eighteenth-century France connoted social and intellectual progressivism.

The founding of the *Annales de chimie* signaled the breaking away of chemistry from physics. Chemistry had begun to claim epistemological independence from Newtonian natural philosophy, and started raising the prospect that knowledge would never be one, but, on the contrary, would develop as a series of partially disconnected intellectual territories. It is in this context that the notion of discipline started to develop, and that it substituted itself for the grand systems that had littered European intellectual history. *No better way than a periodical was found to firm up this call for disciplinary independence.*[20]

In concluding this brief review of the learned periodical's history, it is possible to see that, although conceived to ease communication problems faced by the *Republic of Letters,* it unwittingly achieved a good deal more. It shifted the emphasis from the preservation of the canon to an interest in the movement of human inquiry. It created a new form of legitimacy and authority divorced from obedience. It contributed to the breaking up of the grand philosophical systems in favor of the newer, more limited and modest disciplines. Through all of these shifts in emphasis, printed periodicals supported modes of communication and diffusion that now appear *orthogonal*[21] to the corresponding modes of manuscript culture, as well as its direct, linear extensions to print. The term "orthogonal" attempts to capture the fact that a new medium competing against an older one will both extend its roles in a continuous manner and simultaneously tranform and even subvert it.

The historical detour just completed clearly shows that a new medium can never replace an older one perfectly. As it begins to emerge, a new medium generally emulates the old—emulation being taken here with its double meaning of imitation and competition—and plays by the old rules. While doing so, unexpected consequences ensue. We will remember these lessons as we turn to academic electronic publications.[22]

Academic Electronic Publications: Toward the "Seminar" Form?

For a long time now, research publishing has been contemplating its own doom. A growing number of scholars are producing a growing number of papers in a growing number of journals. The reasons are simple: the research community grows fast, faster than the whole population, and the pressure to publish also increases as promotion requirements get tighter. Meanwhile, subscription costs are rising more rapidly than the general price index, so that both individuals and libraries face difficulties in keeping all of their subscriptions. As a result, libraries go round after painful round of subscription cuts, leaving little choice to the journals but to increase the subscription price, in the hope that it will temporarily compensate for the losses in revenue. Journals also attempt to cut production costs through a more resourceful use of the latest technologies, by lowering quality, and with various expedients. The more common among these include introducing thematic issues to compete with monographs on their market, or multiplying double and even triple issues to reduce the number of printed pages and the mailing costs.[23]

We all know that these problems, in such a complex web of vested interests, both economic and symbolic,[24] will not change without some extraordinary pressure. However, we are fast coming to a point where we cannot ignore or deflect the economic pressure any longer. Electronic journals emerge because they bear the promise, real or not, of some economic relief.

To the best of my knowledge, all electronic journals display one common characteristic: they all are new journals. No existing journal has transformed itself into the new medium.[25] There are good reasons for this situation. Administrators of various grant programs sometimes complain that it would be easier for them to support the transformation of an existing journal than the creation of a new one, given that programs are built nowadays to slow down the growth of journals. Yet there is no reason why a successful journal should want to change its ways, and supporting an unsuccessful venture does not make much sense.

The reality, therefore, is that most electronic publications are and will be entirely new enterprises, and it becomes interesting to see what patterns are at work as they emerge. In particular, it is interesting to examine how they relate to disciplinary structure and scholarly audience.

The advent of the electronic serial rests on a number of technical factors that deeply affect its practical suitability over a long period.

For one thing, until the arrival of the personal computer and its coming into fairly general use, very few people knew how to master those machines. The multiplicity of standards has also adversely affected the penetration of electronic publication. As for networks, both Bitnet and Internet were almost exclusively used by computer specialists until well into the 80s, because they represented an entirely new technical hurdle to overcome. The intricacies of modem connections and the arcane commands of Unix operating systems had to be learned. That around ninety books exist to date (April 1994) to try to help new users "navigate" the Internet is a telling commentary on the difficulties of the system.

Technology is not all. What must be taken into account is something else that has to do with the social dimensions of research. Teresa Harrison and her co-authors put it well when they write:

> Whether these journals succeed or fail will depend on the extent to which a particular journal's design is consistent with the social practices of the discipline it serves and the extent to which it reflects the discipline's needs for information and communication.[26]

The rest of the article uses this important point to justify the fact that the *Electronic Journal of Communication/Revue électronique de communication* was designed to respond to the peculiar needs of communication scholars. The point is well taken, although it bears further questioning.

In the text just quoted, the discipline appears as the unavoidable starting point for the design of any electronic journal. However, we must remember that printed journals fundamentally participated in the invention of disciplines. Within the natural philosophies of the modern age, various opinions have regularly emerged. From mechanism to vitalism, for example, the printed book was the preferred vehicle for achieving this goal in the fashion best suited, simultaneously, to promote individual fame. Lavoisier raised the stakes of intellectual debate when he imported some of the tactics of politics into science, and created a journal to reach his goal. It is as if he had paid attention to his academic colleague, Franklin. Another way to say this is that Lavoisier sensed the role that journals played in recording debates rather than buttressing canons, and he took full advantage of this insight. In so doing, he transformed the largely individual task of creating an intellectual system into a kind of intellectual party. This may be the profound meaning of the phrase "chemical revolutions" that recurs frequently concerning Lavoisier's work.

Inventing a scientific "party" was not enough; its social under-pinnings required serious reinforcements. University chairs originally corresponded to a division of labor within a pedagogic structure that fed into a profession. They were recast as props within a polytechnic pedagogy, where terms like chemistry and physics took on an entirely new meaning. This took place at the newly founded École Polytechnique with some of Lavoisier's supporters, such as Fourcroy. Later, university departments and those periodic, semi-public festivi-ties called congresses or colloquia, with their strange mixtures of cer-emonies, prizes, and communications, both formal and informal, would be invented to complete the trappings of what is now associated with disciplinary structure. In short, if the discipline is the social and insti-tutional translation of a peculiar division of intellectual labor, it could not have been invented without the prior innovation of the printed periodical.

To say, therefore, that an electronic journal must respond to dis-ciplinary needs is very similar to saying that, in the seventeenth cen-tury, a printed periodical had to respond to the needs of the *Republic of Letters*. It is indeed the necessary starting point for any electronic learned journal, but it tells very little about where it is headed. What are the unexpected and unwitting social objects that are going to emerge in its wake? This is the more interesting question if we want to try to peer into the twenty-first century, as the title of this anthology suggests.

Looking at the present trends, two are already clear, and one of them is particularly significant. On the one hand, we see journals appearing that are extremely specialized, and in that trend we recog-nize that small research communities find in the electronic journal an economically feasible way to create a forum all to themselves. This first tendency, whose best examples come from the hard sciences, is very much in line with the existing trends within print culture. The move toward ever greater specialization has been unrelenting since the end of the eighteenth century.

On the other hand, electronic journals also display a repeated tendency to focus on interdisciplinary fields. Cultural studies, post-modernism, disability studies, and, to be sure, reflections about the arrival of digitized documents are but a few examples of interdiscipli-nary ventures that seem to find in electronic journals a congenial sup-port. Those familiar with the Internet will recognize titles behind these generic descriptions, including my own *Surfaces*, whose content is as interdisciplinary as can be, thanks to the good efforts of my colleague, Bill Readings.[28]

To understand this trend, one must reflect upon the nature of interdisciplinary studies in the present organization of knowledge and research. One quick way to dispose of the question would be to say that those intellectual parties called disciplines, because they always have a partial and even biased view on things, can never take in things in their totality. However, a number of important practical problems require the urgent global apprehension of these "things," be they global warming, pollution, or the like. In short, wherever the modern idea of system can be put to use, disciplines will probably be found wanting. This leads to uneasy alliances of variable duration between various disciplines. However, within these temporary, fragile, and fluctuating structures,[27] which oscillate between the multi-disciplinary, the interdisciplinary, not to speak of the trans-disciplinary (for the more ambitious among them), are always found sub-groups that see the opportunities available if these alliances could be made to adhere to . . . a new discipline. The cases of biochemistry and molecular biology are quite telling in this regard, but so are disciplines in the social sciences such as criminology, communication, or even sexology. The interdisciplinary structure also appears to be one of the preferred mechanisms for achieving the spawning of new disciplines by older ones. A complex system of "genetic" inheritance could probably be devised by some new Mendel, if only she could find the equivalent of the two varieties of peas that the good monk from Bratislava had the good fortune to study.

In saying this, a new dimension emerges: the interdisciplinary phase acts as a counterweight to the inherent rigidity of disciplinary structures. If disciplines bear analogies to political parties, it is not unreasonable to suppose that disciplines must also benefit from some sort of party discipline,[29] which is perhaps all that Kuhn was trying to express with the concept of normal science. If no countervailing force were at work, a general social sclerosis would quickly follow, and this is clearly not what we see at work in the scientific enterprise. The interdisciplinary phase is certainly one of the ways in which the disciplinary structure is made more malleable, so to speak.

I will stay a while longer with this image of greater flexibility or fluidity of the disciplinary structure, to try to further interpret the meaning of this interdisciplinary trend in electronic publishing. At the same time, I will go back to the notion of communication inherent in the first printed periodicals. Due to greater and greater delays in publishing, learned journals act less and less as communication tools. Their major roles have more to do with legitimizing knowledge and archiving it. Meanwhile, communication goes on in a rather improvised way. Preprints play a prominent role, but so does private correspondence (again). Telephone calls, congresses, and, nowadays, fax and e-mail complete the spectrum of alternative channels of communication. In arguing that they could significantly reduce publication delays, supporters of electronic periodicals have indicated that they wanted to recover the communication function that had been one of the reasons behind the existence of learned journals in the first place. But again, the logic of the object created pushes its creators beyond their own plans or expectations. The designers of a number of electronic journals were prompt to see that they would not be complete without reader comments. This involved the creation of accompanying discussion lists that could focus on the pieces published in the journal.[30] As a result, communication in the context of electronic periodicals begins to take on an entirely new meaning.

Two consequences can be derived from this important trend. On the one hand, it builds a renewed sense that information can never work fully as information unless it is subjected to commentaries and discussions. Interesting terms then come to mind: for example, exegesis, postil, scholium, gloss, all words related to medieval practices. The appearance of electronic publishing has put us back in touch with the textual wisdom of the Middle Ages[31] and reminded us that no reading can ever be totally solitary, as silent reading induced by print would lead us to believe. *Disputatio* is an integral part of full intellectual appropriation.

The second consequence of this new preeminence granted to purely communicational dimensions of journals is that the distinction between authors and readers begins to subside as the batch-like mode of intellectual production typical of the print medium gives way to the flow-like production of the digitized document. To be sure, the present structure of the research community, and particularly its dominant modes of evaluation, based as they are on individual performance, will ensure for a long while that text integrity and author-reader distinctions are going to remain strong preoccupations in the decades to come. However, the rise of the accompanying communication tool is going to play its role too, and, in my opinion, it is going to slowly transform the electronic journal into some type of electronic *seminar*. At any rate, we can retain the electronic seminar as the probable contour of the learned periodical of the future.

Neither printed periodical nor team, a seminar is a place where structured debate can proceed so as to push theses and theories forward. Like a periodical, it places high emphasis on originality and performance; unlike the periodical, its role is not to promote the individual author, but rather to facilitate debates. Like research teams, seminars build on collective efforts; unlike research teams, seminars do not structure themselves around explicit hierarchies. Access to a seminar is limited by certain rules having to do with recognized levels of competence. Seminars work by reworking and commenting on papers that are either read ahead of time or read as a preliminary step in the seminar dynamics. If seminars have not been the only and universal form of "publishing" so far, it is because access was too limited. Electronic networks change all of this.

How the seminar form will affect the disciplinary structure of research is difficult to say, but one point is certain: affect it will. Exactly as the attempt to emulate letter writing led to discipline formation, the attempt to fulfill the needs of disciplines will probably lead to fundamental reworkings of the research system. What will be interesting to watch are the kinds of political doctrines that will graft themselves on to the seminar form and inspire its evolution as it extends its reach, night and day, to the whole planet.

Meanwhile, Jim O'Donnell has conducted a first, world-wide, seminar on Augustine out of the University of Pennsylvania. My final thesis is that we are going to watch a gradual convergence between experiments of this kind and electronic periodicals, while discrete authors and batch articles will gradually give way to regulated flows of collective intellect: the global seminars.

Notes

1. One of the most common prejudices against electronic publishing has to do with reading. When hearing about an electronic journal, many people react by saying that they do not like to read on a screen, as if electronic publishing were wedded exclusively to screen technology. In fact, the power of electronic publishing is that it brings digital, i.e., virtual, documents to the reader's computer, and it is she who decides how to materialize that document. For browsing and searching information, a computer is more efficient than print. A blind person can make his document speak. As for deep reading and study, it will take a long time before paper and pencil are superseded.

2. The same point is made in Teresa Harrison et al., "Online Journals: Disciplinary Designs for Electronic Scholarship," *The Public Access Computer Systems Review,* vol. 2.1 (1991): 26. *PACS-Review* is both an electronic journal and a paper journal. The former can be accessed on the Gopher of the University of Houston Libraries.

3. Charles W. Bailey, Jr., "Electronic Publishing on Networks: A Selective Bibliography of Recent Works." *The Public Access Computer Systems Review* 3.2 (1992): 13–20. Bailey, "Electronic Publishing on Networks: Part II of a Selective Bibliography," *The Public-Access Computer Systems Review,* vol. 5.2 (1994): 5–14. Good bibliographic notes can also be found in two studies in press by Brenda Danet. The papers are: "Books, Letters and Documents: The Changing Materiality of Texts in Late Print Culture," and "Smoking Dope at a Virtual Party: Writing, Play and Performance on Internet Relay Chat." The latter paper

will appear in *Network and Netplay: Virtual Groups on the Internet,* edited by Sheizaf Rafaeli, Fay Sudweeks, and Margaret McLaughlin (Cambridge: MIT Press, forthcoming).

4. Beyond the titles in Bailey's bibliographies, and in particular those penned by Stevan Harnad, I would like to mention the following titles: Joshuah Lederberg, "Digital Communications and the Conduct of Science. The New Literacy," *Proceedings of the IEEE,* vol. 66 No. 1 (November 1978): 1314–19. Lederberg, "Opinion. Communication as the Root of Scientific Progress," *The Scientist,* vol. 7.3 February 8th, 1993. The latter article is available online. I want to thank Dr. Lederberg for having kindly transmitted these two articles to me. Brian Gaines, "Social Dynamics of Scholarly Publications"; Gaines, "Social and Technical Dimensions of Electronic Journals." These papers can be downloaded by anonymous FTP from cpsc.ucalgary.ca in the pub/KSI directory. Andrew M. Odlyzko, "Tragic Loss or Good Riddance? The Impending Demise of Traditional Scholarly Journals," *Surfaces,* vol. 4.105 (1994): 1–45.

5. For example, the Dutch publisher Elsevier is field testing a scheme called TULIP (The University Licensing Project) to distribute a set of learned journals electronically within a few universities, including the University of Michigan. It rests on the idea of storing digitized images of printed pages as if to preserve their material existence in electronic form. The rather large files that result are then transmitted over suitable networks (generally Unix workstations with X-Windows). A hidden ASCII file allows full-text searching of the articles (and nothing else). Enough has been said to show the awkwardness of this solution. Clearly, it has been invented to make an electronic document behave economically as if it were the same type of commodity as a printed journal.

6. It is poorly named because it is much more a communication than an information highway. This is a recurring theme in communication studies, as the telephone was initially envisioned as a kind of broadcast tool. Much later, ARPAnet, the US. defense network, saw the unexpected development of electronic mail, as did Minitel in France and the internal IBM network. Prodigy, the commercial network, has run into difficulties with its customers because of attempts to limit the quantity of mail one could send.

7. A good deal of my information for this section comes from A. J. Meadows, ed., *Development of Science Publishing in Europe* (Amsterdam: Elsevier, 1980).

8.The original title was: *Philosophical Transactions: giving some Accompt of the present Undertakings, Studies and Labours of the Ingenious in many considerable parts of the World.* It appeared on May 6th, 1665, while its French counterpart started on January 5th of the same year. Both still exist, but the French journal did suffer some interruptions, particularly during the Revolution, unlike its English counterpart.

9. My emphasis, J.-C. G.

10. Oldenburg's emphasis.

11. Quoted by A. A. Manten, "Development of European Scientific Journal Publishing before 1850," in Meadows, 7.

12. Much of what precedes has been stimulated by James J. O'Donnell's brilliant article, "The Virtual Library; an Idea Whose Time Has Passed," in Ann Okerson and Dru Mogge, eds., *Gateways, Gatekeepers, and Roles in the Information Omniverse. Scholarly Publishing on the Electronic Networks. Proceedings of the Third Symposium* held in Washington, D.C., Nov. 13–15, 1993 (Washington, D.C., Association of Research Libraries, Office of Scientific and Academic Publishing, February 1994), 19–31. However, if my argument has any validity, it leads to a revision of O'Donnell's thesis regarding the continuity of the idea of a virtual library from the high Middle Ages to the present.

13. *Giornale de Litterati d'Italia* in the first case; *Miscellanea Curiosa* in the second case. It is interesting to note that three out of these four journals were in the vernacular and not in Latin, despite the fact that the communicational dimension of the periodical should have favored the use of one common language (like English on the Internet nowadays). Complex factors such as the rise of nation states and their reliance on national languages as a tool of identity and as a way to decrease the clerics' quasi-monopoly on written texts are obviously at work here, but exploring this point would take us too far afield.

14. Manten, 8.

15. The printer writes to the reader the following lines: ". . . mais enfin il s'est determine a la huitaine, tant pour satisfaire `a l'empressement des curieux qui le demandent de toutes parts tous les huit jours, que pour ne laisser pas vieillir mille nouveautez qu'il a deja entre les mains, & qu'on luy promet encore des Pais Etrangers." *Journal des sçavans, de l'an M. DC. LXXVIII. Par le Sieur G. P.* TOME SIXIÉME A Amsterdam, Chez Pierre Le Grand. M. DC. LXXIX., p. [3]. This is a Dutch reedition, probably pirated, that testifies to the success of the French enterprise by its very existence.

16. Witness Thomas Shadwell's play, *The Virtuoso,* a satire on the members of the Royal Society of London and their followers in the provinces.

17. Pierre Bourdieu, *La distinction. Critique sociale du jugement* (Paris: Minuit, 1980).

18. It took all of Henry Guerlac's meticulous studies on Lavoisier to start clearing a historical record that had been made quite opaque by the practice outlined in the text. H. Guerlac, *Lavoisier—The Crucial Year* (Ithaca: Cornell University Press, 1961) *passim.*

19. It also allowed for a dynamics of debates that was centered upon institutions and inter-institutionally second. The academies and learned societies began to create an atmosphere very conducive to the later development of the seminar form, to which I will return later.

20. The situation, of course, is quite a bit more complex in its details, and the relationship between chemistry and physics was not resolved once and for all thanks to the creation of the *Annales* . . . In fact, the journal briefly changed its name to incorporate physics at the beginning of the nineteenth century.

21. For the 4th edition of the *Directory of Electronic Serials,* (Washington, D.C.: ARL, forthcoming), Ann Okerson, ed., I have written an essay titled:

"Why are electronic publications difficult to classify? The orthogonality of print and digital media." In it, I try to understand how electronic documents and print relate to one another.

22. This is of course a mere sketch of a much more complex situation. To be pithy, I could say that what is at stake is the role of communication tools in the functioning of social fields. Field, here, is taken precisely in Pierre Bourdieu's meaning of the word.

23. A good survey of research libraries is found in *University Libraries and Scholarly Communication: A Study Prepared for the Andrew W. Mellon Foundation* by Anthony M. Cummings et al. (The Andrew W. Mellon Foundation, 1992).

24. By symbolic, I am referring to the notion of symbolic capital developed by Pierre Bourdieu in his sociological analyses. It involves notions of power, status, visibility, prestige, and authority.

25. I except from this generality the case where a printed journal explores the possibility of a secondary publication in various forms, such as fiches a few years ago, and now in electronic form. I also leave aside the case of an electronic journal later providing a paper version of itself, as did the librarians' electronic journal *PACS-Review*. Moving to paper is still seen as a kind of promotion, as access to greater legitimacy, by many scholars. This is to be expected if we remember that print, at its inception, was often viewed as cheap and inferior publishing compared to manuscript.

26. Harrison et al., 26.

27. A sub-theme could be developed here, that would examine how the dominated and somewhat marginal status of interdisciplinary activities fit nicely with the quest for legitimacy on the side of electronic periodicals.

28. Bill Readings died on October 31, 1994; his duties have been assumed by Terry Cochran.

29. I owe this amusing, but far from insignificant, remark to my wife, Louise Marcil.

30. The actual means to achieve this aim may differ somewhat from periodical to periodical. *Postmodern Culture* uses the constructed virtual space of a MOO, while *Surfaces* relies on a simple "Listserv."

31. Except that, with the scale and efficiency of modern technical means, it might be more apropos to call our age a kind of turbo-Middle Age. Other parameters, such as the ways in which texts are copied *and* modified, the ways in which author and reader roles are modified to the point of becoming interchangeable, as in the case of hypertexts, all point in the same direction.

The Electronic Journal and Its Implications for the Electronic Library

Cliff McKnight
Andrew Dillon
Brian Shackel

It is now more than ten years since the first electronic journal experiments (e.g., EIES, BLEND), and the intervening years have not seen researchers being idle in this field. Indeed, while experiments have continued apace in an attempt to answer various questions, such as the appropriateness of particular interfaces, electronic journals have continued to appear. The third edition of the Association of Research Libraries (ARL) list (Okerson 1993) contains forty-five electronic journals, while the first edition, only two years earlier (Okerson 1991), listed only twenty seven. This might suggest reasonably rapid growth, but in actual fact, represents a high rate of turnover also—sixteen of the original twenty seven do not appear in the latest list. We therefore start this chapter with the assumption that electronic journals will continue to be a feature of the scholarly communication process, although not all will survive.

Our second assumption arises from our experiences in the design, implementation, and evaluation of information technology based systems in general, not just electronic journals. That is, we assume that in order to be acceptable, any system attempting to replace an existing technology must enable users to perform their necessary tasks in a way which is at least as easy as the existing system. The new system must offer at least as much as (and preferably more than) than the existing system; otherwise, motivation to move from the old to the new is not high. In the present context, this means that the successful electronic journals will be those that not only support the scholarly communication process, as well as all the other user requirements satisfied by paper-based journals, but also support additional, enhanced facilities such as tailorable presentation formats, integrated interactive discussion about articles, flexible indexing and retrieval, hypertext linking, and so forth.

Establishing Requirements: From Stakeholders to Users

From a socio-technical perspective it is important to understand systems, as comprising social, or human, and technological sub-systems, and to realize that the success of any technological initiative is a function of the match between these subsystems. Furthermore, the human or social systems extend beyond the obvious users to those whose professional role is influenced in any way by the technology. In the case of academic journals, the stakeholders are clearly more than the readers of academic articles, but also the authors of the material, the publishers, and the librarians who catalogue and manage the storage of journals.

In their own ways, all of these groups will be affected by the shift toward an electronic medium. However, for the purposes of the present discussion we will concentrate on the primary users of journals, the authors and readers, to examine the likely impact of electronic journals, since it is their satisfaction that will largely make or break these developments. Interestingly enough, should the technology be designed sufficiently well to prove acceptable to these users, the remaining stakeholders may be placed in a curious "outsider" position that could dramatically alter their stake in the academic journal system. We will return to this point later. For now, we will concentrate on the user requirements for academic journals, in order to focus attention on the targets that the electronic versions must attempt to meet and eventually exceed.

Users' Requirements of Academic Journals

Requirements for journals among users differ according to their main task, i.e., users as readers or as authors. From a reading perspective, journals serve both current awareness and archival purposes. Scholars browse new issues of journals in order to keep abreast of developments in their field. They refer to earlier volumes to track historical precedence, intellectual propriety, and the rate of progress in a discipline. Readers also use journals as a yardstick of the standards in a field, since most readers have an expectation that prestigious journals will have been rigorously refereed.

Beyond the formal requirements of the readers as scholars, other requirements for the use of journals are important. A survey by Simpson (1988) suggested that many academics like to read while on trains or at home, rather than in their office or even the library. Hence, the portability aspect of paper is a requirement that must be met to some degree by any new journal form.

For authors of academic articles, the user requirements are also diverse. The standard reasons for publishing are to disseminate the results of research, to establish precedence, to advance a discussion, and so forth. However, today's scholar has a variety of other reasons. For example, it is widely accepted in academia that promotion and tenure committees use publications as a performance indicator, and hence there are career pressures to publish. Increasingly, academic institutions are themselves judged by such indicators, and therefore even unambitious scholars find themselves pressured to publish. It is through publishing that a reputation in one's field is established.

In selecting a journal to which a paper will be submitted, scholars typically refer to the proportion of the target population that reads the journal, the belief that the refereeing will be competent and fair, and the extent to which the journal has already published papers on similar topics (Gordon, 1984). Hence, these considerations can be seen as another set of user requirements that the electronic journal must satisfy.

It is indeed conceivable that above and beyond the user as reader or writer, the user as a member of a professional community requires of academic journals that they provide an information dissemination and record keeping resource of the highest intellectual standard for the community. Furthermore, in the days of increased interdisciplinarity, scholars are as likely to define themselves by the journals they use as by any background qualification or intellectual specialism.

Human Factors of Journal Use—The Evidence to Date

The various requirements of users of academic journals need to be considered in terms of the empirical data that have been gathered in recent years. Such evidence provides clues regarding the most suitable form an electronic journal might take.

Negative Human Factors of Paper Journals

It is clear that there are several problems inherent in the paper system that could be improved with electronic delivery. Journals often seem to be missing—either in use by someone else, mis-shelved, gone for binding, not yet delivered, and so forth. Even when journals are available, other problems mentioned are that they are difficult to search through (especially when looking for a half-remembered item of information) and they take up too much space on the shelf. Some readers also complain about the sheer volume of literature and the rate at which new journals appear, making it difficult to keep up with developments.

Burrows (1993) points out that "The main investment in almost all academic libraries is the provision of the shelving and space necessary for direct, open access to as much of the collection as possible." These costs are increasing as the pressure on space forces many universities to implement a policy of charging departments for the space they occupy.

As an information dissemination medium, paper journals are slow. Leading journals often take more than a year to referee, revise, and then publish an article, by which time the work can often be out of date. Furthermore, there is a lack of interaction between information provider and recipient that hampers any true information dissemination process.

The common experience of scholars browsing academic journals and finding extremely relevant material serendipitously is both a flaw and a virtue of the medium. While it is always a pleasant experience to find such work effortlessly and almost by magic, it should be a worry to any serious scholars that their standard information searching behaviors should have failed to point them directly at that piece of work. In other words, if one such relevant article is found by chance, how many more are missed forever?

Positive Human Factors of Paper Journals

The portability of paper renders journals and articles a highly amenable form of information presentation. Given Simpson's (1988) perhaps unsurprising finding that scholars like to read outside of library and office environments, it is clear that paper is a most appropriate medium for delivery.

In readability terms, the standard paper presentation compares favorably with all electronic forms in most empirical tests (see Dillon 1992 for a review). In terms of such outcome measures as speed and accuracy, as well as process measures such as navigation, paper continues to retain dominance over most electronic texts in experimental comparisons.

Paper journals also conform to a certain style that has been shown to be useful for readers as they seek information. Contrary to the naive view of readers as serially ploughing through masses of text due to some form of linear determination found in paper publications (see e.g., Nielsen 1990), the experienced scholar can use the familiar structural representation of the format and the flexible manipulability of the medium to jump through the information space accurately and reliably. Empirical examinations of readers using journals (Dillon, Richardson, and McKnight 1988) indicate that few articles are ever read serially from start to finish, but tend to be subjected to quick scans and jumps through the text—a byproduct (in use) of the very qualities the medium supports.

The purpose of examining journals in terms of requirements and negative/positive usage aspects is to make explicit the criteria electronic journals will be measured against. For minimum acceptance, the new form must maintain the positive and reduce the negative, or increase the positive without increasing the negative. Ideally, a new technology would remove some of the negative and increase some of the positive to be acceptable. It is in this light that we examine some of the attempts at developing electronic journals.

Some Electronic Journal Experiments

In this section, we will briefly describe some past and present electronic journal experiments and consider their implications for the variety of user requirements.

BLEND

The BLEND (Birmingham and Loughborough Electronic Network Development) project (Shackel 1982; 1991) aimed to investigate not only the feasibility of an electronic journal but also the feasibility of supporting the entire communication process—from authoring and submitting, through refereeing and editing, to publishing—via computer. To this end, a central mainframe was used, and the various participants in the process communicated through this machine, with the resulting issues of the experimental journal *Computer Human Factors (CHF)* being stored on it. Users accessed the system via a remote terminal either over the newly developing British Joint Academic Network (JANET) or, mostly, the Public Switched Telephone Network (PSTN).

In at least one respect, *CHF* proved potentially superior to a paper journal. Although each actual article was "read-only" once issued, and could not be altered, there was space allocated for comments on each article, and these comments could then be seen by subsequent readers of the article. The fact that the articles' authors were also part of the "electronic community" meant that they too could read—and respond to—the comments. The resulting dialogue created much more of a feeling of "live" research than is possible in the paper medium, where it is not uncommon for an eighteen-month period to elapse between the submission of an article and its publication in the journal. Indeed, Pfaffenberger (1986, 31) has suggested that "Journal publication, in short, confers reward and recognition more than facilitating genuine communication, which in any case has already taken place within research networks if a field is thriving."

While it might be tempting to think that the electronic medium speeded up the process of publication, this is not necessarily the case. Indeed, Shackel (1991) reported a median publication time of "just over 32 weeks" (i.e., about eight months) for articles in *CHF*, and it is possible that this could be attributed to a "novelty effect." What seems more likely is that the electronic medium more easily supports comment and dialogue than the paper medium, as will be seen in some of the more recent experiments described below.

Quartet

Project Quartet aimed to investigate the implications of information technology for the scholarly communication process. It was therefore somewhat wider than BLEND, being concerned with a broad spectrum of communication activities, including electronic mail, computer based conferencing, electronic document delivery, desktop publishing, and electronic publishing (Tuck, McKnight, Hayet, and Archer 1990). As part of Project Quartet, what was possibly the world's first hypertext electronic journal, *HyperBIT*[1], was designed and built. This was seen as being made available over a local area network (LAN) rather than the wide area network, since it was Macintosh-specific and incorporated graphics. The design was based on the results of various earlier studies by us of journal usage (e.g., Dillon et al. 1988) and, as such, specifically addressed the issue of user requirements. Hence, browsing through author/title lists at either the issue or volume level was supported, as was searching the entire contents of the journal. Each article was structured using the Guide(TM) hypertext system, and cross-references in articles were made into active hypertext links, allowing the reader to move quickly and easily between articles. (A more complete description of the design is given in McKnight, Dillon, and Richardson 1991.)

HyperBIT offered the user several advantages over the paper version. For example, it was always available on the desktop. The entire contents of the journal could be searched in order to locate, say, all articles which mentioned "screen" or referred to work by "Maguire." The ability to move between related articles using the hypertext links was also advantageous, as was a pop-up window facility that provided instant access to the bibliographic details of references without leaving the text. This facility was provided on the basis of observations of many users who would keep a finger permanently in the References section of the article when using the paper version, turning to the section when they encountered a reference in the text and then returning to the text. In this sense, the facility provided an "electronic finger."

Listserv

In recent years, another model of the electronic journal has arisen based on the Listserv software. This name is an abbreviation of "list server," which gives some insight into how the system works. In a typical system, a central computer holds a list of subscribers; when a new issue is available, the system sends subscribers a "contents page" and abstracts via e-mail. Subscribers can then request articles by sending an e-mail message to the server, with the articles being automatically delivered as e-mail by the software.

Although the concept of "issue" is still used in the typical Listserv journal, the issue itself is effectively unbundled since subscribers can request single articles. However, the contents pages and abstracts can be stored for future reference and searching, and articles can be retrieved at any time on demand. Such a system makes effective use of the network "bandwidth" since only requested articles are transmitted. How many academics can honestly say that they are interested in every article of every issue of every journal they receive? Even when the journals are on their shelves, they don't remember what is in them. Shackel (1985, 202), for example, reports on an electronic search of a references and abstracts database: "33 [references] were subsequently used in the preparation of the written chapter. Of these 33, 16 were already known to me, but 17 were new, highly relevant references. . . . In almost all cases the relevant journals were on my bookshelves."

Like BLEND, the Listserv journals have found that they can support discussion of articles. For example, subscribers to the peer refereed electronic journal *Postmodern Culture (PMC)* can also choose to subscribe to a discussion list called PMC-Talk. Indeed, the discussion list not only provides a forum for comment on and debate about the articles in the parent list, it also provides a forum for discussion of the broader issues of postmodemism in general. A further facility offered by *PMC* is PMC-MOO, a "real-time, text-based virtual reality environment in which you can interact with other subscribers of the journal and participate in live conferences" (PMC-list, 1993). At the time of this writing, it is interesting to note that PMC had just begun to be published simultaneously in World Wide Web format, which permits the inclusion of graphics, sound, and video, and includes hypertext links to other documents. However, the PMC-Talk and PMC-MOO services will continue to run.

CORE

The CORE (Chemistry Online Retrieval Experiment) project's aim is to deliver a large majority of the journal literature needed by one academic area, in electronic form to workstations in a library and terminals on the desks of academics. Articles are held in both text and bitmap forms, and a variety of interface options are being investigated. For example, Landauer et al. (1993) report on experiments comparing performance on five different tasks using a SuperBook interface (which allows browsing and provides many hypertext-like features), a PixLook interface (which combines a sophisticated document retrieval engine with bitmap page images), and paper. Not surprisingly, the results suggest that there is no one "best" interface. Rather, particular tasks are supported to a greater or lesser extent by each interface; as the task changes, so the optimum form of interface will change.

The CORE project represents a collaboration among five institutions: the Cornell University Albert Mann Library houses and administers the experiment; the American Chemical Society is providing ASCII and microfilm versions of the last ten years of twenty journals; the Chemical Abstracts Service provides electronic versions of their hierarchical indexing scheme tagged to all of these articles; the Online Computer Library Center (OCLC) is contributing expertise in large database storage, access, and search techniques; and Bellcore (where Landauer and colleagues work) is contributing expertise on text and graphic conversion and transmission, as well as developing prototype user interfaces. At the time of this writing, the project is still running, and we await its results with interest.

TULIP

The TULIP (The University Licensing Program) project, a three-year project scheduled to run until the end of 1995, aims to test the feasibility of networked delivery and use of journals. Elsevier Science Publishers are making electronic versions of forty two of their materials science journals available to the fifteen colleges and universities (including MIT, Harvard, Carnegie Mellon, Cornell, and Princeton) that are participating in the experiment. Each university is providing its own hardware and access and retrieval software. Hence, Elsevier are simply providing a database which Engineering Information, acting as Internet host, archive and customize for each university. The aim is to provide "as much local autonomy as possible" (Elsevier 1992), so that a variety of options can be explored and evaluated. The project will examine the economic, organizational, and technical issues involved in the electronic transmission of journals, as well as consider user issues.

The journals are currently stored as bitmaps, and are distributed with index files and a "dirty ASCII" file. This latter can be searched but not displayed. It is produced by scanning the journals and using OCR software to recover the text. Many people have expressed surprise that it is more cost effective for Elsevier to re-scan and OCR pages that have already existed in electronic form. However, it is likely that this is a temporary expedient in order to get the project off the ground—it was already delayed for some months beyond its scheduled start date. As typesetters move toward a standard format, so will it be easier to produce a "clean" ASCII file directly. As with CORE, results from TULIP are awaited with interest.

OJCCT

The American Association for the Advancement of Science (AAAS) and the Online Computer Library Center (OCLC) have also launched an electronic journal, *The Online Journal of Current Clinical Trials (OJCCT)*. This was due to be launched in April 1992, but was beset by technical problems. In addition to the technical problems facing the project, Wilson (1992, A20) reported that "the AAAS must persuade authors to submit high-quality papers in a new medium that may prove to be largely ethereal" (a problem already reported in the first journal project [Sheridan et al. 1981] and circumnavigated in BLEND [Shackel, Pullinger, Maude, and Dodd 1983]). Indeed, the number of papers on the system does not seem to have reached the expected level, despite its now offering parallel publication in a traditional medical journal. Paradoxically, although the system was designed to be accessed directly by readers, it seems to have received a more enthusiastic reception from the information profession than from end users.[2]

ELVYN

The ELVYN (Electronic Version—Why Not?) project involves the Institute of Physics Publishing (IOPP) and Loughborough University, with support from SCONUL (Standing Council of National and University Libraries). This project is investigating a variety of economic, technical, and user issues involved in the distribution of an electronic version of a paper journal, *Modelling and Simulation in Materials Science and Engineering*, to participating libraries (Pullinger and Meadows 1993). This project has many similarities to the TULIP project: it seeks to involve both publishers and libraries; it allows participating libraries to specify the format in which they receive the electronic version of the journal; and it distributes electronic versions of existing paper journals. This is in contrast to, say, the listserv journals, which effectively bypass the publisher and library (or at least the formal representatives of these bodies). In at least one test site, the publisher's SGML (Standard Generalized Markup Language) files are being converted to the World Wide Web HTML format, with NCSA's Mosaic being used as a client viewer. This allows viewing of full text and color graphics from the user's desktop microcomputer, and could incorporate animation and hypertext links.

The Institute of Physics Publishing also led a consortium of nine publishers in a small project testing journal distribution and usage over SuperJANET, the new British high-speed academic network currently undergoing pilot testing. This project aimed to produce a demonstration system, and was scheduled to run from January to April 1993 (IOPP, 1993), but the project report has yet to appear at the time of this writing.

CAJUN

Also recently started is the CD-ROM Acrobat Journals Using Networks (CAJUN) project. This project involves two journals already in existence, Wiley's *Electronic Publishing: origination, dissemination and design (EP-odd)*, and Chapman and Hall's *Optical and Quantum Electronics (OQE)*. Dissemination will be both on CD-ROM and over the network.

The "Acrobat" referred to in the project title is Adobe Acrobat(TM), which is "a family of products that work together to enable document communications" (Adobe, 1992). The basis of Acrobat is the Portable Document Format (PDF), which is PostScript-based but also allows additional document features such as annotations, hypertext links, and thumbnail views of each page. Like PostScript,

PDF is device and resolution independent, and Acrobat viewers (the applications necessary to read, navigate, and print PDF documents) are available for Macintosh, Windows, DOS, and UNIX platforms. Adobe intends to publish PDF as an open standard.

In the same way that the TULIP and ELVYN projects are important because they explore the role of the publisher and library in the electronic journal, so the CAJUN project is noteworthy because it involves a major commercial software house—indeed, one that has already been responsible for producing the de facto standard page description language, PostScript.

Do Electronic Journals Meet User Requirements?

It is clear from the above that electronic journals meet some of the user requirements of the paper journals. They are less likely to "go missing," more likely to be available on demand or even on the user's desktop (notwithstanding the occasional network crash—the electronic medium has its own varieties of inaccessibility, including the question of long-term archiving, yet to be solved).

In terms of search facilities, the electronic medium offers clear advantages over paper. Modern search algorithms allow very sophisticated searching to be carried out even on the basis of the scantiest piece of half-remembered information. Furthermore, searching need not be limited to bibliographic sources, but can realistically be carried out on large, full-text databases.

The advantage of the electronic medium in terms of storage requirements is also clear. A single copy (plus backup, of course) held centrally takes up less space than hundreds of copies distributed worldwide. Even in the case of *HyperBIT,* which was conceived as being distributable, it would have been easily possible to put the entire contents of the journal (eight volumes with four parts per volume, at the time of the project) on a single CD-ROM.

Some of the interfaces to electronic journals, for example those of *HyperBIT* and SuperBook, are designed to allow browsing, and seem successful in this respect. Even a minimal electronic journal, such as a Listserv journal, allows browsing of the contents page at the title/ author/abstract level, something which many academics do with paper journals. In supporting browsing, such systems also permit the serendipity much valued by academics.

One desirable aspect of the paper journal which does not yet seem to have been tackled in the electronic domain is its portability. The survey by Simpson (1988) referred to earlier suggested that many academics like to read while on trains or at home, rather than in their office or the library. A journal on CD-ROM can be carried easily between office and home but requires equivalent equipment at both places. However, there are certainly portable electronic books being developed, and it may well be that the portable electronic journal will follow behind. The current growth in laptop computers and "note pad" computers, combined with a storage medium such as the smart card, might well support portable electronic journals. However, this would represent a distributed, rather than a truly networked, system.

Although systems like *HyperBIT* allow a reasonable level of graphics, this is achieved by making the system machine-specific. Displaying the same graphics on different systems is difficult, although the World Wide Web protocol supports common graphics formats (e.g., TIFF and GIF) as long as suitable "helper" applications are available to display them.

Those electronic journals that are distributed over the network must also recognize the fact that they are most readily accessible to the academic market. There are many researchers located in industrial research laboratories who have no access to this network. It is to this very market that many commercial document delivery companies are now directing their marketing attention. In America, at least, an increasing number of companies are connecting into the network, but in Britain the take-up rate is very slow in the industrial and commercial sectors. It is probably significant that the forward-looking IOPP is one of the publishers with JANET access.

Although there are an increasing number of electronic journals, not all of these are the subject of peer review. This raises an important issue that must be addressed by the distributors of an electronic journal, that of quality control. In the paper journal system, the process of refereeing acts as an important quality control mechanism. While the refereeing system is open to various criticisms, it does confer an aura of respectability on the journals, to the extent that academic status and recognition rely on publishing in such journals. The early EIES (Electronic Information Exchange System) project (Sheridan et al. 1981) had discovered to its cost that academics could not afford to risk publishing in experimental journals, and the BLEND project had allowed authors subsequently to publish in paper journals specifically because this problem was recognized. The *OJCCT* project appeared to suffer precisely because of this attitude. Hence, if electronic journals are to be successful and attract quality articles, they must be seen to be applying the same standards as their paper counterparts, unlikely to disappear overnight and, perhaps most importantly, recognised by the bodies who for various reasons make judgments of an academic's work based on published output. In this respect, the statement of the recent Joint Funding Council report (1993—the "Follett" report) in Britain that "the [UK] funding councils should make clear that refereed articles published electronically will be accepted in the next Research Assessment Exercise on the same basis as those appearing in printed journals" is very important.

Implications for the Electronic Library

The declining library budget that is a feature of so many academic institutions has put pressure on libraries to purchase "just in time" rather than "just in case." Many librarians have pointed out that the combination of budgetary constraints and developing network services has changed the library's function from a "holdings" approach to an "access" approach.

Librarians were relatively quick to take to the CD-ROM, acquiring and mounting them in the library in much the same way that books were shelved. However, the trend nowadays is for the CD-ROMs to be available across a campus LAN, and for access to be supported by the institution's computing service.

Electronic journals such as the Listserv journals effectively bypass the librarian and call into question the role of the publisher. The argument is advanced that because scholars are both the source of journal articles and their users, the networks allow the distribution function to be removed from the publisher and the library. Librarians typically counter this argument with the observation that the so-called information explosion makes it impossible for the individual scholar to know what is available, and that their role as information intermediary is therefore retained. However, the growth of "information agents" and "selective dissemination of information" (SDI) may tend to undermine the librarian, unless librarians in general change to take the lead in the provision of such services.

This is especially the case in the research community. As was emphasised in the 1989 Cranfield Conference on Information Technology and the Research Process, the growth in electronic facilities will increase considerably the sheer volume of material to be searched/accessed/reviewed, leading to even greater need for SDI and similar support. As Shackel (1990, 159–160) said: "For example, the importance of quick access to knowledge about the current and most recent research is emphasised by Gould (1990). The problem of organizing all the data, which will be accumulated so rapidly when these IT support resources come into widespread use, is another major issue. Obviously, this further development of the 'invisible college' resulting from IT in the future could be helped by librarians and information scientists, but how best to achieve this?"

Projects such as ELVYN have retained a role for both publisher and library. However, even within such frameworks it is not clear that the publisher is "necessary." In most of the test sites, it is also the case that the library requires the active support of the computing service in order to mount the electronic version of the journal and enable its accessibility across the campus LAN. As Sidgreaves (1989) said to the 1988 Conference on The Electronic Campus "the boundaries between libraries and computing centers are becoming increasingly blurred."

From the rapid growth of the electronic journal and other electronic facilities outlined above, it is obvious that there will in time be many changes in the organization of the whole system of scholarly communication. The difficult questions to answer are what and when. A wide range of possible scenarios can be envisaged (cf. McKnight 1991), from very slow evolutionary progress to the extreme of publishers' and libraries' being replaced by direct interaction, via the Internet, between scholars as writers and scholars as readers. We tend to favor the middle range of possibilities, and, in particular, we suspect that the organizational issues may be more influential than the technological possibilities (significant though these are). For example, among the major influences will be the following: the maintenance of quality via the peer review process (relating also to the issue of career status for authors); the problem of copyright control; the vested interest of publishers (including especially the learned society publishers) in maintaining income; the consequent uncertainties regarding how/ whether to attempt the transition from journal volume subscriptions to single article fees (which might well require unacceptable levels of perhaps £10–£50 per article).

Some Remaining Issues

We have largely concentrated on the scholar's needs for electronic journals. However, there are many other important considerations in the development of an electronic journal that need to be taken into account. For example, the question of copyright control is of particular concern for publishers. Although the paper medium is relatively easy to copy using a photocopier, the copy is of inferior quality to the original. In the electronic domain, copying is not only easy and fast but also the copy is identical to the original. If I receive an article over the network, it takes me no more than a few key-strokes to forward a copy of the entire article to someone else. This means that either methods of electronic copy protection must be developed or the concept of copyright must be reconsidered. In real terms, the issue for publishers is not copyright per se (since this is often retained by authors), but rather how to derive a revenue from the electronic journal.

In the paper domain, if scholars order a journal, they either have to pay for it themselves (a personal subscription) or it must be agreed that either the department or the university library will pay. If they receive a Listserv journal, however, it is not clear who pays. Certainly there are costs involved—there is no such thing as a "free lunch"!—but they are costs that are largely transparent to the user. The storage costs are met by the host institution, usually a university, and in this respect we may be witnessing a return to the situation in which universities were also publishing houses. Certainly *Postmodern Culture,* mentioned earlier, received the support of various departments within North Carolina State University, whence it originates, although it has, apparently, since been "acquired" by Oxford University Press. Access to the network is paid for as part of the general funding for computing within a university, and individual scholars do not receive a bill. Hence, it may well prove necessary to develop new costing models for the production and distribution of journals in the electronic domain. Practically all of the current electronic journal projects follow BLEND (Pullinger 1987) in being concerned with investigating economic factors and pricing models, in addition to tackling the technical problems.

Although there are advantages to the development of electronic journals, it must be recognized that such developments exclude a large number of users of the paper journal system—those users in countries that do not yet have a stable network or even an established computer base. Clearly, the hope is that such countries will develop a computing infrastructure eventually. We would not argue that we should not develop electronic journals because they presently exclude such countries, but we must recognize that access for a large number of potential users is currently impossible. For this reason if for no other, the paper journal will be a feature of the academic landscape for some time to come.

Hardware and software have been mentioned in passing, but it is clear that today's decisions about these aspects will have implications for the future, for example with regard to long-term archiving. At a recent exchange of experience meeting organized by the Royal

Society, Mike Lesk of Bellcore made the observation that the United States 1960 Census had been largely lost because it was written on what was (in retrospect) the "wrong" kind of magnetic tape. How many of us have 78 rpm records but no longer own machines capable of running at such speed? Yet medieval manuscripts are still legible!

Conclusions

In such a complex situation, any prediction would be foolhardy. However, there is one scenario that seems to us to have several circumstances in its favor, at least as a transition possibility for the academic world. With academic campuses moving rapidly toward full provision of high-speed wide bandwidth networks, the dissemination of material with good color, graphics, and multimedia quality will soon be possible for electronic journals via these LANs. This might form the basis for an interim solution to the copyright control and income maintenance problems; publishers might sell site license subscriptions to the campus library, (thus combining two familiar journal and software pricing models) and send, say, a monthly file over the network to the central library, for release on the campus LAN and for mounting in the campus' indexed database. Whatever proves to be the eventual scenario, we can be sure of one outcome; the electronic library will certainly evolve to become rather different from the present form, and both librarians and their professional skills will need to change and develop to suit.

We believe that the major determinant of success of the electronic journal and the electronic library lies in their ability to satisfy the needs of the readers and authors, rather than institutional librarians or publishers. This represents somewhat of a shift in the traditional "power base," and requires an appropriate response from librarians and publishers if they are to play a role in the twenty-first century university.

Notes

1. The journal used was *Behaviour and Information Technology (BIT)*, published by Taylor and Francis, whom we gratefully acknowledge for allowing its use.

2. As of Spring 1994, the AAAS had decided to cancel funding of this project, leaving its future uncertain.

References

Adobe (1992). *Adobe(TM) Acrobat(TM) products and technology: An overview.* Adobe Systems Incorporated, November.

Burrows, T. (1993). Serials collection management: The academic library. In H. Woodward and S. Pilling (Eds.) *The international serials industry* (207–231). Aldershot: Gower.

Dillon, A. (1992). Reading from paper versus screens: a critical review of the empirical literature. *Ergonomics, 35*(10): 1297–1326.

Dillon, A., Richardson, J., and McKnight, C. (1988). Towards the development of a full text, searchable database: implications from a study of journal usage. *British Journal of Academic Librarianship 3*(1): 37–48.

Elsevier Science Publishers (1992). TULIP: An irregular update. No. 1, November.

Gordon, M.D. (1984) How authors select journals. *Social Studies of Science 14*(1): 27–43.

Gould, C.C. (1990). Scholarly information needs and RLG's program for research information management. In M. Feeney and K. Merry (Eds.) *Information technology and the research process* (171–181). London: Bowker—Saur.

Institute of Physics Publishing (1993). Electronic journals to be pioneered on SuperJANET. Press release, January 21.

Joint Funding Council (1993). *Joint Funding Councils' Libraries Review Group: Report.* Available from External Relations Department, HEFCE, Northavon House, Coldharbour Lane, Bristol BS6 1QD, UK.

Landauer, T., Egan, D., Remde, J., Lesk, M., Lochbaum, C., and Ketchum, D. (1993). Enhancing the usability of text through computer delivery and formative evaluation: The SuperBook project. In C. McKnight, A. Dillon, and J. Richardson (Eds.) *Hypertext: A psychological perspective* (71–136). Chichester: Ellis Horwood.

McKnight, C. (1991). The electronic journal: A user's view. *Serials, 4*(2): 53–60.

McKnight, C., Dillon, A., and Richardson, J. (1991). *Hypertext in context.* Cambridge: Cambridge University Press.

Nielsen, J. (1990) *Hypertext and hypermedia.* London: Academic Press.

Okerson, A. (1991). (Ed.) *Directory of electronic journals, newsletters and academic discussion lists.* Washington, D.C.: Association of Research Libraries.

Okerson, A. (1993). (ed.) *Directory of electronic journals, newsletters and academic discussion lists.* 3rd ed. Washington, D.C.: Association of Research Libraries.

Pfaffenberger, B. (1986). Research networks, scientific communication and the personal computer. *IEEE Transactions on Professional Communication 29*(1): 30–33.

PMC-list (1993, 21 May). *Postmodern Culture* announces PMC-MOO. Message posted to subscribers to pmc-list@listserv.ncsu.edu.

Pullinger, D.J. (1987). *BLEND-8: Cost appraisal.* Library and Information Research Report 53. London: The British Library.

Pullinger, D.J. and Meadows, A.J. (1993, February). Distribution of an electronic version of a scholarly journal from publisher to libraries. Paper distributed to exchange of experience meeting, Royal Society.

Shackel B. (1982). The BLEND System—Programme for the study of some 'electronic journals.' *Ergonomics* 25(4): 269–284; *The Journal of the American Society for Information Science* 34(1): 22–30; and *The Computer Journal* 25(2): 161–168.

Shackel, B., Pullinger, D.J., Maude, T.I., and Dodd, W.P. (1983). The BLEND-LINC project on 'electronic journals' after two years. *ASLIB Proceedings* 35: 77–91; *The Computer Journal* 26(3): 247–252.

Shackel, B. (1985). Using RAAJ for real. *Journal of Librarianship* 17(3): 200–204.

Shackel, B. (1990). Information exchange within the research community. In M. Feeney and K. Merry (Eds.) *Information technology and the research process* (147–170). London: Bowker–Saur.

Shackel, B. (1991). *BLEND-9: Overview and Appraisal*. British Library Research Paper 82. London: The British Library.

Sheridan, T., Senders, J., Moray, N., Stoklosa, J., Guillaume, J., and Makepeace, D. (1981). Experimentation with a multi-disciplinary teleconference and electronic journal on mental workload. Unpublished report to National Science Foundation, Division of Science Information Access Improvement, 320 pp. (June). (Available from Professor T.B. Sheridan, Room 1-110, M.I.T., Cambridge, Massachusetts 02139, U.S.A.)

Sidgreaves, I. (1989). The electronic campus—an information strategy: Organisation issues. In L.J. Brindley (ed.) *The electronic campus* (65–80). Library and Information Research Report 73. London: The British Library.

Simpson, A. (1988). Academic journal usage. *British Journal of Academic Librarianship* 3(1): 25–36.

Tuck, B., McKnight, C., Hayet, M., and Archer, D. (1990). *Project Quartet*. LIR Report No. 76. London: The British Library.

Wilson, D.L. (1992, June 3). Major scholarly publisher to test electronic transmission of journals. *The Chronicle of Higher Education*: A17, A20.

The Role of Academic Libraries in the Dissemination of Scholarly Information in the Electronic Environment

Lymann Ross
Paul Philbin
Merri Beth Lavagnino
Albert Joy

Networking technology has had a radical effect on the dissemination of scholarly information. Mitch Kapor of the Electronic Frontier Foundation said, "Computer-based communications is a new medium that will be as important as print was in the fourteenth century" (Hyatt 1992, 61). In this chapter, we provide a brief historical overview of the development of the traditional role of the American university library. We address some of the challenges to that role as a result of the rising cost and volume of information, and as a result of the technological revolution. The response to these challenges at the Bailey/Howe Library, University of Vermont, is described. Finally, implications for the library of the twenty-first century are discussed—how the university library of the future might best support and enhance the potential for scholarly communication and information exchange.

An Historical Perspective

The American university as we know it today developed during the nineteenth century. Before the middle of the nineteenth century, the academic library would have been unrecognizable to modern library users. In 1849, only Harvard College owned more than 50,000 volumes (68,000 reported), and only four other academic institutions owned over 20,000 books (Jewett 1850). The academic curriculum of the day was based on the lecture, the textbook, and the recitation.

Research was unknown at American universities, and the curriculum centered on religion and classical studies. The libraries themselves may have been open only a few hours a day, and students would have been able to borrow books only once a week if at all! Preservation of recorded knowledge was a major purpose of the library and the librarian. An anecdote about John Langdon Sibley, librarian of Harvard College from 1856 to 1877, illustrates this philosophy: Sibley was seen one day crossing Harvard Yard with an extremely pleased expression on his face. When queried about the cause of his happiness, he replied, "All the books are in [the library] excepting two. Agassiz has those and I am going after them" (Koch 1912, 274).

In the latter part of the nineteenth century, following the U.S. Civil War, there were great changes in higher education. The Morrill Act of 1862, the Hatch Act of 1887, and the Second Morrill Act of 1890 provided funding as well as a mandate for colleges and universities to change their curricula from the classical model to a more vocational, scientific, and research-oriented curriculum based on the German university model. Because the library was seen as more central to the operations of a modern university, the library gained supporters from the ranks of the faculty, governing boards, presidents, deans, and alumni. The library began to be cited as the "center," the "core," and even the "heart" of the university, and great efforts were made to build the collections of the library.

Along with the collection and preservation of recorded knowledge, access to information gained increasing importance. In 1877, Justin Winsor, appointed librarian of Harvard College following Sibley, stated: "Books may be accumulated and guarded and the result is sometimes called a library; but if books are made to help and spur men on in their own daily work, the library becomes a vital influence; the prison is turned into a workshop" (Annual, 1877, 109). Though some institutions resisted this trend, most universities and their libraries adopted these new models.

The Traditional Role of the American University Library

As a result of these nineteenth century historical developments, a traditional role for the American university library was developed. The library was to acquire and preserve recorded information, and to provide access to that information.

Academic libraries acquire, store, and preserve information for the use of scholars present and future. The materials are selected based on the need to support the instructional and research needs of the institution, and to allow the flow of scholarly information and discourse. This information traditionally has been paper-based and primarily composed of books and serial literature, but also includes maps and photographs. Since the 1930s libraries have collected information in microformats as both a preservation technique and a space saver. To a lesser degree, libraries have begun to collect non-print materials such as film, video, and sound recordings.

Libraries make their collections accessible in many ways. Reference librarians assist users in finding and understanding the library's information resources, through both reference desk service and classroom instruction. Cataloging library materials makes them available by author, title, subject, and other access points. Subject-based pathfinders and finding aids help users identify materials in the library. Libraries also collect indexes to the literature of fields of interest at the college or university. Without access, a library could be compared to a warehouse.

For most of the twentieth century until recent times, the library was viewed as "the" source for scholarly information on campus. Information resources, primarily paper-based, were acquired to support the current and anticipated needs of the university community. This model, has been described as the "just-in-case" model, in which "libraries acquire materials in anticipation of readers' needs, in accordance with an assumption that a particular reader may at some future time wish to consult a particular volume" (Cummings, Witte, Bowen, Lazarus, and Ekman 1992, 107).

The Traditional Role is Challenged

It was universally understood that the library was the best place to store and preserve printed material, and that professional librarians trained to acquire, preserve, and provide access to this medium should manage it. The introduction of microformat and non-print materials into libraries in the 1930s presented new issues for the library, such as the need to provide necessary equipment to view them, but these materials did not represent a serious change in the traditional dissemination of information.

A more serious challenge occurred in the 1970s when there was a dramatic rise in the price and volume of journal literature. This change came at a time when college and university budgets were stagnating or even declining (Cummings, et al. 1992, xvii). As a result, it became clear that individual libraries were incapable of building collections to support all curricular and research needs. Libraries responded to this challenge by investigating regional and national collection building and cooperative cataloging projects—activities that resulted in a dramatic rise of interlibrary loan activities. Two major networks evolved to support these activities at an international level: Online Computer Library Center (OCLC) and Research Libraries Information Network (RLIN). These cooperative ventures were possible only because of developments in computing and telecommunications that libraries to share information in electronic format for the first time.

As increasing amounts of information became available in electronic formats, some began to question whether libraries would continue to play a role in the dissemination of information resources. Such criticism is generally based upon the belief that a library's primary function is to acquire and maintain printed materials. Harlan Cleveland, in an influential essay in the *Futurist*, has argued that information became a commodity to be bought and sold only because it was entrapped in a physical medium: paper. The true nature of information will become apparent as computers release it from its material, paper-based trappings. In its natural form, information will be infinitely extensible and freely interchangeable, and thus outside of the market forces of scarcity and demand. In the future, information will flow freely from the producer to the consumer. Although ten years old, Cleveland's article is a prescient description of today's Internet, where institutions and individuals are racing to provide the network community with free bibliographies, software, essays, dictionaries, fiction, and even pornography (Cleveland 1982).

Others predict that commercial enterprises will replace libraries. They foresee a time when individuals will be able to access digital banks of movies, television programs, newspapers, and books from their living rooms across high-speed computer networks directly from the information providers. The middlemen—video stores, bookstores, and libraries—will disappear.

There are also those within the profession who perceive libraries and librarians as barriers to networked information. A recent article states: "We (librarians) yearn to regulate all information exchange, and we have a morbid fear of losing anything. We traditionally interpose ourselves between the user and the information. And now, just when it appears that technology will finally liberate the user from the tyranny of mediation, the library, in its new guise as information service provider, appears poised to insert itself once again between the information seeker and the information sought" (Atkinson 1993, 211). Others fear that, if we do not aggressively seize control over networked resources, we risk becoming obsolete. Faculty and students will look increasingly to commercial vendors, scholarly associations, campus computing centers, or even remote networked libraries to fulfill their research needs. Those libraries that lack vigilance, that fail to recognize and embrace new technologies, will become irrelevant.

And Libraries Respond

To critics, academic libraries are stuffy and elitist institutions, more interested in preserving our cultural past than in serving the needs of current users. This idea of the library as museum invokes images of heavy oak bookcases, venerable tomes, and stern librarians enforcing a code of silence. While this misconception may reflect nineteenth century realities, it is at odds with the technological revolution currently sweeping the profession.

In the space of ten years, online public access catalogs (OPACs) have replaced card catalogs, CD-ROMs have replaced print indexes, and the Internet has opened the walls of the library to a flood of new information resources. Catalog librarians struggle to describe these dynamic electronic resources. Acquisitions librarians struggle to find ways to purchase traditional materials while saving enough funds from fiscally strapped budgets to expand into the electronic arena. The reference librarian is challenged daily to help patrons who use an ever-expanding array of Internet resources directly and through tools such as Gopher, Archie, Wide Area Information Servers (WAIS), and World Wide Web (WWW) browsers like Mosaic and Netscape. In addition, reference librarians advise on document retrieval, delivery, and file transfer, but increasingly they are called on to provide guidance with managing information through electronic mail, news groups, and discussion forums. Microcomputer labs are also now common in academic libraries. Some university libraries, like that at Iowa State University, are going beyond these more basic services to embrace technology in new and innovative ways. This library has set aside time, staff, money, and space for an Information Arcade where students and faculty may develop and experiment with multimedia tools to integrate text, sound, and images (Rooks 1993, 27).

There is now a real danger that libraries will evolve at a rate faster than their public is willing or able to follow, that the stereotype of the elite preserver of the past will be replaced by that of the insensitive hawker of the future (Franklin 1993). Many within and without the profession openly worry that the fiscal requirements of new technology will be met at the expense of books and other traditional materials (Crawford 1993, 18). Furthermore, as networking increases libraries' potential user base, publishers have begun to place restrictions on the use of their products which threaten to diminish real access for some. For example, access to CD-ROM systems in the library are generally available to non-academic library users. However, as libraries begin to network databases, publishers are enforcing licenses that limit access to certain user groups. It is not uncommon to bar non-academic users from commercial resources. The licensing process may eventually curtail fair use privileges that libraries enjoy under current copyright laws (Ginsburg 1993, 61). It is critical in this situation that libraries maintain a clear vision of their mission, and that they manage technology to meet the needs of all their patrons.

Notwithstanding these potential problems, libraries and their users have realized enormous benefits by embracing the technological revolution. Today, libraries can provide information at the exact time and place needed. As the costs of computer hardware drop, it becomes more affordable for libraries to load databases locally. In addition, libraries can negotiate increasingly competitive volume discounts to commercial services for access to citation and fulltext databases, and document delivery services through the Internet. Servers can be used to provide automated connections to both locally loaded and remote databases. This hybrid approach can provide resources in the library and over a campus network in a manner at once increasingly technologically complicated and at the same time increasingly easy to use.

Sage: A Local Response

The University of Vermont Libraries and Media Services began struggling with this complicated environment in 1991, when individual staff workstations were connected to the newly completed campus network. Library staff were some of the first users on campus to explore the Internet to access and capture information from distant OPACs, commercial databases, and scholarly discussion groups. Yet as the library began to introduce the wonders of these information resources, it became clear that many users lacked either the necessary network connections or technical skills to avail themselves of these riches. Furthermore, resources that were easily accessible from library office desktops were absent from public areas of the library.

In early 1992, the library had a single public access microcomputer connected to the campus network and used for OCLC access. A

```
+------------------MEGA MACHINE MENU------------------+
|     FOR:                           TYPE:            |
|----------------------------------------------------|
|   OCLC (never on Sunday)       |   OCLC [Enter]     |
|                                |                    |
|   Journal & Newspaper Indexes  |   INDEX [Enter]    |
|                                |                    |
|   Library Catalogs             |   LIBER [Enter]    |
|                                |                    |
|   Burlington Free Press        |   BFP [Enter]      |
|                                |                    |
|   HYTELNET Directory           |   CTRL-BACKSPACE   |
|                                |                    |
|   Directory of Country         |   DCS90 [Enter]    |
|       Environmental Studies    |                    |
|                                |                    |
+----------------------------------------------------+
```

Fig. 1

menu was written, using a series of batch and script files, to guide
users to important Internet bibliographic resources such as major
OPACs, a customized gateway to CARL UnCover (Colorado Alliance
of Research Libraries), Hytelnet,[1] and a small number of regional and
national periodical indexes. Despite its limited scope and unsophisticated interface (see figure 1), this station quickly attracted a devoted
cadre of users.

Demand for this single workstation increased to the point where
it could no longer fulfill its primary function—providing public access
to OCLC. A stable and simple-to-use information gateway was needed,
to unite multiple stand-alone databases into one system available from
multiple locations. It needed to manage an array of information
resources that would satisfy the majority of the curricular and
research needs of students and faculty, and allow users to connect to
and disconnect from these services without knowing host connection
protocols.

Working cooperatively with the University of Vermont Computing and Information Technology Division, the menu was reworked to
run on a Novell NetWare server. While this technology would not
provide access for all types of hardware and software, it was an easy
and inexpensive first step toward providing universal access. All public terminals in the libraries, previously only connected to our local
OPAC, were replaced with diskless workstations that could access this
server and all its resources. Similarly, any DOS-based microcomputers
in campus buildings such as offices, classrooms, and dormitories, could
log on through the campus network if they obtained a network card

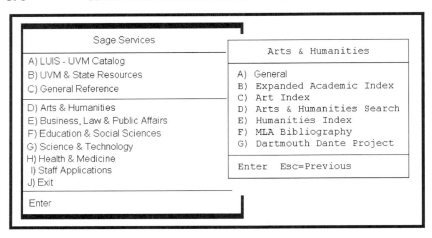

Fig. 2

and network connection. The resulting information gateway was christened Sage (see figure 2). In order to make it easy to use, the menu items were arranged by subject. Through Sage, users can access local information resources—the Libraries' online catalog and the University's Gopher server; commercial services—Dow Jones News/Retrieval Service, LEXIS/NEXIS, CARL UnCover, and selected FirstSearch databases; regional services—indexes to local newspapers (Burlington *Free Press* and Rutland *Herald*) and the Vermont Automated Library System (VALS) network; and cooperative tape loaded databases—the Expanded Academic Index.[2]

Librarians in the reference department built Sage menus using Saber Menu software. Saber Menu was chosen because it is reliable and flexible, and uses less memory than Novell's menu utility. Sage menus can be quickly and dynamically updated to provide for special or temporary needs. Such swiftness was at work in the fall of 1993, when students in an English seminar were required to search the Dartmouth Dante Project, an online data-base providing access to six hundred years of scholarship on Dante's *Divine Comedy*. Many experienced difficulties reaching the project through Gopher. In response, the library quickly created a direct link between Sage and the Dante Project, a process that took less than a quarter of an hour.

Sage has three main components that enhance its usage and management: a help facility, a statistics module, and an authentication program. Each component was designed and developed by librarians in the Reference Department.

Sage Advice is a hypertext help system developed using 1st Class Fusion software. Sage Advice can be used as a tutorial prior to connecting to a service, or users can print portions of it for future reference. As an integral component of Sage, it solves the problem of copying and disseminating the more than forty separate user guides.

The statistical component was written in Turbo Pascal. It can be activated when needed, and records the number of times a menu item is selected. It does not count the number of searches made within a service but does record the length of time an individual spends in the service. The analysis of this data informs the administrator of the busiest times and workstations, and the most popular services. This information can be used to justify staff and equipment, as well as to aid in the selection and removal of information resources.

The authentication program, also written in Turbo Pascal, was essential for managing access to restricted services such as Dow Jones News/Retrieval Service and LEXIS/NEXIS. License agreements for these services limit their use to individuals affiliated with the university. When a restricted system is selected from the menu, a window opens prompting the user to enter their last name and a portion of their library barcode number. The program compares this information with an extract of the patron database from our library management system. If a match is found, a connection to the requested service is established. If not, a message advises the user to ask for assistance at the reference desk.

The Success of Sage and Its Implications for the Future

The popularity of the Sage system has exceeded expectations. The number of services available on the system has doubled from about twenty to forty, while use has increased from an average of over six hundred sessions per day to roughly 1,100. It is now a permanent fixture in the minds of our patrons, who describe items simply as having been found on Sage. One user went so far as to call the support line for her bibliographic database software to see if it supported the uploading of documents from Sage. Some who had resisted automation in the past have accepted Sage, citing its ease of use.

The fulltext services, Dow Jones News/Retrieval and LEXIS/NEXIS, are among the most popular. This is an indication that users will struggle with complex interfaces if they believe that it will repay their efforts. Of the FirstSearch databases, WorldCat is the favorite by a 2 to 1 margin. WorldCat is OCLC's Online Union Catalog and the world's largest bibliographic database, with over thirty million records from some twenty thousand libraries. The most popular Sage service, however, is the University of Vermont's online public access catalog. The popularity of these two catalogs suggests that the scholarly monograph is still a vibrant form of scholarly communication.

Sage has also been successful as an aid to the pedagogic role of the faculty. One romance language professor recounted a story of a student who claimed that he could find nothing relevant to his topic. The faculty member connected to Sage from her office and selected the bibliography of the Modern Language Association (MLA Bibliography). She was then able to show the student that information did indeed exist and was available at the library.

Despite the enormous success of Sage, we are cognizant of its weaknesses, and can already begin to envision the capabilities of the next generation of information gateway. Sage is a victim of its own success. Users from across the campus are pressing for access from multiple hardware and software platforms, and especially for dial-up access from home. Instead of completing Macintosh and Windows versions for the Novell server, the project is now being implemented on a UNIX server. This will provide access not only for Macintosh and Windows but also for UNIX workstations and dial-up users. Eventually, the Novell version will be phased out altogether.

Other weaknesses are more difficult to solve. Organizing the wealth and complexity of information and information sources available through the electronic interface is a great challenge. Sage's hierarchical menu, arranged by subject, is an easy way to organize and search small sets of information, but it quickly deteriorates as it increases in size. Users of Gopher are well aware of the limitations of such menu structures as they wend their way through layers of submenus chasing after an ever elusive document. The Gopher search engine Veronica facilitates the retrieval of relevant items by enabling users to bypass the menus and search for them using keywords. However, it has many limitations of its own. One is a product of Gopherspace itself, which resembles a collective attic, where items have colloquial titles meaningful only to their creators. This loose nomenclature is the foundation upon which Veronica's keyword index is generated. A recent search of Veronica found over 1,200 occurrences of the word "stuff." Gopherspace has no true subject cataloging, nor item description. Given this state of affairs, it is difficult to determine which items are unique and relevant.

Network resources must be clearly identifiable if they are to be fully integrated into the realm of scholarly communication. Equivalents to ISSN or ISBN numbers do not presently exist for electronic materials, while descriptions of physical features (i.e., quarto or folio) are clearly irrelevant. Pagination, perhaps the most basic feature of the printed work, makes little sense in an electronic document, but is often added to comply with current methods of identification. The Internet Engineering Task Force is currently leading an effort to create a system of identification referred to by the acronym URL: Universal/ Unique/Uniform Resource Locator (Lynch 1993). The work of this group is already being implemented in the Internet navigator tools like Gopher and World Wide Web browsers.

Networked information should also be cataloged if it is to become an accepted part of our collections. Assigning subject headings to online documents will enhance users' ability to locate them and to judge their usefulness. This will expand their audience beyond the small loci of cognoscenti studying in a particular field and active on the Internet. The library catalog remains an important finding tool, as it encompasses those materials which the library has committed to making available for use. If it is serious about providing networked resources, it should demonstrate that fact by recording them in its OPAC. Before this can occur, however, standards for describing electronic documents must be established that will build upon libraries' long experience with printed resources (MARBI, 1993). These standards are now being tested and evaluated by an OCLC directed project, "Building a Catalog of Internet-Accessible Materials." The project runs through March 1996 and is funded in part by the U.S. Department of Education, Office of Library Programs.

The increasing number of networked resources creates problems not only of organization and identification but also of use. At present, there are still no standards governing the design of search interfaces. The initial Sage project did not attempt to solve the problem of multiple interfaces. Users are now connected to the native interfaces of the databases accessed. This situation was ameliorated to a certain extent by the decision to use the OCLC FirstSearch service, which provides a common interface to almost half of Sage's offerings. The creation of the Z39.50 standard for the interchange of search retrieval attributes should greatly enhance this capability in the future.[3] Z39.50 implementations such as the library information systems at Dartmouth College, the University of California, and Pennsylvania State University have addressed this problem by providing a common locally developed interface that can be applied to services from many vendors.

A further problem has been an inability to provide consistent links from other databases to local library holdings. This forces our users to disconnect from most of our databases and then reconnect to our OPAC to determine if a journal is owned locally. Many of the FirstSearch databases provide a link to local holdings, and this was a big advantage to using FirstSearch. But not all FirstSearch databases have this feature. Links have also been established to local holdings in the CARL UnCover database through a customized gateway. Other products available from our library management system vendor would provide links to holdings when searching other library catalogs or when searching locally-loaded databases. But until we have consistent, up-to-date, and reliable links in all databases accessed through Sage, users will continue to be frustrated by the extra step necessary to complete their research.

Conclusion

Will the basic role of the American university library change in this age of electronic information? Earlier, we described the traditional role as one of supporting the current and anticipated curricular and research needs of the academic community by acquiring, preserving, and providing access to information resources. Our experience with the Sage project, as well as experiences described in the literature, indicate that this basic role is here to stay for the foreseeable future.

Academic libraries must continue to adapt to changes in information formats and in the electronic tools for their dissemination. With a wealth of information available through networks such as the present Internet, whether freely accessible or purchased, it is important for professional librarians to continue their selecting, organizing, and teaching functions. Now and into the twenty-first century, improvement must be made in areas such as indexing of these resources to increase the user's ability to identify their true content; search structures to allow accurate and useful retrieval of appropriate resources; and search, display, and formatting interfaces to facilitate easy end-user access to and use of the electronic information available. During this period, the teaching role of librarians will be especially in demand, as end-users increase their own skills in information retrieval.

Perhaps the role of the library is not what is changing, but rather the expectations of the users. Users are becoming more sophisticated in their ability to identify and access information that is timely and pertinent to their exact needs, affordable to the individual, and accessible from homes, laboratories, and offices. This increased awareness has led to increased demands on libraries, and we as librarians have a unique opportunity to take advantage of this new interest and sophistication of our users, and to build upon it.

If we hope to be successful in the twenty-first century, academic librarians must continue to be true to the traditional academic role of the library. To accomplish this, we must continue to build and maintain print and electronic resources. The creation of a completely virtual library would not successfully serve disciplines that rely on paper-based materials. Academic libraries must strive to satisfy two very distinct populations: the electronic sophisticates who call librarians "book people," and scoff; and the scholar who fumes at the prospect of dwindling print collections. The future is challenging, and the duality of print and electronic collections will continue into the twenty-first century. Crawford put it well when he foresaw "A future with both print and electronic resources. . . . A future with both prose and hypertext. . . . A future with both librarians as intermediaries and direct access . . . A future with both collections and access. . . . A future with both edifice and interface. . . " (Crawford, 1993 20).

Notes

1. Hytelnet is a hypertext directory to Internet resources developed by Peter Scott at the University of Saskatchewan Libraries.

2. Dow Jones News Retrieval is a news and financial information service. Mead Data Central's LEXIS/NEXIS provides fulltext access to news, legal, business, and medical information. CARL UnCover is the Colorado Alliance of Research Libraries' table-of-contents and journal index. OCLC's FirstSearch service provides a common search interface to over forty databases. Information Access Corporation's Expanded Academic Index is a multidisciplinary index to over 1,500 general and academic publications.

3. Z39.50 is an American National Standard, approved in 1988 by the American Information Standards Organization and the American National Standards Institute. The standard provides a uniform search command language when accessing bibliographic information such as online library catalogs and journal indexes.

References

Annual report of the President of Harvard University to the Overseers on the State of the University, for the academical year 1876–1877. (1877). Cambridge: Harvard University.

Atkinson, R. (1993). Networks, hypertext, and academic information services: Some longer-range implications. *College and Research Libraries 54*(3): 199–215.

Cleveland, H. (1982). Information as a resource. *The Futurist 16*(6): 34–39.

Crawford, W. (1993). Dreams, devices, niches, and edges: Coping with the changing landscape of information technology. The Public-Access Computer Systems Review [Online], 4(5): 5–21. Available e-mail: Listserv@ Uhupvm1 or Listserv@ Uhupvm1.Uh.Edu Message: Get Crawford PRV4N5 F=Mail.

Cummings, A. M., White, M. L., Bowen, W. G., Lazarus, L. O., and Ekman, R. H. (1992). *University Libraries and Scholarly Communication*. Washington, D.C.: Association of Research Libraries.

Franklin, P. (1993). Scholars, librarians, and the future of primary records. *College & Research Libraries 54*(5): 397–406.

Ginsburg, J. C. (1993). Copyright without walls?: Speculations on literary property in the library of the future. *Representations 42*: 53–73.

Hyatt, J. (1992, March 20). Computer crusader. *The Boston Globe*: 61.

Jewett, C. C. (1850). *Appendix to the Report of the Board of Regents of the Smithsonian Institution, Containing a Report on the Public Libraries of the United States of America, January 1, 1850*. (31st Congress, 1st Session, Senate Miscellaneous Documents No. 120). Washington, D.C.: Printed for the Senate.

Koch, T. W. (1912). Some phases of the administrative history of college and university libraries. *Bulletin of the American Library Association 6*(4): 268–275.

Lynch, C. A. (1993, March 24). A framework for identifying, locating, and describing networked information resources [Online]. Available FTP: archive.mcgill.ca Directory: pub/network/uri File: lynch.overview.txt.

MARBI Discussion Paper no. 69 [Online]. (1993, April 30). Available FTP: a.cni.org Directory: /pub/MARBI File: dp69.txt

Rooks, D.. The virtual library: pitfalls, promises, and potential. *The Public-Access Computer Systems Review* [Online], 4(5): 22–29. Available e-mail: Listserv@Uhupvm1 or Listserv@Uhupvm1.Uh.Edu Message: Get Rooks PRV4N5 F=Mail.

The Body in the
Virtual Library
Rethinking Scholarly
Communication

Kenneth Arnold

The Book as Object

If we want a visual analog to the electronic book, we can learn a lot from the Minnesota Center for Book Arts, where art works based on the idea, "book," suggest the open architecture of the Internet. These works of art convey content as form. They are hard to imagine and yet have a gracious logic. Some of them are flights of fancy so tangentially related to the book as we know it that we are aware of their book origins only because they are identified as book arts—a series of fans, for example, or an object that looks like a box kite. Others are more clearly traditional books. One is a book wrapped in barbed wire. Another is a book that unfolds in a fan shape to reveal a landscape. Another has a light in the binding—truly an illuminated text, or perhaps a pun on the computer's backlit screen.

I begin by writing about the book as art because so many fear that the electronic book will obliterate the book as we know it, leaving us with no tangible object of our literate affection. Like the art object, however, the electronic book does not so much replace traditional books as extend our idea of book in new directions. I would suggest that, in the realm of academic publishing that is the subject of this chapter, the e-book actually returns to an earlier mode of scholarly discourse, retrieving the past in a new, friendly form by allowing for more direct and immediate communication among scholars and students.

---

*This chapter draws on two previously published essays by the author: "Rethinking Scholarly Communication in the New University," in *Conference Proceedings, ACLTS, 1993,* published by the Association of Library Collections and Technical Services, 1994; and "The Scholarly Monograph is Dead; Long Live the Scholarly Monograph," in *Visions and Opportunities in Electronic Publishing: Proceedings of the Second Symposium,* edited by Ann Okerson, published by the Association of Research Libraries, 1993.

Most of us know about, and some even remember, monotype, the hot-metal method of composition that was in general use through the 1960s. When I began working at the Johns Hopkins University Press in 1967, I could feel the impression of type on the printed page. The changes that ensued, what we called cold type, were an esthetic shock to our systems. They did not, however, materially affect the nature of our work, which was driven by content. Content as form, the book as art work, is related to the hand-held object most of us cherish only in the most tenuous ways. When is an installation no longer a book? How can you tell? In the electronic environment, we encounter the opposite kind of book—content without form or even materiality. How do we know what we are dealing with? Does it matter? If a producer says that something is a book, perhaps that is all one needs to know. The publisher, of course, wants to know how to make money with it, whatever it is.

A New Way of Publishing

The electronic revolution is about much more than scholarly publishing. It is about a new kind of social order that in fact threatens the very existence of the traditional scholarly publisher. When Michael Jensen at the University of Nebraska Press casually referred three years ago in an e-mail message to "an online society," he was talking about something that clearly exists now in a way just imaginable when he used the phrase. Public policy supports that vision of society. The Clinton administration began, immediately after coming to office, to develop the National Information Infrastructure (NII). Vice President Gore talked enthusiastically and convincingly about tne potential for information technology in American education and business. Investment in this technology has already radically altered the landscape for publishers as some of the largest American communications companies have begun to exploit the potential of fiber-optic highways.

What this revolution means to publishers was articulated in June 1992 by Richard Snyder, then Simon & Schuster chair: "We're not just a publisher anymore, . . . but a creator and exploiter of copyrights. We sell information in any form, in any way you want it. . . . [W]e are out of the confines of print, although that doesn't mean we are out of the print business. We now can sell the same information in various forms. We can take any piece of information—a college textbook or a Securities & Exchange Commission filing—and sell it in print, online, on CD-ROM, on film and on interactive laser discs" (Weyr 1992, 33).

This new kind of publisher makes available to the user only the information the user wants, only when the user wants it, and in the most convenient form. This ability to target and tailor information is at the heart of the electronic revolution. As information becomes more widely and rapidly available, people are going to want to control the flow to suit their own purposes, not the purposes of the supplier (i.e., the publisher). This new set of circumstances challenges the way publishers have traditionally thought. The present book publishing and distribution system is characterized not by precision marketing, although some publishers do that, but by waste. Colin Day, Director of the University of Michigan Press and past president of the Association of American University Presses (AAUP), argued in a private internet communication two years ago that the changes we face as publishers are "Type 2" innovations. By that, he meant that the electronic revolution "bears the seeds of the destruction of our business." His reasoning was based on the problem of maintaining control of copyrights, which generate the revenue stream that pays our costs. ("Type 1" innovations are those that merely change the physical nature of what we sell. The shift from hot metal to cold type is an example.)

Colin Day has stated the issue facing scholarly publishers this way: "The university press community does have to develop and promote a view of how scholarly communication should exploit the strengths of these new technologies while preserving the essential contributions that we make to the process of scholarly communication" (private Internet communication). The new technology has called into question the value publishers have added to the traditional work of scholars, whether disseminated in book or journal form. Some have questioned whether the future will contain publishers—intermediaries between writers and readers—at all. A few netheads have suggested that the writer will also publish and archive in the new environment. Others have acknowledged that some form of intermediary will be required, but that it will emerge from the present library system and combine in one agency the functions of publisher and librarian. I will return to this important question later.

Roots of a New Order

The new technology arrived at a time of crisis for the scholarly communication system. Just as the escalating costs of journals were driving out other library acquisitions, university presses increased the number of titles published in order to compensate for declining library sales. Some presses also shifted their lists toward more general and course markets. Familiar divisions between the nonprofit and for-profit publishing worlds began to blur as university presses ceased to think of libraries as their primary markets. Because the electronic revolution began in libraries and with journals, university presses were caught by surprise when in April 1992 a symposium on scholarly publishing in the electronic networks, sponsored by the Association of Research Libraries (ARL), made it clear to some that the old order was moribund. Journals were already being published online; document delivery systems, along with customized course packs, threatened to destroy both the remaining library market and the developing course market for academic books. The journal model of disseminating information—assemblages of somewhat related materials designed for random access—has now become the paradigm for electronic publishing.

University presses began as the publishers of journals and evolved into publishers of mostly monographs—which I have defined as relatively short, specialized books emphasizing research method as much as or more than content. (Many of my colleagues have disputed this definition, but I believe it describes exactly the sort of book that dominated university press lists until the mid- to late-eighties. It is also the cornerstone of the larger academic publishers who rely on economies of scale, the production of large numbers of narrowly focused books for very small markets, to survive.) These monographs were designed primarily as tools by which scholars could communicate with and evaluate each other on common ground. Clear methodology ensured that one scholar could understand how another scholar reached a particular conclusion. Thereby, the bricks of knowledge were firmly cemented into place. Something like that. Young scholars attained promotion and tenure by participating in this process. Older scholars mentored younger scholars, established schools of thought, controlled what got published through the peer review system. University presses, owned and operated by major research universities, became central to the management of this system. These assumptions on which the system operated have not actually changed, even though nearly everything else has. In a way, the scholars producing work and the universities relying on their presses to validate academic preferment are the last to find out that the government has been overthrown and no one is in charge.

The monograph, as I have argued publicly for several years, is dead as a viable economic base for university presses. Worse yet—and this is not something I have previously said—I do not think that the present system of university publishing can survive at all. Some new form of managing scholarly communication will have to emerge. The question is, what will it look like? The struggle under way is about the control of information, and university presses have few weapons to bring to the field. One example will suffice for the moment. On February 8, 1994, as I was writing the final draft of this chapter, Encyclopedia Britannica announced that the reference work would be offered to universities and some public libraries via the Internet. Using the WAIS search engine and the revolutionary Mosaic software interface, Britannica promised to become state of the art in online retrieval. This happened virtually overnight. By contrast, university presses had been struggling for nearly two years to come up with a way of making all press catalogs available on the Internet and still had not succeeded (although the system was online by June 1994). The difference was capital, and the ability of Britannica to make and execute the decision to develop a system of its own that allowed control of content. Joseph Esposito, president of Encyclopedia Britannica, was quoted as saying that "you just can't make any money licensing your content . . . If you do believe that content is king, it's rather unfortunate that so many of the content providers have put themselves in a position where they're held hostage to the online services" (Markoff 1994, D2). University presses appeared to have no choice but to license content to online services because they lacked the capital and executive ability to create proprietary systems.

In 1991, I suggested that university presses make common cause with campus libraries and computer centers to develop university-based publishing nodes that could take advantage of Internet and short-run printing technologies. When I was at Rutgers as director of the university press, I organized a committee that prepared, in early 1992, a grant proposal to study this new approach to scholarly communication. The essence of the idea was that the university should be at the center of scholarly communication, not the university press as currently operating. Because I had learned that the Andrew W. Mellon Foundation was preparing a report on scholarly communication, we sent our proposal to Mellon. The Mellon report was issued a year later, late in 1992, at which time Richard Ekman, the program officer responsible for the report, indicated that Mellon would not be funding electronic publishing projects for some time to come. Subsequently, in 1993, the Coalition for Networked Information (CNI), which had not previously invited university presses to participate in its deliberations, collaborated with the Association of American University Presses in the encouragement of university-based projects linking libraries, computer centers, and presses—as I had previously proposed. The hitch was that no money was offered to help presses do anything. Sponsorship by CNI, it was hoped, would legitimate the projects and attract funding. Most of these projects were small, content-driven extensions of traditional publishing programs that promised to do little to change the way people used or disseminated information.

By the time CNI and AAUP announced their initiative, I had concluded that it would be necessary to create a larger, more cooperative electronic system in which university presses could function. Local initiatives were unlikely to address the critical question of managing the flow of information in a system that is anything but local. The investment necessary to turn the system around—to bring universities and their presses onto the NII playing field—has to come from the deep pockets of large corporations and foundations. There has been little evidence at the time of this writing that these funding entities have any interest in putting money into the rescue or evolution of the system of scholarly communication, although some foundations—Mellon in particular—have invested in a few projects, such as the Johns Hopkins Press' journal program, MUSE.

My point here is that university presses, acting individually in their university environments, cannot ever move quickly enough with sufficient capital and authority to be players in the new environment. Not only do the presses lack capital and staff to innovate, foundations are clearly not prepared to put large amounts of money into locally based projects that cannot demonstrate large-scale economic value. One or two presses are exceptions, but they are fundamentally different from most university publishers. Oxford and Cambridge University Presses are prime examples of publshers with the capital and the freedom to innovate. Not surprisingly, therefore, Edward Barry, president of Oxford, is one of the key people spending time on the problems of scholarly publishing in the electronic environment. In 1993, the AAUP created an Electronic Caucus, a committee of volunteers charged with monitoring developments in the new publishing environment. Energetically led by Lisa Freeman, Director at University of Minnesota Press, the E-Caucus was quickly overwhelmed by the sheer volume of work to be done. The leadership of AAUP realized that volunteer action would be insufficient for the needs of the press community—and at the same time had to conclude for economic reasons that there were no other options available to the association.

In sharp contrast to the AAUP, the librarians have been extremely well organized around the issue of electronic dissemination and management of information. Ann Okerson, of the Association of Research Libraries, forced the university presses to pay attention to the problem in the first place. The result was a dialogue between librarians and university publishers astonishingly unique in the history of academic publishing. She also focused attention on the critical issue of the ownership of intellectual property raised by the crisis in publishing and the electronic environment.

In an article in *Logos* in 1991, Okerson made the case that universities should reclaim control of the copyrights they generate. This sort of thing was already common in the area of patents and other kinds of intellectual properties created by universities. The copyright system, as she justifiably claimed, was dysfunctional. Richard Dougherty, as long ago as Spring 1989, analyzed the situation perceptively in an issue of *Library Administration and Management*. The publish-or-perish syndrome, he argued, fuels the publishing engine and produces, as a result, too much stuff. Specialization in academe and the reward system that drives scholars to publish create publications, both books and journals, that are unrelated to the demand for the information they contain. In his article, Dougherty argued that the university should become a base for publication very much as I independently proposed in our Rutgers grant application to Mellon. Such an approach would involve the universities more deeply in the system of scholarly communication as both an information and economic enterprise.

In the online HUMANIST Discussion Group back in May 1991, Robin Cover alarmed a number of people by suggesting that the present scholarly publishing system rips off scholars who should take control of their own work and self-publish on the Net. Cover is an anarchist. He questioned the role of the publisher as "authenticator" and owner of academic work. The scholar who produces and uses scholarly work buys it back through university-subsidized programs—or so this argument went. Cover properly noted that publishers did not create this situation. They merely exploited it.

In short, electronic communication systems, arriving with the speed and surprise of Jurassic Park's Velociraptors, immediately called into question the economic soul of the scholarly communications system: copyright itself. It is little wonder that university publishers were alarmed by what appeared to be an assault on their very reason for existing.

The Threat to University Publishing

The 1992 Andrew W. Mellon Foundation study, *University Libraries and Scholarly Communication,* provided little comfort for the university press executive. The report had nothing much to say about university presses, and seemed in fact to assume that they would fade away in the face of new systems of information or knowledge management that would be based in virtual libraries—where, to borrow Stanley Katz's descriptive phrasing in a paper delivered in 1992 in Tokyo, "remote logon, electronic text processing, and computer database technology transform libraries from physical repositories of texts and other materials to electronic nodes on a worldwide information network" (Katz 1992, 2).

The unspoken assumption that began to appear in many discussions of the new electronic knowledge environment, exemplified in the Mellon report, was that university presses would have no significant role to play because somehow the university would become a new publisher embodied in the division best able to manage large amounts of data—the library. As Stanley Katz remarked in his Tokyo paper, "librarians will be the scholar's partner in the creation of knowledge" and will take on "a new, more primary role in the production of scholarly research" (Katz 1992, 5). This was not what I had in mind when I proposed that the libraries and presses cooperate in the production of scholarly information.

I want to use the Mellon report as a vehicle for discussing one aspect of what I think is the most important issue facing the scholarly communications system in the electronic environment: the ownership and management of content. (I will not be discussing the technical aspects of copyrght law, however. My concern is with organizational matters.)

The most alarming statement in the Mellon report is this:

> There are, finally, the proposals that universities (1) claim joint ownership of scholarly writings with members of their faculties, remunerating them and prohibiting them from assigning copyright to a third party; (2) request that faculty members first submit manuscripts to publishers whose pricing practices are, in effect, more consonant with larger educational objectives; and (3) grant unlimited copying to libraries and individual scholars and specify that such permission has been granted in the copyright statement. These proposals, of course, are extensions of the broader proposal that universities reclaim responsibility for disseminating the results of faculty scholarship. (Cummings 1992, 160)

I have previously described the conceptual origins of this remarkable proposal. Several aspects of this paragraph are worth attention.

First, it is not clear to me that universities gave up the responsiblity for disseminating the results of faculty scholarship. University presses are more, not less, numerous than ever, and virtually all of them are wholly owned by research universities that mandate the publication of scholarship in some form. Moreover, as the Mellon report graphically showed, university press publication of scholarship increased (foolishly, as it happens) in the 1980s.

The problem was not that universities stopped publishing scholarship. The problem was that libraries stopped buying it. This is an example of the well-known fact that there are usually two ways, at least, of looking at a situation. Since libraries and university presses are both wholly owned subsidiaries of universities, we might safely say that universities both published and stopped buying the results of scholarship. The Mellon report seems to support this observation. The meaning of the claim that universities have abandoned responsibility for disseminating research is actually more complex than it appears. Claiming responsibility in this instance was actually about who is going to control certain kinds of valuable intellectual property. The argument usually advanced is that the proper management of intellectual property should mean cheap ideas available to all.

The proposal that universities take back copyright had been floated previously without any clear explanation of how this might work in practice, although Brian Kahin proposed quite specific system guidelines under the Harvard-CNI Scholarly Communication Project (see Brian Kahin's chapter in this volume). As expressed by Kahin, taking back copyright (or, to be accurate, taking copyright away from scholars by making their work a form of "work-for-hire") requires that university presses cease to function in a market economy—or that the new form of the university press, based in the library, ignore the demands of market. I have long wanted to ignore the market, as have most university presses, but we have been unable to do it. Kahin calls this "maximum dissemination at the lowest cost" (Kahin 1993). One might also add, at the lowest return to the producer—the scholar.

When this idea was first advanced, I raised the question of joint ownership of copyright with a few of my faculty friends, who mostly responded with wide and rolling eyes. One asked for a copy of page 160 of the Mellon report, so that she could pass it on to her union. Another asked about the place of academic freedom in this system. It is clear to me that most humanities faculty would be aghast at the idea and would fight it fiercely. A serious number of them think of their books as ways of making money for themselves. University presses would similarly fight the proviso that unlimited copying be permitted in universities. The meaning of the suggestion that manuscripts only go to publishers who have correct pricing policies remains a mystery to me. The command economy, such as that once practiced in Eastern Europe and other places, mandated such price rigging without regard to costs, and was a miserable failure. And yet, the idea was being seriously discussed by a committee of the Association of American

Universities studying intellectual property in the academic environment in 1993 and 1994. Chaired by Peter Nathan, provost at the University of Iowa, the committee functioned for some time without a single publisher representative, and, for a time, considered recommending that universities retain faculty copyrights completely. Actions designed to take from scholars and publishers the right to exploit intellectual property would do serious and deadly harm to the system of scholarly communication.

What seems to be wanted, if I understand this paragraph in the Mellon report correctly, is the restructuring of the university press idea with tighter controls over the dissemination of the products. The present system is too difficult to control. Publishers and authors make all sorts of rowdy agreements together, exchange money, deceive customers, etc. At one point the Mellon report notes that, in the culture of print, exchange transactions are the only transactions possible, and goes on to suggest that in the electronic environment other kinds of presumably more democratic transactions will take place in the friendly sharing of resources. The reason for the dominance of exchange transactions in publishing—and indeed, one might note, in the economy as a whole—is the centrality of property rights, including copyright. (More important in Europe are moral rights, which are explicitly excluded by the United States from its adherence to the Berne Convention. The concept of an author's moral rights changes considerably, and perhaps usefully, the terms of the copyright discussion in the electronic environment. It is certainly an issue that will have to be addressed in any revision of copyright law.)

While one might want to change copyright from a property to another kind of right in order to create friendlier transaction models—although I don't know what that right might be like—in the meantime, it seems worth noting that there is a logical reason for this state of affairs, and that publishers did not create it.

Running through the Mellon report is a powerful concern for a situation in which order is threatened. I believe that this reflects a concern important to librarians and publishers as well. As the old, neat system of scholarly communication begins to break down, it is natural that we would want to find some way to prop it up or, failing that, to replace it with something else equally orderly. Or even more orderly. Electronic communications systems tend to be horizontal and therefore difficult to control, even though they seem to promise greater order. Anyone can publish on this system and no one will be able to tell what is good and what is not good. Who is going to provide quality control? Who is going to make sure that all of this stuff is properly archived? Who is going to be the gatekeeper?

The answer advanced in the past couple of years seems to be: the library, which, the Mellon report asserts, is central to the management of scholarly communication and will be for the forseeable future. (Ann Okerson, in her otherwise superb executive summary of the report, goes so far as to assert that the institutional library is the one "indispensable mediator in the dialogue between writer and reader" [Cummings 1992, xxix].) The library has not been splendidly isolated at the center of the dissemination of scholarly communication. It is no more indispensable than the publisher. The library has shared that responsibility with the university press. The new electronic environment seems to be beckoning the libraries, however, to become publishers and, as a natural result, to bring some much-needed order into the messy business of publishing. The institutional imperative is very much at work in the Mellon report and, indeed, in much of which has been written about this subject. But the institutional controls offered are mostly designed to meet the needs of a small part of the traditional knowledge community.

Inventing the Future

Jeremy Bentham's Panopticon, resurrected and reinterpreted for us by Foucault, promised a way of controlling the unruly in society. The round prison building Bentham designed allowed for the constant surveillance of all prisoners. It allowed total social control. What some people want in the new electronic environment is, I fear, a kind of Panopticon, by which the unruly business of communication might be more efficiently managed. The true point of Panoptic architecture was comprehensive knowledge, a pretence perpetuated in electronic systems (as David Lyon notes in *The Electronic Eye,* a recent book on electronic surveillance). The gaze of the machine is relentless and steady. It sees everything. But in fact the new systems will be unruly because the gaze is not one way. Everyone in fact is looking at everyone else, and disorder is inherent. The utopian Panoptic ideal was dystopic, in fact. And the ideal of controlling knowledge in the university is also dystopic, for the essence of university education appears to be its unruliness.

I worry too about entropy, however, and would like to maintain an orderly universe. I think that the solution is not in the transfer of publishing, distribution, and archiving systems entirely to libraries— the Panopticon model. Two years ago, in a paper delivered before a session of the American Library Association meeting, I suggested that the solution lay in a restructuring of the university itself (Arnold 1994).

More than one of my colleagues responded that it was hopelessly idealistic even to discuss such a prospect. It seemed to me that without a restructuring—an integration of university systems to facilitate communication—none of the nifty ideas any of us had would work. I now think that change in the university will be necessary but will probably follow changes in the national structures for the electronic dissemination of information. The university publishers and other publishers concerned with the scholarly communication system will have to solve the problems on their own and outside of the university. When I left Rutgers in Spring 1994, for example, there was still no campus-wide fiber-optic network. The university press itself could not connect to the university, except by modem, because the cost was prohibitive. On the other hand, the head of reprographic services at Rutgers bought three Docutech machines in order to offer customized course packs to faculty at a profit for his university unit. One of his people developed an interactive network for that system, but no one talked to me or the library about how it might have been designed to be useful to us and our work. This sort of Balkanized approach to university systems is common if not universal, and in hard economic times is likely to remain so.

In the humanities, as Douglas Greenberg has recently pointed out, electronic information systems on campuses are going to lag behind those in the sciences, both because of the different ways in which information is used and because there is a deplorable lack of equipment available to humanistic scholars. In fact, he observes in the same paper, the "democratizing influence of technology will operate perfectly in the sciences and fail dismally in the humanities" (Greenberg 1993, 29). The humanities, which are by and large the province of university presses, have already suffered terribly in this crisis and, as I read it, will continue to suffer in the new electronic environment, as will, inevitably, the university presses. Nobody seems to care much about that at the higher levels of university decision-making.

What needs to change is more than technological systems. As the Mellon report notes, tenure and promotion decisions are based on specific forms of publication, particularly through university presses, and there are few signs that universities want to re-examine that system. The allocation of university resources is based on a particular model for the communication of knowledge, and there are few if any signs that that is changing. The producing scholars are not involved in the conversations. The university presses are also left out, as they were in the Mellon report itself.

A new system of knowledge management will only work if scholars and publishers are essential and equal parts of it. That means that they need to be deeply involved in its creation. Even the cooperative symposia sponsored by the ARL and AAUP in the past few years may have been too little and too limited, however needed and valuable. They have identified problems. Solutions, when they have been proposed, have come in small corners of the university world or, more commonly, in commercial settings.

I am concerned that, before we can make much progress at all in the university and nonprofit environment, the systems of electronic communication are going to be taken over by commerce—by the telephone and cable companies, which are already laying the groundwork for providing extensive and sophisticated services nationally, and by the large publishing companies. Universities are likely to end up buying services, because they will not have been able to develop systems of their own. The situation so many librarians now lament, in which they have to buy back research, will be worse, not better, once the commercial companies have networked us all.

The dream of the electronic future is for many the virtual library, a neverland of limitless and free information accessible from the scholar's study. The university press as it has existed for more than a hundred years is in danger of becoming the dead body in this virtual library. The university has always been a disseminator of knowledge through various media, including book and journal publication. The scholar, however, has always been treated as an independent voice in that context. The communication facilitated by all of the institutions involved—publishers, libraries, universities—is between scholars and between scholars and the educated public. All of us are servants in this system. Change needs to be fueled by the needs of scholars and scholarship, not by the needs of organizations. But the commercialization of the electronic future threatens not only the scholar and the publisher, it threatens the library as well. The end result of commercially supplied systems will be expensive and captive to the whims of profit and mass culture.

I do not think that university presses in their present form are essential to the development of electronic systems in universities—although they will undoubtedly continue, at least some of them, to publish effectively as they are presently organized for the ongoing but shrinking print culture of the future. In the future, university presses will publish more than one kind of book; many have worried about the place of the scholarly monograph in that future. I have argued elsewhere that the monograph is a construct designed for the print environment. In the new environment, something else will arise to take the monograph's place—or, rather, to perform the monograph's function. What that is will depend entirely on the way in which information is organized by scholars, publishers, and librarians.

Left alone, the present scholarly communication system will collapse, as will everything else. If the present system collapses before we understand what happened and what is to replace it—if university presses disappear and libraries become prematurely virtual—anarchy may leave us vulnerable to the culture of the trivial that always threatens to overwhelm us.

In 1992, at the first ARL/AAUP symposium on electronics and scholarly communication (known to many as "Woodstock"), I likened university presses to Neanderthals clustered around the fire and electronic librarians to Cro-Magnan humans swooping down from the mountains. I suggested then and suggest now that the E-people contemplate not conquest but intermarriage with the P-people. We need to develop and combine resources in creative new ways. We need to work together to lead our universities toward a new and better system of scholarly communication that retains the virtues of the old. We need to do it now, before yet another group comes over the mountain and consumes us both.

The two keys to the successful development of future structures will be cooperation among the players and control of content. This means in effect that scholars, academic publishers, and libraries will have to work together to find the means to create a new system external to the university itself for the dissemination of scholarly resources. If we look back at the Britannica model, deployed by one company for the management of its own intellectual property, I think we can visualize a national network managed under the auspices of key organizations in the scholarly community, through which university-based scholarly work is transmitted to users. This distribution system would not acquire rights in the work of scholars but would only manage access on behalf of the producers and publishers. For-profit as well as nonprofit publishers of academic work would be included in this system. Individual publishers would neither have to create electronic means of distribution nor license the rights to their publications. The network would operate on a nonprofit basis, charging users low fees permitted by the sheer volume of data. Individual publishers would continue to develop other kinds of products for local and national distribution. This system would meet the librarians' demand for access to cheaper information, provide universities with materials created and controlled by universities and scholars, and allow libraries to retain control of information management and archiving at local sites. Publishers would continue to develop products, add value to content, and manage their businesses for the benefit of the universities or corporations that own them.

The alternative, as I have suggested in this chapter, is a virtual landscape strewn with real bodies, a slaughter of potentially devastating proportions. It is imperative that we recreate a model for scholarly communication that retains the best of the present system. There is not much time in which to accomplish this task. The monograph is a symbol of the serious situation we face. Its disappearance leaves a void that has to be filled. Its disappearance adumbrates our own. Publishers and librarians will become, in the absence of a new vision like the works in the Minnesota Center for Book Arts: objects of admiration and even grace, small triumphs of the spirit adrift on a sea of babble. And, indeed, we might be honored in just that way. I prefer, however, that we see in such art works a metaphor for our collective future: imaginative reconstructions of our lives.

References

Arnold, K. (1994). Rethinking scholarly communication in the new university. In E. Bishoff and C. Chamberlain (Eds.), *Conference Proceedings, ALCTS 1993*. Chicago: Association for Library Collections and Technical Services, American Library Association.

Cover, R. (1991). Internet communication. Humanist Discussion Group.

Cummings, A., Witte, M.L., Bowen, W.G., Lazarus, L.O., and Ekman, R.H. (1992). *University Libraries and Scholarly Communiction: A Study Prepared for the Andrew W. Mellon Foundation.* Washington, D.C.: The Association of Research Libraries.

Dougherty, R. (1989). Turning the serials crisis to our advantage: An opportunity for leadership. *Library Administration and Management* 3(2): 59–64.

Greenberg, D. (1993, April). *Technology and its discontents: Some problems and possibilities for the humanist in the virtual university.* Paper presented at a conference on Changes in Scholarly Communication Patterns, Canberra, Australia.

Kahin, B. (1993, May). Proposed principles for communication and publication of university-based research. Internet communication, unpaged.

Katz, S. (1992, October). *The humanities and the future of the research library.* Paper presented at the Joint Meeting of the Japanese and American Library Associations, Tokyo, Japan.

Lyon, D. (1994). *The electronic eye.* Minneapolis: University of Minnesota Press.

Markoff, J. (1994). 44 million words strong, Britannica to join Internet. *The New York Times,* February 8: Dl–D2.

Okerson, A. (1991). Back to academia? The case for American universities to publish their own research. *Logos* 2(2): 106–111.

Weyr, T. (1992, June). The wiring of Simon and Schuster. *Publishers Weekly* 239(25), (June 1): 32–35.

Equality in Access to Network Information by Scholars with Disabilities[1]

Tom McNulty

The practice of creating special format texts for scholars with print-prohibitive disabilities has a relatively short history, and that history begins with the earliest institutions for the education of the blind, at the beginning of the nineteenth century. The original "accessible texts" were based upon a variety of tactile reading codes; braille, the most well-known and enduring of these early touch-based reading methods, continues to be used by many blind and visually impaired readers (Harris 1986). While the introduction of audio recording technology in the 1930s had a negative impact on the popularity of braille as a means of information storage (That All May Read, 1983), even recorded books' significance pales in relation to the potential impact of network-based text sources, many of which, by their very nature, are accessible to scholars with disabilities.

This chapter will focus upon the needs of print-impaired readers *vis a vis* computerized texts in general, and network-based information sources in particular. The term "print-impaired" encompasses blind and low vision readers, as well as those with cognitive, or learning disabilities, which prohibit access to traditional printed texts. While focusing on the visually impaired and learning disabled populations, the needs of mobility and hearing impaired scholars will also be touched upon in relation to new and emerging trends in network-based text sources.

Early Access to Texts

Until the introduction of the microcomputer and the subsequent shift from paper to electronic text production and storage methods, scholars with print impairments used braille and/or talking books wherever possible. The expense involved in the production of braille imposed limits on the amount of material produced in this medium.

Our nation's inventory of talking book (cassette tape) titles, less expensive to produce and consequently larger than the stock of braille titles, still reflects just a small fraction of the entire output of the paper-based publishing industry. Regardless of the method employed to render printed texts accessible through another sense, whether tactile or aural, accessible texts invariably appear after their printed counterparts, placing the scholar in need of such adaptation at a serious competitive disadvantage. Coupled with the relative scarcity of materials in either of these major text formats, the "after the fact" aspect of rendering print in an accessible format made the scholar's use of assistants, or readers, inevitable.

Unlike other adaptations to regular print, computerized text sources are the first in human history to be immediately accessible to able and disabled scholars alike. That is, in contrast to their printed counterparts, electronic texts and computerized information sources do not need to be re-produced in an accessible format. Rather, a number of microcomputer-based peripheral hardware and software products render the equivalent of the visual computer monitor accessible via another sense. For the braille user, a "soft braille" device converts lines of text into braille on a strip of constantly changing braille "pins." Many visually impaired computer users enlarge portions of the monitor itself with a large-print hardware and/or software product. Still others listen to the text on the computer monitor with special software designed to navigate the screen and read aloud the contents of selected areas. It is not within the scope of this essay to describe in detail the myriad assistive devices available to print-disabled computer users. It is important to keep in mind, however, that each of these and other computer access devices has provided the modern disabled scholar with a degree of independence previously unimagined.

Before proceeding with an examination of obstacles to continued access to network-based information sources, a look at the technology employed to render computerized texts accessible to the print-impaired scholar is in order.[1] In very simple terms, certain characteristics of the technology employed by the earliest personal computers made alternative output options, including but not limited to those identified above, relatively easy to accomplish. Early text-based personal computers utilized BIOS to display information to the screen. The output to the computer's monitor, represented by ASCII and including very little text formatting such as boldface or underlining, was intercepted and acted upon by the synthetic speech, large print, or other adaptive system. In the case of synthetic speech, the screen access software identifies and assembles the characters on the screen, applying rules of phonology of varying degrees of sophistication; the user is then able to listen to the contents of the screen. Soft, or refreshable braille displays, work in much the same way, but instead of converting the numerical (ASCII) text equivalent to speech, braille devices produce temporary braille characters in the form of movable pins or pegs. Another important feature of early personal computer design is the "command line" input principle. Usually prompted by the program being utilized, command line prompts were similarly rendered accessible through alternative output modes, providing the print-impaired scholar with the ability to access most applications and online services without assistance.

As microcomputer technology advanced, graphic information and graphical user interfaces, based upon pixels rather than BIOS, introduced a formidable threat to disabled scholars' continued access to computer-based information. In the next section, the problems of graphic information as well as graphical users interfaces (GUIs) will be discussed, along with screen or menu design. These obstacles to access represent varying degrees of difficulty to circumvent. Beginning with the latter—screen or menu design for enhanced access—the nature of these obstacles will be explored, and possible solutions will be presented.

Obstacles to Access

Reflecting the nature of the microcomputer itself, obstacles to access can be broadly classified as either input- or output-based. Input-based obstacles exert the greatest effect on computer users with physical, or mobility, problems. "For some motor-impaired users, complicated keystroke combinations can be difficult or even impossible to implement. When the keystroke demands the user's holding two keys simultaneously, this can make a system unusable for some people" (Coombs, in press). Special keyboard adaptations, as well as high tech solutions including voice-input technology, allow the physically disabled user to employ an adapted keyboard or, in the case of voice recognition input, to bypass the keyboard entirely.

Obstacles to independent access to the output of the computer pose the greatest threat to the continued independence of the target audience of this essay—the scholar with one or more print-prohibiting disabilities. Output-based obstacles include cluttered or badly designed screens and menus, information presented visually (graphs, illustrations, etc.), and graphical user interfaces that utilize icons instead of the command language described above. While perhaps the easiest type to remedy, the screen or menu design obstacle is also, unfortunately, the most pervasive on all types of online systems, and we will begin our discussion of output obstacles with it.

Screen and Menu Design for Access

In order to get a real understanding of how screen design can adversely affect the presentation of information to a visually impaired user, the interested reader is urged to seek a demonstration of a talking computer. Try dialing in to your library's catalog or other familiar online service; keeping your eyes closed, begin listening to the contents of the monitor as they are read aloud by the synthetic speech system. You will probably encounter some features that are extremely annoying to listen to; many text based systems use characters, such as asterisks or equal signs, to create primitive graphic design elements. A simple line, composed of asterisks, might go unnoticed by the sighted user; the user of synthetic speech, however, hears each of those asterisks spoken aloud by the synthetic speech system unless the system is instructed to omit or to skip over such screen ornamentation. The problem is made real in a statement by Norman Coombs (in press), a professor of history at Rochester Institute of Technology who uses speech to access network-based information sources and services: "For a blind user with speech output, hearing 80 'equal' signs is maddening. The producers [sic] of one CD-ROM product fills the opening screen with literally dozens of 'Wilson Disk' statements. Besides driving a listener to total distraction, when accessed online even at 2400 baud, the system takes an inordinately long time to map the screen which is frustrating to the user."

These kinds of problems, while usually just annoying and only sometimes inhibiting the effective operation of the screen access program, are actually easy to circumvent. Users with any experience with screen access assistive technology will often simply turn off speech temporarily after hearing the third or fourth "asterisk" in a long row of these characters. Also, some access systems provide a "turn ornamentation off/on" feature that ignores repetitive occurences of characters, which are usually visual elements providing no real content. The problem of slowing the adaptive technology is more serious, and designers of CD-ROM and online menus should take into account the needs of the small but constantly growing audience of adaptive technology users.

It has been noted that many of the earliest computerized information sources and services were simply adaptations of their print-based forerunners. The earliest online library catalogs were computerized "card catalogs" as far as most users, and indeed many librarians, were concerned (Basista, Micco, and Rambler 1991). Similarly, at least design-wise, electronic journals patterned themselves after print journals. While it is certainly understandable and indeed to be expected that new technology would not be too quick to abolish previously established text formats, many of the conventions of print pose problems to the adaptation of text for the print-impaired computer user. Remember that, unless otherwise instructed, screen access programs will read from top-to-bottom, left-to-right. Problems arise for the adaptive technology user when she or he attempts to make sense of information presented in columns. Sighted readers have the entire page in view at most times, and the traditional printed page was, after all, designed by and for sighted people. For sighted readers, understanding information presented in columns might, at most, require shifting the gaze from one entry to the name of the appropriate column header. By contrast, visually impaired users generally have only one line of text available at a time, requiring greater concentration. Having to remember each column's heading, for example, can be challenging to some. In cases where entries under column headings are composed of two or more lines of text, the left-to-right output can totally obfuscate the text's meaning, as the synthesis or other adaptation combines bits of text from each column. Again, the user with experience in the use of his or her particular adaptive device will have ways to circumvent obstacles like columns, but in many cases these columns are not really necessary and could be presented in a left-to-right order without posing any inconvenience to the majority of the system's users. The elimination of little unnecessary details, such as identifying the institution or providing the time of day on each screen, can similarly facilitate the disabled user's navigation of the networked system.

One very comprehensive checklist for screen design has been developed by the Royal Blind Society (RBS) of Australia. In a statement of design and layout principles presented at the first Australian Conference on Technology and Disabilities in 1993, RBS Adaptive Technology Services Manager Tim Noonan (1994) offers the following principles, which are intended to facilitate independent use by visually impaired (VI) users without adversely affecting the system for sighted users:

— Field order on each screen is from most to least significant. Listening is sequential from the top of the screen, so order is very important;
— Headings and messages always appear in consistent screen locations. For example, each screen's unique title is on line 1 and the

screen layout type appears on line 2 (such as "list of values" or "update");

— Where possible, only one field should appear on a screen line;

— No ornamental characters or borders should appear on VI screens;

— Highlighting and color should not be used in isolation to provide significant screen information. Punctuation is often used to convey this information. In situations where a cursor is moving from one field to another, highlighting of the current field should be avoided or fields may be verbalised multiple times;

— Each new screen should fully overwrite previous screen information (no pop up windows, etc.). Speech output systems work on a line basis, so old information at the start or end of a screen line causes major confusion;

— Fields which due to their length are too wide for the screen should be identified by the ">" sign, and a means of viewing such fields in full must be available;

— Error messages must always include a bell to attract the user's attention;

—Only one item is displayed on the screen at a time from a vertically scrolling list. This is because most speech programs cannot cope with multi-line scrolling regions over a VT100 style terminal link without re-reading lines multiple times;

— For VI users, menu options are not automatically displayed until the menu key is pressed. This saves time and increases clarity of screens.

Note that these principles for enhanced access are virtually transparent. That is, the much larger population of sighted users will not be aware of any special adaptation, and will in fact benefit from the logical arrangement of data, particularly the presentation of fields in order of most to least important.

The Graphical User Interface

The ubiquitous presence of the graphical user interface, or GUI, has become a concern for computer users with disabilities for a number of reasons. Before going into the specific obstacles encountered by the population of print-impaired scholars, however, a look at the advantages of GUIs for the vast majority of computer users will shed some light on the growing popularity of this computer interface.

As noted above, the earliest text-based personal computers utilized a system that lent itself to adaptation. Sometimes referred to as character-based systems, these computers utilize a text buffer to store information in the form of ASCII characters. All of the information required for the presentation of each character is contained in the ASCII representation of that character. For example, an uppercase "M" is represented by its numerical equivalent "77" in IBM-compatible (text-based) personal computers. By contrast, the graphics-based system utilizes pixels, or dots, to paint an image of the letter "M." The use of pixels makes possible the very popular "wysiwyg" ("what you see is what you get") display of text and graphics that is particularly important to the graphic designer but also appeals to the regular user of word processing and other applications. The use of icons, by which the user is prompted with visual images in lieu of a command line prompt, adds to the popularity of the graphical user interface for many users. With a well-designed graphical user interface, the inexperienced computer user can utilize applications software with little effort.

Perhaps the most widely used graphic computer is the Apple/ Macintosh family of computers, which has always featured the easy-to-use GUI interface. While the various adaptive hardware and software products described above are incompatible with them, Apple/ Macintosh computers have given rise to a series of adaptive programs and devices designed to extend access to print-impaired users. The operations carried out by one of the earliest and most well-known screen access systems for the Macintosh, outSPOKEN by Berkeley Systems, provide an indication of the challenge presented by the use of visually oriented systems. OutSPOKEN employs an interception strategy for converting text to synthetic speech, whereby "information is intercepted, modified and stored in a special 'off-screen buffer' before it is discarded by the screen-writing services" (Boyd, Boyd, and Vanderheiden 1990, 499). Recall that IBM-compatible computers perform much the same operation in the text buffer. The text buffer of IBM-compatible computers is an integral part of the computer's architecture, whereas the "off-screen buffer" employed by outSPOKEN represents a fundamental change in the nature of the system itself.

While much attention has been paid to the evolution of "pictographic" communication "in which visual metaphors completely replace words . . . [i]n reality the most predominant trend is toward pictures accompanied by words" (Boyd, Boyd, and Vanderheiden 1990, 499). Even most icons employed by GUI interfaces are accompanied by labels. Similarly, while most users appreciate the ease of use afforded by icon-driven commands, those who prefer to enter commands from the keyboard are generally provided with this option. In the most recent version of WordPerfect (6.0), this principle of choice is similarly apparent. Users can opt for the familiar WP 5.1 BIOS Interface OR the new graphical user interface. The provision of options, or "redundant" displays (Coombs, in press) allows the user a choice of two or more input methods (keyboard, mouse), extending accessibility to scholars with both physical, or mobility, and print-prohibitive disabilities. The interface options provided by previously character-based applications, such as WordPerfect 6.0, allow the user of adaptive technology to continue using the access technologies she or he is most familiar with. The much larger audience of sighted computer users also benefits from choice, as work styles and preferences differ among this population, and in numbers significant enough to be taken seriously by developers interested in capturing the largest possible audience of consumers.

Content Based Upon Graphics

The earliest personal computers' strictly character-based presentation of information created an environment of equal access for disabled scholars because of the lack of visual information presented. The "full text" of newspaper and journal articles retrieved through online systems simply omitted graphs, charts, illustrations and photographs because the technology could not provide them, not because they were deemed undesirable by providers or users of networked systems. In the very recent past, users of online systems received only straight lines of text which, as we have seen, lends itself to alternative output modes for users with one or more disabilities.

The shift toward the multi-sensory presentation of information represents the greatest threat to the print-disabled scholar's continued access to network-based information sources. A multimedia encyclopedia, for example, might present some text accompanied by sound effects and live action or animated video. Researchers with visual impairments will obviously be excluded from independent access to the visual portions of the vast majority of these multimedia texts. Similarly, scholars with hearing impairments, who have been relatively unaffected by the primarily visual textual mode employed by computerized information sources, will require specially adapted versions of these multimedia texts; information presented aurally will require closed-captioning in order to be fully accessible to this population. Such adaptations, like braille or talking books before them, are sure to be limited to certain texts. The short period of near-universal access to network resources by able and disabled scholars alike is, therefore, most threatened by the proliferation of multimedia text sources.

On a more positive note, some researchers foresee new and emerging technologies coming to the aid of the print-impaired scholar. As multimedia sources proliferate, multisensory approaches to screen access, including synthetic speech accompanied by tactile displays, will be required to ensure maximum access by disabled users of network resources. For example, "breakthroughs in genetically engineered materials and plastic technology offer the potential to develop full-page braille-tactile displays. The ability to display braille and graphic images (with gray scale) could provide blind and visually impaired people with greater access to computer environments" (Schreier 1990, 522). With such a tactile display, visually impaired scholars could identify the shape of a bar graph, pie chart, or other visually encoded information through touch, while reading text with a braille display or synthetic speech. Developments in tactile displays and multimodal adaptive technology, while "in their infancy, . . . have demonstrated that people who are blind can use computers with grapical user interfaces and can begin exploring new capabilities (for instance, drawing; reading flowcharts, schematic diagrams, maps or floor plans; and reviewing or creating musical scores) not available to them on strictly character-based machines" (Boyd, Boyd, and Vanderheiden 1990, 496).

Toward Complete and Continuing Integration

Access to networked information sources, including online catalogs and databases, electronic journals, and academic discussion groups, has had a profound impact on scholarship for able and disabled individuals alike. As new technologies emerge, service providers and systems designers are urged to keep in mind the needs of disabled scholars who, if suddenly cut off from a significant number of mainstream computer applications and services, will have to revert to the use of assistants in order to compete with their peers.

Note

1. The author would like to thank Mr. Richard Banks of the University of Wisconsin, Stout, for his generous contribution of technical assistance and information.

References

Basista, T. H., Micco, M., and Rambler, L. (1991). Designing the OPAC user interface to improve access and retrieval. *Microcomputers for Information Management* 8(2): 87–103.

Boyd, L.H., Boyd, W.L., and Vanderheiden, G.C. (1990) The graphical user interface: Crisis, danger, and opportunity. *Journal of Visual Impairment and Blindness 84*(10): 496–502.

Coombs, N. (in press). Interfacing online services: Alternative inputs and redundant displays. In A. D. N. Edwards, (Ed.), *Extra-ordinary human-computer interaction.* Cambridge: Cambridge University Press.

Harris, E. M. (1986). Inventing printing for the blind. *Printing History 8*: 15–25.

Noonan, T. (1994). Development of an accessible user interface for people who are blind or vision impaired as part of the re-computerisation of the Royal Blind Society (Australia). *Information Technology and Disabilities I*(1).

Schreier, E.M. (1990). The future of access technology for blind and visually impaired people. *Journal of Visual Impairment and Blindness 84*(10):520-523.

That All May Read: Library Service for Blind and Physically Handicapped People. (1983). Washington: Library of Congress. National Library Service for Blind and Physically Handicapped.

Building New Tools for the Twenty-First Century University

Providing Access to Visual Information

David L. Austin

Visual Information: What is it?

Long before humans learned how to write and describe existence on this planet, they drew pictures to help remember valuable lessons for the conduct of life from one generation to another. Visual information of this kind persisted and remained alongside written records for many reasons. Sometimes the people for whom the instructions were intended did not sufficiently comprehend the written word. In other cases, a single picture might supply those qualified to interpret it with more words than many pages of written text.

Visual information exists in three types: descriptive, prescriptive, and aesthetic. Both its original purpose and the way in which others use it determine its classification. Most people automatically think of visual information in its first type, descriptive. In this manner it satisfies the need to tell others, now and in the future, what we see around us. It may be as common as the postcard we send to friends back home, or as pervasive and widespread as a photograph on the front page of our morning newspaper. It may also require a high degree of skill to understand its content and purpose, as in the case of x-rays or radio spectroscopy.

The second type, prescriptive visual information, grew in response to the need for one person to tell another what to do. For example, an architect may draw up an elaborate set of plans to inform a builder where to place a wall, and how long and tall that wall is to be. It may also inform the builder of how many windows carpenters need to frame, what size the windows are, for which glazers need to cut glass, where electricians must put cables and outlets, and where plumbers have to put water and waste pipes. In another case, a composer draws specialized and rigidly ordered pictures, which we call notes, to tell pianists where to put their fingers and how firmly to apply pressure to the keys of their instruments.

The last type, aesthetic visual information, really doesn't need to exist. All the same, we want it, and, whether we acknowledge the fact or not, we need it, since this type enhances our view of the world around us and enables us to live in it more comfortably. Aesthetic visual information helps make livable and comfortable to the eye our daily surroundings, such as the homes in which we live, the streets along which we walk, and our various types of recreation. Best of all, it uplifts and sensitizes our image of life, and gives some of us the sense of contributing something of value to the world in which we live.

We may objectively codify each piece of visual information in three tidy packages, but in truth, visual information takes on a life of its own, and migrates across imposed boundaries. Architects' drawings become descriptive to a student or historian. To a stage designer or a team of architects in charge of renovating an old building, postcards become prescriptive. A photographer who captures terror or joy in a particularly sensitive way may earn a Pulitzer Prize that entitles his or her descriptive work to enter the aesthetic realm. A musician may learn how to play an instrument seldom heard in today's concert halls from a Dutch genre painting of the seventeenth century that shows someone playing a lute or a viola da gamba. Thus, the use of the painting transforms an aesthetic work into a prescriptive document. All this is to say that, although the original purpose of visual information may be isolated into categories, our perception of it and use thereof allows it to achieve a life separate from that intended by its creator. Unlike written documents, even the reason why visual information is preserved may differ radically from the reason for which it is sought and the purpose to which it is put.

The following discussion surveys traditional storehouses of visual information and the ways in which those who organize them provide access for users. Newer sources, such as analog and digital recordings, now provide images for scholars who cannot visit specific collections; a greater benefit exists in the potential to transmit selections of images and even full scale exhibitions in an online environment. The remainder of the discussion focuses on problems and solutions that face us as universal access to visual information becomes a reality in a networked environment.

Traditional Sources of Visual Information

Museums contain a wide variety of primary sources of information for our visible world. The objects they collect and display vary widely from early agricultural tools to today's computers, from fossilized bones of prehistoric creatures to live animals, birds, and fishes in zoos and aquariums, and from gold and jewel-encrusted gospel covers to buildings in an open air museum. In the past, museums have been notably less aggressive than libraries in the application of electronic technology to organize their collections. By the beginning of the last decade of the twentieth century, fewer than ten percent of Europe's museums had implemented some kind of computer system to document their collections (Szrajber 1992). The issue of inventory control and shared access to information about objects and images, however, has important advocates in the museum community (Roberts 1992). The work of the Museum Documentation Association (Roberts 1991) and the International Documentation Committee of the International Council of Museums and the working group on Computerized Interchange of Museum Information (CIMI) of the Museum Computer Network (Bearman and Perkins 1993) will encourage museums to communicate with each other and share information in a way similar to that enjoyed by libraries.

Visual resources collections are often very closely related to museums. The latter often provides the content of slide collections and photograph archives, and museums usually contain their own photographic departments that make transparencies for sale to the public and other collections. The two collections share objectives, but the information contained in a visual resource collection is a step removed from the object, i.e., they contain secondary sources of visual information. Many library collections also contain a variety of pictorial reproductions, including photographs, prints, and slides. Pictures may be located in the archival or special collection section of the library. They may also result from pictures cut from magazines and books, pasted on mounting board, and placed in a file cabinet for the use of patrons. Collections frequently grow up in response to the needs of academic departments of universities, and are independent of the library.

Few of these collections are indexed in any detail, although 3 x 5 card files or in-house database indexes may help to provide access to the images. More often, their care and management is left to the off hours whenever anyone has a moment to spare. Intricate and sometimes arcane systems of filing result, especially at institutions that boast long histories of collecting, and where numerous librarians, curators, or volunteers contribute to the organization of the cabinets.

Lastly, libraries contain interpretive studies of objects and images. Studies such as these aim at placing the object or an image of the object in the context of the culture that created or consumed it. Such studies may be even farther removed from the area of the artifact, but bibliographic collections are the best places to seek out comprehensive interpretive studies. Far too few sources document the place of objects and their surrogates in our libraries.

New Sources of Visual Information

During the last two decades of the twentieth century, reproductions of documents and objects related to visual information began migrating from transparencies and printed images to electronic media. Preservation and access account for two basic reasons for the shift. Access to visual information increases when photographs and drawings of objects can be reproduced. Our current state of knowledge leads us to believe that electronically reproduced images may be more stabile than those that rely upon light and chemicals. The issue of preservation is likewise important to the object itself. If we can accurately establish a known state of an object we will be able to judge the degree to which it deteriorates in the future. This will allow us to determine whether conservation, and perhaps restoration, may be necessary, advisable, or even desirable.

Analog recording of visual information requires smaller start up costs and provides a product for less money than digital recordings. A normal twelve-inch laser video disc can supply as many as 54,000 images per side to end users who need only purchase a relatively inexpensive player to view them on a color monitor. Full-length motion pictures can be disseminated to a wide audience in this medium. Images from a museum or a gallery, however, may require a more sophisticated formatting that allows a viewer to see pictures in random order. Unlike images captured on video tape, analog images can be viewed as still frames, or "frozen," without any deterioration of the medium or the image. Computer programs can also be written that will allow a viewer to automatically fetch a particular image according to words or phrases, such as titles, artists, subjects or medium, which may be imbedded in an obscure portion of the disc.

Analog recordings of visual information have some disadvantages though. Images recorded in this way are available only in the size, color, clarity, and balance of light and shadow in which they were originally photographed. No post-production manipulation of the image, such as zooming in on a detail, can take place. Perhaps the most serious disadvantage to the analog format is that visual information recorded in this way cannot be exported to multiple users over a great distance except as a solid disc.

Information stored in an analog format can be converted to a digital format. In many cases the analog form is still the point of origin for digital form, as in the case of photographs or video recordings. It is now possible to skirt the analog step with digital cameras. Visual information registered in this manner can encompass a richer information content.

Digital registration of visual information, on the other hand, can be compressed, transmitted to multiple users, and manipulated. Libraries, museums, visual resources collections, and even commercial vendors (Slide 1993) have all begun to exploit this technology for various purposes. Museum consortia, such as the VASARI (Visual Arts System for the Archiving and Retrieval of Images) Project and the Conservation Imaging Consortium, or CIC, set their sights at recording ultra-high resolution images of their holdings in the truest color registration possible. Moreover, their image files include such sophisticated approaches as X-ray, raking light, and ultraviolet photographs of objects in their possession, which will enable members to conduct important projects, such as analysis of color changes, and surface and interior degeneration, preparatory to possible restoration of an object (MacDonald 1990; Mazor 1993). Project NARCISSE, on the other hand, is a European initiative that endeavors to make museum and archive holdings available to the public. A networked environment will link text data bases to high quality images from members' collections (NARCISSE, 1993). High-end digital imaging in museums at this time focuses on internal and consortium member use only, probably due to serious concern over intellectual property rights (Braggins 1992). Members of the public community may hope that efforts to broadcast information will soon follow the examples of some members of the natural history world (Croft 1993; Guralnick 1993) who have taken advantage of X Windows systems and the World Wide Web to publish exhibition catalogs of botanical collections and fossil life that make both text and pictures available over computer networks.

Organizations that traditionally subscribe to the concept of free access to information, such as libraries, have also taken the initiative to make various documents available as sources of visual information on computer networks. The United States Library of Congress recently shared digital copies related to the archives of the former Soviet Union, manuscripts from the Vatican Archive, and an exhibit of pictures and documents describing Columbus' voyages to the New World. The British Library, although more cautious in its approach, (Cawkell 1993) intends to provide computer access to its vast holdings of historical visual information. The Bodleian Library's transmission of compressed digital images of manuscripts, photographs, and miniatures over the

Internet (Price 1993) represents one of many university investigations into broader access to specialized collections.

Group Efforts

More activity will follow as other publicly oriented institutions align themselves under the umbrella of database utilities, such as the Research Libraries Group (RLG). Plans are underway to build an RLG Image Database with the cooperation of eight institutions, each of which will furnish 1,000 images from its collection. RLG intends to demonstrate various database interfaces to help users connect text with images early in 1994 (Clarke 1993). No announcement has yet been made concerning obligations of end users who view the product.

In the United Kingdom, De Montfort University (Leicester) became the focal point of the Centre for Image Information when the National Art Slide Library, formerly at the Victoria and Albert Museum, was transferred there. It intends to investigate all forms of images, with an emphasis on new technology. The Centre's plans also include proposals to establish and promote text and imaging standards that will facilitate exchange of digital files (McKeown 1993).

The Getty Art History Information Program has added its support to efforts to record and exchange digital information of art works. A two-year collaboration, in association with MUSE Educational Media, brings together representatives of museums, colleges and universities to consider matters related to quality of images and conditions for educational use of museum images and information on campus networks. The program, known as the Museum Educational Site Licensing (MESL) Project allows a select group of museums and educational institutions to explore and promote the benefits of digital access to museum collections (Getty 1995).

Visual Information of the Future

The advent of two- and three-dimensional computer-aided design programs make it possible to create the appearance of real objects. The computerized recreation of the face of a mummified nine-year-old boy by biomedical visualization specialists (Evenhouse and Stefanic 1993) demonstrates one possible application. Teams of specialists involved in projects such as this and the recreation of the Temple of Horus for the Guggenheim Museum's Antiquities of Egypt exhibit (Alexander 1993), cross the once-sacred boundaries of academic disciplines and the proprietary walls of institutions. Another outstanding example of such cooperative possibilities may be found in the virtual reconstruction of Cluny Abbey, built by two engineering students and based on documentation furnished by archives, art historians, and archaeologists (Dorozynski 1993).

Problems in Presenting Visual Information

Universities are tooling up to provide scholars with more than just text retrieval. Researchers are now able, with the aid of increasingly sophisticated software, to avail themselves of all the resources on the Internet and the World Wide Web. Announcements of various image and sound compression techniques, fiber optic applications, and high resolution monitors appear almost monthly in trade magazines. Journal articles describe academic efforts aimed at expanding and improving access to a wide variety of information (Baker 1993; Webster 1993) with increasing frequency. Several end-user graphic interface programs already enable an individual's workstation to acquire pictures from distant sources. By the end of the twentieth century, most scholars faced with a need for visual information will expect to find swelling numbers of various forms of digital images on their campus.

If we choose to add such resources to our universities' agendas we must begin now to build the access tools that will ensure the success of researchers in obtaining information from the networks. The major ingredients in an efficient system are a uniform and consistent format for the description of an object and its surrogates, and an appropriate vocabulary that helps both those who establish the description and those who seek the digital file described.

Format

In addressing the need for a format, we should look at the least, rather than the most, information necessary to describe an object and its surrogate. So many potential forms of pictorial representations of an object can exist that constructing a single, detailed descriptive document for each could overwhelm our computer systems and tax the patience of the searcher.

Jay Lambrecht's survey of cataloging requirements by bibliographic agencies in North America and Europe shows that agreement on content can be reached by those whose job it is to describe books (Lambrecht 1992). Figure 1 illustrates the minimum level of information the agencies acknowledged as important to provide users. Every other library that has access to the record should feel free to expand upon the basic record, to suit the needs of its own user population.

Element	Recommendation
Title Proper	Mandatory
Parallel Title	Mandatory
Other Title Information	Mandatory
Statement of Responsibility	Mandatory
Edition Statement	Mandatory
Additional Edition Statement	Mandatory
Place of Publication	Mandatory
Name of Publisher	Mandatory
Date of Publication	Mandatory
Extent	Mandatory
Illustration Statement	Optional
Dimensions	Optional
Series Title	Mandatory
Series Parallel Title	Optional
Series Numbering	Mandatory
Standard Number	Mandatory

Fig. 1. Proposed mandatory and optional data elements in a Minimal Level Bibliographic Description

If we analyze the elements necessary to establish a description appropriate to identify both an object and its surrogates we can arrive at a similar minimum level of information (Figure 2).

Many of the basic data fields are the same or very nearly so. For example, data related to elements such as title and statement of responsibility (i.e., author, architect, sculptor) can clearly be seen as information elements also applicable to the organization of objects. Elements related to edition and series are less applicable, except in those cases where replications of the original (i.e., casts or prints) exist. If the term "manufacture" or "construction" replaces the term "publication," the third group of elements is equally applicable to man-made objects. Scholars will find a museum's accession number or a

Object:	Uniform Title
	Title
	Part/Section
	Form/Medium
Artist:	Personal Name/s
	Date/Dates
	Relator Term
Location:	Country
	State/County/Province
	City
	Museum/Collection
Date/s:	
Extent:	Physical Description
Standard Number:	Reference Number
Subject Access:	Personal Name
	AAT Terms
Notes:	General Notes
	Citation/Reference
	Providence Note

Fig. 2. Suggested Minimal Level Data for Objects and Surrogates

reference number from a catalogue raisonné more useful than a standard publication number.

A format that contains a minimal level of information and still provides adequate access to visual information allows flexibility in a way that traditional, full level cataloging cannot. Cataloging records of this kind result in economic benefits for those who originate them, since they take fewer man-hours to produce. They also provide a framework for those who share them after the point of origin, upon which they may expand and shape to fit the needs of their own collections.

At present, the University of Virginia's tri-level cataloging procedure for images approaches this ideal (White 1996). The first level, in its current draft form, establishes the minimum level of cataloging required for all records, and is provided by the library's catalogue department. The second level contains additional fields of information that visual resources catalogers at the university fill in to provide greater depth of access. Researchers are encouraged to use a third level, presumed to be applicable only to their own individual workstations for maximum security for sensitive information. They may add information fields, such as provenance, related literature, exhibition record, and conservation actions, appropriate for their individual projects.

In the museum world, the ROLO (Recording Object Locations Online) system used by the Victoria and Albert Museum also approaches this ideal. A minimum amount of information is entered as quickly as possible into the system to establish inventory control over their vast holdings. More elaborate data related to specific details about the objects will be added later as staff time permits (Seal 1992).

After some revisions, such models will result in time-saving cooperative cataloging by slide and photograph collections. The resultant format will also be a sound basis for a mutually constructed and interchangeable database for objects and their surrogates between museums, visual resources collections, and libraries.

Vocabulary

Before a scholar can examine an object or information about it, including graphic, photographic, and digital representations of it, the object must acquire an acceptable descriptive label or title. Printed material now arrives at our libraries with authors, titles and publication data, but this is not always the case with artifacts in museums, photographs in slide collections, and digital information on computer screens. Images appropriate to medicine and natural sciences may rely upon universally understood title information, supplied by terms from long dead and frozen languages of Greece and Rome. For many of the newer sciences, English has almost unconsciously become the lingua franca.

Providing names and terms to adequately identify images sought by humanists, those who "study the creative works of men and women, [which] include entities and phenomena that exist in space and time" (Wiberley 1988, 2–3), proves more difficult. They see data as something that generates multiple interpretations rather than a single solution. Answers to their problems are liable to change from age to age and country to country. Information system designers should help them arrive at a unique interpretation of an object or phenomena. For them, "designers of computer systems should attempt to produce

systems that assist in the task of forming judgements rather than systems which make final judgements" (Stutt 1990, 73). One of the keys
to providing image seekers with a successful system is the recognition
of a vocabulary that will aid them in their objective of finding the
correct visual information.

Some names of people required to provide access to the objects
and their surrogates already exist in authority files of the United States
Library of Congress and the Avery Library. The *Union List of Artists
Names (ULAN)*, released by the Getty Art History Information Program (Getty 1995), also proves helpful, although further cooperative
authority work to determine a preferred form and its variations will
probably be necessary in the future. Names of a patron or the subject
of a sculptural monument are important, especially to a researcher
from another discipline, and should be treated as points of access
equally important as the names of the creators of an artifact. Data
fields for personal names should therefore include a sub-field for an
occupation title or role name which relates the person to the object.
Occupation titles and role names may be found in the controlled vocabulary of the *Art and Architecture Thesaurus*.

Standard identification of an object's site is important to include,
particularly when the object bears a frequently used name, such as
Notre Dame, Saint Mary's, or Santa Maria. Location is also important
to distinguish for objects smaller than buildings, since they may have
migrated from their original locations. The practice of listing locations
in a hierarchical manner, as set forth in Getty Art History Information
Program's "Thesaurus of Geographic Names," helps avoid confusion
between places with the same or similar names, such as Toledo, in
Nuevo Castilla, España., and Toledo, in Ohio, U.S.A.

Standard access can be provided to images in a collection by
topical means just as it is for printed material. Terms selected from the
hierarchies of the various facets of the *Art and Architecture Thesaurus*
provide several advantages for subject retrieval of image content. First
of all, the *AAT* provides consistency for both index constructors and
index users through a controlled vocabulary. Its hierarchical structure
reflects the arrangement, whole to part, and general to specific, of the
many visual information collections. Solid support in North America
and growing recognition by major documentation centers in England
and on the continent indicate that those who apply the terminology
see its advantages. Efforts to construct a multilingual version will
expand its usefulness. Even the differences between American English
and Anglo English terms and spelling are recognized by the *Thesaurus*,
and appropriate alternates are provided to satisfy the needs of those
two user communities.

Date fields for art works need to tolerate a kind of vagueness, since objects are not always presented to us in nice tidy packages, like printed materials. Construction of cathedrals may have spanned several centuries, dates of other objects may be deduced only through a knowledge of a craftsman's career, or we may only be able to attribute a general date or span of dates based on stylistic comparison. Dates are of relative importance, and they may be subject to future modification and even correction.

A problem also exists for cultural objects (and their surrogates) that do not have a specific name or for which there is not universal accord on a single name. This problem seems to be more appropriate to objects and visual information used by humanities scholars than those in the sciences. In terms of the well-controlled world of bibliography, what is the title of a building, a piece of sculpture, or an ivory crucifix? What good is access to objects and images if those who provide them and those who seek them cannot agree upon what to call them? A practical solution to the problem is the creation of uniform title especially for those objects to which an artist or designer cannot be assigned.

Some labels from which we might choose can be found in the Library of Congress Subject Authority File, but this standardizing mechanism supplies titles only for structures about which someone has written. It is not likely to contain structures such as the Luynes Château or the Église Saint-Sauveur at Luz. For such objects we should rely upon standard indexes, such as Nikolaus Pevsner's *Buildings of England* series, the volumes of the *Guida d'Italia* published by the Touring Club Italiano, the *Dictionnaire des Églises de France,* or Georg Dehio's *Handbuch der Deutschen Kunstdenkmäler*. Occasionally, a generic term such as "medal" or "pulpit" needs to be used as the object name, since no other label may be available for an object. Without such a controlling factor, all images related to a single creative work cannot be drawn together for the benefit of an information seeker.

Rethinking Visual Information Sources

More and more people are discovering that a wealth of visual information may be found in many places, and that it can provide descriptive, prescriptive, and aesthetic information in the same way that texual resources can. They are also beginning to recognize that digitized images and electronic networks promise the imminent possibility of universal access to visual, as well as textual, information. We must therefore shake off our current concept of resource sharing. In an electronic environment, campuses no longer exist by themselves to serve members of their community. Various consortia of universities no longer consider who owns what when it comes to providing access to materials. Boundaries are expanding and shifting daily to include non-university resources. Access to visual information, in whatever form it may be sought, should not limit itself to a single campus or a group of campuses. Networks that provide us with access should be flexible enough to flow between user communities, expand into museums and public libraries, and seek out resources from beyond the perimeters of cities, states, and countries.

References

Alexander, K. D. (1993, Oct. 25, 2:28 p.m.). Virtual reality at the Guggenheim. Message to the recipients of the list. In: CAAH [electronic bulletin board]. [Princeton, New Jersey]: Consortium of Art and Architecture Historians. Message no. 1608.

Baker, J. (1993). The fiber-optic library. *Inform* 7(8): 30–33.

Bearman, D. and Perkins, J. (1993). Executive summary and recommendations of the standards framework for the computer interchange of museum information. Electronic document available through the Coalition for Networked Information via anonymous ftp, or from Perkins, jperkins@fox.nstn.ns.ca, or in *Spectra* 20(2 & 3).

Braggins, D. (1992). Arts & science museum imagery and ownership: Europe vs. U.S. Advanced *Imaging* 7(10): 16–18.

Cawkell, A. E. (1993). The British Library's picture research projects: Image, work, & retrieval. *Advanced Imaging* 8(10): 38–40.

Clarke, Sherman. (1993, Oct. 28, 9:03 a.m.). RLG Digital Image Access Project. Message to recipients of the list. In: CAAH [electronic bulletin board]. [Princeton, New Jersey]: Consortium of Art and Architectural Historians. Message no. 9385.

Croft, Jim. (1993, July 8, 7:08 p.m.). A new botanical WWW server. Message to recipients of the list. In: MUSEUM-L [electronic bulletin board]. [Albuquerque, New Mexico]: University of New Mexico. Message no. 3319.

Dorozynski, A. (1993). Computers bring back a long-lost french abbey. *Science* 261: 544–555.

Evenhouse, R. and Stefanic, T. (1993). Image processing and solid modeling recapture a mummy's face. *Advanced Imaging* 7(10): 40–43.

Getty Art History Information Program (1995). *Visual Resources* 10(4): 357–364.

Guralnick, R. (1993, Oct. 26, 12:54 p.m.). The virtual museum. Message to recipients of the list. In: MUSEUM-L [electronic bulletin board). [Albuquerque, New Mexico]: University of New Mexico. Message no. 4464.

Lambrecht, J. Y. (1992). *Minimal level cataloging by national bibliographic agencies* (UBICM Publications—New Series, vol. 8). Munchen: K. G. Saur.

MacDonald, L. (1990). Europe's growing support for imaging in art. *Advanced Imaging* 5(9): 24–27.

Mazor, B. (1993). Imaging to rescue art and science artifacts in the field. *Advanced Imaging* 8(9): 38–41.

McKeown, R. (1993). The Centre for Image Information: The shape of things to come. *Art Libraries Journal* 18(3): 28–31.

NARCISSE, Project. (1993). Prospectus for Seminaire NARCISSE, 25–26 November 1993, at the Laboratoire de Recherche des Musées de France, Paris.

Price, D. (1993, Oct. 25, 11:20 p.m.). JPEG and GIF Images on Gopher. Message to recipients of the list. In: CAAH [electronic bulletin board]. [Princeton, New Jersey]: Consortium of Art and Architectural Historians. Message no. 0929.

Roberts, A. (Co-ordinator). (1991). *The MDA data standard* (rev. ed.). Cambridge: The Museum Documentation Association.

Roberts, A. (Ed.) (1992). *Sharing the information resources of museums. Proceedings of the Third Conference of the Museum Documentation Association. York, England, 14–18 September 1989*. Cambridge: The Association. See especially: Bibliographic Database Developments and Applications of Systems, by Alan Seal (118); Information Exchange Requirements of Archives and Museums, by David Bearman (119–123); Taking a Second Look at a Bibliographic System, by Rachel M. Allen (124–130); and, Combined Development of Bibliographic and Object-Oriented Systems, by Dr. Leonard D. Will (131–136).

Seal, A. (1992). Evolution at the Victoria and Albert Museum. *Computers and the History of Art* 3(1): 25–32.

Slide Market News. (1993). Saskia Cultural Documents Ltd. makes groups of slides available in the form of CD-ROMs. *Visual Resources Association Bulletin* 26(2): 49.

Stutt, A. (1990). Argument support programs: Machines for generating interpretations. In D. S. Miall (Ed.), *Humanities and the computer. New Directions* (71–87). Oxford: Clarendon Press.

Szrajber, T. (1992). European museum documentation strategies and standards conference. Eliot College, University of Kent, Canterbury, 2–6 September 1991. *Computers and the History of Art* 3(1): 75–83.

Webster, K. (1993). Cornell project saves documents, books—and makes them accessible. *Advanced Imaging* 8(9): 42–46, 100.

White, Lynda (1994). Image cataloging in MARC at the University of Virginia. *Visual Resources Association Bulletin* 21(3): 23–91

Wiberley, S. E., Jr. (1988). Names in space and time: The indexing vocabulary of the humanities. *The Library Quarterly* 58(1): 1–28.

Part VI———————————————

*NAVIGATING THE
NETWORK: AN
INTRODUCTION*

A Short Primer for Communicating on the Global Net

John December

The chapters in this volume trace paths through the interstices of a communications network extending around the globe. This global Net, consisting of interconnected computer networks and telecommunications systems, offers unparalleled opportunities for individuals and groups to communicate, collaborate, and explore new research and education opportunities. Making use of this Net, scholars can communicate one-to-one, take part in work groups, conduct research, and create opportunities for electronic publishing and scholarship. While the invention of the printing press gave those with presses the power to disseminate information over a limited geographic area, the invention of a worldwide computer Net gives individuals the opportunity to disseminate and exchange ideas on an even larger scale.

The components of this Net include tools for information dissemination and forums for computer-mediated communication. People using these tools and forums interact in complex ways to create virtual communities—associations among people who may have never met in person, but who gather online solely because of their common interests. The inner workings and varied forms these tools and forums can take are a testament to human ingenuity in creating forms of communication.

In this chapter, I first survey possibilities for communication on the Net, showing the range of tools and forums for communication. Following this general introduction, I'll introduce specific details for navigating the Net.

Possibilities for Global Communication

The global systems for telegraph communication developed in the nineteenth century provided instantaneous, asynchronous (the sender's transmitting and the receiver's reading of the message could happen at different times) communication across continents. The telegraph changed communication expectations and practices. The telegraph, however, didn't revolutionize scientific or scholarly communication, because the equipment and skills required to send and receive messages wasn't in the hands of scholars on a regular basis, and the code necessary for the composition and reception of messages didn't encourage extended discourse or the expression of complex ideas. So while systems like the telegraph share some of the characteristics of the Net today—instantaneous, long-distance communication—the Net offers much more, both in terms of possibilities for *kinds* of communication, and also in terms of the *deployment* of the technology into the hands of scholars who acquire the necessary skills.

The Net offers not only a kind of telegraph to its participants—electronic mail—but also many other opportunities for communication involving a combination of audience size and time constraints. Electronic mail itself offers possibilities other than just one-to-one communication, such as many-to-many conferencing and one-to-many broadcast of messages. Other specialized tools on the Net offer real-time connections among people in small group or mass contexts. Still other tools provide for the delivery of information—online systems designed so that users can browse, search, and retrieve information from databases. The following chart summarizes the possibilities for communication on the Net. Later in this chapter, I'll explain some of these tools in more detail and define each within the context of the Net's operation.

Possibilities for Communication		
	Time Constraints	
Audience	Synchronous	Asynchronous
one-to-one	talk	e-mail
one-to-many	mbone	email, moderated Listserv, World Wide Web, FTP, Gopher
many-to-many	MU*, IRC	Usenet, Interactive Webbing

talk provides real-time interactive text interchange between two users
e-mail allows a user to send message(s) to another user (or many users via mailing lists)
mbone is a live audio and video multicast virtual network using Internet
Listserv is a mailing-list server for group communication
World Wide Web provides a system to disseminate resources through network-distributed hyptertext

FTP allows a user to retrieve or add copies of files on remote computers
Gopher provides access to resources using a graph of menus
MU* is a family of programs for real-time text-based interchange among groups of people
IRC is a real-time, text-based discussion on a changing set of topics
Usenet provides asynchronous text discussion on a fixed (but expandable) set of topics
Interactive Webbing gives people a common space for network-distributed multimedia writing

The tools and forms described above open up opportunities for:

— communication: among peers as well as between students and teachers; distant experts providing specialized expertise and advice;
— collaboration: in work groups brought together via electronic mail or in real-time or asynchronous online forums; these groups discuss issues, share information, and create knowledge;
— information: scholars contribute to resource libraries of resource materials and information; users can browse, query, and retrieve information from these databases;
— scholarly forums: online scholarly journals, fostering collaborations that extend and develop basic theory and research in a field of knowledge;
— connections: people communicating based on their interests and need for knowledge, in relationships that could have never emerged except through Net forums.

The exciting possibilities the Net offers for communication revolve around its fundamental power to bring people together in online communities of interest. Dreams of a forthcoming "information highway" may yield new variations of technology, but the ability of people to use the Net for communication has already been demonstrated, as the chapters in this volume describe.

For example, the Net can foster projects that develop and disseminate new information and resources. The ProjectH group, described in the chapter by Fay Sudweeks and Sheizaf Rafaeli, produced the following as a result of their online collaboration (ProjectH Information):

1. A database of computer-mediated discussions;
2. A technical report describing the project and its process of collaboration, *ProjectH Overview: A Quantitative Study of Computer-Mediated Communication,* by Sheizaf Rafaeli, Fay Sudweeks, Joe Konstan, and Ed Mabry;

3. An annotated bibliography of Computer-Mediated Communication literature;

4. A forthcoming book, *Network and Netplay: Virtual Groups on the Internet,* edited by Sheizaf Rafaeli, Fay Sudweeks, and Margaret McLaughlin;

5. Two panels on Network and Netplay at the International Communication Association's 1994 convention.

The physical infrastructure that supports this collaboration, knowledge creation, and dissemination consists of complex interconnections among networks and tools. Knowing how to manage the complexities of the operation of these tools is essential for developing the literacy necessary to participate in Net communities.

In the remainder of this chapter, I shall describe how to navigate the Net, for users who may be new to understanding its networks, content, and communities. I shall describe the conduits and connections that make up network infrastructure, and outline methods for Net access. I shall then introduce fundamental concepts important to navigating the Net—network locations and names. Finally, I shall survey, in more detail, the major network information retrieval tools and computer-mediated communication forums.

Navigating the Global Net

The use of the global Net has increased rapidly over the past decade—the Internet portion grew from 213 computer hosts in August 1981 to 727,000 hosts in January 1992 (Lottor 1992), to more than 2.217 million hosts in February 1994 (Rutowski 1994, 9).

The Net has also expanded in terms of the ways people use it. Tens of millions of people in more than 146 countries now use the Net for education, recreation, commerce, scholarship, communication, and community-building. This list of uses grows as new tools and forums for communication develop.

Global Networks: Conduits and Connections

The global telecommunications infrastructure now girding the world developed through a process in which networks came into existence, grew, and merged. Understanding this process and its culmination as today's Net requires understanding how computer networks share information, why people have built them, and the basics of how networks operate.

The purpose of a computer network is to provide a way for people to transfer information via computer. Information shared on a computer network is transmitted according to patterns all computers connected to that network can process. These patterns are called protocols. A network that uses a set of protocols known as the Internet (TCP/IP) protocol suite is called an internet (with a small i). There are more than 23,000 internets worldwide (Rutowski 1994, 9), run by organizations, governments, businesses, and individuals that cooperatively agree to exchange information. The connected set of these individual internets form what is called the Internet (capital I).

Creating global systems like the Internet for sharing information using protocols is nothing new—in fact, the first global electronic network was the nineteenth century telegraph (with Morse Code as a protocol). However, the reasons for building the Internet were different than for building either the telegraph or telephone communication networks. In 1973, the United States Department of Defense's Advanced Research Project Agency initiated a program to build a communications network that would be robust enough to survive a nuclear attack. To accomplish this, developers created the TCP/IP protocol suite with the express purpose of making it operate in a decentralized way. The TCP/IP protocols don't require all the information in a message to flow over the same path. Instead, messages are broken into "packets" or chunks, which might travel different routes to a destination. Thus, if one path is unavailable or busy with traffic, packets can travel over several alternate routes. At the final destination, the packets are assembled to form the message.

The Internet was founded on cooperation as an organizing principle and within traditions of individual autonomy and responsibility. Since the U.S. portion of the Internet was originally funded by the U.S. government, commercial traffic was limited. Today, the restrictions on commercial traffic on the Internet have been largely lifted, because people communicating on the Internet no longer have to rely on government-sponsored conduits. For-profit companies operate TCP/IP networks and give people, companies, and other private and public enterprises access to the Internet. While the early Internet in the U.S. resembled a trunk and branch system of backbone, regional, and local networks, the topology of the Internet now resembles more of a mesh—in which commercial, private, academic, and government networks mix.

The Internet's robust nature and the widespread use of its protocols as a basis for internetworking make it one of the most widely used communication systems in the world. However, the Internet is just one part of the global Net. Other computer networks that do not use the TCP/IP protocol suite can exchange electronic mail with the Internet. The set of all systems that can exchange electronic mail worldwide is called the Matrix (Quarterman 1990). The Matrix includes the Internet as well as Bitnet. Based on IBM's NJE communications protocol, Bitnet connected more than 1,400 organizations in forty nine countries at its peak in 1991–92, and is operated by a single organization, the Corporation for Research and Educational Networking (CREN), a non-profit membership corporation which includes a European counterpart, EARN (European Academic and Research Network) (Corporation for Research and Educational Networking, 1994). Bitnet and Internet exchange electronic mail through a hardware/software interchange point called a "gateway." Another network in the Matrix, called FidoNet, consists of networks of personal computers exchanging information over telephone lines. The Matrix also includes UUCP (a network named after the protocol on which it is based, Unix-Unix Copy Protocol). Within the Internet part of the Matrix are regional networks, such as JANET in the United Kingdom, NYSERNET in New York State, and AARNET in Australia. These networks are the results of government or academic initiatives to provide network connectivity for communication.

The Matrix is not limited to just academic or government-sponsored networks. Many commercial online providers (which are not part of the Internet) are part of the Matrix. Services such as America Online, BIX (a service of *Byte* magazine), CompuServe, Delphi, Prodigy, and others provide e-mail gateways to the Matrix (Yanoff and Chew 1994). These commercial connections to the Matrix illustrate the appeal of the Matrix as a communications system. The key to this appeal lies in the benefit of "critical mass" (Markus 1992). The large number of existing users of the networks in the Matrix lures still more people to construct gateways from their network to the Matrix.

Despite the size of the Matrix, there are many systems that cannot exchange e-mail with the Matrix. Non-Matrix networks include major systems such as France's Teletel (popularly known as Minitel),[1] as well as networks of various sizes used for private or commercial use, such as:

— PANs (Personal Area Networks, networks of portable, usually hand-held devices that can be used for communication, e.g., personal digital assistants interchanging information via wireless communication);
— LANs (Local Area Networks, networks usually located within a single building for an office or an organization);

— MANs (Metropolitan Area Networks, a network for a campus, a
  municipality, or several LANs at one site for an organization);
— WANs (Wide Area Networks, e.g., regional or country-wide networks that may connect several MANs for a corporation or private
  entity);
— GANs (Global Area Networks, globally-distributed networks, such
  as the worldwide system for banking transactions, or a private network run by a multi-national corporation).

With the development of gateways, these unconnected networks
could hook into the Matrix or the Internet. The collection of all these
networks plus the Matrix form the global Net. Since the Matrix forms
the largest connected portion, its critical mass entices developers of
these unconnected systems to build gateways to the Matrix or Internet.
For example, while some commercial online service providers give
just electronic mail access to the Matrix (e.g., CompuServe), other
commercial providers (e.g., Delphi) offer direct access to several Internet
services.

The Net's physical infrastructure is based on increasingly complex collections of switches, wire, fiber optic, microwave, satellite,
cellular, radio, and other systems for telecommunication. Operated by
cooperating organizations and individuals, it challenges expectations
about ownership, cooperation, sovereignty, as well as organizational,
political, and cultural boundaries.

Access: Hardware, Software, and Network Connections

In addition to an awareness of the global extent of networks outlined
above, the user must also know how hardware, software, interfaces,
and tools work together. Many factors affect what a person can do on
the Net, including knowledge, training, and peer and organizational
support. A major factor in terms of hardware and software that deter-
mines how a person can experience the Net is the network access
connection. The following descriptions outline the kinds of access
connections to the Net, and how these connections have an effect on
what a user can do. The kind of connections available to the user are
made available through the network access provider. This provider
might be a commercial service, an employer, or university.

— *Mailbox only:* In this access mode, the user has the ability to send
  and receive electronic mail with others connected to the Matrix.

Examples of this connection include an account on a Bitnet host or an account on a commercial service (such as CompuServe) that offers only e-mail access to the Matrix. Another example is someone operating a FidoNet personal computer bulletin board system. Through gateways, the Bitnet, CompuServe, and FidoNet users can exchange electronic mail with the Internet or other networks in the Matrix (Yanoff and Chew 1994).

— *Online account with full Internet access:* In this access mode, a user has an account on a host computer directly connected to the Internet. This is a common access mode for people who have their accounts at a university (although some universities have only Bitnet accounts) or as part of their employment. By having full Internet access, a person can use all the information and communication protocols that operate on the Internet (explained below) in addition to exchanging electronic mail with other Matrix networks. Using an operating system (such as Unix) that supports multi-tasking (the ability to operate several software applications at once) and a graphical interface (that gives the user a system of graphical menus or icons, such as the X Window System) and a workstation, a person with full Internet access can use many Internet applications and resources simultaneously.

— *Dialup Internet account (modem):* A user who has a full Internet access account (described above) might dial in from home to the host computer. While the user will have full access to all Internet functions, a dialup account will not allow the user to employ multi-tasking or a graphical interface (as described above in terms of workstation access) unless a SLIP account is used (described below).

— *SLIP Serial Line Internet Protocol (SLIP):* An account with this system achieves the same functionality as full Internet access. This is because SLIP allows a user to exchange Internet packets—rather than just a single stream of information about one application—over telephone lines. Users of SLIP are limited only by the software on their computer. Many graphical user interfaces for personal computers, used with a SLIP connection, can give the user a full workstation-like functionality for Net. However, slower modem speeds used with SLIP would yield significantly slower performance than full-Internet access.

— *Dedicated line:* A dedicated line gives full-time full-Internet access to a Local Area Network or a specific computer host. Commercial Internet providers can provide a dedicated line at varying speeds (and varying prices) to organizations or individuals. Dedicated lines are used mainly by businesses and organizations who need fast, continuous access to the Net.

Navigating: Tools and Forums

After gaining some understanding of the composition of the Net and the kinds of access modes available, the next step is to explore what tools are available for accessing information and computer-mediated communication forums. In this section, I focus on tools that are used on the Internet.[2] I shall begin by outlining the concepts and practices behind network locations and machine relationships. Using these concepts, I shall describe the most popular tools for using the Internet. I shall then review specialized tools for networked information retrieval and computer-mediated communication.

Locations on the Net

In order to access information or communicate on the Net, a user must know how to designate network locations. In the discussion below, I define terms for network locations.

Electronic mail address. An electronic mail (or e-mail) address is an identifier for a person's e-mail account or an application that provides services through electronic mail. An Internet e-mail address is generally of the form:

user@host.domain

where *user* is the login id of the person or the name of the application. The *host.domain* part of the address identifies the name of the computer and other information (such as the machine, network, and the kind of computer or network [the *domain* part]). The name of the computer may include several subdivisions separated by periods. For example, the e-mail address

jad@miller.cs.uwm.edu

identifies the user "jad" on the computer named "miller" in the Computer Science ("cs") Department of the University of Wisconsin—Milwaukee ("uwm") in the education domain ("edu"). Other domain designations include "com" for commercial organizations, "gov" for government, and "org" for non-profit organizations.

Not all e-mail addresses are associated with people. E-mail can also be used to deliver information in a way unmediated by direct human interaction. For example, the e-mail address *comserve@vm.its. rpi.edu* is the address of Comserve, a scholarly service for those studying human communication. Messages sent to Comserve will automatically generate replies based on the contents of the body of the e-mail message. Another common auto-reply service, called a Listserv, is discussed in a later section.

While the above examples show the basic structure and concept of an Internet e-mail address, there are many variations, particularly when e-mail is sent through gateways to other Matrix networks (Yanoff and Chew 1994; Adams and Donnalyn 1993).

Host address. As described above, the *host.domain* part of an e-mail address identifies the name of a machine. For example, the computer host on which the Comserve service resides is *vm.its.rpi.edu*. E-mail cannot be sent to a host address. However, the host address of a machine operates in other functions, as will be described below.

Uniform Resource Locator (URL). A URL is a string of characters that uniquely identifies an Internet resource. URLs play a role in the operation of World Wide Web and other network retrieval tools. A URL, just like an Internet e-mail address, is an important, widely recognized identifier and is an internationally-recognized standard, set by the Internet Engineering Task Force, for expressing the location of an Internet resource.

The resource a URL refers to might be a document, a connection to an information service, or a link to hypertext or hypermedia. In general, URLs take the form

scheme://host.domain:port/path

where *scheme* is the method by which this resource is available (for example, one scheme is FTP (file transfer protocol); other schemes are described below). *Host.domain* is the name of the machine, the same as described above for e-mail addresses and host addresses. *Path* includes the name of a file, directory, or other identifying information for the resource. The *:port* identifier is present only when an additional qualifier is necessary to identify the service requested from the host. There are further qualifications to this general form of a URL, but this is the general form.

The Client/Server Relationship

Many applications on the Net operate based on a relationship called "client/server." A server is a software program on a computer host that provides information to a client. A client is a software application that provides an interface to the user that is particular to the user's hardware and software configuration. Since the client communicates in a standard format with the server, a server can provide information to clients that may be running on various platforms on the Net (e.g., Unix, Macintosh, Windows). This client/server model leads to many efficiencies in the development and operation of network applications. The client and server can be located in different parts of the network, and people can create clients for new kinds of hardware, yet access the same server. Generally, a system administrator will obtain and install client software for the applications available at a site or on the network. A user, then, just needs to know how to access and use the clients available.

Basic Tools

As a way to introduce how to navigate the Internet using tools, I'll describe electronic mail, telnet, and File Transfer Protocol—three tools that are commonly used by people to communicate. Historically, these tools were among the earliest developed, and together they constitute the bulk of Internet traffic (for example, these three services made up 40.8 percent of the National Science Foundation backbone packet traffic in May 1994, as opposed the World Wide Web's share of 3.4 percent and Gopher's 2.6 percent).

Electronic mail. E-mail gives a sender the ability to transmit a message to a receiver at an Internet address. Often this message is text, although multimedia extensions to e-mail are available. The sender and receiver must have accounts on computers that are on the Matrix. The user can create a mailing list and send the same text to many users (broadcast). While this broadcasting can be done manually, usually someone will use a software application (such as Listserv, described below) to facilitate group e-mail communication.

Telnet. A user can access a remote computer on the Internet by using telnet. The user issues the command *telnet host.domain port* and connects to the remote host. The *host.domain* part is the host address as described above, and *port* is an additional qualifier to identify the service requested. *Port* is usually a number set by the provider of the service (this number is arbitrarily set within specific constraints, and similar services often use the same numbers, for traditional or technical reasons). A telnet service usually consists of a menu interface that presents information—an online card catalog or weather information, for example. One telnet service is the

Weather Underground service provided by the University of Michigan *(telnet downwind.sprl.umich.edu 3000)*. The computer accepting the telnet request might admit any user or only those who enter a specific identification or password. In addition to information systems like the Weather Underground, telnet can also be used to connect to conferencing systems.

Here is a sample telnet session showing how to access the Empire Internet Schoolhouse, a selection of K–12 resources, projects, and discussion groups:

```
$ telnet nysernet.org
Trying 192.77.173.2 ...
Connected to nysernet.org.
Escape character is '^]'.
SunOS UNIX (nysernet.org)
login: empire
You are empire login 4 of 10.
Enter your terminal type below.  Some common ones are:
vt100, vt200, vt300, sun, xterm, wyse50
If you're not sure, try vt100.
Terminal Type [vt100]: vt100
```

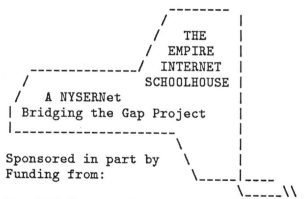

```
Sponsored in part by
Funding from:

The IBM Corporation
The New York State Science and Technology Foundation
The National Science Foundation
The National Science Foundation
Press [enter] to continue
Press q to quit
```

File Transfer Protocol (FTP). FTP is a way to send or retrieve copies of files to or from a remote host. The files might be documents, graphics, sound files, movies, or executable programs. As with telnet, the computer accepting the FTP request might accept any user or only those who enter a user identification and password. FTP is used extensively for sharing information on the Internet. "Anonymous" FTP is a means by which anyone on the Internet (or, through e-mail gateways, anyone on the Matrix), can obtain a file from an FTP server running on a remote host.

For example, the following shows how to get the anonymous FTP resource called "internet-cmc.txt" whose URL is

ftp.rpi.edu/pub/communications/internet-cmc.txt

```
command                                    comment
$ ftp ftp.rpi.edu                          ftp.rpi.edu is the host name
Name (ftp.host.dom:yourid):  anonymous     Login  as ''anonymous''
Password: YOURID@YOURHOST.DOMAIN           Enter your email address
ftp> cd /pub/communications                change to path (identifying the
                                           location of the resource on
                                           the host
ftp> get internet-cmc.txt                  internet-cmc.txt is the file name
ftp> quit                                  End ftp session
$
```

A user without a direct connection to the Internet might not have an FTP client that can perform the access shown above. Users on the Matrix, however, can obtain files at FTP sites via e-mail, by creating an e-mail message with a specific list of commands and sending it to an FTP mail gateway service. The following shows the commands a user would place in an e-mail message to obtain the same resource described above via e-mail.

```
command                                comment
$ mail ftpmail@decwrl.dec.com          send email to this host
Subject: ftp request                   anything as a subject is ok
connect ftp.rpi.edu                    ftp.rpi.edu is the host name
chdir  /pub/communications             change to path (identifying the
                                       location of the resource on the host)
get internet-cmc.txt                   internet-cmc.txt is the file name
quit                                   Ends ftp session
.                                      Ends letter (Unix Mail)
$
```

Network Information Retrieval Tools

Along with the three basic tools (e-mail, telnet, and FTP), there are a variety of specialized tools used on the Net for locating and retrieving information.

Archie.   Archie provides a way for a user to search anonymous FTP sites for files with names that match a given string of characters. The user, through an Archie client, queries an Archie server, and the server reports the location of files that match the pattern. The Archie client displays the addresses of computer hosts that have files matching the pattern. Also displayed is a description of where on those computers the files reside (the pathname). If an Archie client is not installed or not available, a user can telnet to a machine running an Archie server or use Archie by electronic mail.[3]

The following illustrates how to telnet to an Archie server to find files at FTP sites that match the string "internet-tools."

```
command                              comment
$ telnet Archie.internic.net         Archie.internic.net is the host name
Trying 198.49.45.10 ...
Connected to ds.internic.net.
Escape character is ']'.
InterNIC Directory and Database Services
SunOS UNIX (ds)

login: Archie                        login as ''Archie''

Welcome to the InterNIC Database Server.

Archie> prog -s internet-tools       look  for files matching string
  internet-tools

# Your queue position: 1
# Estimated time for completion: 00:04

working... -# Your queue position: 1

[list of  sites]                     a long list of sites scrolled by

Host  uceng.uc.edu     (129.137.189.1)    this  is a  host that has a match
Last updated 12:18  4 Mar 1994

Location: /pub/wuarchive/doc/EFF/Net_info/CMC_List      directory match
FILE   817 bytes 19:19 26 Jan 1994 internet-tools.Z      a file name match
FILE   347 bytes 19:19 26 Jan 1994 internet-tools.txt.Z  a file name match

Host anubis.ac.hmc.edu (134.173.32.18)    another host with a match
Last updated 16:03  4 Mar 1994
```

The above example generated a long list of sites that have files with names matching the string *internet-tools.* The last two sites, *uceng.uc.edu* and *anubis.ac.hmc.edu,* are shown. The user could then obtain files from these hosts by using anonymous FTP and the path and file names shown. By putting this information together, the Uniform Resource Locator for one of these resources can be constructed:

ftp://uceng.uc.edu/pub/wuarchive/doc/EFF/Net_info/ CMC_List/internet-tools.Z

Since Archie locates FTP resources, Archie and FTP can be used in conjunction with each other to locate and retrieve information from the Internet. While an excellent way to share information, FTP sites are difficult for users to browse, even using Archie, because the file name is often the only information available about the contents of a file.[4]

Gopher. A Gopher client presents the user with a system of menus and selections. These menu selections can point to another Gopher, a menu, a document, a search function, or a link to a telnet connection. As with Archie, a user accesses a Gopher client as the interface to a Gopher server. If a Gopher client is unavailable, telnet or electronic mail can be used to access some Gopher servers. Since the Gopher is a simple interface (menus) that can be easily used from nearly any terminal, Gophers are enjoying wide popularity as campus-wide information systems and information systems for organizations and corporations. The development of "Veronica," a tool that locates Gopher menu entries in Gophers worldwide, makes information retrieval from Gophers much easier. The relationship of Veronica to Gopher is analogous to the relationship of Archie to FTP sites: Archie finds files at FTP sites; Veronica finds menu entries on Gophers.

The following shows how to telnet to the Gopher at the University of Minnesota:

```
command                                    comment
$ telnet consultant.micro.umn.edu          telnet to the host
Trying 134.84.132.4 ...
Connected to hafnhaf.micro.umn.edu.
Escape character is ']'.
login: Gopher                              enter ''Gopher'' as the login
                                           name

Internet Gopher Information Client 2.0 pl11
Root Gopher server: hafnhaf.micro.umn.edu
-> 1. InformationAboutGopher/              This is the first menu entry
   2.  Computer Information/
   3.  Internet file server (FTP) sites/
   4.  Fun  Games/
   5.  Libraries/
   6.  Mailing Lists/
   7.  News/
   8.  Other Gopher and Information Servers/
   9.  Phone Books/
  10.  Search Gopher Titles at the U of MN <?>   this menu entry is for a
                                                 search
  11. Search lots of places at the U of M <?>
  12. UofM Campus Information/
  Press ? for Help, q to Quit              use commands to navigate
```

World Wide Web (WWW). The World Wide Web is a system of network-distributed hypertext. Hypertext is text which is not constrained to a linear structure. This means that hypertext can contain "links" to other text. On the World Wide Web, these links can be to hypertext documents, documents at FTP sites, Gopher menus, or a variety of network resources.

The World Wide Web uses hypertext as a "glue" to link files, Gophers, telnet servers, FTP sites, or Usenet newsgroups (described below). Just as with Gopher and Archie, accesses to a World Wide Web server is through a client or by using telnet. For WWW telnet connections, see the list of WWW sites on the Yanoff Internet Services List (ftp://csd4.csd.uwm.edu/pub/inet.services.txt). Once in one of these WWW telnet interfaces, a user can obtain a resource by entering the command "go" followed by the URL for the resource. For example:

go http://info.cern.ch/hypertext/WWW/Clients.html

The "HTTP" indicates that this resource is accessible through the Hypertext Transfer Protocol (HTTP). The Clients.html list will then show the WWW clients available.

The "Mosaic" WWW client gives the user a hypermedia (graphics, sound, motion pictures) interface. WWW viewed using a Mosaic client is a rapidly growing form of information publishing and retrieval on the Internet. People with little or no training in the details of Gopher, Usenet (discussed below), FTP, telnet, or WWW can use these applications through the point-and-click operation of Mosaic.

Just as Archie and Veronica provide ways to search the information spaces created by FTP sites and Gophers, the World Wide Web Worm (WWWW) is a searching tool for WWW. The WWWW gives the user an interface to search the WWW for URLs matching given string of characters. The URL for the WWWW is http://www.cs.colorado.edu/home/mcbryan/WWWW.html.

Computer-Mediated Communication (CMC) Forums

In the preceding discussion, I covered a variety of tools to locate and retrieve information from the Net. Another class of tools provide ways for people to communicate with each other, either in real-time or asynchronously (a form of communication which the sender and receiver need not be simultaneously logged on for the message to be received). Information retrieval tools use files as a basic unit for conveying information. CMC forums also use files, but these files are distributed through e-mail or the "Usenet"news distribution system. Other CMC forums employ "conversations" of asynchronous text interchange as a basis for sharing information. In the descriptions below, I begin with describing two asynchronous file-based CMC forums and then describe two forums for synchronous text interchange.

Listserv. A Listserv is a software program that provides users with a way to participate in online discussions or obtain information by electronic mail. In response to a command e-mailed to it, a Listserv server will respond with a text file or other appropriate action. Since it is based on e-mail, a Listserv is accessible to anyone on the Matrix.

A common use of Listserv is to set up mailing lists for asynchronous computer conferencing and computer-mediated scholarship. Kovacs (1993), in *The Directory of Scholarly Electronic Conferences,* lists over 1,200 electronic conferences on subjects ranging from anthropology to the physical sciences. Strangelove (1992) lists over a hundred electronic journals, some peer reviewed, distributed through Listserv or electronic mail.

Usenet news. Usenet is a system for asynchronous discussion about subjects separated into "news-groups." Despite its name, Usenet is not a computer network; rather, it is a system for distributing discussion among cooperating computers. Usenet extends across the Matrix, with computers receiving Usenet news feeds located on the Internet, Bitnet, or on systems sharing information through the UUCP (Unix-Unix Copy) protocol. Usenet newsgroups and articles propogate through these networks according to a scheme determined by the cooperating computer system administrators who operate Usenet news servers.

Similar to the systems described above, the user interacts with a Usenet news client program which communicates with a Usenet news server. The client displays the newsgroups from which a user can choose, and offers the reader a variety of options to access and read articles (scan for keywords in article subject lines, list all articles, show articles with a specific range of article numbers) or contribute (called "posting") articles to newsgroups. New newsgroups are added according to a system for newsgroup formation defined and operated by the Usenet community.

The discussions that take place on Usenet cover a wide variety of topics. These topics are identified by a hierarchical naming system which allows for increasing specialization. For example, the newsgroup *soc.culture.indian.telugu,* is for discussion related to the culture of the Telugu people of India. Similarly, there are other newsgroups whose names begin with *soc.culture* covering other groups. The first part of the newsgroup name, such as *soc* (which stands for "society"), are the root hierarchies for the newsgroups. Other top-level root hierarchies include: *sci* (science), *comp* (computers), *rec* (recreation), and *alt* (an alternative hierarchy which allows a less formal process for group formation), and others such as special-interest academic *ieee* (Institute of Electrical and Electronics Engineers), or regional *capdist* (The capital district of New York State). As of 1993, there were more than two thousand newsgroups (Spafford 1993a; Gilmore and Spafford 1993). Some newsgroups (approximately 360) are moderated, so that only articles approved by a moderator can be posted (Spafford 1993b).

The day-to-day traffic of Internet newsgroups involves much discussion (for example, more than a hundred articles were posted to the *alt.folklore.urban* newsgroup in a single day). Discussion proceeds on topics or off-shoots called "threads." Within this maelstrom of the Usenet discussion, members of the newsgroups often encounter similar questions by new users. From this need to codify and transmit group knowledge, the tradition of "Frequently Asked Questions" (FAQ) lists with answers has evolved. These "FAQs" help provide answers to questions that are often relevant to new members. The FAQs also summarize accumulated knowledge and codify the specialized knowledge of experienced users. These FAQ lists are often periodically posted to the newsgroup and maintained by a FAQ editor or group of editors. The "official" (as defined by group members) FAQ will often be placed in the Usenet FAQ FTP site on the host computer *rtfm.mit.edu*. There are over 750 files of FAQ material on *rtfm.mit.edu*.

Internet Relay Chat (IRC).   Internet Relay Chat is an application that allows many users to exchange real-time text in discussion areas called "channels." A person uses an IRC client to access a particular IRC server. IRC servers are available around the world, and the resulting real-time discussions range across many topics.

Aside from learning the interface itself (consisting of commands to list, create, join, or leave channels, among others), the user should observe IRC activity before participating. Because IRC happens in real-time, without provisions for storing text, the resulting social context has many qualities of a pre-literate or oral culture (December 1993). Common uses for IRC include recreational and educational interaction. IRC "channels" with names such as *chat, romance, talk, india, 30plus, russian,* and *sex* illustrate the focus of existing IRC culture on social interaction.

There are written texts that describe IRC and the communities that develop on it (see Uniform Resource Locator http://eru.dd. chalmers.se/home/f88jl/Irc/ircdocs.html). The user should become familiar with the practice of obtaining a nickname and specialized IRC jargon (e.g. "bots," "flooding"), in addition to the intricacies of using the interface itself.

Here is a sample of the start of an IRC session. This session assumes that the user has obtained and installed an IRC client, accessible through a command called "irc."

```
$ irc
* Connecting to port 6667 of server netserv2.its.rpi.edu
* Welcome to the Internet Relay Network decemj
  This is IRC-II, version 2.2.9, with RPI extensions to allow anonymous
userids.
  Please report problems to Kenny Zalewski (zalewk@rpi.edu).
  ANONYMOUS USERIDS have been disabled on RPI local servers
  For information about anonymous userids, please read the file
  /dept/acm/packages/irc/Anon-Userids.
* If you have not already done so, please read the new user information
*   with /HELP +NEWUSER
* Your host is netserv2.its.rpi.edu, running version 2.8.16
* Your host is netserv2.its.rpi.edu, running version 2.8.16
* This server was created Fri Mar 18 1994 at 19: 31:10 EST
*   umodes available oiws, channel modes available biklmnopstv
* There are 2433 users and 1365 invisible on 125 servers
* There are 70 operators online
* 1202 channels have been formed
* This server has 13 clients and 2 servers connected
* - netserv2.its.rpi.edu Message of the Day -
* - Welcome to netserv2, RPI's central IRC server
* - Rensselaer Polytechnic Institute
* - Troy, NY  12180
```

Once the session has started, the user has a variety of options available. As the introductory text above shows, the user can read new user information by using the /help command once in the IRC session. Here is a brief summary of basic commands:

command	comment
/list	shows all the current channels available
/join *channel name*	enters the user into channel name
/quit	end the IRC session

Since IRC provides real-time interchange versus the asynchronous interchange of Listserv or Usenet, IRC offers a different dimension for communication. This dimension includes creating a common, asynchronous event for group identity formation. There have been weddings as well as funerals on IRC. Since IRC channels can be created by any user, and there are provisions for private or restricted channels, IRC can be used for scholarly or special-interest purposes of groups.

MU*s. The term MU* refers to a family of applications that allow users to engage in real-time text discussion and navigate in virtual environments that contain persistent (i.e., that continue to exist after a session is over) objects. This is in contrast to what happens when a user quits IRC—traces of IRC activity and conversation are gone (unless saved through some storage facility not directly available to IRC users). In many kinds of MU*s, however, the user has the capability to create or change a virtual project or landscape or to undergo permanent changes in the state of their own online persona or profile in the MU*. A popular form of MU*, called a MUD (Multiple User Dungeon/Dialogue/Dimension) allows a user to create a persona (a character) and interact with others on the MUD. The origins of MU*s go back to role-playing games such as Dungeons & Dragons and other computer games. Like these games, MU*s give rise to a variety of communities and cultural and language practices.

Navigating in a MU* begins with using a MU* client to connect with a server. Some MU*s allow for telnet access, but telnet access often limits what a user can do. An example of a MU* called a MOO (Object-Oriented MUD) is Diversity University MOO, an experiment in interactive learning. Below, you will see what a user encounters when connecting with Diversity University.

```
$ telnet erau.db.erau.edu 8888
Trying 155.31.1.1 ...
Connected to erau.db.erau.edu.
Escape character is '^]'.
                        Welcome to
                    DIVERSITY UNIVERSITY
              Running version 1.7.6 of the LambdaMOO server
              Address:  erau.db.erau.edu (155.31.1.1) 8888
 Diversity University  is an experiment in interactive learning through
 internet.
 We are attempting to create a practical learning environment containing as many
 areas of  study as we can accurately provide.  If you would like the help us
 create this monolith of learning, we could use the help.
 As one of many participants in this experiment, Embry-Riddle Aeronautical
 University  (ERAU)  has agreed  to temporarily allow  this program on their
 system.  ERAU  is in no way responsible for  the content of the material that
 may be  placed in this environment.  Your feedback  on this experiment would be
 appreciated.  You may e-mail  your   comments   to: comments@db.erau.edu
        Login Commands:
        connect guest       | to have a look around
        @who                | to see who is online
        @quit               | to exit Diversity University
        connect guest
```

By using the command "connect guest," at this point, a user can tour Diversity University (DU). As in many MU*s, a user navigates DU by using commands. These commands provide the user with movement, information, or communication with other people in DU. The best source of information on how to use these commands is on DU itself. A user can enter an extensive help system through the @help command. For a general introduction to MU*s, see the MUD FAQ at URL ftp://ftp.math.okstate.edu/pub/muds/misc/mud-faq/.

A text map shows the geography of the Diversity University virtual space:

```
       ----------1------------------------2------------------------3------------
 |   ------------------------   ----JASON_ROAD____   _____(Jason's Ct.->)
 | |          .-----------------.| | Football field   | |                  | |
6| |      |Cllge of Agrcultr||   |_____|  |  (Gym)           | |6
 | |      |_____------'|  ____BOB_STREET____   |                  | |
 | |               Villa   | |   Northern         | |                  | |
5| |(grad dorm)   Villekulla | |      Quadrangle    | |  (Pool)          | |5
 |  |_____|  |_____|   |_____| |
 |   ------------------------   ____7th_STREET____   _____
 | |      |Cfetria|      ____|  |.-------.f.------.|  | .--.__.--. .-------.|W|
4|M|      '-------: Dorm |Hlth|  ||Student|s| Admin||  |(          | |    ||E|4
 |O|Hotel Schl   | 2   |Ctr.|  ||Union  |a|      ||  |[ Library  | |Educatn||S|
 |G|_____|------|____|  ||_____/ '------'|  |[_____| |    ||T|
 |U|                            ____LSU_STREET____   |.-----.           ||H|
 |E|.-----------..----------.  | |               | ||Engl.|.-----.::::::::|E|
3|'||  Business ||Communcatn\|H|  |S||      ||    |.------.|I|3
 |S||_____||____ ____||0|  |A||_____||Cltrl||     ||M|
 | |.------. .--------''-----.|U|  Southern Quad  |N|.------.|Studs|| Law ||E|
 |R||Engin-| | Tech Complex ||S|  |D||Hist.||     ||_____||R|
 |U||eering| |   _____/|T|  |0||_____||_____|.-----.| |
2|N||_____| '---'._____.|0|  flag!pole    |Z|.----. .----. |Poli ||S|2
 | |.-----------.  | Medical ||N|  | ||  |_|Soc | |Sci ||T|
 | ||Archtcture|  | Complex ||  |S||Psych_ Work| |_____/|R|
 | |'-----------'  _____||S|  .'N'.  |T|_----'_'----'_____|I|
 | |(Construction .--------.||T|  W-+-E  |  ____JEANNE'S_LANE____ P|
 | |.--. trailer| | Science || |  '.S.'  | |.---------.        | |
1| ||__|<--'     |  Bldg.  || |  | || M&DA   | Ampithtr | |1
 | |_____'---------'| |                    | |'---------'_____| |
 |_____6th_STREET_____|
       1                         2                         3
```

Communities and Communication

Communication on the Net is growing increasingly sophisticated and complex in terms of interface, integration with information-sharing protocols, and functionality. The WWW client Mosaic has been called the "killer application" (Markoff 1993) for the Internet because it integrates FTP, news, Gopher, HTTP, WAIS, and other networked information in a graphical interface that is easy to use. A similar, integrative interface for CMC forums (e-mail, mailing lists, IRC, MU* and other person-to-person communication protocols and forums) is the next step in evolution of Net communication.

Net tools, forums, and connections are the products of communities of people who share information and communication. These are communities in the true sense of the word—involving relationships, shared experiences, practices, rules, conventions, stocks of knowledge, jargon, and expectations. Because of the cooperative nature of the Net, members of communities influence how they operate. A user venturing into these communities for the first time must find out "what is going on" by observing, exploring, and acting responsibly according to community standards. Over time, the user will learn community traditions and gain the community's wealth. This wealth might be in stores of information (like the Usenet FAQ lists) or in dynamic connections with others (as in IRC). A user must be critical of the information and processes on the Net—to judge the value and veracity of information as well as the ethics and morality of Net activity.

Getting Started

The above discussion presents just a short overview of ways to navigate the global Net. Since the Net is changing rapidly, a user can best build knowledge about Net information and communities by accessing information and discussion on the Net itself. There are a number of starting points for exploration listed in December (1994a). Among introductory essays, Jean Armour Polly's "Surfing the Internet" article gives the new user a good initial overview of the possibilities and resources on the Net. This guide's Uniform Resource Locator is (ftp:/ /nysernet.org/pub/resources/guides/). The Electronic Frontier Foundation's guide, written by Adam Gaffin, *The Big Dummy's Guide to the Internet* (URL ftp://ftp.eff.org/pub/Net_info/Big_Dummy/) is available for free on the Net, and provides detailed instructions for accessing many Net resources and communication.

Notes

1. France Telecom is expected to provide a gateway link from Teletel to the Internet in 1994. When this happens, Teletel will become part of the Matrix, increasing the number of people in the Matrix significantly.

2. A longer list of tools, forums, and associated network documention is in December (1994b).

3. See December (1994b) for references to documentation on how to use Archie via e-mail or obtain clients.

4. It is possible for information providers to place descriptive entries for a file name in an Archie "what is" database. However, the majority of files at FTP sites do not have such entries.

References

Adams, R. and Frey, D. (1993). !@:: A directory of mail addressing and Networks, 3rd Ed. Sebastopol, Cal.: O'Reilly and Associates.

Corporation for Research and Educational Networking (1994, April 18). "CREN: History and Future," Gopher://info.cren.net/00/cren/cren-doc/cren-hist-fut.txt.

December, J. (1993). Characteristics of oral culture in discourse on the net. Paper presented at the twelfth annual Penn State Conference on Rhetoric and Composition, University Park, Pennsylvania, July 8, 1993.

December, J. (1994a). Information sources: The Internet and computer-mediated communication. ftp://ftp.rpi.edu/pub/communications/internet-cmc.

December, J. (1994b). Internet Tools Summary. ftp://ftp.rpi.edu/pub/communications/internet-tools.

Gilmore, J. and Spafford, G. (1993, November 30). Alternative newsgroup hierarchies, Part I and Part II. ftp://rtfm.mit.edu/pub/usenet-by-group/news.lists/.

Kovacs, D. (1993). Directory of scholarly electronic conferences. ftp://ksuvxa.kent.edu/library/.

Lottor, M. (1992, January) Internet growth (1981–1991). Request for comments 1296. ftp://nic.merit.edu/documents/rfc/rfc1296.txt.

Markoff, J. (1993, December 8). A free and simple computer link. *The New York Times.*

Markus, M. L. (1990). Toward a critical mass theory of interactive media: Universal access, interdependence and diffusion. In J. Fulk and C. Steinfield (Eds.), Organizations and Communication Technology (194–218). Newbury Park, Cal.: Sage Publications.

ProjectH Information, http://www.arch.su.edu.au/PROJECTH/index.html.

Rutowski, Anthony. (1994) A year in the life of the Internet. *Internet Society News* 2(4):6–11.

Spafford, G. (1993a, November 29). List of active newsgroups, part I and part II. ftp://rtfm.mit.edu/ pub/usenet-by-group/news.lists/.

Spafford, G. (1993b, November 30). List of Moderators for Usenet. ftp://rtfm.mit.edu/pub/usenet-by-group/news.lists/.

Strangelove, M. (1992, July). Directory of electronic journals and newsletters. ftp://ftp.cni.org/pub/net-guides/strangelove/.

Quarterman, J. S. (1990). The matrix: Computer networks and conferencing systems worldwide. Bedford, Mass.: Digital Press.

Yanoff, S. and J. Chew. (1994). Inter-network mail guide. ftp://csd4.csd.
uwm.edu/pub/internetwork-mail-guide.

LIST OF
CONTRIBUTORS

Kenneth Arnold was, until April 1994, Director of Rutgers University Press. After twenty-seven years in university and print publishing, he decided to establish New Century Communications, which focuses exclusively on networked publications in the scholarly communication system. He is also a partner in the newly formed PubComm Group, which is developing copyright protection software for network publishing. He works and lives in New York City.

David L. Austin, Architecture and Art Librarian at the University of Illinois at Chicago, earned his Bachelor of Music and Master of Arts degrees from the University of Michigan. He later pursued his academic training in librarianship at the University of California, Berkeley. Previous publications of his include *Henri Sauguet. A Bio-Bibliography.* His current research in problems related to locating prints, slides, and photographs led him to address the broad problem of access to visual information in a universal context and, more specifically, to construction of an index of the *Conway Library Microfiche,* which focuses on architecture, sculpture, and decorative arts.

Sheryl Burgstahler is an Assistant Director within Computing & Communication at the University of Washington and an active member of EDUCOM's special interest group EASI (Equal Access to Software and Information). She currently directs DO-IT (Disabilities, Opportunities, Internetworking, and Technology), a project to recruit students with disabilities into science, engineering, and mathematics academic programs and careers, which is primarily funded by the National Science Foundation.

Michael Day (Mday@silver.sdsmt.edu) is an Assistant Professor of English at South Dakota School of Mines and Technology. He teaches technical communications using the Internet and has created stylistic revision software for writing classrooms. *Eric Crump* (LCERIC@mizzou1. missouri.edu) is the Assistant Director of the Writing Center at the University of Missouri. He manages several electronic mail discussion forums, including one that focuses on the development of learning environments. *Rebecca Rickly* is a member of the English Composition Board at the University of Michigan.

John December is a PhD candidate in communication and rhetoric in the Department of Language, Literature, and Communication at Rensselaer Polytechnic Institute.

Deborah Everhart holds a Ph.D. in medieval English literature from the University of California, Irvine. She is currently Co-Director of the Labyrinth at Georgetown University. Her work in global net-working over the past few years has included not only the conception and development of the Labyrinth, but also the founding of Interscripta and Arthur-Net, both of which have quickly become important Internet forums involving hundreds of scholars. She has taught at Southern Methodist University, the University of California, Irvine, and Georgetown University. She also developed and directed the English/ESL computer lab at Mission College in Santa Clara, California, and she has conducted extensive research on the effect of computers in the writing process. Her publications include articles on Chaucer's poetry and an English translation of Haimo of Auxere's Latin commentary on the Book of Jonah. She is currently writing a book on the abbess Heloise and the feminine reception of authority in the statues of the Paraclete.

Brian R. Gaines is Killam Memorial Research Professor and Director of the Knowledge Science Institute at the University of Calgary. His previous positions include Professor of Industrial Engineering at the University of Toronto, Technical Director and Deputy Chairman of the Monotype Corporation, and Chairman of the Department of Electrical Engineering Science at the University of Essex. He received his BA, MA, and Ph.D from Trinity College, Cambridge and is a Chartered Engineer, Chartered Psychologist, and a Fellow of the Institute of Electrical Engineers, the British Computer Society, and the British Psychological Society. He is editor of the *International Journal of Man-Machine Studies* and *Knowledge Acquisition,* and of the "Computers and People" and "Knowledge-Based Systems" book series. His research interests include: the socio-economic dynamics of science and technology; the nature, acquisition and transfer of knowledge; software engineering for heterogeneous systems; and expert system applications in manufacturing, the professions, sciences, and humanities.

William Graziadei obtained his Ph.D. in 1970 from Boston College. After a three-year postdoctoral fellowship in immunology and virology at Yale University, he joined the faculty of the State University of New York at Plattsburgh. He has been Professor of Biology since 1980, and was the recipient of the 1978 Chancellor's Award for Excellence in Teaching. He has since been nominated twice for a Distinguished Teaching Professorship. From 1979 to 1992 he served as Coordinator of the In Vitro Cell Biology & Biotechnology Program, a national and international training program cooperatively sponsored by SUNY Plattsburgh and the William H. Miner Agricultural Research Institute. It was during this time that he began to extensively employ computer applications and telecommunications in teaching-learning. He recently completed a sabbatical in the use of authorware and laser discs for presentations, lessons and assessments. He serves as project director and co-coordinator of the Teaching-Learning Center programs and activities as well as a faculty tutor. In addition, he participates as an instructor in telecommunications and multimedia workshops for faculty and as a discussion leader during the Round Table segments. Finally, he organizes an all-campus seminar/demonstration program on the Use of Technology in Education and recruits faculty from various disciplines as participants.

Jean-Claude Guédon is Professor, Department of Comparative Literature, University of Montreal. He is also Founder and co-editor of *Surfaces,* a refereed, electronic journal that started publication in Fall of 1991.

Laura J. Gurak is an Assistant Professor of rhetoric and technical communication in the Department of Rhetoric at the University of Minnesota. Her research involves the rhetorical dynamics of online communities in cyberspace. She has published and presented on both the methodological and rhetorical issues raised by computer-mediated communication technology.

Jack P. Hailman is Professor of Zoology at the University of Wisconsin-Madison. His principal research concerns the behavior of birds (with some research on the behavior of other animals and some research on non-behavioral topics about birds). He has published nearly two hundred research papers, book chapters and notes, and is author, co-author or co-editor of more than a half dozen books and monographs.

He was Review Editor of *Birdbanding* and New-World editor of *Animal Behaviour,* and serves currently on editorial boards of several journals including the e-mail journal *Psycoloquy.* He has been elected fellow of several professional societies, including the American Ornithologists' Union, and was recently elected to Det Kongelige Norske Videnskabers Selskab (Norway's national academy of sciences). He founded and manages the network Titnet, and was the first instructor at the University of Wisconsin-Madison to network fully a class of over a hundred students.

Linda Harasim is an Associate Professor in the Department of Communication at Simon Fraser University, British Columbia, Canada. She has designed, implemented, and evaluated networking applications in Canada, the United States, and Latin America. She has edited *Online Education: Perspectives on a New Environment* (Praeger, 1990), *Global Networks: Computers and International Communication* (MIT Press, 1993), and, with coauthors Starr Roxanne Hiltz, Lucio Teles, and Murrary Turoff, recently published *Learning Networks: A Field Guide* (MIT Press, 1995).

Teresa M. Harrison and *Timothy Stephen* are Associate Professors of communication in the Department of Language, Literature, and Communication at Rensselaer Polytechnic Institute. They are co-directors of "Comserve" a network-based information and conference service for the communication discipline.

Susan Hockey is Director of the Center for Electronic Texts in the Humanities (CETH), which is sponsored by Rutgers and Princeton Universities. She moved to the United States in October 1991 after sixteen years at Oxford University Computing Service where her most recent position was Director of the Computers in Teaching Initiative Centre for Textual Studies. She is the author of four books and numerous articles on humanities computing. She is currently Chair of the Association for Literary and Linguistic Computing and a member (past chair) of the Steering Committee of the Text Encoding Initiative.

Brian Kahin is Director of the Information Infrastructure Project and Adjunct Lecturer in Public Policy at Harvard University's John F. Kennedy School of Government. He also serves as General Counsel for the Annapolis-based Interactive Multimedia Association and directs the Association's Intellectual Property Project.

J. L. Lemke is Professor of education at the City University of New York, Brooklyn College School of Education. He is the author of *Using*

Language in the Classroom (Oxford University Press, 1989) and *Talking Science: Language, Learning and Values* (Ablex Publishing, 1990). Professor Lemke began his academic career in theoretical physics (Ph.D., University of Chicago), later shifting his research interests to the role of language in the communication of science, linguistic discourse analysis and multimedia literacy, and social semiotics. He is co-editor of the international research journal *Linguistics and Education*. His new book *Textual Politics: Discourse and Social Dynamics* was published in 1995 by Taylor and Frances (London) and Falmer Press.

Peter Lyman, formerly University Librarian at the University of Southern California, is now University Librarian at the University of California, Berkeley. As a political scientist, he has been conducting research on the sociology of knowledge in digital and networked environments for fifteen years in an effort to understand the relationships between information and power.

Cliff McKnight is Reader in Information Management in the Department of Information and Library Studies, and *Brian Shackel* is Emeritus Professor and Founder of the HUSAT Research Institute, both of Loughborough University of Technology. *Andrew Dillon* is Associate Professor of Information Science at the School of Library and Information Science, Indiana University.

Tom McNulty is Coordinator of Disabled Student Services at Bobst Library, New York University. He is co-author of *Access to Information: Materials, Technologies and Services for Print-Impaired Readers* (Chicago: American Library Association, 1993), and Editor-in-Chief of *Information Technology and Disabilities,* a quarterly electronic journal devoted to the application of adaptive technologies in a variety of settings.

David L. Rodgers was Director of the Division of Electronic Products and Services at the American Mathematical Society. He was previously Manager of Systems Development at *Mathematical Reviews* and Project Manager for the e-Math project. He is now Research Scientist with the School of Information and Library Studies (SILS) at the University of Michigan. *Kevin W. Curnow* is User Support Specialist for the e-Math System. *Drury R. Burton* is Systems Manager at *Mathematical Reviews*. *Greg S. Ullmann* was Software Engineer for the e-Math project. *William B. Woolf* is Associate Executive Editor for the American Mathematical Society and Principal Investigator for the e-Math project.

Lyman Ross is Reference Librarian and Online Database Coordinator, *Paul Philbin* is Head, Systems Department, and *Albert Joy* is Collection Development Librarian at the University of Vermont Libraries & Media Services. *Merri Beth Lavagnino* is Library Systems Director, University of Illinois at Urbana-Champaign.

Duncan Sanderson completed his Ph.D. in Sociology at Laval University (Quebec City) and then undertook post-doctoral research in the area of the organizational implications of new network technologies at the Centre for Information Technology Innovation. His research interests include the user-centered design of computer supported collaborative work technologies, the management of telework, the technology implementation process, and organizational issues that may appear with the introduction of groupware technologies.

Carolyn P. Schriber received her Ph.D. in History in 1988 from the University of Colorado at Boulder, where her field of specialization was twelfth-century Anglo-Norman church history. She is the author of *The Dilemma of Arnulf of Lisieux: New Ideas Versus Old Ideals* (Bloomington, Ind.: Indiana University Press, 1990). She has also published articles and reviews in *Comitatus: A Journal of Medieval and Renaissance Studies; The Journal of the Rocky Mountain Medieval and Renaissance Association; Locus: An Historical Journal of Regional Perspectives; The Journal of the American Academy of Religion; The Dictionary of National Biography: Missing Persons Supplement* (Oxford University Press, 1993); and *The St. James Press Guide to Biography* (Chicago: St. James Press, 1991). Currently she is an Assistant Professor of history at Rhodes College in Memphis, Tennessee.

Fay Sudweeks is a researcher at the Key Centre for Design Computing, University of Sydney, Australia, and a doctoral candidate in collaborative design at the University of Sydney. Her research area is in computer-mediated communication and her current interests are in interactivity, identifying typicality using associative neural network techniques, and social and linguistic aspects of computer-supported collaborative work. She has co-edited books on artificial intelligence, design and creativity, and co-authored papers on mediated group dynamics, Internet resources, CMC, neural networks, and categorization. *Sheizaf Rafaeli* is a Senior Lecturer (Associate Professor) at the School of Business Administration, Hebrew University of Jerusalem, Israel, where he has been head of the Information Systems area since 1986. His interests are in computers as media. He has published on this topic in journals such as *Behavior and Information Technology, Communication Research*, and *Computers and the Social Sciences*. He authored a book on electronic spreadsheets, and is currently completing a book on information systems for the Open University.

Jeff Taylor is Associate Professor and Chair of the Labour Studies Program at Athabasca University in Athabasca, Alberta, Canada.

John Unsworth is an Associate Professor of English at the University of Virginia, a founding co-Editor of the electronic journal *Postmodern Culture*, and Director of the University of Virginia's Institute for Advanced Technology in the Humanities.

INDEX

AARNET, 112, 427
ABSnet (online discussion group), 169
abstracts, electronic publication of 171
academic disciplines, 340–341, 343–345
academic societies, 21, 60
ACN (online discussion group), 279, 287
Acrobat, Adobe, 331, 360
action, 42
adaptive technologies, 26, 233, 240,
    400–401, 407
  braille, 237–238, 399–401, 407
  disk drives, 236
  keyboards, 236
  monitors, 237, 239
  printers, 237
  Morse Code input, 236–237
  scanning, 236, 238
  speech recognition systems, 237
  speech synthesizers, 238, 239, 400
  word prediction software, 238
  voice output, 237
Advanced Research Project Agency
    (ARPA), Department of Defense, 429
African-American studies, 20
African studies, 20
America Online, 430
American Association for the
    Advancement of Science, 359, 366
American Chemical Society, 358
American Historical Association, 243
American Information Standards
    Organization, 381
American Mathematical Association, 18,
    22, 177–179, 181–182, 184, 185–188,
    318
  Committee on Electronic Products and
    Services, 185–187

Electronic Products and Services,
    185–186
Preprint Service, AMS, 184, 186–188
American National Standards Institute,
    381
American Physical Society, 30
American Ornithological Union, 170
Americans with Disabilities Act of 1990,
    233
Andrew W. Mellon Foundation, 85, 387,
    388
Anglo-American Cataloging Rules, 89,
    195
Anglo-Saxon studies, 243
Annales de chimie, 340–341, 349
AOUnet-l (online discussion group), 169
Archie, 101, 220, 438–439, 447
Architectural Barriers Act, 240
ARPAnet, 99, 220, 348, 373
Art and Architecture Thesaurus, 419
ASCII, 86, 348, 359, 400, 401, 405
Aspects, 297, 299, 309
Association for Computational
    Linguistics, 85
Association for Computers and the
    Humanities, 85
Association for Literary and Linguistic
    Computing, 85
Association of American Publishers, 87
Association of American Universities,
    391–392
Association of American Universities
    Task Force on a National Strategy
    for Managing Scientific and
    Technical Information, 60
Association of American University
    Presses (AAUP), 385, 387–388, 395